DS 480.853 .D384 1995
Regional powers and small
De Silva, K. M

210983

DATE DUE

MAR 1 1999	
JAN 0 2 2001	
FEB 1 1 2003	
DEC - 2 2003	
BRODART	

D1442930

Regional Powers and Small State Security

Regional Powers and Small State Security

India and Sri Lanka, 1977–90

K. M. de Silva

THE WOODROW WILSON CENTER PRESS
Washington, D.C.

THE JOHNS HOPKINS UNIVERSITY PRESS
Baltimore and London

Editorial offices:

The Woodrow Wilson Center Press

370 L'Enfant Promenade, S.W., Suite 704

Washington, D.C. 20024-2518

Telephone 202-287-3000, ext. 218

Order from:

The Johns Hopkins University Press

Hampden Station

Baltimore, Maryland 21211

Telephone 1-800-537-5487

2 4 6 8 9 7 5 3 1

Library of Congress Cataloging-in-Publication Data

De Silva, K. M.
Regional powers and small state security : India and Sri Lanka, 1977–1990 / K.M. De Silva.
p.   cm.
Includes bibliographical references and index.
ISBN 0-8018-5149-1 (cloth)
1. India—Politics and government—1977–   2. Sri Lanka—Politics and government—1978–
3. India—Foreign relations—Sri Lanka.   4. Sri Lanka—Foreign relations—India.
5. National security—India.   6. National security—Sri Lanka.   I. Title.
DS480.853.D384   1995
327.5405493'09'048—dc20   95-8097
CIP

WOODROW WILSON INTERNATIONAL CENTER FOR SCHOLARS

Board of Trustees

Woodrow Wilson Center Press

Contents

Preface

This book emerged from work I have been engaged in for some years now, the writing of a political biography of J. R. Jayewardene, Sri Lanka's first executive president (1978–88), along with a coauthor, my American colleague Howard Wriggins. In our research for this biography we have had unrestricted access to the papers of President Jayewardene. At the time of his retirement in early 1989 and the establishment of the J. R. Jayewardene Centre, based avowedly on the U.S. model of presidential libraries, Jayewardene decided to transfer his papers including those relating to the last phase of his administration of this library. I discovered that the documents transferred included his correspondence with the Indian prime minister during the period 1987–88. I asked for and was given the same freedom to use this material as with the rest of his papers. Reading through them I realized that there was a strong case for a monograph on India's intervention in Sri Lanka in the 1980s. Without this entirely serendipitous development, President Jayewardene's decision to retain this documentary material in his library, it would not have been possible to write this present book in the form it has taken.

The papers included most of the telegrams and letters exchanged between President Jayewardene and Prime Minister Rajiv Gandhi in this vitally important period 1987–89, as well as most of the letters they wrote to each other and a mass of secret and confidential material relating the negotiations they conducted after the signing of the Indo–Sri Lankan peace accord of 1987. There are gaps in this correspondence, which likely can only be filled by a search through the files of the presidential secretariat in Colombo, but those gaps are relatively small, and it has been possible to fill them adequately by interviews with some of the principals involved in the negotiations between the two countries.

The access I have had to the Jayewardene–Rajiv Gandhi correspondence for the period 1987–89 has been an enormous advantage in the interviews that form the basis of many of the chapters of this book. The correspondence was so much like a set of clues to solving a series of very

ix

complicated crossword puzzles. It enabled me to focus my questions to those I interviewed much more accurately than would have been possible without them. Wherever I thought it appropriate I have quoted extensive extracts from these documents. In some instances an important letter or document is printed in full.

I am fully aware that this will be seen as a book based on Sri Lankan sources. Nevertheless the correspondence between the two heads of government at a crucial period of their complex relationship has given us glimpses into the Indian sources that would not have been normally available to scholars for years to come. Given the penchant of the Indian bureaucracy to protect official papers well beyond the thirty-year rule introduced in Britain under Prime Minister Harold Wilson, it would take several decades before an Indian scholar would have access to papers in New Delhi and Madras, essential for the study of the Indian part of the story. If the publication of this volume and others based on the Jayewardene manuscripts were to hasten this process, the world of scholarship would be greatly benefited. I have endeavored to overcome the limitations of access to Indian official documents and correspondence by interviewing as many of the principal figures on the Indian side of the negotiations as I could. These included Rajiv Gandhi and some of the Indian officials who were privy to the negotiation process in the years from 1983 to 1989. A list of these persons is included in the bibliography.

In Sri Lanka I have had several interviews with President Jayewardene and the three persons directly involved in the negotiations with India at a political level: Lalith Athulathmudali, Gamini Dissanayake, and Ranjan Wijeratne. It is a matter of deep personal regret to me that each of the three has suffered violent deaths at the hands of assassins. I was saddened also by the assassination of Rajiv Gandhi. He had given me one interview and had agreed to give more time for discussions at another interview on a later date. Those discussions never took place.

Besides the people who granted me interviews, others gave me copies of papers in their possession. Gamini Dissanayake gave me access to some of his papers relevant to India's Sri Lankan policy. H. L. de Silva, president's counsel (P.C.), lent me his copy of the official minutes of the discussions in Thimpu, Bhutan, in July and August 1985.

This book studies four areas: first, the question of regional power/ small state security relationships in parts of the world that were integral but distinct units of the British Empire; second, conflict resolution and mediation in the context of acute ethnic tensions; third, the internationalization of ethnic conflict; and finally, though not specifically, personal relationships at a leadership level in neighboring states. In that sense it is a study of tragedy, for so many of those who played important roles in the contentious issues analyzed in this book died violent deaths.

The research and data gathering that went into the writing of this volume has benefited from the work involved in the production of volume 2 of the political biography of J. R. Jayewardene. Some of the data from interviews are common to the two books. Special mention must be made of an interview with General Vernon Walters conducted by Howard Wriggins. Many if not most of the interviews cited in the notes were conducted by me specifically for the purpose of this book; a few chapters in this volume are based on material in the biography, but much more detail is provided here even on those. The biography stops at the end of 1988, while the analysis here goes on to 1990 and 1991 up to the time of the assassination of Rajiv Gandhi.

Acknowledgments

I have incurred many debts, institutional and personal, in the course of the three years or more I took to write this book. I need to begin by thanking the United States Institute of Peace in Washington, D.C., for the grant given to the International Centre for Ethnic Studies (ICES) in Sri Lanka to help finance some part of the research and travel expenses—to India—incurred in the writing. Much of the first draft was written when I was a Fellow of the Woodrow Wilson International Center for Scholars in Washington, D.C., in 1991–92. I would like to express my thanks to that institution for providing such a congenial atmosphere for my work, apart from excellent library and other academic resources, all of which enabled me to complete a first draft much earlier than I might have done without those advantages. I am especially grateful for the enthusiastic support I had from Mary Brown Bullock, director of the Asia program of the Woodrow Wilson Center. I am very appreciative of the assistance I had from Susanne Jones, who converted my very difficult handwriting to a workable draft on her word processor, and from two very energetic and extremely helpful research assistants, Vanessa Saldanha and Dallas Brennan, provided by the Center. I must also acknowledge the help rendered by some of my colleagues at the Wilson Center, Robert Frykenberg and Granville Austin in particular, through their responses and criticisms when I inflicted on them many of the problems I encountered in the course of my work and some of the issues I was engaged in examining.

In New Delhi, my work would have been very much harder but for the support I had from a number of people, and much less pleasant but for the hospitality I enjoyed from many persons. In that latter category are Palitha and Nedra Abeykoon, at whose home I often stayed and where I actually conducted an interview with a guest while others were involved in their conversations, and Stanley Kalpage, with whom I stayed on a number of occasions when my old friend of university days was Sri Lanka's high commissioner in India. Among my Indian friends I would like to mention two in particular, Narendra Kumar, formerly managing director of Vikas Publishers, who arranged for my interviews with the late Rajiv Gandhi and with Romesh Bhandari and S. K. Singh, and V. A. Pai Panandiker, whose Centre for Policy Research has been an academic home away from home during my frequent visits to Delhi for interviews. Indeed some of the interviews were arranged by him.

At the ICES the earliest drafts of the chapters of this book were prepared by Sepali Liyanamana and Bernadine Perera with their customary cheerful efficiency. Between them they prepared and virtually completed a second draft of the book on my return from Washington in August 1992. When it was necessary to revise the second draft comprehensively, that was done expeditiously and with exemplary competence by Iranga Silva and Dilrukshi Herath. Kanthi Gamage, librarian of the ICES, has helped me in the preparation of the bibliography, while the preparing of the several copies of this typescript was in the capable hands of Samarakoon Bandara. I have also had the enthusiastic assistance of others at the ICES, especially Nalini Weragama and Eranganie Karunaratne, whenever I asked for it. I am deeply grateful to all of them, especially to Dilrukshi Herath for the many hours she devoted to preparing the final version.

The present study emerged from three papers I wrote for an International Conference on Peace Accords and Ethnic Conflict organized by the ICES in Colombo, Sri Lanka, 25–27 July 1991. The papers were "The Prelude to the Indo–Sri Lanka Accord of July—Negotiations Between India and Sri Lanka, November 1984 to mid-1987"; "The Making of the Indo–Sri Lanka Accord of July 1987—The Final Phase, June–July 1987"; and "The Breaking of the Indo–Sri Lanka Accord, August 1987 to the End of 1989." Revised versions of these papers were subsequently published. "The Prelude to the Indo–Sri Lanka Accord of July 1987" appeared in *Ethnic Studies Report* 10, no. 1 (January 1992): 1–16; and "The Making of the Indo–Sri Lanka Accord: The Final Phase—June–July 1987" in *Peace Accords and Ethnic Conflict* (of which I was a joint editor) (London: Pinter, 1993), 112–55. The material contained in these papers and articles appears in this book in a substantially revised and expanded form.

Many friends and colleagues helped me in the revision and expansion of these articles, some through incisive critical comments and suggestions and some by helping in the search for documents and other research material. These include my colleagues at the International Centre for

Ethnic Studies in Kandy, S. W. R. de A. "Sam" Samarasinghe and Gerald Peiris. A number of persons who read and commented on the three articles encouraged me to expand them into a book.

Once the writing of the book began in earnest I had the support of a number of friends who helped by commenting on the contents of several draft chapters. I would like to express my gratitude to all of them and to four of them in particular, who read the whole volume in draft form for me and in the process saved me from many errors of fact and interpretation and helped improve the language and the clarity of my arguments. They are Margaret Gunaratne, Tissa Jayatilleke, Howard Schaffer, and Howard Wriggins. I am deeply grateful to them for taking on such a heavy burden and sacrificing so much of their time for detailed comments on this monograph. The two maps were prepared by Matthew Kania, cartographer, based on the initial work of Gerald Peiris. Needless to say no one is in any way responsible for any errors that may appear in this book. The responsibility is mine.

Finally I need to thank my wife, Chandra, for all her help given, as usual, ungrudgingly, by taking on more than her fair share of household responsibilities so that I could spend more hours than would otherwise have been possible in the research and the writing and revising of this book. I have enjoyed listening to her critical comments on the foibles of some of its principal figures. Her assistance in the writing of this book, as in practically everything else I write, has been invaluable.

Sri Lankan Provincial Boundaries, 1821–89

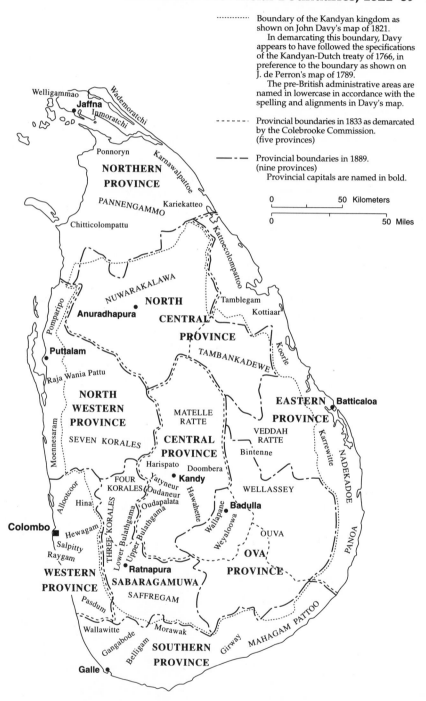

··········· Boundary of the Kandyan kingdom as shown on John Davy's map of 1821.
In demarcating this boundary, Davy appears to have followed the specifications of the Kandyan-Dutch treaty of 1766, in preference to the boundary as shown on J. de Perron's map of 1789.
The pre-British administrative areas are named in lowercase in accordance with the spelling and alignments in Davy's map.

------- Provincial boundaries in 1833 as demarcated by the Colebrooke Commission. (five provinces)

—·—· Provincial boundaries in 1889. (nine provinces)
Provincial capitals are named in bold.

N

ANDHRA PRADESH

Nellore

14°N

Tirupathy

KARNATAKA

Bangalore

Madras

Mangalore

Vellore

INDIA

Pondicherry

Salem

Chidambaram

TAMIL NADU

KERALA Coimbatore

Thanjavur

Tiruchirapalli

Velankannai

Palni

10°N

Madurai

Jaffna

10°N

Cochin

Kovilpatti

Rameswaram

Tirunelveli

Mannar

Trincomalee

Trivandrum

Anuradhapura

Kanya Kumari

Batticaloa

SRI LANKA

INDIAN OCEAN

Kandy

76°E

Colombo

6°N

Sri Lanka and Southern India

Galle

6°N

80°E

0   50   100 Kilometers

0   50   100 Miles

Regional Powers and Small State Security

1

Introduction

FEW INTERNATIONAL RELATIONSHIPS in any part of the world are quite so asymmetrical as that between India and Sri Lanka, whether one considers population or physical size. India has nearly fifty times Sri Lanka's population of seventeen million and is a large subcontinental state 1.2 million square miles in extent, while Sri Lanka is a small island of twenty-five thousand square miles. Inevitably, therefore, the wider issue of regional power/small state relationships figures prominently in, indeed dominates, any discussion and analysis of the themes of this book.

Linked to this issue are conflicting visions of the essentials of national security from the time these two neighbors emerged from colonial to independent status in 1947 and 1948 respectively. The second chapter deals with this topic in some detail. The issues it analyzes are essential to understanding the ramifications of decisions taken by the two countries from the 1970s onwards. This forms the essence of chapters 3 and 4.

The island's ethnic conflict of the mid- and late 1970s and 1980s is the third interlocking theme in this book, and, to the extent that it provided India with the opportunity to intervene in the island's affairs, our analysis here is also a case study in the internationalization of ethnic conflict. The complexities of the island's ethnic conflict[1] are not dealt with at any great length in this book; here we will merely refer to some of its salient features.

The island's recent political history provides a remarkable contrast to the peaceful and smooth transfer of power from British to Sri Lankan rule. That transfer of power was unique for South Asia in being negotiated rather than extracted after agitation, strife, and violence. Sri Lanka has not lived up to the promise of its early years of independence (1947 to

1

1956) when an emphasis on pluralism and secularism seemingly stabilized the orderly and uneventful transfer of power.

The fundamentals of a stable political order with its emphasis on pluralism and secularism were systematically challenged by populist nationalists through a reassertion of indigenous values emphasizing an ethnic identity based on language and religion. In the period from 1956 to 1964 and again from 1970 to 1977 the country witnessed a second phase in the transfer of power, this time from the English-educated elite to the vernacular-speaking elites. The tensions generated erupted into violence during three distinct phases: 1956–58, 1975–77, and from 1983 to the present day.

There have been, by and large, five major interconnected areas of dispute between the two principal contending groups, the Sinhalese majority and the Tamil minority. These are language rights; employment in the state service; connected to this, in the early 1970s, controversies over admissions to universities; settlement of farming families on state-owned land; and devolution of power to regional centers.

Sri Lanka provides a classic example of the destabilizing effects of linguistic nationalism on a plural society. In the period from 1955 to 1961, a fundamental and unilateral change in language policy destroyed the peace of the country after a decade of stability following upon a peaceful transfer of power. The second period of violence began in the mid-1970s and continues to the present day when a separatist movement led by a section of the Tamil population has met strong resistance from the Sri Lankan government.[2] The confrontation has become increasingly more violent. The nature of the separatist demands and the responses they provoke are reviewed in considerable detail in chapter 5.

Sri Lanka has two Tamil minorities. The indigenous Tamils, who have lived in the island almost as long as the Sinhalese (that is, over two thousand years), at present constitute 11 percent of the island's population; the Indian Tamils, as they are called, are a smaller group, about 5 percent of the population. The latter are comparatively recent immigrants brought to the island as plantation workers by the British, or migrants to the island in British times because of the much higher standard of living in the island and the greater economic opportunities available there by way of employment and trade for people from southern India. Until very recent times the two Tamil groups have had little in common except their language. Both groups are mainly Hindus, but the rigors of the Hindu caste system had kept them apart, the bulk of the plantation workers being regarded as "low" caste by the Sri Lankan or Jaffna Tamil elite; there is also the class element, the Indian Tamils being, in the main, plantation workers.

Throughout the twentieth century those who ruled India, whether British viceroys or Indian politicians, have been deeply interested in the fate of the Indian community on the island, especially in insisting that the bulk of them be absorbed by Ceylon or Sri Lanka as its citizens. The controversies over these issues have been acrimonious since 1928 when they first began.[3] Agreement was reached on the terms of a settlement of this question between India and Sri Lanka as long ago as 1941, but the failure of the Indian authorities to sign an agreement they had initialed in that year saw the first postindependence Sri Lankan government take unilateral measures in 1948 and 1949 to decide the issue of citizenship. Eventually, in 1964 and 1974, an agreement was reached between the two governments on the citizenship question; in 1988 the residual issues stemming from the earlier agreements were finally settled. India's interest in the problems of Sri Lanka's larger Tamil minority is a more recent development, something that emerged and grew in the 1970s and 1980s.

The situation is neatly summarized in a recent article by Myron Weiner:

> When Sri Lanka became independent there was no clear notion as to what constituted Sri Lankan citizenship. In the 1949 [*sic*][4] elections anyone who was a British subject in Sri Lanka including [the resident Indians] could vote. But the new government lost no time in introducing the Ceylon Citizenship Act of 1948 and the Indian and Pakistani Residents (Citizenship) Act of 1949. These Acts along with various agreements subsequently signed with the Indian government in 1964 and 1974, added up to a set of policies to end all further migration into Sri Lanka, to expatriate [*sic*][5] as many of the Indian Estate workers as Indians would accept.[6]

"The Sri Lankan government was hardly alone," Weiner adds,

> in wanting the expatriation of migrants who had entered when the country was under colonial rule. Many post-colonial regimes regarded their migrants as an illegitimate presence if the migrants did not belong to the dominant indigenous ethnic community. Uganda and Burma expelled their Indian and Pakistani settlers, and in Indonesia large numbers of Chinese were massacred or expelled. Sri Lanka, however, had a democratic government. It sought to remove the Indians through legitimate means, in accordance with

the law and with due regard for its international obligations. However one may fault successive Sri Lanka governments for their policies of seeking to expatriate the Indian community, one should note that the Sri Lanka government at no point engaged in the forcible expulsion or killing of estate workers. Its repatriation policies were constrained by whatever agreements were reached with India.

This study of India's involvement in Sri Lanka's affairs in the period from 1987 to 1991 is a contribution to the growing literature on managing ethnic conflict in deeply divided societies, especially the involvement of regional powers in such disputes. Several recent examples spring to mind: Turkey in Cyprus, Israel and Syria in Lebanon, Vietnam in Cambodia. No doubt other examples will emerge from the burgeoning ethnic conflicts of central and eastern Europe in the future. This book is also a case study in the usefulness or otherwise of accords and treaties in mediating ethnic conflict.[7]

Sri Lanka's ethnic conflict is a much more complex business than a simple straightforward confrontation between a well-entrenched minority—the Sri Lankan Tamils—and a powerful but insecure majority—the Sinhalese. Although, at present, the Sinhalese majority and the Sri Lankan Tamil minority play the principal roles in this intricate political drama, they are not the only players, as the frequent and increasingly ferocious clashes (1984–91) between the Tamils and the smaller Muslim minority show. Most Sinhalese believe that the Tamil minority has enjoyed a privileged position under British rule, and that the balance must of necessity shift in favor of the Sinhalese majority. The Sri Lankan Tamil minority are an achievement-oriented, industrious group that enjoyed and continue to enjoy high status in society, have considerable influence in the economy and a still significant if diminishing presence in the bureaucracy, and are well placed in all levels of the administrative system. The Tamils, for their part, would claim that they are now a harassed minority group, the victims of frequent acts of communal violence and calculated acts and policies of discrimination directed at them. These two contending perceptions lie at the core of the current political crisis in the island, and have rendered the governance of Sri Lanka's multiethnic society more than ordinarily difficult.

Devolution and Separatism

Two issues figure prominently in the mediation of the Sri Lankan conflict: devolution of power and a remodeling of the postindependence Sri

Lankan polity, and the demand of the Sri Lankan Tamils—as distinct from Sri Lanka's Indian Tamil minority—for the creation of a Tamil-dominated region covering the island's Northern and Eastern Provinces. Chapter 5 of this book seeks to explain why these issues figure so prominently in the debates and discussions on Sri Lanka's ethnic conflict and why it is necessary—indeed essential—to go back, briefly, to the island's troubled history.

In recent times the Sinhalese and the Sri Lankan Tamils have had sharply different perceptions on the nature of the Sri Lankan state and diametrically opposed attitudes to decentralization and devolution of power to regional units of administration. Although the early proponents of decentralization (from the 1920s on) were Sinhalese, the situation has changed since independence. The main political parties of the Sri Lankan Tamils have become the principal if not sole advocates of decentralization and devolution. These demands have provoked strong opposition from the Sinhalese, both in the mainstream political parties and in pressure groups representing Sinhalese-Buddhist opinion. Many of them fear, if not believe, that schemes of devolution of power are likely to lead to political fragmentation of the island and threaten the island's territorial integrity through the reemergence of a Tamil state—a Tamil kingdom had existed in the northernmost parts of the island and parts of the east coast from the thirteenth to the early seventeenth century—and the linking of such a state to Tamil Nadu in southern India.

Then again, the results of the policies of centralization vigorously pursued by the British during their rule in the country (1796–1947) have proved to be an enduring political legacy, because postindependence regimes have been both reluctant and unable to repudiate it. These centralizing processes were initiated in 1815–18 with the subjugation of the last independent Sinhalese kingdom, the kingdom of Kandy, and the fusion of its territories with the narrow coastal strip the British had conquered from the Dutch. However, it was not until 1832 that a unified administrative system for the whole island was set up, in the course of which the existing traditional regional and subregional administrative boundaries were eliminated and replaced by new provincial boundaries. The objective behind the action was avowedly political: to hasten the breakup of the Kandyan kingdom and to weaken national feeling in the Kandyan areas. The Kandyan kingdom had successfully resisted Western invaders—the Portuguese and Dutch—since the middle of the sixteenth century, and had defeated and destroyed a British expeditionary force in 1803. In 1832 the island was divided into five zones of administration in the form of provinces. When changes in these boundaries came between 1845 and 1889, they were mostly a belated recognition of traditional boundaries. By 1889 there were nine provinces. With only minor adjustments to their boundaries, introduced largely for purposes that can only be described as administrative convenience, this structure has survived to the present day. In the 1950s the district—a smaller administrative entity within a province—replaced the province as the largest unit of administration. Even so, the province survived, bereft of all administrative energy and purpose, a remnant of a British system that refused to fade away, and eventually received another lease on life in 1987–88.

The pressure for revival of the provincial structure has been an integral part of Tamil separatist agitation in Sri Lanka. The case for Tamil separation was built on the modern doctrine of self-determination of peoples. Linked with it, in time, was the concept of the "traditional homelands" of the Tamils, "homelands" that needed to be protected from "outsiders," themselves citizens of the same country. This concept first emerged in the early 1950s. Every version of it since that time has been built on a foundation of pseudohistorical data. It is a claim based on a hazy "historical" memory of statehood in centuries past, remembered and now interpreted (and generally misinterpreted) as a continuous and continuing tradition of independent statehood and an unbroken national consciousness.[8] In less than a decade after its first enunciation, this theory—refined as the notion of "the traditional homelands" of the Tamils—has become an indispensable and integral part of the political ideology of the Tamil advocates of regional autonomy and separatism. The definition of boundaries of the "homelands" came in the mid-1950s and generally encompassed the Northern and Eastern Provinces.

As a result of its overt separatist connotations, the concept of "the traditional homelands" of the Tamils has generated hostility from the Sinhalese. The Eastern Province was an integral part of the Kandyan kingdom, and it contains the main ports of that kingdom: Trincomalee and Batticaloa. Furthermore, the Tamils are a minority in that province, and neither its Muslim population nor the Sinhalese favor linking it with the Tamil-dominated Northern Province. All these issues are reviewed in considerable detail in chapter 5 of this book.

Indian Involvement in Sri Lanka's Ethnic Conflict

India has had three roles in Sri Lanka's ethnic conflict. The first, which began with Indira Gandhi's return to power in 1980, was that of a covert supporter of Sri Lankan Tamil separatist activists operating in India, mostly in Tamil Nadu. As we shall see, this covert support continued until 1987. The Tamil Nadu factor is an important facet of India's complex role in regard to Sri Lankan affairs. Seldom has a constituent unit (a province or a state) of one country influenced the relationship between it and a neighboring country with the same intensity as and to the same extent that Tamil Nadu did and continues to do in the case of India's relations with Sri Lanka. The India–Tamil Nadu–Sri Lanka tripartite relationship is thus unique in international affairs. Admittedly, India's own role is a more complex one than merely reacting to the pressures of domestic policies in Tamil Nadu. Tamil Nadu governments have provided Sri Lankan Tamil separatist activists with sanctuaries, training, and bases. Not only did the central government connive in this, it also tolerated the provision of training facilities and the existence of camps and bases in other parts of the country. These began with Indira Gandhi in the early 1980s, that is to say, well before the riots of July 1983 in Sri Lanka.

India's role of mediator—the second of the three roles—began under Mrs. Gandhi as a calculated political response to the anti-Tamil riots of July 1983 in Sri Lanka, and continued under Rajiv Gandhi. The third role, that of active participant, began in late 1987 and continued to the middle of 1990. That too is almost unique in the history of mediation in ethnic conflict. Rarely if ever has a mediator taken on the role of combatant, and the presumed guardian of an ethnic minority's interests waged a bitter war against sections of that minority, in a neighboring state at that.

Mrs. Gandhi's assumption of power as prime minister in 1966 saw a further recovery of Indian morale after the debacle of 1962 in the conflict with China. She took over as prime minister after the sudden death of Lal Bahadur Shastri against the background of India's diplomatic success in Tashkent after the war with Pakistan in 1965. India's position in South Asia became immeasurably stronger after its successful intervention in the conflict within Pakistan leading to that country's dismemberment and the creation of Bangladesh.[9] In a recent study on India, Lloyd I. and Susanne Hoeber Rudolph capture the essence of the new situation:

The Indian state's relative independence of the international system at the global level is complemented and reinforced by its leading role in the South Asian system. Its present dominant position followed the formation of Bangladesh in 1971, a development made possible by an Indian military victory over Pakistan. The South Asian region differs significantly from South East Asia, Latin America, Africa and the Middle East in two crucial aspects: the predominance of one power, India, and the small degree of political fragmentation . . . . India's relative position among South Asian states is characterized by a degree of asymmetry not present in the other four Third World regions . . . . India leads its region decisively (by ratios of 2:1 or more) in GNP, population, armed forces, military expenditures, installed energy, and world trade; Brazil is the only other single country to lead its region in all six measures, and Brazil's proportions and ratios are substantially lower than India's.[10]

Paradoxically, India's growing strength and the decisive shift in her favor of the balance of power in the region did little to reduce the sense of insecurity among her leaders, Mrs. Gandhi in particular. Their fears about India's continuing vulnerability were greatly exaggerated. Despite the lack of any solid basis for them they were shrewdly exploited to argue the case for "increased outlays for the defence industry and armed forces," and to produce by the early 1980s a "bureaucratic military elite which irrespective of any change in government, became assertive in the formulation of the state's domestic and foreign policies."[11] The objective was to turn India into a world power and "to persuade the world to give India its rightful place in international diplomacy."[12] Commenting on this last point, the Indian publicist Ravi Rikhye noted sardonically that "One of the most enduring (but least endearing) illusions that Indians have about their country is that we are a natural super power and must take our rightful place in that club."[13]

Indian critics of this transformation of the country into a military state have pointed out that she faces no serious security threat from any external source. The balance of power in the region has shifted so decisively in her favor vis-à-vis Pakistan since 1971 as to make the latter no credible threat to India. Nor is China any longer a formidable, let alone menacing, challenge. Yet the "budget for military research has quadrupled since 1982. Larger allocations were made to expedite the country's nuclear and ballistic-missile programme and [for] sophisticated weapons from abroad."[14]

A well-researched *Time* magazine article on the militarization of India made the point that "since 1986, India has ranked as the world's largest arms importer; in 1987, it purchased from abroad weaponry valued at

5.2 billion dollars, more than Iraq and Iran combined and twelve times as much as Pakistan."[15] It has the world's fourth largest army. This massive expansion of her "military capabilities [has] definitely fuelled the power-ambitions of its privileged elite." A "climate of psychological insecurity . . . helped the ascendancy of the hawks in the formulation of neighbourhood policies."[16] Among India's neighbors, none felt the impact of this "imperial" outlook on its internal affairs and external policy more than Sri Lanka in the period covered by this book, the 1980s through 1990–91.

Separatism and Its Victims

Historians are likely to view the 1970s and 1980s as a period when separatist agitation threatened the stability of many parts of South Asia, India and Sri Lanka in particular. Mrs. Gandhi returned to power in 1980 after suffering her first electoral reverse in 1977, the first defeat of an Indian prime minister and government since independence, to face a divided opposition. She confronted, however, a resurgence of separatist sentiment in the Punjab and Assam. Her response to the first was characteristically aggressive and cynical, an attempt to manipulate the separatist forces in the region through a policy of dividing and ruling. It was effective to deal with Assam at this stage by a mixture of force and deft diplomacy. As for the Tamil separatist agitation in Sri Lanka, she countenanced the use of Indian territory—Tamil Nadu in particular—by separatist activists from that neighboring country. She paid a terrible price for all this in aggravating the Punjab crisis and making that state virtually ungovernable for nearly a decade, and in her own assassination by Sikhs from her own personal bodyguard at the end of October 1984. And her son, who inherited the problems caused by her Sri Lankan policies, was assassinated in May 1991 in Tamil Nadu by Tamil separatist activists from Sri Lanka.

It is not that Sri Lanka's own political leadership of the 1980s handled the challenges posed by separatist agitation with greater skill than their Indian counterparts. But in their case it could be said that their freedom of movement in that regard was constrained by Indian pressures. Some of the most powerful of these latter were from the state of Tamil Nadu, from both government and opposition groups. All of them lent their support to separatist agitation among the Tamils of Sri Lanka. The Indian central government, whether under Mrs. Gandhi or her son Rajiv, did not feel strong enough to assert its own authority against the political pressures of Tamil Nadu. Mrs. Gandhi did not think it necessary to do so.

Within Sri Lanka itself separatism took its toll among the political leaders. President Ranasinghe Premadasa, who tried to work and come to terms with the Liberation Tigers of Tamil Eelam (LTTE), the main Tamil separatist group, was assassinated by them on 1 May 1993 in Colombo. Two Sri Lankan defense ministers, men who gave leadership to the struggle against the LTTE, were also assassinated by them: Lalith Athulathmudali in May 1993, and Ranjan Wijeratne in March 1991. Gamini Dissanayake, who was closely associated with efforts to resolve the problem through Indian mediation in 1987 and 1988, was assassinated in October 1994. President J. R. Jayewardene himself had narrowly escaped assassination on 18 August 1987, not at the hands of the LTTE but by a Marxist nationalist group, the Janatha Vimukthi Peramuna. This group was exploiting a backlash against him for coming to terms with India through a peace accord signed on 29 July 1987 in an attempt at managing, if not resolving, the Sri Lanka conflict. Thus our study has a macabre aspect, with violent death stalking the corridors of power in both India and Sri Lanka and claiming a succession of very distinguished victims, two blown up by suicide killers,[17] two shot by assassins, and one killed in a massive blast set off by a timing device.[18]

Notes

1. On Sri Lanka's ethnic conflicts there is a large and growing literature. The following works will be useful to the reader: K. M. de Silva, *Managing Ethnic Tensions in Multi-Ethnic Societies: Sri Lanka, 1880–1985* (Lanham, Md.: University Press of America, 1986); Stanley J. Tambiah, *Sri Lanka: Ethnic Fratricide and the Dismantling of Democracy* (Chicago: University of Chicago Press, 1986); Sinha Ratnatunga, *The Politics of Terrorism: The Sri Lanka Experience* (Canberra: International Fellowship for Social and Economic Development, 1988).

2. For discussion, see S. W. R. de A. Samarasinghe, "The Dynamics of Separatism: The Case of Sri Lanka," in Ralph R. Premdas, S. W. R. de A. Samarasinghe, and Alan B. Anderson, eds., *Secessionist Movements in Comparative Perspective* (London: Pinter, 1990), 48–70.

3. On the theme of Indian migration under British rule, see Hugh Tinker, *A New System of Slavery: The Export of Indian Labour Overseas, 1830–1920* (London: Oxford University Press, 1974); Tinker, *Separate and Unequal: India and the Indians in the British Commonwealth, 1920–1950* (London: C. Hurst, 1976); Tinker, *The Banyan Tree: Overseas Emigrants from India, Pakistan, and Bangladesh* (Oxford: Oxford University Press, 1977). For a more recent survey, see C. Z. Guilmoto, "The Tamil Migration Cycle, 1830–1950," *Economic and Political Weekly*, 16–23 January 1993.

4. These elections were held in 1947, not 1949.

5. The technical term used is "repatriate."

6. Myron Weiner, "Rejected Peoples and Unwanted Migrants in South Asia," *Economic and Political Weekly* 21 (August 1993):1738–39.

7. K. M. de Silva and S. W. R. de A. Samarasinghe, eds., *Peace Accords and Ethnic Conflict* (London: Pinter, 1993).

8. K. M. de Silva, *The "Traditional Homelands" of the Tamils—Separatist Ideology in Sri Lanka: A Historical Appraisal,* Occasional Paper no. 4. (Kandy: International Centre for Ethnic Studies, 1994).

9. Richard Sisson and Leo E. Rose, *War and Secession: Pakistan, India and the Creation of Bangladesh* (Berkeley: University of California Press, 1990).

10. Lloyd I. Rudolph and Susanne Hoeber Rudolph, *In Pursuit of Lakshmi: The Political Economy of the Indian State* (Chicago: University of Chicago Press, 1987), 4. This point has recently been made by several other commentators on South Asian politics. India has 79 percent of the region's GNP, 72 percent of its land area, and nearly 60 percent of its total trade.

11. Anirudha Gupta, "A Brahmanic Framework of Power?" *Economic and Political Weekly* 7 (April 1989).

12. Ibid.

13. Ravi Rikhye, *The Militarization of Mother India* (Delhi: Chanakya Publications, 1990), 82.

14. Gupta, "Brahmanic Framework."

15. *Time,* 3 April 1989, quoted in Gupta, "Brahmanic Framework."

16. Gupta, "Brahmanic Framework."

17. Rajiv Gandhi and R. Premadasa.

18. Ranjan Wijeratne, Sri Lanka's foreign minister and minister of state for defense, 1989–91.

Part I

2

India and Sri Lanka, 1947–79:
Conflicting Visions of Security

ON 31 JULY 1987, the Indian high commission—that is, the Indian embassy—in Colombo published the following news bulletin on an agreement signed between India and Sri Lanka in Colombo two days earlier.

Indo–Sri Lankan Agreement Signed in Colombo

The Prime Minister of India, Mr Rajiv Gandhi paid a two-day visit to Sri Lanka and had talks with the Sri Lankan President, Mr Jayewardene in Colombo on the afternoon of July 29. The two leaders were together without aides for about 45 minutes. According to reports, practical steps to implement the proposed Indo–Sri Lankan agreement were discussed. The discussion also covered Indo–Sri Lankan cooperation in political, cultural and educational fields.

Earlier Mr Rajiv Gandhi arrived in Colombo on the morning of July 29. He was received by the Sri Lankan Finance Minister, Mr Ronnie de Mel at Katunayake Airport. Mr Gandhi later flew in a helicopter to meet Mr Jayewardene and his cabinet colleagues.

The two leaders signed the historic agreement later. After the signing ceremony they also addressed a joint press conference. In the evening the Sri Lankan President and Mrs Jayewardene hosted a dinner in honour of Mr Rajiv Gandhi and Mrs Sonia Gandhi.[1]

This bland announcement was more suited to the early nineteenth century than to the latter part of the twentieth, when news—especially bad news—is flashed across the globe in seconds. There was an air of

15

unreality about the news bulletin because it ignored every aspect of the dramatic events associated with the signing of the agreement—the violence in and around the city of Colombo, the deserted streets through which the Gandhis had been whisked for the ceremony, and above all the guard of honor ceremony at their departure, when a naval enlisted man had swung the butt end of his rifle at the Indian prime minister. The latter would certainly have been seriously injured if not killed had the blow struck him on the head as it had been intended to. That incident had provided photographers and television crews assembled for the occasion with the pictures of a lifetime, and minutes later television viewers in the Western world were shown the attack, sometimes frame by frame, to capture the incident in all its horror, and generally as the first news item of the day.

Less than four years later—on 21 June 1991—Rajiv Gandhi was assassinated in India. The assassins were a group of Tamils from Sri Lanka. They had succeeded in doing what that infuriated Sinhalese sailor had failed to do on 30 July 1987.

These two events, both focusing on an Indian prime minister and his country's relations with the small island neighbor to the south of the Indian subcontinent, encapsulate the tensions, suspicions, fears, and indeed hatred that have governed relations between the two countries in recent years. The fundamental issue was the conflicting visions of security of the two neighbors after 1947–48, when they gained their independence from the British.

Sri Lanka's geographical location emphasizes its proximity today as in centuries past to a large regional power or powers in the Indian subcontinent. The India of today is a much larger and more powerful political entity than any Indian state or states that impinged on Sri Lanka's affairs either in the distant past or since the sixteenth century, with the single exception of the British *raj*. Despite its proximity to the Indian subcontinent, Sri Lanka or Ceylon as it was then called was never part of the *raj*. By contrast, Burma was part of the *raj* until 1937, and Ceylon was administered by the Colonial Office as a crown colony. This separation from the *raj* has had a profound impact on the political thinking and the strategic vision of several generations of Sri Lankans, and especially its influential politicians, beginning with its first postindependence prime minister, D. S. Senanayake. His strategy for the country's survival in the postindependence situation was based on the assumption that the most likely threat to its independence would come from India.[2]

As he saw it, the stark choice the country faced was between survival as a small but independent partner of the Commonwealth and absorption by an independent India. Senanayake believed that Nehru's ambition was to make independent India the dominant power in the region, and that the latter's continuing interest in Sri Lanka was solely on account of its strategic importance, the naval base in Trincomalee and air bases in other parts of the island.

The defense agreements between Britain and Sri Lanka signed prior to the grant of independence in February 1948[3] were part of a process of adjusting to the uncertainties of a new pattern of international politics in South Asia when India would become an independent state. Because of Britain's strategic interests in the Indian Ocean, Sri Lanka was a vital link in securing British ties with Australia and New Zealand.[4] For Senanayake they served a different but not less important purpose in offering security against any possible threats from India to Sri Lanka's independence.

Senanayake's policies survived his death in 1952, but not the defeat of his party, the United National Party (UNP) in 1956. S. W. R. D. Bandaranaike, the leader of the Sri Lanka Freedom Party (SLFP) who had led the Mahajana Eksath Peramuna (MEP) coalition, of which his party was the core, to victory in 1956, had been a member of the Board of Ministers and the cabinet that had endorsed Senanayake's objectives in negotiating the transfer of power, and supported the signing of the defense agreements with Great Britain. After he crossed over to the opposition in 1951, however, he became a vigorous and persistent critic of the agreement and a strong advocate of nonalignment. Naturally Nehru found him a congenial ally.[5] After his victory in 1956 he persuaded Britain, in late 1957, to hand over control of its air and naval bases in the island to the Sri Lankan government. Nevertheless, neither party formally abrogated the defense agreements signed prior to independence.

The emphasis in Sri Lanka's foreign policy after 1956 has been assessed and its salient features have been outlined and analyzed in a number of monographs and articles, and it is not intended to deal with them here. What is important is to note that Sri Lanka had moved out of range of Britain's defense umbrella just at the time when the protection it offered was becoming insubstantial. The time had come to think of a national defense policy for the new strategic situation—the power vacuum created by Britain's abandonment of her traditional role in the Indian Ocean region.[6] Neither the SLFP-dominated governments of the periods 1956 to 1965 and 1970 to 1988, nor the UNP-led coalition of 1965 to 1970 did anything to develop even a modest defensive capacity against any external threat, or for that matter even against internal turmoil. The outbreak of the first Janatha Vimukthi Peramuna (JVP) insurrection in 1971 saw a marked increase in defense expenditure, but it was not sustained beyond 1972, largely because the insurrection was speedily crushed. (As we shall see, this Marxist-nationalist group recovered its strength in the 1980s and posed a deadly threat to the state.) More significantly, without considering the long-term implications of its actions or inaction Sri Lanka took shelter under the security system that India was in the process of constructing.

Such regional security arrangements as Bandaranaike may have had in mind in 1956, regional cooperation among India, Pakistan, Burma, and Sri Lanka, were beyond the capacity of these nations to devise. The passions and hatreds that developed over the partition of the *raj,* and of course the Kashmir issue, kept India and Pakistan apart and drew Pakistan into its alliance with the United States. In the mid- and late 1950s Burma had ambitions of building a Buddhist bloc and of giving the religious enthusiasms generated by the *Buddha Jayanthi*—the 2,500th anniversary of the death of the Buddha—a political content. These proved to be chimerical as Burma's prolonged civil war and ethnic conflicts aggravated the political instability that had been its fate ever since it became independent in 1948. No wonder then that Bandaranaike found an association with Nehru's India so agreeable and useful. Whatever differences there were in regard to their respective attitudes to the role of ethnicity and religion in the processes of state building and consolidation in their own countries—and the differences were indeed very substantial—they had a common anxiety to steer clear of the entanglements of the Cold War. In regard to this latter, Bandaranaike followed where Nehru led, as did the leaders of a number of countries then emerging from colonial rule. Nehru's prestige as a world leader was at its height during this period.

But even if a small state like Sri Lanka could afford to ignore its external environment, India could not. She had inherited much the larger portion of the *raj* after the partition, and was in the process of consolidating it into a cohesive state. India confronted the revived strength of powerful precolonial forces such as language, culture, religion, and ethnicity, forces that were intrinsically divisive in their impact on the

Indian polity. The implementation of the recommendations of the Boundaries Commission of 1955 has a dual significance. Through them Nehru's India came to terms with the divisive pressures of linguistic nationalism allied to regional identities, and they also constituted the second and more decisive phase in the submergence of "princely" India in the modern Indian polity.

India's "Natural" Boundaries

Nehru's India and Nehru himself had inherited from the *raj* a belief in India's "natural" boundaries. This faith was one that most prominent Indians shared with Nehru, including even some of his most mettlesome critics such as the well-known Indian writer, Nirad Chaudhuri, the author of the classic *Autobiography of an Unknown India*. In an essay published in 1985, Chaudhuri claimed:

> No country is more clearly demarcated by geography, and yet no country is more open to invasions. Therefore, India, too, needed to have her natural frontiers, which, ideally, should run along the Hindu Kush, its south-western extension, the main Himalayas, and their extension to the south-west.[7]

This extract from Chaudhuri is important not merely for its clear exposition of the concept of India's "natural frontiers" but also for its reference to another familiar theme, fears about India's vulnerability. This latter was the natural result of Indian concern with the recent past, when colonial powers fought for supremacy on Indian soil, the triumph of the British, and the construction of the *raj*. Indeed, as an Indian political analyst points out, India's politicians and strategists were all acutely aware of this:

> The events of the second World War, especially the Japanese sweep through archipelagic and mainland South-East Asia in a remarkably short time, had driven home the lesson to India's nationalist elite that India's eastern flank and the seaward approaches to the subcontinent were as important for India's defence as the land boundaries of the north-west and the north which had been traditional concerns of strategists during the days of the British *Raj*. . . .
>
> The events of the [second world] war also increased Indian awareness of, and concern with, its maritime strategy and the great importance of the Indian Ocean to the defence of the Indian peninsula.

The lesson that India had lost its independence to European colonists because of the latter's control of the sea was relearnt by the Indian nationalist elite as a result of the experience of the second world war.[8]

K. M. Panikkar popularized this latter view in the last days of the Second World War in his study, *India and the Indian Ocean: An Essay on the Influence of Sea Power on Indian History.* He warned that

an exclusively land policy of defence for India will in future be nothing short of blindness. No other policy was required in the past, as the Indian Ocean was a protected sea—a British lake. . . . But today the position is different. The freedom of India will hardly be worth a day's purchase, if Indian interests in the Indian Ocean are not defended from India, especially, as in the changed circumstances. . . . the British fleet will be in no position to maintain that unchallenged supremacy which it possessed for 150 years. . . . As a free nation it is [India's] sacred duty to organize herself in every way for the defence of her freedom. This . . . is primarily an Oceanic problem. Unless India is prepared to stand forth and shoulder the responsibility of peace and security in the Indian Ocean, her freedom will mean little. She will be at the mercy of any power which has command of the sea, as it will be impossible for us to require of Britain or any other country to defend the Indian Ocean for us.[9]

In its commitment to the defense of this inheritance, Nehru's India was assuming, tentatively at first, but with greater conviction with the passage of time, the strategic vision of the *raj,* especially the conception of the South Asian region as "a political unit knit together for defense."[10] When, in practical terms, it meant an attempt to assert rights to disputed boundaries imposed by British proconsuls on weak neighbors in the nineteenth and early twentieth centuries, Nehru's India came into conflict with the People's Republic of China, with whose revolutionary leaders Nehru had cultivated a warm friendship. For some time, a common Asian identity and rejection of colonialism had drawn them together until disputes over India's borders with China led to the outbreak of hostilities in 1962.

Thus the defense thinking of the *raj* lived on, a lively presence in Delhi, and by no means a ghostly one. It has drawn India into conflict with many of its South Asian neighbors, and more important, with China.

Since 1959, relations between the two Asian giants have been seriously affected by conflicting interpretations on the "true frontiers" of the *raj* in the Himalayan region. The following passage from *India and the China Crisis* by American scholar Steven A. Hoffman provides a succinct summary of the issues in the conflict. He draws a contrast between the Indian and British viewpoints on this:

> Underpinning them all was the fervent belief that an Indian nation had existed through time—defined by culture, common experience, custom and geography—long before the British had created and imposed their own state structure on the subcontinent. . . . Crucial to the British view had been the belief that India existed as a viable political unit only because of British military and administrative power.

More specific to the issue of national boundaries was the Indian assumption that

> India's traditional and customary boundaries had long existed and had evolved naturally, since they were based on the activities of populations and cultures and on geographical features such as mountain ridges and watersheds. The British had chosen to reinforce these boundaries, or to deviate from them, for strategic reasons and because their knowledge of Indian geography was not complete. More important, however, was that, when acting as definers of borders, the British were not basing their thinking on historical evidence. That was why they could wittingly or unwittingly sacrifice Indian interests when formulating frontier and border decisions.[11]

For the smaller South Asian states the return of China to the world stage as an independent state was a source of quiet satisfaction, although none of them yet regarded China as a counterweight to India. If at all, it was a counterweight to the colonial powers who still controlled parts of Southeast Asia. Influential sections of Sri Lanka's political elite saw China as a benign influence in South Asian affairs, and a reassuring one. Indeed, for Sirimavo Bandaranaike, the widow of S. W. R. D. Bandaranaike and the country's sixth prime minister, friendship with China was a vitally important facet of her government's foreign policy in the 1960s and 1970s.

The Sino-Indian war of 1962 was in every way a turning point in the evolution of South Asian security systems. For one thing, India emerged from the shadow of this defeat intent on building up its ground and air strength to face the new challenge from its mighty Asian rival, China. Furthermore, for many Asian countries, Pakistan in particular, China became a far more effective counterweight to India than any Western ally; China was both closer and more consistent in the support it gave.

Over the 1960s South Asia felt the impact of contemporary changes in great-power relations. The most significant of these changes was the rift between China and the Soviet Union. During and in the aftermath of India's China war, the Soviet Union and the United States, each for its own special concerns, had supplied India with arms to save her from further humiliation at the hands of China. India, the major regional power in South Asia, and its principal rival, Pakistan, were drawn into extra-regional alliances, the latter because of opposition to India over Kashmir and other issues. This in turn had repercussions on the strategic situation and strategic vision of the South Asian states. Despite Pakistan's membership in U.S.-sponsored security alliances such as the Southeast Asia Treaty Organization (SEATO), and the arms assistance she received from the United States, the latter was generally anxious to maintain neutrality on the Indo-Pakistani dispute. On the other hand, there was less hesitation on the part of the Soviet Union in its support of the Indian position on the Kashmir dispute.

After the Sino-Indian war of 1962, a reappraisal of Indian defense policy led to a substantial increase in expenditure on the expansion and modernization of India's armed services. When the Indo-Pakistani war of 1965 broke out, there was an unusual situation in which both sides used weapons supplied by the United States. The United States responded to the outbreak of war between the two states, one an ally and the other a friendly state, by suspending arms supplies to both. Although China threatened to intervene on Pakistan's side, she did not do so, but there was no hesitation on the part of the Soviet Union in her support of India. Indeed, the Soviet Union took the initiative in the diplomatic negotiations that brought the hostilities to an end, and in the signing of the Tashkent declaration by the two belligerents in 1966.

The sudden death of Nehru's successor, Lal Bahadur Shastri, in Tashkent just after the completion of the negotiations there, paved the way for the 1966 election of Nehru's daughter, Indira Gandhi, as India's prime minister, thus beginning the second phase of over four decades of the Nehru-Gandhi family's dominance in Indian politics. Mrs. Gandhi figures prominently in this book. The next two parts of this chapter are devoted to an analysis of her strategic vision and her relations with Sri Lanka during the first phase of her prime ministership (1966–77) and especially with her Sri Lankan counterpart, Mrs. Sirimavo Bandaranaike, during the latter's second term in office (1970–77). Mrs. Gandhi's protagonist in the events of the 1980s that form the substance of this book was J. R. Jayewardene, the first executive president of Sri Lanka. He makes a brief entry in this chapter but figures more prominently in chapter three.

Mrs. Gandhi's Strategic Vision

These events of 1965 and 1966 led to a strengthening of the extra-regional alliances in South Asia. Disappointed at the U.S. suspension of arms supplies in 1965, Pakistan turned even more to China as a reliable source of military supplies. India, in turn, looked to the Soviet Union—again, as a more reliable and regular source of military supplies and the transfer of technology—for a systematic and purposeful program of modernization of her security services and the indigenization of arms production. Under Mrs. Gandhi, an Indo-Soviet link confronted the Sino-Pakistani alliance; the Soviet Union saw India as the most effective check on the expansion of U.S. and Chinese influence in South Asia.

While the major regional powers of South Asia were locked into alliances with extraregional powers, the smaller states were anxious not to be drawn into their conflicts. These smaller states remained committed to nonalignment as the principal feature of their foreign policy. For Sri Lanka, an alternative to India's security umbrella appeared in the late 1960s when she was offered membership in the newly formed Association of Southeast Asian Nations (ASEAN). But the UNP-led coalition of this period would not commit itself to this, and certainly there was no national consensus on ASEAN as there was for nonalignment. The SLFP, and to a greater extent the Marxist left, regarded ASEAN with deep suspicion as a neoimperialist venture serving U.S. strategic interests and inimical to Sri Lanka's status as a "nonaligned" nation.[12]

In the 1970s the Sino-Soviet rift was a very conspicuous feature in Asia's strategic landscape, with a marked visibility in the affairs of South Asia. This shift in strategic orientation saw the Indo-Soviet and Sino-Pakistani alliances assume an unusual prominence in regional politics there. In another overlapping development, superpower rivalries intruded into the Indian Ocean through increased naval activity seeking to fill the vacuum caused by the departure of the British navy, and, on the part of the United States, an anxiety to protect the sea routes to and from the oil-rich Persian Gulf to Europe and the Far East.

All this occurred against the background of continued disharmony between India and Pakistan, and simmering discontent within the latter, especially in its eastern wing, where the Bengali-speaking majority sought to resist the power and demands of a Pakistani state dominated by the western wing. The growing dependence of India on the Soviet Union and of Pakistan on China aggravated these existing tendencies. India was intent on exploiting discontent in the eastern wing of Pakistan, to weaken her rival and if possible to dismember her. The Indo-Soviet treaty of 1971 greatly strengthened India in fashioning her intervention in Pakistan's civil war. Within twenty-five years of its creation the state of Pakistan was divided once more, demonstrating this time—in the birth of Bangladesh—the superior strength of language and culture as points of identity in a state that was constructed, at the time of the partition of the *raj*, on the basis that religion was the principal bond of identity of the Muslim minorities.

The regional ramifications of the birth of Bangladesh were equally far-reaching. The balance of power in the subcontinent shifted decisively and dramatically in India's favor with her successful intervention in the civil war in Pakistan, and the support she gave to Bangladeshi independence. Neither China—which had threatened to intervene but did not—nor the United States—which had used some bluster in what came to be called a tilt in Pakistan's favor—had been able to save Pakistan from dismemberment. However, Bangladeshi independence strengthened rather than reduced Pakistan's dependence on China as an ally. The smaller states— such as Sri Lanka—had to accommodate themselves to this new strategic situation, of a powerful and more self-confident India.

A surprising by-product of this fundamental change in the strategic situation in South Asia in India's favor was an even greater emphasis in Indian political and defense circles on strengthening India's security forces. It set in motion a trend of events that reached its maturity in the mid- and late 1980s, when, apart from a "dramatic acceleration of India's fighting capacity," security became the "end-goal of defense and foreign policy planning," and with all this a notable "shift became visible in India's treatment of its neighbors."[13]

India's arrogation of the presumed strategic role of the *raj* with its axiom of subcontinental defense based on the essential strategic unity of the region was an established fact by the late 1960s. India's neighbors— in particular Pakistan, but increasingly Bangladesh, Nepal, and Sri Lanka as well—regarded this as an encroachment on their own strategic interests. For many of them, Pakistan in particular, the main security threat was from India itself. As a critic of these politics saw it a generation later, India's "immediate concern [was] to establish primacy in the region whereby its neighbours should accept that their national security cannot stay apart from but must become complementary to India."[14]

Sri Lanka had begun taking shelter under India's defense umbrella in the 1960s as a purely voluntary act, on the rebound, as it were, from Britain's reduction of her traditional imperial defense obligations in the Indian Ocean. In the 1970s and 1980s, with Indira Gandhi reflecting the views of the exponents of India's assumption of the mantle of the *raj*, India decided that small South Asian neighbors like Sri Lanka *must* take shelter under that umbrella, and that a search for an alternative would be regarded as an unacceptable, if not intolerable, challenge to the now dominant regional power. This policy was made explicit with regard to Sri Lanka in 1983.

The speed with which Indian assistance had arrived to support Mrs. Bandaranaike's left-of-center government when it was threatened by the JVP insurrection of 1971 was as significant as the eagerness with which it was done. But the implications of this hardly registered in the minds of Sri Lanka's national political leadership of that period.

India's main interest in the late 1960s and early 1970s, so far as Sri Lanka was concerned, was in what it regarded as the increasing Chinese influence in the island. The signing of a maritime agreement between Sri Lanka and China in early 1973, conferring "most favored nation" status on each other and making provision for ships of the two countries to carry cargo and passengers to and from the ports of either country, was regarded in New Delhi as ominous evidence of the intensification of that influence. India was extraordinarily sensitive to the possibility of any foreign power or influence—China on this occasion, but later the United States—gaining access to Trincomalee on Sri Lanka's east coast, acknowledged to be one of the world's finest natural harbors. The signing of the Sino–Sri Lankan maritime treaty was viewed in India as potentially the prelude to moves by Beijing to obtain facilities in Trincomalee for its war and maritime fleets. There was no evidence at all that China had any such ambitions or that Sri Lanka would cooperate in helping her to fulfill it, but the rumors persisted in Delhi, despite firm denials in Colombo.

The almost obsessive concern of Indian diplomats and politicians with the port of Trincomalee provides striking evidence of the durability of late-eighteenth- and early-nineteenth-century British assessments of its strategic value,[15] rather than an accurate evaluation of the actual value of the port to the British during their rule in the island. Lord Nelson's comment that it was the finest harbor in the world is quoted with remarkable frequency, but not the fact that Trincomalee did not flower into an important naval base after the British captured it.[16] As early as 1812, Trincomalee was a desolate and impoverished place. In G. S. Graham's study *Great Britain in the Indian Ocean,* published in 1967, the subsection on Trincomalee carries the pithy but wholly appropriate title, "The Rise and Fall of Trincomalee."[17] It was only in the Second World War after Japan had captured Hong Kong and Singapore that Trincomalee reverted to its early-nineteenth-century position of a base for the British East Indies fleet.[18]

Although the Indian government made no public statements to this effect, it was an open secret that Indian military strategists believed Sri Lanka should be brought under India's defense umbrella more emphatically than had been the case up to that time, not only because of its strategic location in the Indian Ocean, but also because of Sri Lanka's very friendly ties with China. Indian strategists thought it unwise to trust Mrs. Bandaranaike's left-of-center coalition to remain neutral in the event of another Sino-Indian confrontation, believing that it would endanger India's security if China were to gain a foothold in Trincomalee harbor. They remembered how Pakistani aircraft carrying reinforcements to East Pakistan during the Indo-Pakistani war of 1971 had been permitted to refuel in Colombo on the way to Dhaka. Although Sri Lanka denied the charge when Indian sources made it, the fact is that it actually happened. And Sri Lanka was one of the last countries in Asia, and one of the last non-Muslim states in the world, to grant recognition to Bangladesh, seen at that time as an Indian satellite state. Sri Lanka's recognition of Bangladesh came only after the Indian troops there were withdrawn.

The early 1970s were a period of aggressive Chinese diplomatic activity in the island. While China welcomed the return of Mrs. Bandaranaike to power in 1970, the strong Communist Party (Moscow wing) presence in the cabinet and the conspicuous lack of a committed pro-China figure in it were seen as a distinct disadvantage at a time of intense rivalry between the People's Republic of China and the Soviet Union. There were, of course, a few individuals in the legislature who were seen as either supporters of China or ideological sympathizers, but that was small compensation for the lack of a cohesive party with representation in the legislature. The JVP insurrection of 1971 was a setback for China, because of suspicions of a Chinese role in it through North Korea (seen at that time in Sri Lanka as a Chinese proxy), and it took a year or more for China to recover its influence with the government. By the middle of 1972 that recovery was complete, partly as a result of India's dismemberment of Pakistan and the creation of Bangladesh, partly with the growth of a small but seemingly influential group within the SLFP with strong Chinese sympathies if not links. That recovery was consolidated with the return to the island of Mrs. Bandaranaike's elder daughter and the daughter's first husband, Kumar Rupesinghe,[19] who were seen to be the leaders of a radical group with an ideological commitment more akin to the Chinese than to the Russian version of current Marxist orthodoxy. The Janavegaya movement, as it came to be called, had become a powerful and controversial influence within the government.

China's efforts at strengthening its influence in the country became a matter of controversy in the island throughout 1973. While the Sri Lankan prime minister herself was committed to the maintenance of close ties with China, she recognized the need to place limits on China's influence in the country. When there were allegations of a Chinese attempt to bribe representatives of the government parliamentary party into supporting the small but very vociferous pro-China lobby in Parliament in early 1974, she used considerable pressure in securing the virtual recall of the then Chinese ambassador in Colombo, Ma Tzu-Ching.

It was with these matters in mind that J. R. Jayewardene, leader of the opposition, speaking to a group of journalists and parliamentarians of the UNP on 3 April 1974, urged that Sri Lanka should strengthen her ties of friendship with India, and also establish new ones, particularly in regard to economic development. He went on to state that "on our part this needs a foreign policy of strict neutrality and non-alignment. The government must see to it that Sri Lanka does not become the breeding ground for political developments like the Naxalite movement in India." "It is obvious," Jayewardene continued, "that India cannot look on unconcerned if those in authority are used as pawns in international political maneuvers of the big powers."[20] Clearly he was referring to the powerful—and growing—Chinese influence in the country, and especially within the Bandaranaike family circle and therefore at the highest levels of the government.[21]

Then as in the mid- and late 1980s, an Indian "obsession with security" rendered its "policy makers acutely psycho-pathetically insecure. They fancied external threats from all directions."[22] Much of the illogicality of all this stemmed from the essential contradiction of a poor, if very large and populous, Third World country, taking on the mantle of the nineteenth century's superpower, Great Britain.

Superpower naval rivalry in the Indian Ocean was accelerated in the early 1970s. The United States established and developed a naval base and communications center on the island of Diego Garcia, causing concern among many of the littoral states. Few, if any, were more critical than India of the conspicuous U.S. presence in the Indian Ocean through its base at Diego Garcia.

In December 1971, at the twenty-sixth session of the UN General Assembly, Sri Lanka presented a resolution declaring that the Indian Ocean, "within limits to be determined, together with the air-space above and the ocean floor adjacent thereto, is hereby designated for all time as a Zone of Peace." All external powers were called upon to eliminate "all bases, military installations, and logistical supply facilities, the disposition of nuclear weapons and weapons of mass destruction . . . and great power rivalry." In 1972 the UN General Assembly appointed an ad hoc committee chaired by Sri Lanka to recommend ways and means of implementing this declaration. Two years later the United Nations recognized the need for convening an international conference to implement it. At this stage, the concept was widened to include a variety of proposals for nuclear-free zones embracing or in some cases limited to the littoral and hinterland states. Differences developed in the committee over the scope of the projected zone, and even on the advisability of holding the proposed international conference.[23] While India supported the resolution in its original form, it had strong reservations about its subsequent interpretations. The Indian objections were based on the contention that, while the original resolution treated the Indian Ocean as a water body, by 1973 the ad hoc committee sought to include the adjacent land mass; furthermore, the original acceptance of the concept by the superpowers was not conditional on reciprocal obligations by the littoral and hinterland states as it became after 1973–74. The Indian Ocean Peace Zone concept, in its later permutation, was perceived by India as inimical to its primary objectives of boosting its naval strength in the region and acquiring a blue-water naval capability. The smaller littoral states viewed India's change of emphasis, if not change of mind, on the Indian Ocean Peace Zone as a bid to establish an Indian-dominated ocean, to convert the Indian Ocean into an *Indian* ocean.

A Cordial Relationship, 1974 to 1977

When Mrs. Gandhi arrived in the island on 27 April 1974 for two days of talks with Mrs. Bandaranaike, few people anticipated the dramatic improvement in relations between the two countries that occurred from that point for the duration of the tenure of office of the two leaders as prime ministers of their countries.[24] Nor could they have predicted that the warm personal ties that developed between the two leaders and their immediate families would have such important consequences for relations between the two countries in the 1980s, when Mrs. Bandaranaike was out of power and Mrs. Gandhi returned to power in 1980 after her defeat at the hands of the Janatha coalition in 1977. But this is to anticipate events.

Two thorny issues dominated the discussions: the Kachchaitivu problem, and the question of voting rights of Indian plantation workers resident in the island. Kachchaitivu is a tiny uninhabited islet a few acres in extent in Sri Lanka's northern territorial waters. Although Sri Lankan rulers had exercised effective control over the islet from the fifteenth century at least, India had not acknowledged Sri Lanka's claims even when the subcontinent was under British control. Sri Lanka, for its part, had always dismissed India's claims on the ground that there was no historical evidence to support it. By the 1970s the islet had gained additional significance because it was situated in an area where there were believed to be substantial deposits of oil. Apart from that, and its access to rich fishing grounds, the islet has some religious significance to Roman Catholics. A festival staged there attracts Roman Catholic devotees from Sri Lanka's northern region and from India as well. It is also the point of entry for illicit immigrants from South India to Sri Lanka, who then disappear into the remoter parts of the country.

India's attitude to this problem was distinctly ambivalent, neither asserting its claims unambiguously nor acknowledging Sri Lanka's. On the other hand, the Dravida Munnetra Kazhagam (DMK) government in Tamil Nadu had been urging the Indian government to annex the islet. This attitude was by no means confined to the DMK in Tamil Nadu. Members of Mrs. Gandhi's own party had expressed much the same views. During her negotiations with Mrs. Bandaranaike, Mrs. Gandhi conceded Sri Lanka's rights to the islet, and used the opportunity to initiate moves for a comprehensive demarcation of maritime boundaries between the two countries.

The second issue was more complex, and one with a longer history of negotiations between the two countries.[25] In 1964 Mrs. Bandaranaike had successfully negotiated an agreement with her Indian counterpart, Lal Bahadur Shastri, which provided for repatriation of 525,000 Indian residents in Sri Lanka to India over a fifteen-year period, along with their natural increase, and the absorption of 300,000 as citizens of Sri Lanka. The future of the remainder, amounting to about 150,000, would be negotiated later on by the two countries. The political benefits to all parties were considerable, not least to the Indians in Sri Lanka, 300,000 of whom would become Sri Lankan citizens. But two parties—the Indian government and the Indians in Sri Lanka—had reservations about the principle of compulsory repatriation of those who opted for and obtained Indian citizenship.

The agreement was implemented by the UNP-led coalition of 1965–70, which placed a more liberal interpretation on its provisions. Thus those who were granted Indian citizenship were permitted to remain in the island, if necessary to the end of their working days, to be repatriated to India thereafter or at a time to be determined by the Sri Lankan government. Mrs. Bandaranaike, as leader of the opposition, was very critical of this decision. In her view, it had undermined one of its basic principles, reciprocity between the grant of Sri Lankan citizenship and repatriation of those granted Indian citizenship in a ratio of five to three (five persons being granted Indian citizenship for every three granted Sri Lankan citizenship). If this formula had been adhered to, 217,750 would have been repatriated to India by 1974 and Sri Lanka would have given citizenship to 131,250.

The discussions of 1974 brought to a successful conclusion the settlement originally negotiated in 1964. India agreed to a 10 percent increase in the annual intake of repatriates so that the process could be completed within the fifteen-year period envisaged by the treaty of 1964. Thus the problem of "statelessness" of the bulk of Indians resident in Sri Lanka would be eliminated once and for all. For the moment, the more urgent requirement was an agreement on how to deal with the balance of 150,000 left over for later consideration in terms of the 1964 pact. The decision was that there would be an equal division of these people into Indian and Sri Lankan citizens.

Not all the stateless were covered by this 1974 agreement: a number variously computed at between 50,000 and 75,000 were left over for further consideration, the last of the stateless. But much more important for Mrs. Bandaranaike was that the Indian government accepted the principle that those who were granted Indian citizenship must be repatriated to India as soon as they were given such citizenship, and that the process of repatriation should be expedited in order to make up for the time lost between 1965 and 1970.

Mrs. Bandaranaike reciprocated her Indian counterpart's conciliatory policy by making an important shift of emphasis in Sri Lanka's foreign policy. The tilt in favor of China was adjusted. In its place one saw a deliberate attempt at reaching a congruence of views on regional and foreign affairs between Sri Lanka and India. Thus by the middle of 1974 Mrs. Gandhi no longer had reason to fear that Sri Lanka's friendship with China posed a security threat on India's southern frontier. Sri Lanka, for her part, acknowledged India's predominant role in regional security matters.

From the mid-1970s Indo–Sri Lankan relations came to be dominated by Indian responses to Sri Lanka's ethnic conflicts, Sinhalese versus Tamils. The mid- and late 1970s mark the beginning of the second phase in the postindependence violence in the island. The first phase was in the mid- and late 1950s. At that time India had treated it as a matter of Sri Lanka's domestic politics and therefore not for diplomatic or political intervention. It was the heyday of India's perception of itself as the conscience of the Third World, and Nehru acted with a restraint in regard to domestic turmoil among India's smaller neighbors (with the possible exception of Nepal) that his daughter and successor did not show. In the 1970s the situation had changed. After the intervention in East Pakistan and the creation of Bangladesh, India was in a more self-confident mood, having recovered fully from the debacle of 1962, the humiliating defeat inflicted by China.

The other factor that influenced the relationship between the two countries was the Tamil Nadu connection and its impact on the Sri Lankan situation. Within the Indian union, Madras, or Tamil Nadu as it became later, had been one of the main centers of separatist tendencies. The rise of the Dravida Kazhagam (DK) and later the Dravida Munnetra Kazhagam in the early 1950s reflected the same powerful force of linguistic nationalism that had transformed the politics of Sri Lanka in the same period.[26] The DK and the DMK (which came to power in Tamil Nadu in 1967) were even more conscious of the rights of Tamils in South Asia than the Congress-dominated state government of Madras had been, and acted with much less restraint in demonstrating their concern about these, so much so that the increasingly turbulent politics of Sri Lanka's Jaffna peninsula (the main concentration of the Tamil population in the island) in the early 1970s began to be treated as an integral part of the internal politics of Tamil Nadu. Tamil politics in South Asia thus had a regional rather than a purely local impact. The DMK, effectively checked from pursuing its separatist goals in India, took vicarious pleasure in giving encouragement and support to separatist tendencies among the Tamils of Sri Lanka.

There was a noticeable intensification of separatist agitation from 1974 to 1975, as well as an increase in terrorist activity, of which the shooting in 1975 by Velupillai Prabhakaran, now leader of the Liberation Tigers of Tamil Eelam (LTTE) of Alfred Durayappa, a fellow Tamil, the SLFP Mayor of Jaffna (the administrative capital of the Northern Province) was the most significant incident. The Sri Lankan security forces found the search for actual and potential troublemakers a frustrating experience because the local population would not voluntarily help in apprehending these young men; besides, when there was the slightest chance of capture, they moved across the Palk Strait to Tamil Nadu, which served them as a refuge and as a bridgehead for raids into the Jaffna peninsula.

It was at this point—the passage between Jaffna and the Tamil Nadu coast—that smugglers entered the picture both as transport agents for fugitives and as sources of ready money. The safe houses established on both sides of the Palk Strait for the traditional smuggling trade were now put to other uses, as havens for men on the run and as transshipment points for arms for the separatist cause. Very soon the more politically conscious smugglers and the terrorist groups had joined forces. Each needed and used the other. There was the inevitable metamorphosis of the smuggler into "guerrilla" and "freedom fighter"; indeed some of the most dynamic and powerful leaders in recent times who emerged from this blending of clandestine trading activity and aggressive and violent political agitation had been smugglers.[27]

Despite the cordial relations between the two prime ministers, Mrs. Gandhi and Mrs. Bandaranaike, the Indian government generally did not cooperate in apprehending Sri Lankan Tamil activists wanted in that country for serious breaches of the law. Quite often the center was under pressure from the Tamil Nadu government, which was able to thwart all efforts to apprehend such Sri Lankan lawbreakers.

Indeed, in the years 1975 and 1976 the compatibility of views between the two prime ministers had reached a point where critics in Sri Lanka felt that the personal friendship between them and their families had an unhealthy effect on the country's internal policies. A year earlier, in June 1974, Mrs. Bandaranaike had used emergency powers to place a ban on public meetings organized by the principal opposition party, the UNP, the first but not the only time in Sri Lanka's postindependence history that one of the two principal governing parties had taken such strong and undemocratic measures against its rival. The ban remained in force for a year. Then in 1975 came the emergency imposed on India by Mrs. Gandhi, during which a large number of her political opponents were arrested and kept in jail for varying periods of time. Mrs. Gandhi's imposition of emergency rule in India came as a great shock to the democratic world and led to widespread criticism. The Sri Lankan government under Mrs. Bandaranaike was one of the very few that made any public statements in support of Mrs. Gandhi's period of rule under emergency powers.[28] Both governments faced a general election in 1976 or 1977; both leaders sought to postpone the election,[29] Mrs. Bandaranaike following her Indian counterpart's example. Eventually Mrs. Gandhi changed her mind and decided to face the country at a general election in early 1977, despite the fact that she had the votes in Parliament to secure a postponement. Mrs. Bandaranaike was compelled to hold the election as scheduled in the middle of 1977, once she found that she did not have the votes for yet another postponement after the one she secured in 1975.[30] Eventually both went to the polls, and both suffered defeat, Mrs. Bandaranaike more comprehensively than Mrs. Gandhi, even though, unlike Mrs. Gandhi and Sanjay Gandhi, Mrs. Bandaranaike and her son did not lose their seats. But while Mrs. Gandhi returned to power in 1980, Mrs. Bandaranaike has had a long spell in the political wilderness.

Notes

1. This bulletin was issued in Colombo on 31 July 1987.

2. Colonial Office series (hereinafter CO) 882/30, 55541/47, 141, D. S. Senanayake to Creech Jones, 28 February 1947.

3. CO 54/986/6, D. S. Senanayake to G. H. Hall, 16 August 1945.

4. See H. Duncan Hall, *Commonwealth: A History of the British Commonwealth of Nations* (London: Nostrand, 1971), 801.

5. Vijaya Samaraweera, "Foreign Policy," in K. M. de Silva, ed., *Sri Lanka: A Survey* (London: C. Hurst, 1977), 330–52.

6. The completion of this process extended to the early 1970s. See Denis Healey, *The Time of My Life* (London: M. Joseph, 1989), 278–300.

7. Nirad C. Chaudhuri, "My Vision of the Real East-West Conflict," *Encounter* 65 (September/October 1985): 7–15; quotation, 9.

8. Mohammed Ayoob, *India and Southeast Asia: Indian Perceptions and Policies* (London: Routledge, 1990), 8–9.

9. K. M. Panikkar, *India and the Indian Ocean: An Essay on the Influence of Power on Indian History* (London: Allen and Unwin, 1945), 90–91, cited in Ayoob, *India and Southeast Asia,* 19–20.

10. Guy Wint, *The British in Asia* (London: Faber, 1947), 22.

11. Steven A. Hoffmann, *India and the China Crisis* (Berkeley: University of California Press, 1990), 25–26.

12. Both sides of the Marxist ideological divide of this period, the Soviet Union and the People's Republic of China, were strongly opposed to the creation of ASEAN. On the other hand, as Mohammed Ayoob has shown (*India and Southeast Asia,* 10–11), India's initial response to the establishment of ASEAN was one of enthusiastic approval.

In regard to Sri Lanka's moves to join ASEAN, it was the Soviet ambassador to Colombo who protested against it to the Ministry of Foreign Affairs. See comment by Ben Fonseka, a senior Foreign Service officer (then retired) on the keynote address by Shelton Kodikara on Geostrategic Perspectives of Indo–Sri Lankan Relations, in Shelton U. Kodikara, ed., *Dilemmas of Indo–Sri Lankan Relations* (Colombo: Bandaranaike Centre for International Studies, 1991), 33.

13. Anirudha Gupta, "A Brahmanic Framework of Power in South Asia?" *Economic and Political Weekly* 7 (April 1990): 712.

14. Ibid.

15. For discussion of British assessments of the strategic value of Trincomalee see Gerald S. Graham, *Great Britain in the Indian Ocean: A Study of Maritime Enterprise 1810–1850* (Oxford: Clarendon Press, 1967), 312.

16. Ibid., 317, for discussion of the downgrading of Trincomalee in the early nineteenth century.

17. Ibid., 305–28.

18. H. A. Colgate, "The Royal Navy and Trincomalee: The History of Their Connection, c. 1750–1958," *Ceylon Journal of Historical and Social Studies,* 1st ser., 7, no. 1 (1964): 1–17; see particularly 15.

19. Rupesinghe left Sri Lanka in the late 1970s and was associated with the Peace Research Institute in Oslo, Norway, for many years. Currently he is secretary general of International Alert, a London-based organization.

20. See the J. R. Jayewardene MSS for a typescript of this brief talk.

21. Jayewardene was focusing attention on divisions within Mrs. Bandaranaike's own family, the rivalry between her then son-in-law Kumar Rupesinghe and her daughter Sunethra, who were seen to be leading a radical political group with pro-Chinese leanings, and her young son Anura, who had just returned after his studies in London. Anura's views were more conservative.

22. For a stimulating critique of Indian defense and strategic concepts, see Ravi Rikhye, *The Militarization of Mother India* (Delhi: Chanakya Publications, 1990).

23. For a discussion, see Selig S. Harrison and K. Subrahmanyam, eds., *Superpower Rivalry in the Indian Ocean: Indian and American Perspectives* (New York: Oxford University Press, 1989), 223–30.

24. Mrs. Gandhi addressed the House of Representatives on this occasion. For the text of her speech, see *Times of India,* 29 April 1973.

25. See Shelton U. Kodikara, *Indo-Ceylon Relations Since Independence* (Colombo: Ceylon Institute of International Affairs, 1965), 123–25, 220–37. See also Hugh Tinker,

The Banyan Tree: Overseas Emigrants from India, Pakistan and Bangladesh (Oxford: Oxford University Press, 1977), passim.

26. See Marguerite R. Barnett, *The Politics of Cultural Nationalism in South India* (Princeton: Princeton University Press, 1976); Eugene F. Irschick, *Politics and Social Conflict in South India* (Berkeley: University of California Press, 1969); G. Palanithurai and K. Mohanasundaram, *Dynamics of Tamil Nadu Politics in Sri Lankan Ethnicity* (New Delhi: Northern Book Centre, 1993).

27. One of the most prominent of these smugglers turned political activist was S. Yogachandra, alias Kuttumani. He was arrested in Tamil Nadu in 1974 on charges that he had smuggled twenty thousand detonators to Sri Lanka.

28. See the speech of T. B. Illangaratne, Sri Lanka's minister for trade, public administration, and house affairs, at a banquet in his honor by Y. B. Chavan, India's minister for external affairs, in which he gave emphatic support to the Indian government. The *Ceylon Daily News* of 13 February 1976 reported Illangaratne as having said, "No group should be allowed to destroy democracy by utilizing the freedom it affords in the name of democracy."

29. On 6 January 1976, H. R. Gokhale, union minister of law, justice, and company affairs, was asked whether the government had decided to postpone the general election and some Assembly elections scheduled for 1976. When Gokhale gave an evasive answer, he was pointedly asked about the government's reaction to a resolution adopted by the All India Congress Committee (AICC) at a meeting in Chandigarh calling for a postponement of general elections for one year. Gokhale's answer to this supplementary question was as follows: "The attention of the Government has been drawn to the resolution of the AICC. The reaction of the Government can be known when the Government makes a decision. Ultimately, it is the House which has to decide" (*Lok Sabha Debates*, 6 January 1976).

30. The parliament of 1970 was elected for a five-year term, the firmly established practice under Sri Lanka's constitution of that period. In adopting a new constitution in 1972, Mrs. Bandaranaike's government secured an extension of the life of parliament by a period of two years, that is, to the middle of 1977. In 1976 and up to early 1977, Mrs. Bandaranaike tried very hard to get another postponement.

3

J. R. Jayewardene: A Change in Style and Substance, 1977–79

Background

SRI LANKA'S NEW HEAD of government, elected to office in the landmark general election of 1977, was one of the country's most experienced politicians. Seventy-one years old at the time he became prime minister, J. R. Jayewardene was the oldest head of government in Sri Lanka's history. Few people in the ranks of his party (or any party in the country) had longer experience than he in the subtleties of decision making in foreign policy, and in the mechanics of formulating foreign policy. It went back to the time he was a cabinet minister in the first decade of Sri Lanka's independence, 1947 to 1956. Some of that early experience had left its mark on him and one could discern evidence of the outlook of that period as he grappled with the problems of the late 1970s and the 1980s.

A significant part of that background has received less attention than it deserves. Jayewardene had been and continued to be one of the most Indophile of Sri Lanka's politicians. As secretary of the Ceylon National Congress in the late 1930s and early 1940s he had initiated moves to build close links with its Indian prototype. These efforts took its delegates to sessions of the Indian National Congress, where he himself appeared in the political "uniform" of that party, Gandhi cap and all. This latter was quite unusual for Sri Lankan politicians of that period. The prominent role he played in the affairs of the Ceylon National Congress brought him into contact with Jawaharlal Nehru in the immediate preindependence phase of the politics of their two countries. Indeed, a unique feature of Jayewardene's career was his association, for good or ill, at an official level, with all three members of the Nehru-Gandhi political dynasty, Nehru himself, his daughter Indira Gandhi, and Nehru's grandson Rajiv Gandhi. That was due mainly to the remarkable length of his political career.

As finance minister in the first postindependence government of Sri Lanka (1947–52), Jayewardene had two major foreign policy initiatives to his credit. D. S. Senanayake, the country's first prime minister, had no expertise in foreign affairs and was always ready to let others in the cabinet handle them for him, although the portfolio of foreign affairs was in his charge.[1] The first of Jayewardene's initiatives began in January 1950 at a Commonwealth Foreign Ministers Conference held in Colombo, where he sponsored the case for a regional equivalent of the Marshall Plan—which had so successfully stimulated the postwar recovery of Western Europe—for Southeast Asia.[2] Among the delegates was Jawaharlal Nehru, who led a distinguished Indian team which included V. K. Krishna Menon, then India's high commissioner in London. The details of Jayewardene's successful negotiations on this occasion need not detain us here.[3] The fact is that the Colombo Plan that emerged from these discussions was in large measure due to Jayewardene's skillful diplomacy. Nehru originally damned the proposal with faint praise in tones of frosty condescension. Sri Lanka's and in particular Jayewardene's initiatives in the events that led to the establishment of the Colombo Plan were ungrudgingly acknowledged by other contemporary Commonwealth politicians.

Jayewardene's notably constructive role in the negotiations that led to the Colombo Plan was the prelude to an even more memorable achievement at San Francisco in September 1951, in the formal sessions that culminated in the signing of a peace treaty with Japan.[4] Although the U.S. government, the prime mover in this conference, was anxious that the prime minister should lead the Sri Lanka delegation to San Francisco, Senanayake chose to send his finance minister instead. Jayewardene was now presented with an unexpected opportunity to test his skills in a wider diplomatic arena than a Commonwealth ministerial conference, an international peace conference of major significance.

Three Asian countries were not represented at the conference, each for a different reason. India was not present ostensibly because it felt the treaty did not give Japan the full freedom it was entitled to; Burma because the proposed treaty did not provide for adequate reparations; and China because the People's Republic of China and the Chiang regime in Taiwan each claimed the right of representation, so the decision was taken to invite neither. Although representatives from Indonesia and the Philippines were present, they had not indicated whether they would sign the treaty. Japanese armies had ravaged their lands and it was too soon for the people of these countries to forget and forgive the sufferings inflicted on them.

Jayewardene's speech on that occasion was brief—it lasted a mere fifteen minutes—but it proved to be the highlight of the conference. In that speech he called for magnanimity to a fallen foe, and couched the argument in terms of his religious (Buddhist) beliefs: "[We] believe in the words of the great Teacher, the founder of Buddhism," Jayewardene asserted, "that hatred ceases not by hatred but by love."[5]

The *San Francisco Chronicle* reported that his speech "touched off a roar of acclamation that shook the very windows of the Opera House Conference room."[6] The Japanese prime minister, Shigeru Yoshida, who had been watching the proceedings, impassive and inscrutable, burst into tears.

The whole mood of the conference changed. The Asian representatives had been reticent and hesitant to express their views, some because of obviously mixed emotions that burdened the minds of those recently freed from Japanese rule, such as the people of the Philippines and Indonesia. Now there was instead a readiness to support the treaty in a spirit of reconciliation. The treaty was eventually carried by forty-eight votes to three, but the Asian votes cast in its favor were more important to those who drafted the treaty than all the others put together. The political impact of the treaty was so much greater as a result of it.

Jayewardene's speech had captured headlines in the United States— and in Sri Lanka and Japan—and was prominently reported in all the most important journals of the day. None were more gratified than the Americans and the Japanese, but the latter's gratitude lasted longer than the former's and when Jayewardene became the prime minister and executive president of Sri Lanka twenty-five years later those memories were still fresh. The Japanese reciprocated Jayewardene's sentiments in a practical form, as a tribute to an act of generosity when Japan needed support— moral and political—most.

In the 1950s, in the early years of the Cold War, most people tended to look at issues in ideological terms, as black or white, with little or no respect for any shades of gray. To Sri Lanka's very vocal Marxist left, support for the Japanese peace treaty was an ideological act, taken on ideological terms, all the worse for the fact that Sri Lanka was represented at San Francisco at all at a time when India had refused the invitation extended to her. Worse still, Jayewardene had argued passionately in favor of signing the treaty, and appeared to have done so at the bidding of John Foster Dulles, the Republican architect of the treaty, and Dean Acheson, the U.S. secretary of state.

Among the Marxists the most critical group were the Communists, who were upset at the attack on the leader of the Soviet delegation, Andrei Gromyko, and the generally calculated discomfiture of the Soviet Union at Jayewardene's hands on this occasion. At a time when the Korean peninsula was still the center of a fratricidal struggle, exacerbated by great power rivalries, they viewed the signing of a peace treaty with Japan as an unforgivable error of political judgment to which the United National Party (UNP) had been led by its commitment to the Western powers. Looking back on Jayewardene's own career they saw this as one more piece of evidence of his pro-American sympathies.

Earlier speaking in Parliament, Jayewardene had made his own position very clear:

> In the world today, there are really two principal factors, the United States of America and the USSR. We have to follow either the one or the other. There can be no half-way house in the matter. We have decided and we intend to follow the United States of America and its democratic principles.[7]

A Reappraisal of Priorities

Of the twenty-one years after his defeat—and loss of his seat—in 1956, Jayewardene was either out of Parliament (1956 to 1960) or in the opposition (1960–64, 1970–77) for sixteen of them. He was in the cabinet from 1965 to 1970, but had little influence on the making of policy. For the next eleven years, 1977 to 1988, he was head of government, first as prime minister (1977–78) and then as the country's first executive president.

Jayewardene's views on foreign policy had changed over the two decades since 1956 in which he had little or no influence on the making of policy. As leader of the opposition from 1970 to 1977, he had generally paid little attention to foreign policy issues. While he understood the strength of Mrs. Bandaranaike's commitment to nonalignment, and appreciated her role as a moderate in the councils of the nonaligned nations, he was strongly opposed to what he regarded as her excessive concern for foreign affairs at a time when domestic policy, especially the parlous state of the economy, should have taken higher priority. He had opposed the holding of the nonaligned nations summit in Colombo in 1976, regarding it as an expensive luxury, an aspiration to grandeur that was mere self-delusion because it diverted attention from more urgent domestic problems. He had made this an important campaign issue at the general election of 1977. Indeed, his criticisms had been so strong that it took him over a year after becoming head of government to make any public statement on his attitude to nonalignment.

There were other reasons as well for his reluctance to speak on foreign policy, to explain and underline the assumptions of national purpose and action that formed its basis. The first of these was clearly a lack of conviction on his part about nonalignment as it was seen to operate in practice within the nonaligned nations movement, or its practical utility in ensuring the security of small states in a changing world situation. Under normal circumstances his studied reticence about nonalignment would not have caused too many problems. But he had inherited from Mrs. Bandaranaike the chairmanship of the nonaligned nations movement, and so his reluctance if not refusal to speak out on this theme caused difficulties for the officials of the Ministry of Foreign Affairs who had played an enthusiastic role in the summit conference of 1976. Called on to sustain the secretarial apparatus of the movement until 1979, when it would be transferred to Cuba, these officials viewed Jayewardene's reticence with some concern. The combined efforts of a large number of people were required to persuade him that a public statement endorsing the principle of nonalignment was called for.

At the time he became prime minister he was as much an Indophile as he had been in his early years. His attitudes changed in response to Mrs. Gandhi's efforts to impose India's hegemony over Sri Lanka, and once Tamil Nadu became a haven for Tamil separatists from Sri Lanka and a source of support for them. He was more sympathetic to the West, and the United States in particular, than his predecessor Mrs. Bandaranaike had been, and much less committed than she to the principles of non-alignment. He was intent on a thorough reappraisal of governmental priorities. He would concentrate on urgent domestic problems, in particular in overhauling economic policy and providing a more congenial climate in which business confidence could be rebuilt, to stimulate the country's economic recovery after what he saw as seven lost years of muddled and disastrous socialist economic policies.

The appointment of a foreign minister, the first in the island's post-independence history, was indicative of the priorities he attached to the responsibilities of the head of government, the important point being that the Ministry of Foreign Affairs was no longer part of the direct responsibility of the head of government as it had been since 1947. To that extent there was an inevitable and perhaps intentional reduction in political status and importance of that ministry. However, as with heads of government the world over, Jayewardene would keep the more important pronouncements on foreign policy for himself, and would intervene directly whenever he felt it necessary to do so. A. C. S. Hameed, minister of foreign affairs, was not merely in the shadow of the president, he was often overshadowed in his own area of responsibility by his cabinet colleagues. The fact that he was a Muslim carried no particular advantage or disadvantage to Jayewardene.[8]

Occasionally Ranasinghe Premadasa, as prime minister, would be the chosen spokesman of President Jayewardene on foreign affairs, especially during visits overseas. As we shall see, Premadasa was sent on missions to the People's Republic of China in 1979, and to the Association of Southeast Asian Nations (ASEAN) countries in 1981. These interventions were admittedly sporadic, but they all formed part of a pattern of administration in which the foreign minister had to share the responsibilities of speaking on behalf of the country in matters of foreign relations with others in the cabinet quite apart, of course, from the president himself. Other ministers led regular overseas missions with a distinct foreign policy content. One obvious case was Ronnie de Mel, the minister of finance, who was given charge of negotiations on foreign assistance and over the years developed an expertise in the economic aspects of foreign policy that assumed great importance with the liberalization of the Sri Lankan economy. Foreign aid negotiated annually under the auspices of the World Bank and the International Monetary Fund became an essential and indeed an indispensable part of the development process and, just as important, in balancing the annual budget. Previously, because of the importance assumed by bilateral trade agreements with the communist countries of central and eastern Europe and barter agreements with other countries, the minister of trade was the principal figure in negotiations on the economic aspects of foreign relations. Once the patterns of trade changed so fundamentally after Jayewardene assumed power, that role in the economic aspects of foreign policy declined sharply, but the one area of responsibility still left to him was among the most important aspects of foreign relations, the biennial trade negotiations with the People's Republic of China. The first such negotiation took place in 1977, very early in the life of the new government, when Trade Minister Lalith Athulathmudali led a mission to Beijing for this purpose. Athulathmudali found that the trade negotiations presented no difficulties at all. More important, the Chinese government used this occasion to convey a political message of great importance to the new government wishing it well and hoping the UNP would consolidate its position in the country. The Chinese, still greatly concerned with the need to check the growth of Soviet influence in general in South Asia, were relieved that the Communist Party (Moscow wing) presence in the Sri Lankan cabinet, which had been a feature of the United Front (UF) government under Mrs. Bandaranaike, was now at an end.[9]

Relations with India—Jayewardene and Desai

The importance of good relations with India became evident to Jayewardene less than a month after he became prime minister in July 1977, with the outbreak of the first of the anti-Tamil riots of his presidency. The disturbances could be justifiably attributed to the misguided policies pursued by the previous government. From the mid-1970s, Indo–Sri Lankan relations had come to be dominated by Indian responses to Sri Lanka's ethnic conflicts, Sinhalese versus Tamils. The other factor that influenced the relationship between the two countries was the repercussions of the politics of Tamil Nadu on the Sri Lankan situation. The turbulent politics of the Jaffna peninsula were increasingly developing a regional dimension because of links established with Tamil Nadu parties. Separatist tendencies among the Tamils of Sri Lanka thus received encouragement and support from Tamil Nadu. Separatist agitation had intensified in 1974 and 1975 and with it came, almost inevitably, an increase in the number of incidents of political violence. Despite the cordial relations between the two prime ministers, Mrs. Gandhi and Mrs. Bandaranaike, the Indian government generally did not cooperate in deporting Sri Lankan Tamil political activists who had escaped to Tamil Nadu after serious breaches of the law, including murder and gang robberies. Quite often the Tamil Nadu government was able to thwart these efforts at apprehending lawbreakers. The victory of the Janatha government at the elections of 1977 in India had a special significance in inaugurating an all-too-brief two-year period when India's relations with her neighbors improved markedly. Indeed these relations were never better than they were with Morarji Desai as prime minister.

The first official encounter between the elderly prime ministers of India and Sri Lanka, an octogenarian and a septuagenarian, came as early as August 1977. When the riots broke out in Colombo, the Indian high commissioner, Gurbachan Singh, claiming that some members of the Indian community were in danger, urged the new prime minister to permit an Indian emissary (perhaps a cabinet member) to come to the island to review the situation. This Jayewardene refused to do. But in an exercise in personal diplomacy an invitation was extended to an Indian businessman known to him, S. A. Chidambaran, to visit the island to see for himself how the government had handled the riots. On his return to India, Chidambaran wrote to Jayewardene on 5 September 1977 as follows:

He [Desai] was happy that you sent for me to enable him to get first-hand information on the recent developments in your island. He is now convinced that they [the riots] are an internal matter and reflect nothing against India or Indians. . . . He expressed to me that he was aware that the situation was in safe hands and wished you all success in your efforts at handling the situation. His sympathies are fully with you in the steps you are taking to bring normality to the island speedily.[10]

The two prime ministers soon developed as close an understanding as had Mrs. Gandhi and Mrs. Bandaranaike, so there was a continuation of the very friendly relationship between the two countries established by their predecessors. For Jayewardene the principal advantage was that under Desai and the Janatha government there was very little talk about India's neighbors posing security threats to her interests, or about the smaller among them having to take shelter, either through compulsion or voluntarily, under India's defense umbrella. Instead, purposeful efforts were made to reduce the tensions between India and its neighbors that had been the order of the day under Mrs. Gandhi, and to reduce suspicions about India's intentions as well.

The warm relationship was strengthened by the visits of the two heads of government to each other's countries. When Jayewardene made an official visit to India on 27 October 1978, he set the tone for their mutual cordiality with his statement, in response to the welcome address of the Indian president Sanjiva Reddy, that

> I am a friend of India and its people; an admirer of its noble heritage, a follower of its greatest son [the Buddha] . . . our meetings will only help to further the understanding and co-operation that exist between us already.[11]

That same evening, at the official banquet given in his honor by the Indian president, Jayewardene made a calculated reference to the hard measures taken against the then opposition by the predecessors of the present heads of government in their two countries.

> In all the countries that attained freedom after the second world war, in Africa and Asia only your nation and our nation have preserved the democratic traditions without any interruption. We were the first to change our governments by constitutional process. We have done this on several occasions and I have been at the receiving end of several of those changes. Today, I am the President of Sri Lanka by the choice of its people and not by any constitutional or military coup.
>
> Your country too has set an example to the democratic world by changing its Government by the democratic process. I will not go into recent history, but there are many parallels that can be drawn between events that took place in your country during the last two years and the events that took place in our country during the same period.
>
> You may not know but my one and only son was put into jail and up to date he has not been charged for any offence. My nephew who is my Private Secretary, was put into jail. Up to date he has not been charged for any offence.
>
> I was not put into jail because our opposition was too powerful to put the leader of the opposition into jail, as they did in the case of Morarji Desai.[12]

The reference to the common adversities suffered under the previous regimes in their two countries helped establish an emotional and personal bond between Jayewardene and Desai, a bond that grew in strength over the brief period in which the latter was prime minister of India. Within a few weeks of his return home, Jayewardene was playing host to Morarji Desai, who was an honored guest at Sri Lanka's Independence Day celebrations on 4 February 1979. Unlike India's Republic Day celebrations, Sri Lanka's Independence Day celebrations seldom had a foreign dignitary sharing the honors with the head of state. The invitation to Desai was thus something special. He was lodged at President's House. Two days after his appearance at the independence celebrations, he addressed the Sri Lankan Parliament. He was also the chief guest at the foundation laying ceremony for the Kotmale Dam, one of the main dams being constructed as part of the massive Mahavali River project.

The cordiality in their relationship was now so firmly established that it could survive an offer by Desai during his visit to mediate in the "Tamil problem" if he was requested to do so by the "right people." Jayewardene did not take up the offer—the situation was not so bad as to warrant such a request—but the fact is that it was the leader of the opposition, A. Amirthalingam, the leader of the Tamil United Liberation Front (TULF), who found it necessary to back away from the offer. He indicated a preference that the problem be solved at an all-party conference within the country, but added somewhat hastily that he had no objection to a mediatory role for the Indian prime minister if the government of Sri Lanka agreed to it.[13] From Jayewardene there was no response at all.

Nor was Jayewardene particularly perturbed when Charan Singh, India's deputy prime minister under Desai, on a visit to Sri Lanka as a state guest, startled his Sri Lankan minister in attendance, Gamini Dissanayake, with a request for a quick visit to Trincomalee, something that was not on the agenda. Dissanayake was given permission to take his guest on a helicopter tour of the famous natural harbor.[14] Jayewardene could understand Charan Singh's curiosity about a port that figured so prominently in the calculations of India's politicians no less than in those of her strategic thinkers.

Jayewardene and the Nonaligned Movement, 1977–79

Part of Mrs. Bandaranaike's legacy to Jayewardene was the chairmanship of the nonaligned movement. As we have seen, his aversion to this role was especially marked in the early months of his administration, and it caused much worry to his officials because some of the forms it took. He held back from a commitment to host a ministerial meeting of the Coordinating Bureau of the Non-Aligned Countries in Colombo in mid-1979, because of his original opposition to the nonaligned summit conference in 1976. Eventually he was persuaded that this conference was an inescapable obligation, an essential preliminary to the next nonaligned summit in Havana late in 1979, and that it was organized on a much smaller and less elaborate scale than a summit meeting of the nonaligned nations.

He looked forward to the time when he could hand the job over to Fidel Castro, who was scheduled to take over from him in September 1979. Thus Jayewardene was more than a little disturbed when diplomatic efforts were initiated in May 1979 to secure a postponement of the conference beyond September 1979 and into 1980, in the hope that a majority among the nonaligned states could be persuaded that some country other than Cuba should take over the chairmanship of the movement. This move was led by Sudan and Somalia. Jayewardene, like many of his advisers, saw the hand of President Anwar Sadat of Egypt in this.[15] Jayewardene was in an embarrassing position, as it was an open secret that those who wanted the meeting postponed wished to see him continue as chairman well into 1980.

These efforts came to an end one month later, when the ministerial meeting of the Coordinating Bureau met in Colombo.[16] Jayewardene was relieved that he would soon be free of the responsibilities the head of government of Sri Lanka took on as the "chairman" of the group of nonaligned nations. He used the occasion of the meeting to make a firm but— so far as his critics were concerned—belated statement on Sri Lanka's continuing commitment to nonalignment:

> Non alignment runs like a golden thread through the fabric of our country's foreign policy though changes may take place in the quality, colour and shape of that fabric from time to time. At no stage has our country deviated from that policy. At no stage, I will make bold to say, will it do so in the future.[17]

He had made much the same point in Kathmandu in November 1978, but he repeated it here in Colombo because of doubts being expressed in some quarters about the strength of his commitment to this principle. Indeed, this was one of those rare occasions when he used the services of a speechwriter for an official policy statement.[18] Jayewardene may have had deep reservations about Sri Lanka's role as chair of the movement, something he regarded as akin to a gaudy ribbon on the chest of a down-and-out and decrepit man, but he had no reservations at all about the need to adhere to a policy of nonalignment, and of steering clear of great-power rivalries and entanglements.

He returned to the theme a few months later, in Tokyo in September 1979:

> We in Sri Lanka believe that non-alignment provides the best hope for a better order in international relations, based on the true independence of states, equality in state relations and peaceful coexistence between all states in the world irrespective of ideological and other divisions.[19]

Despite his anxiety to get the Havana conference over with, he chaired the meeting there, in September, with his customary savoir faire. Part of the effectiveness of his personal diplomacy on this occasion lay in articulating the essence of nonalignment as the vast majority of its members saw it and in linking this to the vision of the movement's founding fathers. He used the occasion also to reiterate his—and the country's—commitment to nonalignment as the guiding foreign policy principle successive governments had adhered to, "because it [was] rooted in a set of fundamentals which no government can vary or seek to vary, unless it chooses to destroy our political and philosophical heritage."[20]

A Search for Small State Security: A Balancing Act, October 1979

For all his personal satisfaction with the way he had managed the sessions of the nonaligned conference, Jayewardene left Havana—for Mexico on an official visit and then on to Tokyo—in a mood of disenchantment. The disenchantment was due to two reasons. The first was the concerted attempt by a group of radical states to shift the movement away from its original ideal of neutrality between the two rival power blocs to a pro-Moscow position. While Sri Lanka and the other moderate states had been successful in preventing this both in Colombo[21] and in Havana, Jayewardene realized that it would be a long battle now that Cuba was chair of the movement. The second was the power wielded by the Arab bloc, which succeeded in getting the conference to concentrate heavily on the Middle Eastern situation at the expense of problems of greater interest to the bulk of the nonaligned nations. And this at a time when the economies of most of the countries represented at the conference were grievously affected by the second oil shock of the 1970s, which came in 1979. The Arab-dominated Organization of Petroleum Exporting Countries (OPEC) would not yield to the pressure from the poorer countries of the world—all of whom were represented at Havana—for a special rate for the oil purchased by them.

The reappraisal of priorities in foreign policy initiated toward the middle of 1979 reflected Jayewardene's views rather than those of the minister of foreign affairs or the latter's ministry.[22] After his return from Havana he had given public expression to his revulsion at the authoritarian excesses of many African states; more than once he had said there was nothing in common between him and the African dictators he had met at Havana.[23] Nor was he particularly enamored of the Arab bloc. A mammoth petition to be presented to OPEC was being prepared in Sri Lanka under the auspices of the government, asking for a special rate on the sale of oil to the so-called Third World of developing or less developed countries. Jayewardene realized that this petition was not likely to be anything more than an exercise in moral pressure, and he had no great faith in its effectiveness. But it would serve the purpose of being an open expression of an Asian country's dissatisfaction with OPEC.

The essence of Jayewardene's reappraisal was a greater emphasis on an Asian outlook in Sri Lanka's foreign policy. This had two facets, one political and the other economic. Politically, it called for an astute understanding of the complex relationships the major Asian powers, China and India, were engaged in evolving with their neighbors no less than with each other and the superpowers. At the time this reappraisal was being fashioned, Morarji Desai's position within the Janatha coalition had become untenable. He was compelled to resign as prime minister on 15 July, setting in motion a train of events which led to the collapse of the coalition. Jayewardene, like most others, believed that Mrs. Gandhi would return to power and that the smaller states of South Asia would then be under greater pressure than they had been since her defeat in 1977 to acknowledge India's dominant role in the region.

As he saw it, small nations like Sri Lanka, too small to be balancing elements on their own in these evolving relationships, could do much better as units of a group or groups of states seeking to ensure that no single regional power (e.g., India or China) dominated its neighbors either by itself or in association with a superpower (e.g., India, or for that matter Vietnam, in association with the Soviet Union). An essential part of the political equation in his reappraisal of foreign policy was thus a conscious search for identity with smaller or medium-sized states in South and Southeast Asia, such as the ASEAN countries and Pakistan.

In his calculations in this reappraisal, the economic aspects of foreign policy played as important a role as the political. In economic affairs, the primary emphasis was on closer ties with the more economically advanced Asian nations, Japan principally, and with South Korea,[24] Singapore, and Hong Kong. He regarded them—in particular Singapore—as role models for Sri Lanka. There was an affinity between the economic policies that had helped these countries to develop so rapidly and the policies introduced in Sri Lanka in 1977. Thus the emphasis on a much greater solidarity with the ASEAN nations that was an important feature of this reappraisal of the national interest in foreign policy focused on its economic dimension as well. As in politics, so in economic affairs, the primary objective in his reappraisal of policy was a search for support from a countervailing force against the emerging economic giant of the world and Asian scene, OPEC.

In implementing this new policy, he kept relations with Japan very much at the center and very much under his own control. The Japanese had responded to his massive electoral victory of July 1977 with a warmth and enthusiasm that surprised him. To his great delight the speech he had made at the Japanese Peace Conference more than twenty-five years earlier in support of Japan was still remembered in that country, and he reaped the benefits of this throughout his period in office. This became clear when he made his first official visit following the Havana summit. The royal family and the government of Japan received him with great warmth when he arrived in Tokyo. Emperor Hirohito struck a note that was to become very familiar to Jayewardene in the latter's relations with Japan throughout his period of office, with his reference to his San Francisco speech: "Our people were profoundly moved by it at that time and they will never forget it in the future. I wish to take this opportunity to convey to him our gratitude for it."[25] This demonstration that public memories lasted so long in Japan was especially gratifying to him.

After his visit to Tokyo, Japan's direct bilateral assistance to Sri Lanka increased substantially. Japan had been a member of the Sri Lanka Aid Consortium, set up under the auspices of the World Bank, from its inception in 1978. From that time onward Japan had been one of the principal sources of economic assistance to Sri Lanka.

In March 1981 the Japanese crown prince, Prince Akihito and Princess Michiko visited Sri Lanka, thus further strengthening the special relationship between the two countries. The crown prince's response to the toast at a banquet given by Jayewardene included a reference once again to his speech in San Francisco:

> Your generous sentiments towards the Japanese people were well exemplified in your speech on the occasion of the Japanese Peace Conference held in San Francisco 30 years ago when you quoted the words of the Buddha: "hatred ceases not by hatred, but by love." I can well imagine how the Japanese who listened to your speech were filled with deep gratitude to Your Excellency and to the people of Sri Lanka. Your visit to Japan, the year before last, reminded the Japanese people of your contribution to the Japanese Peace Conference, which we shall not forget.[26]

The first major diplomatic mission to the People's Republic of China after the new government took office was assigned to the prime minister, R. Premadasa. Both sides treated the visit as a matter of great importance. An advance party, led by a senior Foreign Ministry official with considerable experience of China, spent a month in China making preparations for Premadasa's visit in September 1979. In the effusiveness of the welcome he received, and the great publicity in the Chinese press, Premadasa's visit to China was treated as an event of very great importance by the Chinese government. Many persons in the Sri Lankan delegation were struck by the fact that the elaborate arrangements made to welcome Premadasa were considerably in excess of Sri Lanka's own importance in world affairs.[27]

For his part, Premadasa, in an important policy statement made orally to his Chinese hosts, explained the Sri Lankan government's perception of the nature of the relationship it desired with China. This statement, prepared for him by the Foreign Ministry, made two principal points: Sri Lanka desired a strong China that would play a constructive role in the affairs of South and Southeast Asia; and no single power or combination of powers should dominate the politics of South and Southeast Asia. Though Premadasa did not make it explicit, it was evident to his listeners that he was thinking of a South Asia under Indian domination or a Southeast Asia threatened by Vietnam. And of course there was the role of the Soviet Union in both areas, acting either on its own as it was doing in Afghanistan (through its pliant Communist Party clients there) or through an ally such as Vietnam.

The UNP government was also eager to establish a close relationship with its Chinese counterpart. In the past, relations between the two had not been very good, but under the leadership of Jayewardene the party was intent on making a fresh start. Indeed, the Chinese had responded with great enthusiasm to these overtures, and a change in outlook of the Chinese government vis-à-vis the new UNP government had been noticeable since the latter came to power in July 1977. As we have seen, the first explicit indication of this concern to maintain a friendly link with the new UNP government had come very shortly after the new government took office, when the minister of trade, Lalith Athulathmudali, went to Beijing for negotiations on the rice-rubber pact. Premadasa urged China to boost this new relationship with a tangible gesture on the lines of its generosity to the Sri Lanka Freedom Party (SLFP) government of the past. This was, in effect, a plea for economic aid to the new government in the form of a substantial grant or loan.

His Chinese hosts responded positively on both counts. They identified their policy objectives in South and Southeast Asia, and Chinese leaders informed their visitors that, in relation to these regions, there was an essential compatibility of views between the two governments. And they realized that this new more friendly relationship with a UNP regime should be strengthened by a generous response to the new government's economic program of reconstruction.

Jayewardene treated the reestablishment and maintenance of a good and constructive relationship with the West as a matter of prime importance. Mrs. Bandaranaike had indeed moderated her views regarding the West in the last phase of her government, but unlike Jayewardene she was never really comfortable in sustaining that moderation. This reluctance flowed partly from the nature of her own party, the SLFP, with its wide range of intrinsically incompatible political views and a strong left-wing presence (some pro-Moscow and others pro-China), partly from the nature of her government, a left-of-center coalition in which at least a fourth of the ministers found a friendly relationship with the United States difficult to visualize. Indeed, to many of them a friendly association with the United States would have been anathema. Jayewardene had no such difficulties either personally or from his own political party, in which there were many who welcomed a close association with the United States and Great Britain.

Jayewardene's early years in office straddled changes of government in both the United States and the United Kingdom, changes that had a powerful ideological connotation in each country: from James Callaghan and the Labour Party to Margaret Thatcher in the United Kingdom, and from Carter to Reagan in the United States. These changes made hardly any difference to him, and he did not need to make any adjustment of policies to accommodate himself to them. His first approach for support in the daunting task of economic reconstruction he was embarking on had been to the British prime minister, James Callaghan, who had responded with a most encouraging promise of strong support.[28] Callaghan's government had been one of the earliest supporters of the gigantic multipurpose Mahavali scheme, and its firm commitment to finance the construction of the Victoria Dam helped to get this scheme, on which Jayewardene set such great store, started early. Indeed, it was much more enthusiastic in this regard than the Carter administration in the United States. Margaret Thatcher's government endorsed this in a very practical way by making a grant of £100 million—first promised by the Labour government—for the construction of the Victoria Dam.

The political aspects of the relationship with the West brought the new government into closer cooperation with the United States, beginning with support for a strong U.S. naval presence in the Indian Ocean, and thereafter to diplomatic support for the U.S. stand on the Soviet invasion of Afghanistan. When the Iran hostage crisis broke out, the U.S. government turned to Jayewardene, as one of a small group of nonaligned moderates, for assistance in making an appeal to Ayatollah Khomeini to release the hostages. He strongly sympathized with the plight of the hostages, and sent his minister of foreign affairs to Teheran with a personal letter to the Iranian leader on this futile mercy mission.[29] For Jayewardene's critics the ineffectiveness of this exercise was overshadowed by his readiness to play a mediatory role on behalf of the United States at a time when few Asian states were anxious to do so.

Notes

1. In the Soulbury Constitution (1947–72), under which the country attained independence, the portfolio of defense and external affairs came directly under the prime minister. Generally the prime minister had a deputy minister (or parliamentary secretary, as the post was designated in the Constitution) to handle some of the routine affairs of the two ministries.

2. At this time the term Southeast Asia covered both South and Southeast Asia; the territorial limits covered those of Admiral Lord Louis Mountbatten's Southeast Asia Command.

3. For these, see K. M. de Silva and Howard Wriggins, *J. R. Jayewardene of Sri Lanka: A Political Biography,* vol. 1, *1906–1955* (London: Blond/Quartet, 1988) (hereafter *JRJ*, vol. 1), 226–32.

4. See *JRJ*, vol. 1, 233–44.

5. Ibid.

6. 8 September 1951; see also *New York Times,* 7 and 8 September 1951; and *Newsweek,* 17 September 1951.

7. *Hansard* [House of Representatives], vol. 8, 1950, col. 293.

8. The fact that Hameed was a Muslim did not bother Jayewardene, but it apparently did bother Morarji Desai, the Indian prime minister, who, on an official visit to Sri Lanka in 1979, pointedly asked Jayewardene why he did not appoint a Sinhalese to that important position. Jayewardene related this incident to the author in early February 1979, shortly after Desai's visit.

9. Discussion with Lalith Athulathmudali, October 1979.

10. S. A. Chidambaran to Jayewardene, 5 September 1977. J. R. Jayewardene MSS, file 10 XXVII.

11. J. R. Jayewardene, *Selected Speeches and Writings* (Colombo: H. W. Cave, 1979), 186.

12. Ibid., 188–89.

13. *Daily Mirror,* 17 February 1979.

14. Gamini Dissanayake, interview with the author, 6 May 1991.

15. Discussion with J. R. Jayewardene, May 1979. The same information was also provided by senior officials of the Ministry of Foreign Affairs.

16. Three controversial issues came up for resolution: the position of Egypt in view of demands from large sections of the Arab bloc that it be suspended from membership because of the Camp David Accords; the question of who should represent Kampuchea, the Heng Samrin government or the Khmer Rouge; and the question of Cuba's succession to the position of chairman of the movement. A compromise was reached in regard to the first, the second was swept under the carpet, and the third was not resolved at all.

17. Text of speech issued by the Presidential Secretariat, Colombo, 15 June 1979.

18. The speechwriter used on this occasion was Ernest Corea, former Lake House journalist and at this time Sri Lanka's high commissioner in Canada. He later became ambassador to the United States.

19. Jayewardene went to Tokyo from Havana after the nonaligned nations summit there in September 1979. Text of speech issued by the Presidential Secretariat, Colombo, 20 September 1979.

20. Ibid.

21. At the Colombo meeting in June 1970 some of the Arab states pressed for the suspension of Egypt from the nonaligned movement. From the outset, Sri Lanka sought to avoid any discussion of this issue. While Sri Lanka as chairman played a rather low key role, India spoke out forcefully against it, as did a large group of moderate states. A compromise was negotiated: there would be no discussion of Egypt's suspension, but the Camp David Accords and the peace treaty with Israel were condemned.

22. This reappraisal had begun in May 1979, prior to the June meeting of nonaligned nations' foreign ministers in Colombo. Discussion with J. R. Jayewardene, May 1979.

23. J. R. Jayewardene, interview with the author, October 1979.

24. Very early in the life of his government, Jayewardene had initiated moves to establish diplomatic links with South Korea.

25. *Ceylon Daily News,* 12 September 1979.

26. *Ceylon Daily News,* 5 March 1981.

27. This review of Premadasa's 1979 visit to China is based on discussions with members of the Sri Lankan delegation and officials of the Ministry of Foreign Affairs.

28. James Callaghan to Jayewardene, 14 September 1977, J. R. Jayewardene MSS, file 10 XXXVIII.

29. J. R. Jayewardene, interview with the author, 27 November 1979.

4

Coping with Mrs. Gandhi, 1980–83

The Fall of Desai and the Return of Mrs. Gandhi

IN INDIA the self-destructive factionalism of the Janatha government was reaching its denouement. On 15 July 1979 Morarji Desai resigned, and on 20 July, after a fortnight of bitter wrangling, Charan Singh was invited to form a government, for which he had been promised support by the Indira Congress. The Lok Sabha was due to meet on 20 August, when the new government would seek a vote of confidence. On the previous day Indira Gandhi withdrew her offer to support a Charan Singh government, whereupon Charan Singh resigned and the president decided to dissolve the Lok Sabha. The president's call for fresh elections gave Indira Gandhi and her party an unexpected opportunity of returning to power much earlier than she had had reason to hope when she was defeated in 1977. By October all the indications were that Indira Gandhi would be back in power as prime minister soon.[1]

Political groups in Sri Lanka were making their own assessments of the likely impact of her victory on Sri Lanka. Most of these assessments were based on the fact that she had forged an electoral alliance with the M. Karunanidhi faction of the Dravida Munnetra Kazhagam (DMK) in Tamil Nadu, a group well known for its outspoken support of the principal Tamil political group in the island, the Tamil United Liberation Front or the TULF, the acronym by which it was known. By October 1980 there were signs that the TULF was hardening its position in its negotiations with the Sri Lankan government in the belief that with Indira Gandhi in power and dependent on Karunanidhi's support there would be greater pressure from India on the Sri Lankan government on behalf of the Tamil minority.

Just as important, Mrs. Gandhi's victory was certain to be hailed by Mrs. Bandaranaike as a harbinger of her own eventual return to power. Indeed immediately after the news of Mrs. Gandhi's sweeping victory was received in December 1979 posters went up in all parts of Colombo and some of the other towns of the island with a brief and poignant political message—"India today, Sri Lanka tomorrow." The hitherto dispirited Sri Lanka Freedom Party (SLFP) was seeking to extract as much propaganda effect from Mrs. Gandhi's victory as possible.

Jayewardene realized that he and his government would be in for more difficult times now that Mrs. Gandhi was back in power. He was perturbed by some of Mrs. Gandhi's comments on India's neighbors during the election campaign; she had accused her Janatha rivals of being too soft on India's neighbors, and even referred to Nepal as a province of India, in total disregard of that country's independent status. But he was intent on building a new and, if possible, amicable working relationship with her.

That was not to be. From the outset it was clear that there was an element of personal animosity in Mrs. Gandhi's attitude to Jayewardene, something that went back to 1977 and the Sri Lankan election of that year. Jayewardene and the United National Party (UNP) had eagerly, if somewhat tactlessly, exploited the stunning defeats suffered by her and her son to draw a parallel with the situation in Sri Lanka where a similar mother-and-son combination faced an election campaign against his own party. She had responded to the UNP's landslide victory in July 1977 with the comment that "foreign forces"—she did not specify what these were—had helped in this. Mrs. Gandhi was in the political wilderness at this time and her comments were seen in Colombo as being guided by her personal friendship with Mrs. Bandaranaike. Nor would she have found his specific reference to the harsher aspects of her rule, in his speech of 27 October 1978 in New Delhi, any more palatable. In fact she resented the friendship that had developed between Desai and Jayewardene and the latter's references to the common link of a successful electoral triumph against the two women prime ministers.

Once she came back to power in 1980, she took it upon herself to comment on Sri Lanka's internal politics in matters totally unconnected with the island's Indian minority or even with the problems of the Tamils.

Generally these were related to Mrs. Bandaranaike's tribulations as she faced a Commission of Inquiry on charges of abuses of power. Suffice it to say here that the commission held against Mrs. Bandaranaike, and she faced the usual penalty imposed on persons found guilty of such charges—the loss of a seat in Parliament and civic rights for a specific period. The Sri Lankan government either completely ignored Mrs. Gandhi's undiplomatic and imprudent comments on these developments or, on occasion, pointedly left the response to the youngest member of the Sri Lankan cabinet.

The Return of Indira Gandhi

The unraveling of the intrinsically unstable Janatha government, through personal conflicts exacerbated by some not very important policy issues, had fateful consequences for South Asia. In Sri Lanka President Jayewardene watched in dismay as Prime Minister Desai lost his hold on the fractious coalition that had sustained him in office over two difficult years. The Sri Lankan president braced himself for the return of Indira Gandhi to power. He realized that the cordial Indo–Sri Lankan relationship that had been an important feature of his own years in office would be under some strain, primarily because Mrs. Gandhi was much less concerned about the sensitivities of India's neighbors than Desai had been, and much more attracted to India's hegemonic strategic vision. He was not aware at that stage of the Soviet Union's own contribution to the downfall of the Janatha government[2] but he realized that with Mrs. Gandhi in office there would be greater emphasis on the maintenance of the Indo-Soviet alliance.

The Soviet invasion of Afghanistan came in the last week of 1979, an event that served to underline the differences between India and her neighbors at this expansion of Soviet power and its intrusion to the borders of South Asia. In January 1980, when Mrs. Gandhi took office again after an absence of nearly three years, she came determined to strengthen India's links with the Soviet Union, which she felt had been weakened by the Janatha government. For her and her principal advisers, the Soviet alliance was the pivot of India's defense and foreign policies, and the essential means of realizing Indian aspirations for regional supremacy. They were aware of the dangers from the Soviet invasion because of the inevitability of its provoking countervailing U.S. measures. Thus Mrs. Gandhi could not, and did not, condemn the Soviet invasion as unequivocally as many of the leaders of India's neighboring states would have liked her to do. The Afghan issue became a major point of difference between Mrs. Gandhi and President Jayewardene, since the latter was deeply perturbed by this extension of Soviet power into the borders of the South Asia region, and upset by Mrs. Gandhi's failure to take the lead in opposing it. We shall return to this theme later on in this present chapter.

By the time Mrs. Gandhi returned to office, there were signs of a distinct improvement in relations between India and the United States and China as well. The Carter presidency had seen Iran and India as two "regional influentials" with whom the United States could coordinate its strategic interests in the Indian Ocean region.[3] The fall of the Shah of Iran had put an end to the once stable and close U.S.–Iran relationship; there were few difficulties with regard to India under the Desai regime. Washington's disappointment with what it had regarded as India's pro-Soviet posture over Afghanistan and New Delhi's concern with the renewal, following the difficulties of the Carter years, of the U.S.-Pakistan security relationship, had both introduced severe strains in U.S.-Indian ties. But by 1982 the two countries had concluded that they should live with their differences and seek to put their relations on a constructive course. Mrs. Gandhi's visit to Washington that year seemed to confirm that position on the part of both governments.

Although Sri Lanka was seen as a friendly country and had been one of those the United States had relied on during the delicate negotiations over the U.S. hostages in Teheran, the United States did not let its friendship stand in the way of its more important strategic objective of improving relations with India.[4] Thus when the Indo–Sri Lankan relationship deteriorated rapidly in the early 1980s with Mrs. Gandhi in power, the United States did very little to help Sri Lanka when that help could have mattered greatly.

Yet despite all the efforts taken by the United States to improve relations with India, Mrs. Gandhi remained as suspicious of U.S. intentions and strategic concerns, especially in the Indian Ocean region, as she had ever been. Indeed, the rapid and increasing flood of U.S. armaments to Pakistan for diversion to the Afghan resistance was treated as a matter for deep concern by New Delhi. Mrs. Gandhi and her advisers—most of whom were pro-Soviet—believed that this had tilted the strategic balance in favor of India's rival, Pakistan, which was benefiting from the flow of arms from China as well. The fact is that Mrs. Gandhi and her closest advisers continued to see the United States as the only obstacle to India's securing the sort of domination of the region that the *raj* had in its day. Under Indira Gandhi, India had been one of the most vocal critics of the establishment of the U.S. naval base at Diego Garcia; there was no change in this attitude once she came back to power in 1980. Indeed, the U.S. naval presence in the Indian Ocean, the renewal of links with Pakistan, both of which stemmed from the burgeoning Afghan crisis, and India's unhelpful attitude toward that crisis—as Washington saw it—limited the scope for any substantial improvement in U.S.-Indian ties.

From the mid-1970s, Beijing was intent on improving its relations with India.[5] There were several factors behind this, the most important being the fact of India's preeminence in South Asia after the dismemberment of Pakistan in 1971. India was much stronger after that time, a point that China recognized even if it was not publicly conceded. The two Asian giants were wary of each other. China, for her part, could no longer afford a policy of brinksmanship because the potential costs of another outbreak of war were seen to be greater than they were in the early 1970s. The Janatha government of Morarji Desai had been determined to correct what it believed was India's unbalanced alignment with the Soviet Union, and very shortly after taking office Desai decided to improve relations with the United States and China, albeit while being careful to maintain cordial ties with the USSR—a course he characterized as "genuine nonalignment." Moscow was extremely upset at Desai's opening to Beijing, and it eventually resulted in the decision taken to help anti-Desai forces in India to destabilize the Janatha government.[6]

The Soviet occupation of Afghanistan in December 1979 increased Chinese concern with South Asia. Beijing saw Moscow's move as part of a bold "southern strategy" designed to secure warm-water ports on the Indian Ocean: Afghanistan was a stepping stone to Iran, Pakistan—especially Pakistan's Baluchistan province with its ports on the Indian Ocean—and the Persian Gulf. While aimed primarily at winning strategic superiority over the United States, Moscow's southern strategy was seen in Beijing as part of a Soviet drive to encircle China, and therefore a grave threat to China's security. Beijing had moved quickly to support Pakistan in the face of the increased Soviet threat. Nevertheless, while China would provide diplomatic and material support for Pakistan, it sought to avoid undertakings that might drag it into a major war.

Diplomatic support for Pakistan was intended to discourage India from supporting Soviet designs in South Asia. This was balanced by efforts at improving Sino-Indian relations and encouragement of Indo-Pakistan relations. Beijing's decision for war with Vietnam in 1979, and for a policy of sustained pressure on Vietnam after that, created additional incentives for Beijing to improve relations with India. After the Soviet invasion of Afghanistan, Beijing made a determined effort to improve relations with India. The principal difficulty this policy confronted was that India would do nothing to undermine her strong relations with the Soviet Union, or take any measures that would seem to endorse Beijing's policy of "antihegemonism" directed against the Soviet Union.

As Indira Gandhi saw it, or preferred to see it, Beijing's "antihegemonism" was intended to weaken Soviet influence in the region and Asia in general. That would work against India's principal concern, the Soviet Union's readiness and ability to support her in the power politics of South Asia. Besides, antihegemonism would strengthen Pakistan, India's most persistent opponent. More specifically in relation to the rest of South Asia, the strategic vision of the Jayewardene government appeared to coincide with China's on a number of critically important issues such as Afghanistan, Vietnam, and the need for a strong U.S. presence in the region, all of which Indira Gandhi saw as evidence of China's influence in South Asia.

Jayewardene and the Soviet Invasion of Afghanistan

Few events in recent years have had a more destabilizing influence on the security of South Asia than the Soviet intrusion into Afghanistan. Jayewardene was greatly disturbed by what he saw as the ruthless extension of Soviet power to the border of Pakistan and the great security threat it posed to the whole region. Sri Lanka, like most other South Asian states, strongly condemned the Soviet Union on the Afghanistan issue. India was seen to be out of step with the rest of South Asia, and much of the rest of the nonaligned world, on this issue. The mutual distrust between President Jayewardene and Mrs. Gandhi in regard to their respective strategic visions stemmed in important part from this, and its implications for the hegemony India sought in the region.

At the first meeting for the Sri Lankan cabinet for 1980 there was a brief discussion of this event, and Foreign Minister A. C. S. Hameed was asked to prepare a statement to be issued on behalf of the government.

The statement eventually submitted by Hameed fell far short of what the cabinet wanted. Its tepid language did not reflect adequately the sense of deep concern of the Sri Lankan government at the invasion of an Asian neighbor by a superpower and the threat posed to the security of South Asia by this breach of the regional peace. The cabinet—with Jayewardene giving the leadership—proceeded to draft a statement of policy condemning the Soviet invasion in more forthright terms.

Jayewardene believed—quite wrongly as it turned out—that the original statement reflected the views of officials in the Ministry of Foreign Affairs, and that this was indicative of a reluctance to make an emphatic condemnation of the Soviet Union even when the national interest required them to do so.[7] He did not know that the original draft presented to the cabinet was Hameed's and that the officials in the latter's ministry had taken a much firmer line.

The result, however, was that Jayewardene was more reluctant thereafter to rely on the expertise of the Foreign Ministry in the enunciation of foreign policy, and in initiatives on foreign policy. This decision had far-reaching consequences in the mid- and late 1980s, when policy toward India was conducted by the president's office, or by cabinet ministers chosen by him, in preference to the foreign minister and without the benefit of the institutional memory of that ministry.

More significantly, India's early (and seeming) acquiescence in this extension of Soviet power to the borders of South Asia created serious doubts in Jayewardene's mind about Indira Gandhi's and India's commitment to the principles of nonalignment. The invasion of Afghanistan led to a renewal of American ties with Pakistan, which had been weakened in the aftermath of the creation of Bangladesh. The military and naval challenge and response between Washington and Moscow—between American sea-based power and Soviet land-based power—aggravated superpower tensions in the Indian Ocean, and with each escalation of such tensions the U.S. naval presence became more visible. The base at Diego Garcia became more important than ever before in U.S. strategic considerations. Military assistance to Pakistan—to be funneled to the Afghan resistance—increased exponentially, with a corresponding reinforcement of India's sense of insecurity at the prospect that Pakistan was becoming stronger militarily.

Despite differences of policy over regional and international affairs in the wake of Mrs. Gandhi's return to power, relations between Sri Lanka and India remained friendlier than India's relations with its other neighbors, Pakistan, Bangladesh, and Nepal. But the differences on policies in regard to the problems of the Indian Ocean, and relations with the Soviet Union and China, widened.

With regard to the first, differences between India and Sri Lanka[8] had emerged in the early 1970s. They became wider and sharper in the mid-1970s, and now in the first half of 1980 they became wider still. India's main aim was to see the elimination of all foreign bases in the Indian Ocean area. Since Jayewardene took office as prime minister, Sri Lanka, like the Association of Southeast Asian Nations (ASEAN) states, had been more interested in establishing a balance of influences there, so that no one country would be able to dominate the region. Now in the wake of the Soviet invasion of Afghanistan Sri Lanka feared that the elimination of all bases could result in a domination of the region by the Indian navy, and that the Indian Ocean could be converted into an Indian lake, or an *Indian* ocean. Since it seemed quite unlikely that either the United States or the Soviet Union would reduce its presence in the Indian Ocean area, Sri Lanka was more interested in seeing that there was no escalation of superpower rivalry, if not activity. In regard to this, the Indian attitude was seen to be ambivalent in view of her close links with the Soviet Union.

Sri Lanka had a vital interest in the improvement and eventual normalization of relations between India and China, because tensions between the two inevitably led to pressures and counterpressures on Sri Lanka. The improvement in relations between India and China that had begun with the Janatha government in power had received a setback with the outbreak of war between China and Vietnam. Now the Soviet invasion of Afghanistan aggravated the situation. A large purchase of arms by India from the Soviet Union in June 1980 soon became a major setback to any prospects of normalization of relations between India and China. As China saw it, these purchases were not justified on the basis of India's current defense requirements since Pakistan was far too weak to pose a serious threat to India. For China—as for Sri Lanka—the most serious threat to the security of the region came from the Soviet presence in Afghanistan, and the purchase of arms from the Soviet Union only aggravated an already dangerous destabilization of the region.

Inevitably, the Soviet invasion of Afghanistan became a serious impediment to any move at a reconciliation between the Soviet Union and China. Earlier there had been tentative moves, initiated by China, to reach some settlement of existing differences. If these had been pursued, it might have led to much better relations between the two countries in the 1980s. As it was, the Afghan invasion strengthened Chinese suspicions of Soviet motives, and renewed its fears for the security of China's huge land frontiers with Russia. Naturally it also strengthened links between China and the United States. All these developments impinged on China's relations with India and intensified India's sense of insecurity.

We turn next to the ASEAN group of states. The Soviet invasion of Afghanistan confirmed all their fears and suspicions of Soviet expansionism in association with Vietnam. It also increased their suspicions of India because of the latter's close ties with the Soviet Union and its failure to make any forthright condemnation of that invasion or the continued Soviet presence in Afghanistan.

Jayewardene's first personal meeting with Mrs. Gandhi came in September 1980, when he traveled to New Delhi for the Commonwealth Asia-Pacific Regional Conference. There he made what became a controversial speech in which he urged India to take over the leadership of the nonaligned world through a return to the high moral and ethical standards that had governed India's policies in the days of Mahatma Gandhi and the two Nehrus, Motilal (Mrs. Gandhi's grandfather) and Jawaharlal. The background to the speech was the recent death of Marshal Josif Broz Tito (in June 1980), which had removed from the scene the last of the founding fathers of the movement. At the time he made the speech India was isolated in the councils of the Third World and, although he did not say so on this occasion, he believed her isolation would continue until there was a return to the principles that guided Indian foreign policy in the 1940s and 1950s.

All but one of the Indians present on the occasion were greatly impressed by the speech, and deeply touched by his references to India's historical leadership role in the Third World. No one there was more enthusiastic in his appreciation of this speech than Indian president Sanjiva Reddy.[9] The exception was Mrs. Gandhi, who was upset and annoyed at what she thought was a deliberate attempt to exclude her from the compliments showered on India's leaders. She felt that Jayewardene had made an invidious comparison between her and her predecessors.

For his part, Jayewardene found Mrs. Gandhi a very cold person, withdrawn and unapproachable. He found it difficult to get to know her. He realized that the tragic death of her son and closest confidant, Sanjay Gandhi,[10] was partly responsible for this but there was more to it. There were signs, he believed, of a failure of judgment and a lack of imagination in much that she was doing then. She seemed isolated within her party, and had no really trusted aides.

Sri Lanka and the ASEAN States

This failure to establish a close understanding with India under Indira Gandhi provides the background for Jayewardene's next diplomatic venture: throughout 1979 and 1980 he was calculating the advantages and disadvantages of a link with ASEAN. At the same time Sri Lanka had been approached by Bangladesh to support moves it was making to call together a South Asia Regional Council (SARC). This body later became the nucleus of the present South Asian Association for Regional Cooperation (SAARC). In May 1980, Ziaur-Rahman of Bangladesh had formally proposed the establishment of such an organization, and the Sri Lankan government had agreed to give its support to the venture. Disappointment with India's foreign policy turned Jayewardene's mind to an effort actively to seek for Sri Lanka an association with—if not membership in—ASEAN.

The advantages of membership in ASEAN, as Jayewardene saw it, were more economic than political, although the latter were not without significance: access to a huge market, to advanced technology, and to capital investment in Sri Lanka from ASEAN sources, especially a shift of labor-intensive industry from the ASEAN region to Sri Lanka. In foreign policy, too, there was now a much greater coincidence of views between Sri Lanka and the ASEAN states, especially after India's recognition of the Heng Samrin regime in Kampuchea.

In September 1980 he intended to broach the subject of Sri Lanka's association with ASEAN with Malaysian prime minister Hussein Onn, who was due to visit Sri Lanka soon. If the latter gave his approval, the process of active negotiation was expected to begin with the other ASEAN powers as well. Onn was scheduled to visit Sri Lanka in the early part of 1981, but the visit was postponed until later in the year because his health was deteriorating. He never recovered, and died later that year.

There were other ASEAN nations with which Sri Lanka had built very close ties, Singapore in particular. The links were so close that Dr. Goh Keng Swee, first deputy prime minister of Singapore, had been invited by Jayewardene to make a confidential report to the Sri Lankan government on the state of Sri Lanka's economy, and to make recommendations on how current shortcomings in it could be overcome. He presented his report to Jayewardene on 6 December 1980.[11]

On 29 January 1981, Singapore prime minister Lee Kuan Yew arrived in the island for a three-day visit. Planned originally as a private visit, it turned out to be a business visit as well. Foreign affairs loomed large in the discussions, as was seen by the presence of the Singapore foreign minister, Dhanabalan, in the entourage. Lee Kuan Yew's main aim was to gain Sri Lanka's support for the ASEAN viewpoint at the forthcoming nonaligned nations foreign ministers conference in New Delhi in regard to three issues: Kampuchea, Afghanistan, and the Iran-Iraq War. On all three, Sri Lankan and ASEAN views were very similar.[12]

Naturally enough, the Singapore leader's main interest was in Kampuchea, over which ASEAN policy had by then developed in some detail. The ASEAN states sought the establishment of a viable and neutral Kampuchea (i.e., neutral as against both Vietnam and China) that could stand on its own. This was not very far from Sri Lanka's own view. Singapore was concerned that India, whose attitude on Kampuchea and Afghanistan was more pro-Soviet than that of many (if not most) of the nonaligned nations, would try to foster the cause of the Heng Samrin regime in Kampuchea, which India had recognized.

Sri Lanka supported the ASEAN states on these issues at the nonaligned nations foreign ministers conference in New Delhi in June 1981. India was suspect to the ASEAN states as well as to others, not only because of its pro-Moscow inclinations in regional and international affairs, but also because it was a regional power with its own ambitions and political imperatives in the Indian Ocean. Thus India's attempt to identify the Diego Garcia base, in the official communiqué, as a disturbing element in the peace of the region, only strengthened these suspicions. Eventually, Sri Lanka, in association with the ASEAN states and other moderates, succeeded in deleting the reference to Diego Garcia from the communiqué.

The Sri Lankan government had a special interest in the Indian Ocean issue because a resolution of the UN General Assembly in 1972 had appointed Sri Lanka as the chair of a committee that was expected to convene a conference on the special problems of the Indian Ocean, the Indian Ocean Peace Zone Conference as it came to be called.[13] That conference had still to be held because the superpowers, in particular the United States, were reluctant to participate. Jayewardene's government had inherited the chairmanship of the committee, and his foreign minister, A. C. S. Hameed, was anxious to convene the conference in Colombo.

Without U.S. support there was no hope of success in this. The ASEAN states were not very enthusiastic about holding the conference.

We need to return to Sri Lanka's efforts to join ASEAN, the first stage of which was to secure observer status. The actual negotiations were left in the hands of Premadasa, who visited the ASEAN states in early 1981 for this purpose. In Manila he exceeded his brief in making a public statement to this effect. The bid was unsuccessful. Sri Lanka had been a good prospect for membership in 1967–68 when ASEAN was being formed; now that organization was well established, and Sri Lanka was no longer such an attractive prospect for ASEAN to take a bold decision to extend its reach westward to the southernmost fringes of the Indian subcontinent. The reasons for the rejection of Sri Lanka's approaches for membership in ASEAN were never revealed, but the rejection constituted a failure of Jayewardene's diplomacy. It was only after this rejection by ASEAN that Jayewardene really committed himself to supporting the SARC concept then being put forth by Bangladesh.[14]

Sri Lanka and the Western Powers

There was, in fact, an obvious compatibility of views between Jayewardene's government and the United States on a wide range of issues involving the Asian region: beginning with the opposition to the Soviet invasion of Afghanistan; on the Kampuchea issue; and—whatever Colombo's public rhetoric may have been—on the question of bases in the Indian Ocean. This compatibility of views disturbed India under Indira Gandhi, and there was a strong suspicion in New Delhi's South Block—the section of the administrative complex that housed both the prime minister's office and the Ministry of External Affairs—that the United States was actively seeking facilities in the port of Trincomalee. With the establishment of a base at Diego Garcia there really was no need for such facilities in Trincomalee, but the rumors and allegations persisted in India to the point that Donald Toussaint, the U.S. ambassador in Sri Lanka, felt compelled to issue a forthright public denial in August 1981 that the United States had any such plans. Toussaint declared: "The US government has no plans or policy to develop Trincomalee into a military base or facility. Nor has the US government ever discussed such a policy with officials of the Sri Lanka government either present or past, either here in Sri Lanka or elsewhere."[15]

The speech was made in Kandy, at a formal occasion, in the presence of Jayewardene himself. It had no apparent effect on Delhi, where the United States had also sought to reassure the Indians on that score.

Indian suspicions of Jayewardene and his government's pro–United States attitudes arose also from the expanded facilities granted to the United States for its Voice of America (VOA) relay station in the island,[16] and in the choice of a consortium consisting of Oroleum (Pvt) Ltd., Singapore Oil Tanking, West Germany, and Tradinaft, Switzerland to restore to commercial use a complex of oil tank farms in the vicinity of the strategically important port of Trincomalee. The Indian government believed that there were covert links between the constituent firms of this consortium and U.S. interests, and expressed fears that there were concealed political and strategic dimensions in this transaction.

Sri Lanka's relations with Britain developed a political dimension in 1982 when Argentina invaded the Falkland Islands. Most of the nations of the nonaligned group, even those belonging to the Commonwealth, either sympathized with or supported Argentina on this issue. Sri Lanka's foreign ministry itself was inclined to take this view, but Jayewardene intervened directly and instructed Sri Lanka's UN representative to vote with Britain. He was more consistent on this than his many critics gave him credit for: to him a single thread ran through these three crises— Afghanistan, Kampuchea, and now the Falklands—the use of force and an invading army. For his part he was not afraid to stand up for what he believed was right, even if it meant standing against the conventional wisdom of the nonaligned nations' political thinking as expressed in the United Nations. As we shall see, Sri Lanka paid a heavy price, in the mid- and late 1980s, for Jayewardene's idiosyncratic reaction on the Falklands issue. Mrs. Gandhi was uncharacteristically less than forthright on the issue. It was said, at that time, that she was influenced by her excellent relationship with Mrs. Thatcher (the two "iron ladies") and thus did not condemn the British.

In 1981 Sri Lanka was celebrating the fiftieth anniversary of the introduction of universal suffrage in the country seventeen years before independence. Sri Lanka was the first country in Asia to enjoy the privilege and benefits of universal suffrage, and Jayewardene's government decided to make the occasion one of national celebration. The choice he made of the two sets of guests to be invited that year reflected the importance he attached to the countries they came from: the crown prince and princess of Japan, and Queen Elizabeth II and Prince Philip of Great Britain. The queen and her husband were the guests of honor at the principal celebrations. They were making their second royal tour of the country, the first having been in 1954 when Jayewardene was a cabinet minister under Sir John Kotelawala. In that combination of guests one found a celebration of the special relationship with Japan and a renewal of warm ties with Great Britain, symbolizing not merely the Commonwealth link but also a wider association with the West. At a personal level, that combination also symbolized a dynamic link between his policies of the 1970s and early 1980s and the most creative and imaginative aspects of the foreign policy decisions of the early 1950s. He had then played a crucially important role in the diplomacy over the ratification of the Japanese peace treaty in 1951, and in the formative years of the Commonwealth link he had been one of the prime movers in the creation and establishment of the Colombo Plan mechanism for economic and technical assistance.[17]

Riots of July 1983[18]

The period from around August 1982 to the end of May 1983 had been one of intense political activity in Sri Lanka. This prolonged period of political campaigning and the unusual frequency of electoral contests kept political passions and rivalries inflamed and overheated throughout these months. Inevitably, too, communal tensions were aggravated by all this, especially because in the early months of 1983 political violence erupted with greater frequency than before in the north of the island.

Yet there were signs of conciliatory moves afoot. Jayewardene had announced his intention to summon the All Party Conference for the resolution of outstanding issues in Sri Lanka's ethnic conflict the UNP had spoken of in its manifesto for the election of July 1977. This proposal was explicitly intended to move to a wider national forum beyond the bilateral talks between the government and the TULF that had been a feature of the years 1981 and 1982 but had ended in an impasse. A round-table conference for this purpose was announced for the end of July 1983. One of the principal groups invited, the TULF, was in one of its frequent moods of introspection, unable to decide whether to participate (or at least to put up a show of doubt to satisfy its own electorate). It was scheduled to meet at its annual conference in the third week of July, where policies for the immediate future were to be determined.

While the TULF convention was in progress at Mannar, thirteen soldiers were killed in Jaffna in a Liberation Tigers of Tamil Eelam (LTTE) ambush on 23 July. It led almost immediately to army reprisals there and subsequently to the worst outbreak of ethnic violence in the island since 1958. The symbolism and purpose of the attack could not be missed. It was timed to coincide with the TULF convention, to upstage the latter, and to serve as a warning that a conciliatory response to the government's proposals would be quite misplaced in the current mood of youth opinion in the north; 23 July was also the sixth anniversary of the UNP's return to power in 1977. Thus in one decisive move the armed separatist activists had once again attacked the principal advocates of constructive change in the troubled ethnic scene in Sri Lanka with deadly effects on prospects for a settlement.

Although the riots that broke out in Colombo and several other parts of the island in the wake of the killing of the thirteen soldiers in Jaffna took virtually everyone by surprise, the fact is that for several weeks perceptive observers of the Sri Lankan scene had been living in fear of such an outburst. Jayewardene himself was aware of the dangers of this situation. On 6 June 1983, on the eve of his departure from the island for an official visit to Egypt and the Vatican, he had appealed to the Sinhalese people for restraint in the face of provocations in the form of violence in Jaffna, and had urged them to refrain from attacking Tamils in their midst. On his return from this visit he found the situation as combustible as it had been when he left. The annual *gam udava*[19] ceremony, held in this occasion at Nikaveratiya in the North Western Province in the last week of June, gave him the opportunity for another appeal, in a speech that was televised during prime time. Throughout June there had been isolated incidents; fortunately every one of these had been contained.

When the news of the ambush reached the country at large, Jayewardene and the government feared a violent eruption of rioting in the Sinhalese areas. Little did they realize that some of their own decisions in the wake of that incident would create a situation that would get so completely out of control, or that the normal machinery for the maintenance of law and order would fail so comprehensively in the face of this wholly unprecedented outbreak. The scale of the rioting took everyone, including Jayewardene and the government, by surprise.

Bringing the bodies of the thirteen soldiers killed on that occasion for burial or cremation at the principal cemetery in Colombo proved to be a serious mistake. Who recommended it we do not know, but the consequences proved to be disastrous, for it provided a crucial focal point for the violence that followed. But the outburst might not have been so ferocious if the arrival of the bodies had not been delayed for five or six hours. That delay enabled the crowds to increase prodigiously in size, and provided opportunities for mischief makers to gain an advantage they might not have had if the bodies had arrived at the time they were expected to and the next of kin permitted to remove them to their respective home towns or villages.

The delay of five or six hours, with the crowds increasing in numbers with every hour, was a critically important factor in explaining why a containable situation assumed the proportions of an uncontrollable outburst of ethnic hostility. The riot began in the vicinity of Colombo's principal cemetery and quickly spread to other parts of the city, especially to the residential areas in which Tamils lived; the mobs moved next to the suburbs. Over the next two days it spread to other parts of the island, to many of the important towns in which there was a Tamil population. The violence soon engulfed the plantation areas. The simmering ethnic tensions of the previous few weeks were brought hideously to the boil.

Sinhalese mobs did not distinguish between Sri Lankan Tamils and Indian Tamils in their ferocious, vengeful outburst of indignation against terrorism in the north. In fact few of the victims of these assaults had shown any outward sympathy for the separatist movement, or indeed for the TULF. Tamils living in the Sinhalese areas had voted in large numbers for the UNP. Yet they faced the rage of the mobs. Colombo City and its residential areas were the principal target of the arson and destruction that followed. There was little doubt that much of the violence reflected a ferocious mood of disapproval of the government's handling of the terrorist threat. Jayewardene himself came to believe this in the heat of the moment and many of his decisions that week were governed by that belief. For the first time since he had come to power in 1977, Jayewardene was in very real danger of being overthrown by the upsurge of anti-Tamil feeling that swept the Sinhalese areas of the country.

There was a self-destructive aspect too, most evident in the senseless burning of factories and shops owned by Tamils in Colombo and its suburbs. These had provided employment for thousands of Sinhalese. The Roman Catholic areas in the north and northwest of the city and the Roman Catholic suburbs between Colombo and Negombo on the route to the airport were among those most seriously affected. That was one of the principal differences between the riots of 1983 and those of 1958. This new development reflected the deep chasm that had emerged over the years among the Roman Catholics themselves—between the Sinhalese and Tamil Roman Catholics—and the anger directed against the Roman Catholic Church in the north where some of the younger and more activist clergy were well known for their avowed sympathy for the separatist cause.

Given the extent of the physical destruction of property—houses, shops, and factories—that occurred in Colombo and its suburbs and elsewhere in the country, the death toll estimated at between five hundred and six hundred was much smaller than was feared.

What distinguished the riots of July 1983 from previous disturbances was the role of the security forces. The breakdown in law enforcement in the early days of the riots had no precedent in the past; it took the government nearly a week to reestablish its authority and quell the violence. The security forces were either generally indifferent to or ignored their peacekeeping role, repeatedly refusing to intervene when their intervention could have saved lives and property. The machinery of law and order had almost totally collapsed.

Senior government officials recalled that the heart of the problem was the role of the army. Even in August 1977 some units of the army had been reluctant to fire on Sinhalese mobs and had to be coaxed into doing so. But by and large the army had been an effective instrument of law enforcement at that time when the loyalties of the police were suspect. On this occasion the roles were reversed. Soldiers in mufti actively encouraged the mob gathered near the cemetery on the first day of the riots, and prevented the police from quelling the violence.

Many of the Tamils, their houses destroyed or in danger of destruction, their lives threatened, took shelter in refugee camps. Sadly, some remembered their stays in similar camps in the mid-1950s and 1977. Then again there was a dreary journey by steamer from Colombo across the seas to Jaffna. Some had painful memories of the same journey in the mid-1950s.

Despite the comments of some contemporary observers of these incidents, foreign and local, suggesting a link between the mobs and influential government politicians, no firm evidence has yet emerged to support that contention. The fact is that the mobs that roamed the streets of Colombo and the other towns of Sri Lanka on that fateful week were composed of people professing a wide range of political views and included supporters of the UNP. Anyone who saw them at work would have sensed the operation of something like a mass of visceral antagonisms, a frightening force fed on a diet of rumors, tensions, fears, and paranoia, and a fearsome rage directed against the Tamils—any Tamils—on the assumption that they were all communally responsible for the terrorist outbreaks in the north and for the incident that sparked off this vengeful fury. The country's political structure was shaken to its foundation.

A state of emergency had been in force since the middle of May 1983. Now, in the aftermath of the riots, curfews were imposed under the emergency regulations. The curfews were at first ignored by both the mobs and the security forces. It took a few days before the security forces began the business of restoring order, tardily and hesitantly at first, but within a week with professional competence; soon curfews and emergency regulations became vigorous instruments of peacekeeping. But the government had made an important concession to Sinhalese opinion, an admission on state television by Jayewardene himself, that the policy of conciliating the TULF and separatist forces was a mistaken one, and a promise was made of firm and effective steps to curb separatism.

Thus one very significant change of policy flowed from the riots of July 1983. In August 1983 Parliament approved the Sixth Amendment to the Constitution, imposing a ban on political parties that advocated separatist policies and penalties on individuals who advocated separatism. Twenty years earlier India had introduced a similar ban through the Sixteenth Amendment to the Indian Constitution, which had a prompt quieting effect on irresponsible separatist talk in South Asia. An important and inevitable consequence was that all TULF members of Parliament forfeited their right to sit in the national legislature unless they took an oath abjuring the advocacy of separatism. None of them chose to take such an oath.

The riots of July 1983 exposed the flaws in the administrative system that had been built up under Jayewardene, as did no other incident during his whole administration. While an outbreak of communal violence had been expected through much of the early part of 1983, it was evident that little had been done to build an administrative mechanism to deal with such a crisis if it did break out. As in the past, there was resort to a state of emergency, followed by a curfew. But when these proved to be patently ineffective, there were no contingency plans and certainly no team of politicians or administrators identified as a crisis management group to assist the president in a situation such as this.

The scale of the violence and its rapid spread into the heart of Colombo's residential areas had not been anticipated. Nor had the extent to which the normal security mechanisms, the police and the armed services, failed to cope with the outbreak, and to which units of the army failed to cooperate in containing the situation. It was clear that the normal political direction of the law and order machinery had also broken down. No cabinet subcommittee had been set up for such an eventuality; certainly there was no equivalent of a National Security Council. Senior public officials who saw Jayewardene at work on that occasion recalled him as shaken by the unfolding events, more than a little bewildered, and somewhat confused as to what steps could be taken to bring the situation quickly under control.

Jayewardene himself has been criticized for not imposing a curfew as soon as the riots broke out. But the fact is that even when a curfew was imposed neither the army nor the police seemed willing to enforce it. More inexplicable was his silence for three days when the country was waiting to hear him on the radio and see him on television. Jayewardene's own explanation, given on several occasions, was that nothing he could have said would have had any influence on the rioters. It was a confession that, within a few months of his election as president for a second time, his authority had been eroded by an upsurge of communal feeling.

Had any group in the army felt emboldened to oust him from power on this occasion, they might well have succeeded in doing so. The riots and arson first erupted less than half a mile from Jayewardene's private residence at 66 Ward Place. Although he was vulnerable there, he did not move to a more secure point. His own house became a haven for some of his Tamil neighbors.

That last week in July 1983 saw Jayewardene's prestige in the country reach very nearly its nadir. He was to face more serious crises later on, as we shall see later in this book, but on each such occasion he very quickly established his own command over the situation and gave clear leadership to those who had to carry out his instructions.[21] On this occasion there was evidence of a failure of nerve. How else does one account for the succession of dubious decisions taken: the delay in addressing the nation on the crisis; the fact that even when he did so for the first time there was not a word of solace for the Tamils, the victims of the riots, mostly people in no way associated with the separatists, and a great many of whom had voted for him; and the decision to introduce the Sixth Amendment, whose effect was to drive the moderate TULF out of Parliament and into the arms of the Tamil Nadu politicians, leaving the field clear for the more extremist elements among the Tamils.

Above all, Mrs. Gandhi was provided with a totally unanticipated opportunity for intervention in the affairs of Sri Lanka, and Jayewardene, whose political authority had suffered badly as a result of the riots, locally as well as internationally, found himself dealing with a relentless adversary intent on extracting every possible benefit from the advantageous situation in which she found herself.

Notes

1. For the background to the collapse of the Janatha government, see Inder Malhotra, *Indira Gandhi: A Personal and Political Biography* (London: Hodder and Stoughton, 1989), 211–13; Pupul Jayakar, *Indira Gandhi* (New Delhi: Viking, 1992), 388–90. See also Arun Gandhi, *The Morarji Papers: The Fall of the Janata Government* (New Delhi: Vision Books, 1983).

2. For discussion of this, see Arun Gandhi, *The Morarji Papers*, 27–31. See also Subramaniam Swamy, "The Bear Hug," *Illustrated Weekly of India*, 17 March 1985, 14–17.

3. This point is made in Riaz M. Khan, *Untying the Afghan Knot: Negotiating Soviet Withdrawal* (Durham, N.C.: Duke University Press, 1991), 23.

4. Ibid.

5. See Lillian Craig Harris, "China and the Northern Tier: Shoring up the Barrier to Soviet Southward Expansion," *Contemporary China* 3, no. 4 (1979): 22–27.

6. Arun Gandhi, *Morarji Papers*, and Subramaniam Swamy, "Bear Hug."

7. Jayewardene, interview with the author, January 1980.

8. For a discussion on this, see Selig S. Harrison and K. Subrahmanyam, eds., *Superpower Rivalry in the Indian Ocean: Indian and American Perspectives* (New York: Oxford University Press, 1989), 223–30.

9. Based on the recollections of Sri Lankan officials who were present on the occasion.

10. Sanjay Gandhi was killed in the crash of the small airplane he was flying on 30 June 1980.

11. A copy of this document is available in the J. R. Jayewardene MSS.

12. J. R. Jayewardene, interview with the author, January 1981.

13. See Harrison and Subrahmanyam, *Superpower Rivalry*, 223–30.

14. On the diplomatic negotiations that led to the formation of SARC and later the South Asian Association for Regional Cooperation (SAARC), see Bhabani Sen Gupta, ed., *Regional Cooperation and Development in South Asia*, 2 vols. (New Delhi: South Asian Publishers, 1986).

15. *Sunday Observer*, 16 August 1981.

16. The Indian government was kept informed of the negotiations and the then Indian foreign minister, P. V. Narasimha Rao, was provided with a draft of the agreement for scrutiny. Despite all this, Indian suspicions remained. Ernest Corea, interview with the author, Washington, D.C., 20 May 1992. Corea was Sri Lanka's ambassador to the United States at this time.

17. For discussion of these themes see *JRJ*, vol. 1, chaps. 16, 17 (see chap. 3, n3).

18. On the riots, see T. D. S. A. Dissanayake, *The Agony of Sri Lanka: An In-depth Account of the Racial Riots of July 1983* (Colombo: Swastika [Pvt], 1983) and Sinha Ratnatunga, *The Politics of Terrorism: The Sri Lanka Experience*, (Canberra: International Fellowship for Social and Economic Development, 1988), 11–68. There are also some discerning eyewitness accounts in the essays in James Manor, ed., *Sri Lanka in Change and Crisis* (London: Groom Helm, 1984).

19. Literally, a village reawakening celebration, part carnival, part educational exhibition, and entirely political.

20. This point has eluded most commentators in the riots, but it is one of the most significant.

21. A parallel comes to mind in the masterful Tunku Abdul Rahman's failure of nerve during the Malaysian riots of 1969. See Karl von Vorys, *Democracy Without Consensus: Communalism and Political Stability in Malaysia* (Princeton, N.J.: Princeton University Press, 1975), 308–38.

5

Devolution, Regionalism, Separatism, and "Traditional Homelands"

An Enduring Legacy

THE FREQUENCY with which schemes for the decentralization of administration and devolution of power[1] will figure in later chapters of this book make it necessary to sketch some of the salient features of these and related issues here. To understand why these issues are at the core of the current ethnic conflict in Sri Lanka, and why there is so much controversy over them, one needs to go back to the recent—and not so recent—history of the country.

Sri Lanka, we must emphasize, was not part of the *raj*. It was administered by the Colonial Office, and the administrative and political policies pursued in the colony of Ceylon—as Sri Lanka was called under British rule and until 1972—were affected as much by administrative experience in the Colonial Office tradition as by British experience under the *raj*. Unlike the situation in a great many colonies, the British in nineteenth-century Ceylon deliberately pursued and encouraged policies of centralization. The reasons for this lie in the country's geography and its recent history. It was easy to envisage and maintain a centralized political structure in a comparatively small and compact island. Thus the forces of geography suggested the advantages of centralization while the facts of history made it a political imperative. There had been a long and successful tradition of Sinhalese resistance to Western colonial powers, Portugal first, then Holland and Britain itself. The years 1815–18 when the British established their control over the whole island constitute, in every way, a decisive turning point in the country's history.

75

This time was the first since the early and mid-fifteenth century, when a Sri Lankan (Sinhalese) ruler had effective control over the whole island for about fifty years, that the process of unification had been successfully introduced. However, one had to go further back in history, to the eleventh century in fact, for a period of political control from the national capital comparable to the period of British rule (1796–1947) in Sri Lanka in length of time and in the consistent pursuit of centripetalism as a desirable objective of state policy. To the legatees of the British, at independence in 1948, this centralized structure coincided with their vision of an idealized historical pattern, so it was easy to envisage it as part of a heritage to be preserved. Thus the British policies of centralization have proved to be surprisingly difficult to change. Controversies over attempts to deviate from them form the stuff of the diplomatic negotiations between Sri Lanka and India analyzed in later chapters of this book.

British policies have proved to be enduring in a number of ways, not least in the survival of the administrative boundaries of the provinces carved out by the colonial power between 1832 and 1889. Some of them were modified later on, but the changes made were generally not very significant. More important is the fact that the nine provinces created by the British have remained to the present day. Not a single new province has been created since 1889, despite the massive demographic changes the country has seen since then, not to mention the transfer of power from British to Sri Lankan hands.

A unified administrative system for the whole island was established in 1832, eliminating the existing historical, regional, and subregional administrative boundaries and replacing them with a new system, and dividing the island into five zones of administration in the form of provinces.[2] The avowed objective in all this was political: to hasten the breakup of the Kandyan kingdom (the last independent Sinhalese kingdom, and one that had successfully resisted Western invaders since the mid-sixteenth century) and to weaken "national" feeling there by attaching its low-lying and littoral regions to parts of the maritime regions conquered by the British from the Dutch.[3] In all but one of the new provinces the administrative capital was located on the coast.

These provinces were never intended to be anything more than administrative units. They did not embody political identities despite the political motivation behind their creation.[4] In the 1950s the district (a smaller administrative division) began replacing the province as the largest unit of administration. Even so, the nine provinces survived, bereft of all administrative energy and purpose, a remnant of a British system that did not fade away. They were revived in 1987–88 as a result, in part at least, of Indian pressure on the Sri Lankan government.

In the first half of the nineteenth century, aspirations to centralization were thwarted by the peculiarities of the island's physical features and the inadequacies in the means of communication. As a result, provincial administrators and those at the district level in the more isolated parts of the country enjoyed a great deal of independence and the principal officials there had considerable scope for individual initiative in matters of administration. But Colombo was able to establish tighter control over the provinces by the last quarter of the nineteenth century because of rapid improvements in communications by road and sea, and through the introduction of the railway and the telegraph.

By the beginning of the twentieth century, the island's administrative system was, if anything, overcentralized. Critics of the system, especially Sri Lankan politicians, sought changes that would make it more responsive to popular opinion. Decentralization in some form was regarded as essential for this purpose. Nevertheless there was no noticeable shift of emphasis in the administrative structure in response to these criticisms, that is, no deliberate policy of decentralization even at the end of the 1920s, when the Donoughmore commissioners arrived in the island from London to examine the island's constitution and administrative system. The report of the Donoughmore Commission is celebrated because of some pathbreaking recommendations, such as the introduction of universal suffrage to the island (a recommendation implemented in 1931) and a power-sharing arrangement in which elected ministers were part of a Board of Ministers (with three British officials also holding ministerial posts). That report also proposed an expansion and democratization of the island's local governmental institutions as a remedy for overcentralization, a recommendation that was entirely in keeping with the British experience and political tradition.

In the last two decades of British rule in the island, the Donoughmore Commission's report became the point of departure for several attempts, ineffective though they proved to be, to give some formal shape to decentralization and democratization at the provincial or district level. During this period (1931–47) and the first years of the postindependence phase (1947–51), the most prominent political figure associated with these attempts was S. W. R. D. Bandaranaike, as the minister in charge of local government affairs before independence (1936–47) and as cabinet minister and aspirant to the prime ministership (1947–51). He was the principal advocate of a system of provincial councils (modeled on the British county councils) as the apex of the island's modern local government system. In 1940 the national legislature of this period—the State Council as it was called—gave its formal approval to the principle of establishing provincial councils. However, the legislation required for this purpose was never presented for the legislators' consideration; indeed it was never even prepared.

Although interest in the scheme of provincial councils revived after independence, the consensus that had existed in the 1940s on this had evaporated in the face of new and more urgent concerns, and in any case the first cabinet of postindependence Sri Lanka gave it very low priority. The establishment of these provincial councils inevitably called for a reduction of the powers of ministries under the control of Bandaranaike's cabinet colleagues, none of whom showed much willingness to accept a diminution of their own political and administrative authority. Furthermore, Bandaranaike was seen to have established a solid political base through the expansion and revitalization of local government institutions, and the extension of this system through powerful regional councils was perceived as a calculated attempt to strengthen his position further. These provincial councils came to be viewed as institutions that could give him an overwhelming political advantage, as the prime minister's main political rival within the government, and in the coming struggle for the succession.

More important, once the Federal Party emerged on the political scene in 1949 as an important "ethnic" political party and a very vocal Tamil pressure group, it made the establishment of a federal system the main plank of its political platform. As a result decentralization, which up to then had been viewed as a matter of administrative efficiency and therefore noncontroversial, became acutely controversial. This was partly, at least, because of the deliberate ambiguity in which the Federal Party's demands and objectives were couched: these latter could be and were interpreted, by both its supporters and critics, as a claim for a separate Tamil state. Thus federalism was soon linked with the issue of separatism. Thereafter, proponents of any scheme of regional, provincial, or district councils have confronted an almost impregnable barrier of suspicion. The inevitable weakening of the unified political structure bequeathed by the British, inherent in any scheme of devolution of power, was viewed as a positive encouragement to separatist sentiment among the Tamils.

Resistance to Decentralization

Our study in this volume concentrates on the 1980s, and on efforts on the part of the Sri Lankan government, often under pressure from India, to extend the scope of political initiatives on the devolution of power. As we shall see, one of the problems was a lack of political will before the early 1980s. We need, at this stage, to review some of the constraints that faced the Sri Lankan government in attempting a fundamental change in the country's administrative structure. One of these was undoubtedly the conflicting perceptions on the part of the Sinhalese and the Tamils on the usefulness of devolution of power as a political and administrative device in the management of ethnic conflict. To this theme we shall presently turn in some detail, beginning with the Tamil minority and the separatist aspirations in the north of the island that form part of the debate. Later in this chapter the special problems of the Eastern Province are reviewed, along with the reason there was so much opposition to its linkage with the Northern Province as an integral part of the "traditional homelands" of the Tamils.[5]

There is also the parallel but subsidiary debate on the politically acceptable or viable size of the unit of devolution—district or provincial units. The pressures that emerge from these contentious issues stretch the limits of political action available to Sri Lankan politicians in power perilously close to the breaking point, where the alternatives that loom ahead are either major outbursts of extraparliamentary agitation or a split in the governing party. Thus two attempts at introducing such legislation were abandoned in the face of extraparliamentary agitation, as in 1958, or fear of a split in the government Parliamentary Party, as in 1968.[6] The first successful attempt at introducing such legislation came in 1980 with the District Development Councils Act of that year. There was no extraparliamentary agitation on that occasion and no threat of a party split.

The current debate on devolution of power in Sri Lanka, and the passions that discussions on regionalism and regional autonomy arouse, illustrate two vital themes. The first is the dilemmas that confront the political establishment in the recently independent nations of Asia and Africa in conceding legitimacy to regional loyalties. Those involved in the political establishment in these nations, as legatees of departing imperial powers, passionately protect this inheritance in the shape of the state bequeathed to them at the transfer of power, and regard centralized authority as an essential political and administrative instrument at their disposal. They often justify this position by arguing that centralization is essential for the introduction and management of processes of social change designed to eliminate poverty. In that situation anything likely to encourage or lead to communal or ethnic fragmentation is regarded with the utmost suspicion. More important, once the threat of separatism appears as an objective fact of political life the choice is between the tolerance of cultural traditions and ethnic identity falling well short of secession—in fact, permitting the full expression of such cultural traditions—and the suppression of secessionist demands by armed force, where necessary, if there are signs that secessionist aspirations are striving for fulfillment. India's treatment of Sikh agitation for autonomy and Sri Lanka's responses to Tamil separatist activity provide excellent examples of this phenomenon. However, regionalism divorced from separatism is recognized as having advantages, if not positive value, in generating political participation in decision making at the grassroots level, a principle immanent in the two abortive attempts at establishing provincial and district level councils, in 1957 and 1968 respectively, and in the more productive but equally controversial exercises which led to the District Development Councils Act of 1980. The debate and controversies over the Provincial Councils Act of 1987 are discussed later.

Second, and more specific to Sri Lanka, is the question of location. The Jaffna region in the north of Sri Lanka, the principal area of Tamil settlement in the island, is close to Tamil Nadu in southern India, a great reservoir of sentiment favoring Tamil separatism from India, which has encouraged, nurtured, and protected Tamil separatist groups from Sri Lanka. Thus devolution of power to provincial councils is opposed by Sinhalese because of fears that the councils could serve as a spur to separatist pressures rather than acting as an effective check on these in the north and east of the island. Large sections of the Sinhalese view the Tamil pressure for devolution of power as the first step in an inevitable progression to separation of the Tamil majority areas of the country from the Sri Lankan polity. The fact is that the Sinhalese, although a majority of the population of the island, nevertheless have a minority complex vis-à-vis the Tamils. They feel threatened by the more than fifty million Tamil-speaking people in present-day Tamil Nadu in southern India. For although the Sinhalese outnumber the Tamils by more than five to one within Sri Lanka, they in turn are outnumbered nearly six to one by the Tamil-speaking people of South Asia. The burden of history contributes greatly to the disquiet and apprehensiveness the Sinhalese feel about southern India: the popular perception of events of centuries past; the abiding historical memory (with a recorded history stretching back over two thousand years) of southern India as the single most powerful and persistent threat confronting Sri Lanka and the Sinhalese over the centuries.

In the early years of independence, the Tamils of the north and east of the island had showed little inclination to identify themselves with those of Tamil Nadu. Nevertheless the Sinhalese feared this possibility and the campaign for a federal structure for the island served to aggravate these fears. Those in the forefront of the Tamil agitation for devolution of power have always been vague, deliberately or unconsciously, in the terminology of their arguments, and the distinctions of provincial autonomy, states' rights in a federal union, and a separate state have been blurred by a fog of verbiage and obfuscation. The situation has been aggravated by the close links established in more recent times between Tamil political groups, ranging from the Tamil United Liberation Front (TULF) to various separatist groups, with the government and opposition in Tamil Nadu, and even more by the establishment of training camps in Tamil Nadu for guerrillas and terrorist groups who made forays into the northern and eastern coastal regions of Sri Lanka. The result is that decentralization, which was and should be a purely Sri Lankan matter, has taken on a cross-national dimension, of which India's role as mediator in the recent political negotiations between the Sri Lankan government and representatives of Tamil opinion was the most conspicuous feature.

Moreover, the capacity of devolution of authority to regional units, be they districts or provinces or something larger, to reduce ethnic conflict is more limited than enthusiastic advocates of it are willing to concede. Nothing in the contemporary history of India, Pakistan, or Nigeria, to name just three countries, as they grapple with the issues of devolution and ethnic conflict, justifies any complacency in regard to the capacity of devolution of power, by itself, to help reduce the tensions in ethnic conflict. The situation in Sri Lanka has its own peculiarities. For one, pressure for decentralization of administration is limited to the Tamils, and largely to the Tamils living in the north and east of the island, where they are either a majority (the north) or a substantial minority (the east). There is no pressure, in fact there is strong opposition, from all other ethnic groups and all other parts of the island. Quite apart from the Sinhalese majority, there is the Muslim minority, especially those living in the Eastern and Northern Provinces, who are greatly concerned about the submergence of their own identity under a Tamil-dominated devolutionary system in the north and the east of the island. In other words, devolution of power to units larger than a district or a province is perceived as threatening the smaller group (the Muslims) in areas in which a larger minority (the Tamils) would be likely to dominate the affairs of a large territorial unit, a province, or a regional unit linking provinces. Thus attempts at managing Sri Lanka's ethnic rivalries and tensions through district or provincial level councils are always caught up in the jostling among the minorities themselves as they jockey for positions of advantage in the race for political and economic gains.

Where an ethnic (or religious) minority is concentrated in a region or regions of a country, and where in addition it constitutes the overwhelming majority of the population there, as in the case with the Tamils of the Jaffna peninsula and Jaffna district in Sri Lanka (and to a lesser extent in the other component districts of the Northern Province) geography and demography combine to provide an ideal breeding ground for a separatist movement. Ethnic cohesion and a heightened sense of ethnic identity, important ingredients for the emergence of separatist sentiment, has existed in Jaffna and the Jaffna district since the mid-1950s; indeed some would argue that they had been present since the 1940s in the last decade of British rule. However, the striking feature of the emergence of Tamil separatism in Sri Lanka, in contrast to contemporary separatist movements in Burma or Thailand, is its late development. The transition from expressions of separatist sentiments (in the late 1940s and early 1950s) to a full-fledged separatist movement took over twenty-five years and was the result of the operation of a number of factors. These included a perceived threat to the ethnic identity of the Tamils from political, economic, and cultural policies (such as the unilateral change in the language policy introduced in 1956 and a similar unilateral change in university admissions policy introduced in 1970 and 1971[7]); perceived grievances of a political or economic nature or both; and a sense of relative deprivation at the loss of, or the imminent loss of, an advantageous or privileged position.[8]

Separatist agitation went through several stages and phases, from peaceful political pressure in the mid-1950s, to civil disobedience in the early 1960s, to violence, and that violence itself from sporadic acts to more systematic attacks directed against state property and police and security forces in the early 1970s.[9] The avowed objectives of the agitation could vary from securing greater autonomy for a region or a people within the Sri Lankan polity to pressure for conversion of its unitary structure to a federal or quasi-federal one. The final phase was a full-fledged separatist movement bent on independence.

Many of the essential ingredients of separatism had emerged by the 1970s, including a leadership that had taken a public position advocating separatism. More important, bands of militant agitators were intent on converting the traditional political leadership's public utterances and political rhetoric—the leadership was not known for any steadfast adherence to that cause—into a program of action, to be systematically implemented with the leadership's consent if possible, but without that consent or even acquiescence if necessary. They were equally intent on "selling" the legitimacy of their political cause to the Tamil masses and to the world at large. Thus grievances of the literati and the rest of the elite were more than adequate, in the absence of widespread mass social and economic discontent, to generate public support for separatism.

The case for Tamil separatism in Sri Lanka was built on the modern doctrine of self-determination of peoples. In time, it became linked with the concept of the "traditional homelands" of the Tamils, "homelands" that needed to be protected from "outsiders," themselves citizens of the same country. The concept of the Tamil "traditional homelands" was itself based, as we shall see, on a fragile foundation of pseudohistorical data and the demography of the "homelands," past and present.

The Sinhalese, the majority group, and the Sri Lankan Tamils, the island's most significant minority, have sharply different perceptions of the nature of the Sri Lankan state, and diametrically opposed attitudes to decentralization and devolution of power to regional units of administration. Although the early proponents of decentralization (from the 1920s on) were Sinhalese, the situation has changed since independence. The main political parties of the Sri Lankan Tamils have become the principal if not the sole advocates of decentralization and devolution. These demands have provoked strong opposition. The opposition has been strongest from the Sinhalese both in the mainstream political parties, and in pressure groups representing Sinhalese Buddhist opinion. Many of the latter fear, if not believe, that schemes of devolution of power are likely to lead to political fragmentation of the island, and that they are therefore a potent threat to the island's territorial integrity through the reemergence of a separate Tamil state and the linkage of such a state to Tamil Nadu.

The Federal Party and the "Traditional Homelands" Concept

The concept of the "traditional homelands" of the Tamils of Sri Lanka, which figures prominently in the negotiations between Sri Lanka and India in the mid- and late 1980s, emerged in the 1950s. Every version of it since then has been constructed on a foundation and with a superstructure of "historical" data. It is also inextricably linked with the political ideology of the Federal Party, and its successor, the TULF, was immanent in the principal resolution adopted when the Federal Party was established in 1949. At the first national convention of the Federal Party in 1951 a claim was made that "the Tamil-speaking people in Sri Lanka constituted a nation distinct from that of the Sinhalese in every fundamental test of nationhood," and the "separate historical past" of the Tamils was emphasized as an essential part of this.[10]

This claim was to a large extent based on a hazy "historical" memory of statehood in centuries past, remembered and newly interpreted (and generally misinterpreted) as a continuous and continuing tradition of independent statehood and an unbroken national consciousness. In less than a decade after its first enunciation, this theory, refined as the "traditional homelands" of the Tamils, had become an indispensable and integral part of the political ideology of the Tamil advocates of regional autonomy and separatism. Some recent studies by Tamil scholars take this concept of a Tamil "homeland" for granted. Their books have very little by way of definition of the boundaries of these "national areas" of the Tamils, except for occasional references to the Northern and Eastern Provinces.[11]

The definition of the boundaries came in the mid-1950s. It was based on a single piece of "historical" evidence, contained in a document prepared by Hugh Cleghorn, a British academic, who had been in the island in the very early days of British rule in the last years of the eighteenth century, first as political troubleshooter and later as the island's first colonial secretary. This document, entitled "Notes from Mr Cleghorn's Minute dated 1st June 1799, on the Administration of Justice and of the Revenues under the Dutch Government," was first published in the government's *Ceylon Almanac and Annual Register* in 1855. It was subsequently reprinted elsewhere, in 1883 and again in 1891. It was known to be a fragmentary, if not defective, version of an original that had disappeared from the records that should have been in Colombo. The original itself was not located till the 1930s. A Sri Lankan scholar, Dr.

(later Professor) Ralph Peiris, published this fuller version of the Cleghorn Minute in 1954 under the title "Administration of Justice and of Revenue on the Island of Ceylon under the Dutch Government (The Cleghorn Minute)."[12]

The document immediately attracted scholarly attention and critical comment. More important, Tamil politicians and ideologues looking for historical data and evidence in support of their case for the "traditional homelands" of the Tamils seized on one short extract from the Cleghorn Minute. It read as follows:

Two different nations, from a very ancient period, have divided between them the possession of the island. First the Cingalese [*sic*] inhabiting the interior of the country, in its southern and western parts, from the river Wallouve [Walawe] to that of Chilaw [*sic*], and secondly the Malabars [Tamils], who possess the northern and eastern districts. These two nations differ entirely in their religion, language and manners. The former, who are allowed to be the earlier settlers, derive their origin from Siam, professing the ancient religion of that country.[13]

The last sentence, an egregious solecism, would have alerted readers to the limitations of this extract as historical source material, but ideologues of Tamil separatism generally omitted it in their resolutions and documents on the theme of "traditional homelands." They relied heavily on this extract. One sees this in claims advanced by the Federal Party, its successor the TULF, and other Tamil separatist activists in defining the territorial limits of the "traditional homelands" of the Tamils. This single extract from the Cleghorn Minute in support of their territorial claims has gained the status of scriptural sanctity among the advocates of a separate state for the Tamils of Sri Lanka, accepted almost as an act of faith, in the face of scholarly criticism of its reliability as a historical source.[14]

From the outset, the concept of the Tamil-speaking peoples of Sri Lanka sought to bring the Muslims, who were mostly Tamil speakers, under the umbrella of Tamil politics, on the assumption that a common language linked them despite a fundamental difference in religion. The Muslims have persistently rejected this linkage because of its assumption of a Tamil tutelage over them. Nevertheless it constantly reappears in Tamil agitational activity. It was also linked with a purposeful opposition by the Federal Party and its successors in the leadership of Tamil politics to the entry of Sinhalese into the parts of the country regarded as "traditional" Tamil areas. Thus, at the inaugural convention of the Federal Party (Ilankai Thamil Arasi Kachchi or ITAK) in April 1951, a resolution urged:

> Inasmuch as the Tamil-speaking people have an inalienable right to the territories which they have been traditionally occupying, the first national convention of the ITAK condemns the deliberately planned policy of action of the Government in colonizing the land under the Gal-Oya reservoir and other such areas with purely Sinhalese people as an infringement of their fundamental rights and as a calculated blow aimed at the very existence of the Tamil-speaking nation in Ceylon.[15]

We shall return to the theme of the Gal-Oya project and settlement of peasants there later on.

The Agitation for Eelam—A Tamil State in Sri Lanka

The mid-1970s marked the emergence of separatism as a destabilizing factor in Sri Lankan politics. At the beginning the main advocate of a separatist program was the TULF as the successors of the Federal Party. At a convention held on 14 May 1976 at the village of Pannakam near Vaddukodai, a suburb of Jaffna, the vague and disconnected separatist aspirations of the 1950s were given a more coherent form, and a program of action for the establishment of Eelam, a Tamil state in Sri Lanka was announced.[16]

The principal resolution there—the Vaddukodai resolution as it came to be called—claimed that the

> Sinhalese people have used their political power to the detriment of the Tamils by (inter alia) . . . making serious inroads to the territories of the Tamil kingdom by a system of planned and state-aided colonization and large-scale regularization of recently encouraged Sinhalese encroachments calculated to make the Tamils a minority in their own homeland.

As with the Federal Party in the 1950s, the claim in the 1970s for a separate state looked back to the distant past and endeavored to link the present with that past through a misinterpretation of historical data. Once more the emphasis was on a continuing tradition of independent statehood and unbroken national consciousness. Above all, the territorial dimensions of "Eelam" were defined in the Vaddukodai resolution in terms that clearly showed an (unacknowledged) dependence on Cleghorn:

> Whereas throughout the centuries from the dawn of history, the Sinhalese and Tamil nations have divided between them the possession of Ceylon, the Sinhalese inhabiting the interior parts of the country in its southern and western parts from the river Walawe to that of Chilaw and the Tamils possessing the northern and eastern districts [the TULF resolves that] Tamil Eelam shall consist of the Northern and Eastern Provinces (of Sri Lanka).

In its manifesto for the general election of July 1977, the TULF elaborated further the concept of the "traditional homeland of the Tamils." The claim now was that "Even before the Christian era the entire island [of Sri Lanka] was ruled by Tamil kings." From this claim, which was in fact a falsification of history,[17] the manifesto proceeded thus:

> From this background of alternating fortunes [of the Sinhalese and Tamil rulers of ancient Sri Lanka] emerged, at the beginning of the 13th century, a clear and stable political fact. At this time, the territory stretching in the western sea-board from Chilaw through Puttalam to Mannar and thence to the Northern Region, and in the east, Trincomalee and also the Batticaloa Regions that extend southwards up to Kumana or the northern banks of the river Kumbukkan Oya were firmly established as the exclusive homeland of the Tamils. This is the territory of Tamil Eelam.

Tamil Eelam, the manifesto asserted, is the successor to the Jaffna kingdom.

A Tamil kingdom was in fact a historical reality, but its life had been short—from the thirteenth century to the early part of the seventeenth—and except during the brief heyday of its power in the fourteenth and early fifteenth centuries it seldom controlled anything more than the Jaffna peninsula, some adjacent regions on the coast, and some parts of the interior. Set against Sri Lanka's recorded history of over two thousand years, the independent existence of this kingdom was a brief episode during a period of political decline of the Sinhalese kingdoms of that period. At times the kingdom of Jaffna had been very powerful; at others it had been reduced to the status of a satellite of the expanding Dravidian states across the Palk Strait; and at others it had been subjugated by the

Kotte kingdom, the principal political entity in the island in the fifteenth and early sixteenth centuries. Generally it acknowledged the suzerainty of the principal Sinhalese kingdom. It disappeared from the historical scene in the early seventeenth century, and while its memory was kept alive in the twentieth century there was neither an unbroken "national" consciousness nor a continuing tradition of independent statehood among the Tamils of Jaffna in particular or of Sri Lanka in general.

There were also contradictions and ambiguities in the claims made in the 1970s and 1980s. The Vaddukodai resolution defined the boundaries of Tamil Eelam in terms of people: "Tamil Eelam shall consist of the people of the Northern and Eastern Provinces." The TULF manifesto of 1977 adopted a territorial definition and extended the territorial limits to cover part of the North Western Province in addition to the Northern and Eastern Provinces. The lack of consistency in these claims was demonstrated afresh in the amendment to the Statement of Government Policy in the national legislature moved on 18 August 1977 by A. Amirthalingam as the leader of the TULF and leader of the opposition, in which he referred to the "mandate given by the people of Tamil Eelam to the Tamil United Liberation Front for the restoration and reconstitution of a free sovereign socialist state of Tamil Eelam."

On that occasion there was no reference to the boundaries of the state, no reference to provinces or to people, no reference to the exclusive rights of the Tamils to such territory, and no reference, implicit or explicit, to that extract from the Cleghorn Minute which plays such a vital role in the claims of Tamil politicians, but merely a reference to the Tamils' "traditional occupation of a separate and well-defined territory in the Northern and Eastern parts of Ceylon."

Eight years later the TULF reliance on the extract from Cleghorn's minute was at last made explicit, in the TULF letter dated 1 December 1985 to Prime Minister Rajiv Gandhi of India. That document contained a section with the subtitle "The Integrity of the Tamil Homeland," which included the following:

> The Northern and Eastern provinces have been traditionally recognized as Tamil-speaking areas from the days of British rule. This was the position at the time of the British conquest of the Maritime Provinces of Ceylon. Sir [*sic*] Hugh Cleghorn in a report to the Colonial Office in 1799 stated as follows:—

Two different nations, from a very ancient period, have divided the Island. First, the Sinhalese in its Southern and Western parts, from the river Walawe to that of Chilaw; and secondly, the Malabars in the Northern and Eastern Districts (Malabars is used to refer to the Tamils).[18]

The letter brought up once against the equivocal concept of the "Tamil-speaking peoples" in which the Muslims, as a Tamil-speaking group, are involuntarily yoked to the Tamils. The TULF argued that in the Eastern Province "75% of the population have Tamil as their mother tongue [and in] the combined Northern and Eastern provinces the Tamil-speaking people form over 86 per cent of the population."

From that specious piece of statistical information they proceeded to invoke the Indian experience in support of the claim for a Tamil homeland encompassing the Northern and Eastern Provinces: "In the same way that India has solved its multi-lingual problem by creating linguistic states the Tamil linguistic area, i.e., the Northern and Eastern provinces should be made into one unit."

The TULF letter was written during negotiations then being conducted through the mediation of the Indian government for a political settlement of Sri Lanka's ethnic conflict, and was clearly aimed at influencing the Indian government's policies. As we shall see, one of the immediate consequences of the ethnic disturbances of 1983 was the application of diplomatic and political pressure by India on behalf of the Tamils of Sri Lanka for a more thoroughgoing scheme of decentralization and devolution of power than that introduced in the island through the District Development Councils Act of 1980.

The problem at this stage was the unit of development. This unit had been the district since the decentralization exercise of 1980–81 and indeed in all political negotiations on devolution of power since the early 1960s. The upshot of India's mediatory effort was the presentation of a set of proposals by the Sri Lankan government for a radical restructuring of the administrative system, in which the key feature was a system of provincial councils, nine in all, based on the provinces of British times but modeled as regards their legislative powers and administrative author-ity on the states of the Indian union, with the significant difference that the Sri Lankan provincial councils would operate within the framework of the country's constitutionally entrenched unitary system.

One of the most controversial features of this endeavor to reshape the structure of the Sri Lankan polity in the 1980s is the attempt to create a supraprovincial regional unit by the fusion of, or a linkage between, the Northern and Eastern Provinces. The pressure for this came from the TULF and various other Tamil separatist groups, in the aftermath of the riots of 1983, and was a revival of a concept of regionalism introduced into the national political debate by the Federal Party in 1956–57. The Bandaranaike government of that latter period had agreed to this concept, but the storm of opposition that erupted from within and outside the government compelled a hasty—and indeed ignominious—withdrawal of the offer. When a proposal to create a regional unit encompassing the Northern and Eastern Provinces was introduced by the TULF in late 1983, it immediately won the backing of the Indian government. As in 1956–57, so in 1983–84 the Sri Lankan government found itself hastily abandoning plans it might have had to consider this demand, once it became evident that there was a division of opinion within the cabinet, and almost unanimous—and vehement—opposition from the principal opposition party, other Sinhalese groups, and powerful sections of the government.

The Eastern Province

The Eastern Province, whether in its form of the period 1832 to 1873 or in its present form, consists of territories that were integral parts of the Kandyan kingdom at the time it was ceded to the British in 1815. Most of the eastern seaboard had never been part of the short-lived Jaffna kingdom. At the height of the latter's power, part of its southern boundary had extended close to Trincomalee, but this had been only for a very brief period. Nor was the Batticaloa area part of the Jaffna kingdom. Indeed, not only was the eastern seaboard part of the Kandyan kingdom, but for much of the nineteenth and the early twentieth centuries, the Tamil population there was concentrated in and around Trincomalee and the Batticaloa lagoon. These littoral settlements were—as in the eighteenth century—in the nature of a thin strip of habitation confronting two powerful forces of nature, the sea on the one side and the forbidding wilderness of the almost impenetrable forests of the dry zone on the other. The overwhelming difficulties of access by land intensified the isolation of this region; land communications improved only in the late nineteenth and early twentieth centuries. More important, these settlements had a large Muslim population.[19]

The littoral regions of the present Eastern Province are the home of over a third of Sri Lanka's Muslims. Some of them are descended from immigrants from the coast of southern India, but a substantial number, perhaps the large majority, are descended from Muslim refugees from Sri Lanka's own west coast who fled the persecution of the Portuguese and were afforded a safe haven on the east coast—and elsewhere—by Sinhalese kings of the period. While they were, and still are largely, a Tamil-speaking group, they maintain an identity distinct from the Tamils through their religion.

In the 1880s Sir Ponnambalam Ramanathan, a distinguished Tamil lawyer-politician, caused a stir by arguing that the Muslims were, in the main, Tamils who had converted to Islam. Spokesmen for the Muslims passionately rejected this position; they responded by reasserting their Arab or Indo-Arab origins and insisting that their Islamic faith separated them from the Tamils with whom they shared only a common language. Echoes of this controversy reverberated in the aftermath of the language controversies of the 1950s, when the concept of the "Tamil-speaking peoples" of Sri Lanka became part of the political jargon of those tumultuous times. Muslims rejected this concept then as they do now—and as they did at the end of the nineteenth century—because of its implications of a subordinate role for them vis-à-vis the Tamils, and the assumption of a Tamil wardship over them.

Nevertheless, we have seen TULF politicians—and radical groups to the left of them—persisting in treating the Muslims as part of the Tamil-speaking population, especially in claims for the "traditional homelands" of the Tamils encompassing the Northern and Eastern Provinces. And this despite the frequency of violent clashes in recent years between the Tamils and Muslims in the Eastern Province (and in Mannar in the Northern Province where there is a large Muslim presence). Islamic fundamentalism, which emerged as a significant political force in the politics of the Muslims in the Eastern Province in the late 1980s, sprang up largely as a reaction against the political pressure on the Muslims from Tamil separatist groups operating there.

The interior of the Eastern Province was sparsely populated and conained Sinhalese settlements in *purana* (i.e., traditional) villages; its people eked out a hard existence in this forested region. These Sinhalese settlements, although smaller in population than either the Tamil or Muslim ones, and few and far between, were scattered throughout the Trincomalee and Batticaloa districts. (The present Amparai district of the

Eastern Province was created only in 1960.) Writing in 1921, S. C. Canagaratnam, a Tamil official of the Kachcheri (secretariat) at Batticaloa, observed that "[o]ne of the saddest features in the history of the [Batticaloa] District is the decay of the Sinhalese population in the West and South. At one time there were flourishing and populous Sinhalese villages here, as is evidenced by the ruins and remains dotted about this part of the country."[20]

Canagaratnam also made the point that "The whole District formed part of the Kandyan Provinces when the Sinhalese Kings held sway and Batticaloa was then known as Puliyanduwa."

It is precisely in this part of the present Eastern Province that the massive multipurpose Gal-Oya irrigation project—which the Federal Party pointedly refers to in its political resolutions of the 1950s as a prime example of state-sponsored settlement of Tamil homelands—was established. This was the first new major irrigation project and settlement scheme after independence, and the first new major scheme since the eleventh century, the last great age of Sinhalese irrigation engineering.

Retrospect

The "traditional homelands" theory has, as we have seen, several versions. One of these, as propounded in the TULF election manifesto of July 1977, speaks of these regions as "exclusively the homeland of the Tamils." This claim to exclusivity has caused profound concern among other ethnic groups in the country, indeed more concern than other variants of this theory, because of its implications: nearly 30 percent of the land area of the country, and over half of its coastline with its marine resources, to be reserved for a minority who constitute only 12.6 percent of the island's population. The share of the national resources thus claimed is grossly disproportionate to their numbers vis-à-vis the rest of the population, and even more so when two other factors are considered.

Tamil politicians and publicists who protest against alleged Sinhalese encroachments into the "traditional homelands" of the Tamils have seldom shown any sensitivity to the grievances of the Kandyan Sinhalese over the massive presence of Indian—almost entirely Tamil—plantation workers, a process of demographic transformation of historically very recent origin, one that has converted parts of the core area of the old Kandyan kingdom into a multiethnic community. In some areas, for example in parts of the Nuwara Eliya district, the Indian Tamils outnumber the local Sinhalese population. Tamil politicians of the Federal Party and the present TULF see no contradiction in advocating the preservation of the "traditional homelands" of the Tamils from Sinhalese encroachment, while at the same time championing the cause of Indian Tamils who were settled in Sinhalese areas by British planters to meet a demand for cheap, regimented plantation labor that the local population was unwilling or reluctant to meet. Population increase through immigration of Indian labor was actually greater than the natural increase of population during some decades of the late nineteenth and early twentieth centuries. Most if not all of these immigrants moved into the Kandyan areas to the tea and rubber plantations there.

Second, there is the demographic reality of a vital Tamil presence in other parts of the island. In 1971, 29.2 percent of the Sri Lanka Tamils lived outside the Northern and Eastern Provinces; this figure had increased to 32.0 percent at the 1981 census and is probably higher today. The Tamil areas of the north are poor in economic resources, and since the late nineteenth century have exported labor, generally skilled labor and professionals, to the Sinhalese areas and especially to Colombo City and its suburbs. There are, in fact, more Tamils in Colombo and its suburbs than in the town of Jaffna.

And finally, from the 1930s, when the systematic regeneration began of the dry zone of the ancient Sinhalese kingdoms, the core of which lies in the present North Central Province and its peripheral regions, the Tamils who lived to the north and northeast looked on this process of economic development with a mixture of fear and anxiety. The ebbing of the jungle tide that had submerged this region for centuries, and the moving frontier of Sinhalese settlement, represented, or were seen to represent, a potent threat to the majority status the Tamils enjoyed in the north and some parts of the northeast of the island.

These fears and anxieties became more pronounced after independence and lie at the heart of the mythmaking connected with the political pressure for a demarcation of a region or regions as the "traditional homelands" of the Tamils. That pressure ignores the facts of history as well as the hard economic reality that the forests of these regions could not serve forever as a buffer between the two ethnic groups, one—the Tamils—anxious to preserve their ethnic dominance of these regions, and the other moving in to do battle with the forests and the anopheles mosquito in a historic return to the heartland of the hydraulic civilizations of old. Resources of land and water are scarce in all the dry zone regions, and the preservation of an uninhabited no-man's-land in the face of unprecedented population pressure is as unreasonable as it is inequitable. Moreover, as Gerald H. Peiris points out, while "state-sponsorship" has "admittedly been a vital element in land settlement schemes," this was necessarily so because such schemes "were meant for the poorest segment of the population—the landless peasantry. But neither in this nor in state responses to . . . encroachment [on state lands] do we find any evidence of discrimination against the Sri Lanka Tamils."[21]

Political myths such as that of the "traditional homelands" of the Tamils, like any other myths, meet a social purpose, the emotional needs of a people facing rapid change in their fortunes and a perceived threat to their identity. Their capacity to believe in such myths will not be diminished by demonstrations by scholars that the supporting evidence provided is flawed and full of contradictions. The myths will survive; they will change; change will transform and even transmogrify them, especially where such myths—like the one we have analyzed here—are not peripheral to but integral parts of the ideology of a political party, or in this instance, of political parties claiming to represent the interests of an ethnic group.

Notes

1. There has been no precision in the definition of terms used in this debate either by politicians or academics. Thus "decentralization" and "devolution" are used as interchangeable terms. In this present chapter a distinction is attempted between the two. Decentralization generally refers to efforts at giving greater autonomy to regional or district level units of government departments and to the development of informal mechanisms for delegation of authority to administrative organizations at a regional or district level. Devolution of authority generally means the transfer of power to elected regional bodies, a genuine second tier of government between the central government and local governmental bodies.

Many scholars in other parts of the world do not see the need for this distinction and use the term decentralization to cover both these meanings. See, for example, Brian C. Smith, *Decentralization: The Territorial Dimension of the State* (London: Allen and Unwin, 1985).

2. There were between thirty-two and thirty-five such units in the period 1815 to 1832. They were reduced to five.

3. For discussion of this see K. M. de Silva, *A History of Sri Lanka* (London: C. Hurst, 1981), 315–26.

4. Even at the end of the nineteenth century their boundaries were rather ill defined, with over four hundred miles of boundaries still unsurveyed. See Sir J. West-Ridgeway, *Administration of Ceylon* (Colombo: Government Printer, 1897), 52–53. I owe this point to Professor G. H. Peiris.

5. See Gerald H. Peiris, "An Appraisal of the Concept of a Traditional Tamil Homeland in Sri Lanka," *Ethnic Studies Report 9*, no. 1 (1991): 13–39, and K. M. de Silva, *The*

"Traditional Homelands" of the Tamils—Separatist Ideology in Sri Lanka: A Historical Appraisal, Occasional Paper no. 4 (Kandy: International Centre for Ethnic Studies, 1994).

6. See K. M. de Silva, "Democratization and Regionalism in the Management of Sri Lanka's Ethnic Conflict," *International Journal of Group Tensions* 19, no. 4 (1989): 317–38.

7. See S. W. R. de A. Samarasinghe, "The Dynamics of Separatism: The Case of Sri Lanka," in Ralph R. Premdas, S. W. R. de A. Samarasinghe, and Alan B. Anderson, eds., *Secessionist Movements in Comparative Perspective* (London: Pinter, 1990), 48–70 for an excellent summary of the issues. The problems emerging from the constitutional changes of 1972 are reviewed in K. M. de Silva, *Managing Ethnic Tensions in Multi-Ethnic Societies: Sri Lanka, 1880–1985* (Lanham, Md.: University Press of America, 1986), 247–55.

8. See de Silva, *Managing Ethnic Tensions,* 261–71.

9. See Samarasinghe, "The Dynamics of Separatism."

10. See K. M. de Silva, *The "Traditional Homelands,"* 6–7.

11. Chelvadurai Manogaran, *Ethnic Conflict and Reconciliation in Sri Lanka* (Honolulu: University of Hawaii Press, 1987); A. Jeyaratnam Wilson, *The Break-up of Sri Lanka: The Sinhalese-Tamil Conflict* (London: C. Hurst, 1988).

12. See *Journal of the Royal Asiatic Society (Ceylon Branch),* n.s. 3, no. 2 (1954): 125–52.

13. Ibid., 131.

14. Aylwyn Clark's recently published biography of Hugh Cleghorn, *An Enlightened Scot, Hugh Cleghorn 1752–1837* (Edinburgh: Black Ace Books, 1992), makes no mention at all of this controversial minute.

15. K. M. de Silva, *The "Traditional Homelands,"* 7.

16. Most of the documents relating to the years 1976–77 are printed in the appendix to K. M. de Silva, *Managing Ethnic Tensions,* 394–413. The resolution and manifesto of 1976 are based on a misinterpretation of historical events and data. See K. M. de Silva, *The "Traditional Homelands,"* 12–15.

17. There is no evidence of any extensive Tamil settlements in the island earlier than the tenth century A. D. Permanent Tamil settlements in part of the north of Sri Lanka became fairly extensive only in the eleventh century. See K. Indrapala, "Early Tamil Settlements in Ceylon," *Journal of the Royal Asiatic Society (Ceylon Branch)* 13 (1969): 43–63.

18. TULF 1 December letter.

19. On the demographic patterns of the Eastern Province, see V. Samarasinghe, "Ethno-Regionalism as a Basis for Geographical Separation in Sri Lanka," *Ethnic Studies Report* 7, no. 2 (1988): 24–51.

20. S. C. Canagaratnam, *Monograph of the Batticaloa District of the Eastern Province, Ceylon* (Colombo: Government Press, 1921), 102.

21. Gerald H. Peiris, "An Appraisal of the Concept of a Traditional Tamil Homeland in Sri Lanka," mimeographed paper presented at a conference on "The Economic Dimensions of Ethnic Conflict in Sri Lanka," 8 August 1985, at the International Centre for Ethnic Studies, Kandy, Sri Lanka.

Part II

6

Mrs. Gandhi and the Sri Lankan Imbroglio, July–August 1983

Mediation with Muscle

THE RIOTS OF JULY 1983 in Sri Lanka, described in the previous chapter, gave Mrs. Gandhi an unexpected opportunity for intervention in the affairs of the island. She very swiftly initiated action that set India on the way to assuming the role of intermediary in Sri Lanka's ethnic conflict. The maneuvers she engaged in to launch this process in late July and early August 1983 have been treated in lively and exact detail in a monograph by a well-informed Sri Lankan journalist.[1] This chapter will concentrate on some of the salient features of her intervention, two in particular: the dispatch of her foreign minister to Colombo on 29 July 1987 and shortly thereafter the appointment of an Indian mediator.

For conflict resolution specialists and international relations experts alike, the Indian intervention in Sri Lanka's ethnic conflict, initiated by Mrs. Gandhi, provides a classic case study. Conflict resolution specialists will see in Mrs. Gandhi's actions in the imbroglio, commencing in the last week of July 1983, the beginning of an Indian involvement that went through the three phases of resolution, management, and—as later chapters of this book will show—settlement. In essence it is a study of the failure of a mediator in each of these phases. International relations experts will see in it the operation of two themes, the regional power/ small state relationship in an acute form and the internationalization of ethnic conflict in all its ramifications. The Sri Lanka–India relationship has few parallels in international affairs unless one looks at the superpow-

99

ers and their involvement and intervention in the affairs of smaller neighbors on their borders or in the periphery of their spheres of influence: for instance, the United States in the Caribbean or Central America and the former Soviet Union in the Baltic states. Many of these issues in international relations relevant to our study will be discussed in this and later chapters. We need to concentrate our attention here on the conflict resolution aspects of the study.

From the outset, Mrs. Gandhi's statements and actions made it clear that she regarded India as a principal mediator rather than a neutral one. Here James Laue's definition of the distinction between the two roles fits the Indian situation with an unusual degree of accuracy: "The principal mediator is a mediator with muscle, one who is a principal in the dispute; the neutral mediator in an international conflict would be a truly uninvolved third party, with little or no actual or implied power over the disputants."[2]

Throughout the period covered by this book, India never abandoned her role of being a principal in the dispute and the protector of the interests of the Tamil minorities in the island. The result was that India was at once a negotiator and an advocate. The distinction between these two roles was blurred to the point where it often disappeared altogether. There was one other consequence, best stated in the form of another extract from James Laue, this time a concise statement on the essence of conflict resolution:

True resolution of conflict satisfies the underlying needs and interests of the parties by joint agreement. Real conflict resolution does not sacrifice any of the parties' important values. If a conflict is resolved, none of the parties will later wish to repudiate the agreement, even if power conditions change so they might be able to do so. Voluntary compliance is another major criterion. It is really not a resolution unless the agreement is self-implementing. If agreements have to be enforced, they may be managed, settled, planned or controlled, but these differ from full resolution. A final criterion for determining whether a conflict is resolved is whether the outcome meets some mutually agreed-upon standards of fairness and justice.[3]

The Indian mediation effort eventually failed because it fell far short of the exacting requirements of successful conflict resolution outlined by Laue.

Just prior to the outbreak of the riots the Indian government had expressed concern through an official spokesman—Shankar Bajpai, a secretary at the Ministry of External Affairs—at some hard measures announced in Sri Lanka in response to the burgeoning political violence in the north of the island.[4] The Sri Lankan government responded testily to these Indian criticisms and protested that it was an unwarranted, deliberate, and wholly unacceptable attempt to interfere in the country's internal affairs.[5] With the outbreak of the riots the Sri Lankan government could no longer adopt such a defiant tone; indeed, it succumbed to Indian pressure for a role in the resolution of the Sinhalese-Tamil conflict in the island.

The pressure began just two days after the outbreak of the riots. It took the form of a telephone conversation between the Sri Lankan president and Mrs. Gandhi on the situation in the island. The upshot of that fateful conversation was that Jayewardene found it necessary to invite Mrs. Gandhi to send an official representative to observe the situation in the island on the spot and to report back to her. Mrs. Gandhi chose a senior cabinet minister, P. V. Narasimha Rao, the minister for external affairs, for this purpose. He was rushed to the island on 29 July, accompanied by a small group of officials including Shankar Bajpai. Parts of Colombo were still in flames when Narasimha Rao met President Jayewardene at President's House in Colombo. Bajpai recalled that Jayewardene was clearly disconcerted by the tragic events of the previous few days, the killings in Colombo, and the widespread destruction of property.[6] Jayewardene himself gave his Indian visitors a vivid description of the damage done by the mobs, the lives lost, the shops, factories, and houses burned, including the houses of some of his friends. Narasimha Rao returned to India somewhat shaken by what he saw but with a more accurate assessment of the situation than Delhi had received up to that time from alarmist reports reaching India through journalists and other sources.

In Sri Lanka, Jayewardene's associates and critics alike were surprised at the speed with which he had succumbed to Mrs. Gandhi's pressure and agreed, if not volunteered, to accept an Indian cabinet minister as a visitor to the island at a time when the violence in the city of Colombo had scarcely abated. Naturally they drew a contrast between his firm refusal to concede a similar visit by a highly placed Indian politician in August 1977, when the request was made by the then Indian high commissioner in Colombo. Instead he had invited an Indian observer of his own choice, a businessman, not a politician. This time his position was altogether weaker; moreover, the riots of August 1977 were a minor episode in comparison to the events of July 1983, and instead of a sympathetic Morarji Desai he now confronted a hostile Mrs. Gandhi. Realizing that his position was at its weakest at that time, she moved very quickly to extract a political advantage—to India's strategic interests—that may not still have been available once Jayewardene regained his usual dominance over the Sri Lankan political scene.

In seeking to intervene in Sri Lankan affairs as a self-appointed mediator in a major ethnic conflict, Mrs. Gandhi was underlining India's presumed right, as a regional power, to influence the settlement of a potentially (and actually) destabilizing domestic conflict in a neighboring state. Because one of the parties to the conflict—the Tamil minority—had linguistic, cultural, and religious ties with a neighboring state of the Indian union, the conflict itself was seen in India as a regional rather than a purely local one. The fact was that Tamil Nadu opinion was inflamed by the anti-Tamil riots in Sri Lanka and Indira Gandhi could hardly ignore this in devising her policies on the Sri Lankan situation. But there was a personal factor as well. General elections were due in India in late 1984 and Indira Gandhi's party's electoral base was eroding in many parts of India, including some of its strongholds in southern India. She was very anxious to mollify Tamil Nadu opinion in order to retain, if not secure, her and the Congress Party's position there. This explains to a large extent the speed with which she intervened when the riots of July 1983 broke out, the choice of G. Parathasarathy as a mediator, and the very significant change in the basis of India's declared interest in the affairs of Sri Lanka.

In choosing Parathasarathy for this tough diplomatic assignment, she was signaling to Tamil Nadu and the Tamil United Liberation Front (TULF) that she had picked a southern Indian Tamil, albeit a Brahmin, who would be very sensitive to their concerns. To them it was a reassuring choice. Parathasarathy, the quintessential establishment man, with a background in journalism, diplomacy, and administration, was a trusted adviser to Nehru and Mrs. Gandhi, especially to Mrs. Gandhi, for whom he conducted delicate negotiations on many sensitive matters, political and even personal. An example was Parathasarathy's somewhat heavy-handed intervention in the matter of a biography of Mrs. Gandhi being written in 1977–78 by Dom Moraes, the well-known expatriate Indian poet and writer. In a neat little thumbnail sketch of Parathasarathy's career, Moraes provided some of its essential details:

G. Parathasarathy, known to his intimates as GP . . . had been an excellent cricketer and had very nearly played for India. He had later become an outstanding diplomat, had been Vice-Chancellor of the Jawaharlal Nehru University in Delhi, and most recently, head of the Planning Commission.[7]

Moreas painted a not very flattering picture of Parathasarathy's attempts to get Mrs. Gandhi to go back on a promise to extend her support to him (Moraes) in writing the biography. To this he added a mordant description of Parathasarathy's efforts, in association with D. P. Singh, a well-known lawyer, to get him to exclude certain sensitive issues (as they saw them) from the biography he was writing. Moraes reports the lawyer as saying, "the party may not like it if you print certain things she tells you."[8]

What is important for our purposes is not merely the success Parathasarathy and Singh achieved in limiting Moraes's access to Mrs. Gandhi, but the author's sardonic assessment of the role played by her advisers in general. He stated that "this confirmed my view that in all the ground round her, advisers bulge up like mushrooms after rain, sometimes because she wants them, sometimes not, and that in the end she tends to disregard all the advice and to do exactly what she thinks or feels is sensible."[9]

More relevant for Sri Lanka in 1983 would have been Parathasarathy's role in the affairs of Kashmir and the negotiations with Sheik Abdullah, after he was released from jail in 1972, which led to the signing of the Kashmir Accord.[10] Abdullah had begun his talks with Mrs. Gandhi and these were continued with Parathasarathy as "the Prime Minister's representative."[11]

A great many Indian politicians and bureaucrats resented the influence Parathasarathy had with Mrs. Gandhi.[12] This included the cabinet rank (i.e., the status of a cabinet minister for protocol purposes) he enjoyed, which raised him above the level of other officials and politicians.

On previous occasions of ethnic conflict in Sri Lanka, India's principal concern had been with the safety of the "stateless" Indian residents in the island, and with Indian citizens generally, both categories being largely plantation workers. This was quite clearly a legitimate Indian interest.

The presence in the island of large numbers of plantation workers with Indian citizenship was the result of a concession made—with the knowledge and approval of the Indian government led by Mrs. Gandhi herself—by the United National Party (UNP) governments (of 1965–70 and 1977 onward) whereby they were permitted to remain in the island for the duration of their working lives. Under Mrs. Bandaranaike's governments such persons were required to leave the island once their status changed from "stateless" to Indian citizen. With her return to power in the early 1980s, Mrs. Gandhi had initiated a fundamental change in the avowed nature of Indian interests in Sri Lanka, from a legitimate concern for the safety of Indian citizens or "stateless" persons of Indian extraction, most if not all of whom were Tamils, to Tamils in general, indeed to Sri Lanka's Tamil minority.

Strong ties had developed since 1964 between the Indian Tamils, represented by their political party *cum* trade union, the Ceylon Workers Congress (CWC), and the UNP, which had been strengthened and reinforced in the 1970s by participation in a common struggle against the Sri Lanka Freedom Party (SLFP)-led United Front (UF) coalition in the years 1974–77. In this situation they made little difference to the political responses from India in general and Tamil Nadu in particular. This early tentative association had been consolidated by the electoral support given by the Indians to the UNP at the general elections of 1977, and had survived the attacks on the Indians by Sinhalese mobs during the ethnic disturbances of 1977 as well as in 1981.

Jayewardene had persuaded CWC leader S. Thondaman to join the Parliamentary Select Committee appointed in 1977 for reform of the Constitution. The latter had used the advantageous position this gave him to secure a constitutionally guaranteed improvement in status for his community. All eight fundamental rights in Article 14(1) of the new Constitution were extended to the stateless Indians resident in the island. In addition, one of the long-standing grievances of the Indians in the island, the distinction between citizens by descent and citizens by registration, was eliminated. Article 26 of the Constitution abolished this distinction, and thus removed the presumed stigma of second class citizenship for the Indians who had obtained it under the terms of the Indo–Sri Lankan agreements of 1964 and 1974. In December 1977 an administrative decision of the new government had removed the bar (imposed from as early as 1937) on workers resident on plantations from voting in local government elections in areas where the plantations were located. The distinct improvement in legal status of Indian Tamils in Sri Lanka ushered in by the new Constitution was consolidated when the CWC leader, S. Thondaman, joined the cabinet in September 1978. Through this decision, Jayewardene brought the Indian Tamils within Sri Lanka's "political nation" for the first time since the 1930s. Thondaman became a trusted ally of his and an influential member of his government, while the CWC alliance with the UNP helped to strengthen the latter's electoral position throughout the 1980s and early 1990s.

President Jayewardene and his cabinet hoped that this fundamental change in the attitude to the Indian Tamils resident in Sri Lanka would help improve relations between Sri Lanka and Tamil Nadu, and through that with India. He was to discover that this did not happen. Generally Tamil Nadu politicians looked sympathetically at the cause of Tamil separatists in the north of the island, and ignored the substantial gains made by the Indian Tamils resident in other parts of the island under the Jayewardene government.

As for the Jayewardene government's relations with the leadership of the Sri Lankan Tamils, the passage of the District Development Councils Act in August 1980 and the establishment of a second tier of government in the island nearly sixty years after it was first recommended were intended to mark a watershed in relations between the two communities. Considering that two previous attempts (in 1958 and 1968) at introducing such legislation had failed in the face of extraparliamentary agitation and internal bickering within the then ruling party or coalition, there was good reason to believe that there would be attractive political advantages in this creative political initiative.[13] This new institutional framework of democratic administration at the district level was in the process of construction in the early 1980s. The fact is that these councils did give the restless Jaffna peninsula a brief period of peace, despite occasional outbursts of ethnic violence (in 1981, for instance) and an ongoing conflict between security forces located in Jaffna and Tamil separatist activists and terrorists. As in the past, the latter were using safe houses if not "bases" in Tamil Nadu.

Indian Pressure on Mrs. Gandhi, Tamil Nadu, and the Lok Sabha

To be fair to Mrs. Gandhi, she faced very great pressure from Tamil Nadu politicians of all parties for some positive action by the Indian central government in regard to the attacks on and killings of Tamils in Sri Lanka and the widespread destruction of Tamil-owned property in the riots of July 1983. Similar demands arose from legislators from both houses of the Indian Parliament almost as soon as the riots broke out.

As a parliamentarian from the south of India herself—she held the Chikmaglur seat in Karnataka in the Lok Sabha, the lower house of the Indian parliament—she was more than ordinarily sensitive to the intensity of feeling in Tamil Nadu and Pondicherry (a Union territory comprising largely Tamil-speaking areas formerly held by France) on the Sri Lankan riots. There had indeed been a vast outpouring of public sympathy— partly engineered by the Tamil Nadu government itself—which took the form of *bandhs* (work stoppages) and massive demonstrations. Demonstrations virtually laid siege to the small Sri Lankan consulate in Madras, and effigies of the Sri Lankan president were burned by the score in various parts of Tamil Nadu and Pondicherry. Workers of all grades in state government institutions were encouraged to participate in these. The Tamil Nadu government itself had taken the lead in them, partly to steal a march on the opposition parties, who were intent on using the emotional upsurge to their own political advantage.

On 26 July, M. G. Ramachandran, the Tamil Nadu chief minister, urged the prime minister to raise the issue at the United Nations and to draw world attention to the riots in Sri Lanka.[14] On 31 July Mrs. Gandhi received a sixteen-member all-party delegation from Tamil Nadu, led by Ramachandran. After listening to them with great sympathy she assured the delegation that "the entire country shared the concern and anguish of the Tamil Nadu people over the tragic happenings in [Sri Lanka]," and that her government was "dealing with this as a national issue affecting the whole country, not merely as a problem concerning Tamil Nadu alone."[15] She informed them that, as a symbolic gesture of the central government's sympathy and solidarity with the people of Tamil Nadu, all central government offices in the state would also close on Tuesday 2 August during the one-day *bandh*. Reporting this decision, a well-known Indian journalist, G. K. Reddy—of whom we shall hear more later in this book— stated: "This is the first time ever that the Central Government is officially participating in a bandh called by a State Government, since it is aimed at focussing national attention on a sad event that transcends party politics and parochial considerations."[16]

She was associated at these talks with three of the most important members of her cabinet: External Affairs Minister P. V. Narasimha Rao, who had just returned from a fact-finding mission to Sri Lanka, Finance Minister Pranab Mukherjee, and Defence Minister R. Venkataraman (a Tamil), evidence of the importance she attached to the meeting.

Mrs. Gandhi's principal domestic political concern was with the Indian Parliament, in particular the lower house. The Sri Lankan situation was raised in both houses almost as soon as the news of the riots broke out. On 27 July, Narasimha Rao made the first of what was to be a succession of official statements on Sri Lanka. Speaking on this occasion in the Lok Sabha, he explained the Indian government's response to the news coming from Sri Lanka. The emphasis, very correctly, was on attacks on Indian nationals and Indian property, and protests were made against attacks on both. But he stressed also the importance of "working in friendship and cooperation" with the government of Sri Lanka, because "[w]e, in India, know full well both the necessity and the difficulty of safeguarding a nation's unity and integrity. We understand the problems facing the Government of Sri Lanka. We also value our relations with this friendly neighboring country."[17]

The next day Mrs. Gandhi announced, after the telephone conversation with President Jayewardene referred to earlier, that she was sending Narasimha Rao to Sri Lanka to make an on-the-spot survey of the situation and for discussions with the Sri Lankan president.

The Sri Lankan situation remained very much at the top of the Lok Sabha's agenda through much of August. On 12 August Mrs. Gandhi made an official statement on the Sri Lanka riots, and this was debated on 16 August in the Lok Sabha and on 18 August in the Rajya Sabha, the less powerful upper house of the Indian Parliament. At the time she made her statement she had already secured the appointment of G. Parathasarathy as her special envoy to mediate with the Sri Lankan government, and in response the Sri Lankan president had sent his own special envoy for discussions in Delhi, his brother H. W. (Harry) Jayewardene, a distinguished civil lawyer.

The official record shows that twenty speakers participated in the Rajya Sabha debate on 16 August, and almost as many when the Lok Sabha debated the prime minister's statement at its meeting on 18 August. Mrs. Gandhi herself made two interventions in the debates (on 16 and 18 August), and P. V. Narasimha Rao made two interventions also, in both cases one in each of the two houses of the Indian Parliament.

While the debate was proceeding A. Amirthalingam, the TULF leader, arrived in Madras and proceeded to Delhi, where he had two separate discussions with Mrs. Gandhi and her senior officials. In addition he addressed a well-attended press conference on 17 August. This was a public relations exercise for both Mrs. Gandhi and Amirthalingam; the one to demonstrate her sympathy for the cause of the Tamils of Sri Lanka, and the other to display the easy access to and support he had from the highest levels of the Indian government. Mrs. Gandhi had shown as clearly as possible that her role (and that of the Indian government) was not that of a neutral mediator, but of a principal mediator.

We need to return to the debate. Speaker after speaker condemned the Sri Lankan government for letting the situation get out of control in the island, and for its patent failure to control the security services and get them to put down the disturbances as soon as they broke out. There was, in all the speeches, justifiable outrage at the killings in Sri Lanka of defenseless Tamils, but the emotions that ran high explain to some extent the tendency to exaggerate the scale of the violence one noticed in most of the speeches, as well as the susceptibility to giving credence to the wildest rumors emanating from Indian and other sources in both Sri Lanka and India. They also explain the intemperate personal attacks on President Jayewardene and some of his ministers, the former for his apparent failure to bring the situation under control expeditiously, and the latter for alleged complicity in the riots.

Two other aspects of the debate need special mention. The first was a call for Indian intervention on the East Pakistan model of 1971 when Bangladesh was created, and on the model of the Turkish intervention in Cyprus leading to the creation of a de facto separate state in the northern part of that island. A full-throated chorus of anti-American sentiment from many of the speakers was the second important element.

References to the East Pakistan or Bangladesh analogy would emerge from time to time, as it did on this occasion, from Indian (generally southern Indian and in particular Tamil Nadu) parliamentarians as well as from the TULF leadership later on. Even those speakers who referred to East Pakistan and Bangladesh generally stopped short of advocating the creation of a Tamil mini-state in the north and east of Sri Lanka through a surgical strike of Indian armed might. But one speaker, Mura-soli Maran, a Dravida Munnetra Kazhagam (DMK) legislator from Tamil Nadu and the nephew of M. Karunanidhi, the great rival of M. G. Ramachandran in Tamil Nadu politics, speaking in the Rajya Sabha, urged the use of Indian security forces to create a Tamil state in Sri Lanka. The analogy he used was Cyprus and the Turkish intervention: "To get a permanent solution we should send our forces there and carve out a home land for the Tamils there. We should recognize the Tamil Eelam movement there. Otherwise if we keep quiet history will not pardon us."[18]

The most egregious assertions had to do with the alleged U.S. involvement in the riots in Sri Lanka. Some Indian legislators saw an American hand in the riots as part of an attempt to destabilize Sri Lanka, a first step in the destabilization of India. Others, of a more sophisticated outlook, argued that the United States would benefit from the instability resulting from the Sri Lanka riots; yet others, taking a cue from this, expatiated on the threat to the security of India from it all. G. C. Bhattacharya, a member of the Rajya Sabha, asserted that the United States "wants to replace even Mr. Jayewardene with their chosen," General in the army. . . . They want absolute military dictatorship as in Pakistan. They want to make Sri Lanka a cantonment of America. . . . Mr. Jayewardene, his government and army are totally in their pockets."[19]

Bhattacharya claimed that he had proof (which he did not present) that "in Sri Lanka the separatist movement is the handiwork of American imperialism" and argued that "American submarines were present in Sri Lanka a day before the ethic violence took place." Arguing that Trincomalee was "the most affected area" and one from which "almost all the Tamils have either been killed or driven away," he asserted that "This area is so much affected because they [the Americans] want [it] . . . to be free from Tamilians so that . . . [it] could be safe for their military base."[20]

That speech, for all its grotesqueness, was in essence a caricature. As with all caricatures its exaggerations and distortions reflected a reality, in this instance a mood and an attitude that affected a great many Indian legislators, and the higher bureaucracy, especially in the Ministry of External Affairs. These were views which Mrs. Gandhi shared in more temperate form, and views which we shall presently see influenced her relations with the Jayewardene government in Sri Lanka.

Mrs. Gandhi's speech in the Lok Sabha on 18 August was, as could be expected, a mature politician's clever response to match the mood of the house on that day. She was constructive especially when she said

The basic need of the hour is to bring a sense of security among the people of Sri Lanka. This in turn can restore confidence in their living together and in working out permanent solutions which are satisfactory to the Tamil minority as well as the Sinhalese majority.

The need for that permanent solution also needs to be undertaken as quickly as possible.

This can best be attempted at the conference table. As I have previously said, it is for the Sri Lankan government to decide how and when a conference of Tamil leaders can be brought [*sic*]. But because of our profound concern, we have offered to help in whatever way we can. To arrive at any settlement, it is necessary for both sides to talk to each other. To facilitate this process of dialogue and to give effect to our good offices, I have offered to send a special envoy to meet President Jayewardene and others. During my telephone call last evening President Jayewardene agreed to my suggestion. Accordingly I have asked one of our distinguished and experienced diplomats, Shri G. Parathasarathy to undertake this delegate [*sic*] and important task. He will visit Colombo next week.[21]

She was always concerned with the need to mollify Tamil Nadu opinion expressed with so much passion in that part of the country and more particularly in the two houses of the Indian Parliament.

During the repeated discussions in this House, hon. Members have expressed their strength of feelings at the course of events. All sections of the people all over the country share these feelings, which transcend party and other differences. I am particularly aware of the deep emotions of our brothers and sisters in Tamil Nadu over these tragic happenings. As I said in the other House the agony of the Tamils in India and elsewhere is that of our entire nation. The brutality and insensate violence to which the Tamils of Sri Lanka have been subjected were vividly described by Mr. Amirthalingam in his talks here. My government and I [have] personally been conveying our own anguish and concern to the Government of Sri Lanka.[22]

The part of her speech that caused most concern for the government of Sri Lanka was its first three paragraphs, in which she referred to her talks with A. Amirthalingam. Her references to the latter[23] were much less fulsome than in her speech in the Rajya Sabha on 16 August and those of many others who participated in the debate in the Lok Sabha, but, coming as they did from the Indian prime minister intent on initiating a mediatory process in Sri Lanka, they only served to impair the efficacy of the latter from the outset:

Mr. Speaker, Sir, last week I informed the House about the outcome of my talks with president Jayewardene's Special Envoy. Immediately afterwards Mr. G. [*sic*] Amirthalingam, the leader of the opposition, in the Sri Lanka parliament and Secretary-General of the TULF the main party representing the Sri Lanka Tamils, left for Delhi. Since his arrival on August 14, he has had talks with the Foreign Minister and other members of our cabinet and parliament members of various parties. Yesterday, I once again telephoned to [*sic*] president Jayewardene.

I would like to inform the House of the result of the latest developments. On behalf of the TULF, Mr. Amirthalingam has also welcomed our offer of good offices, which, he said has introduced a basic change in regard to negotiations between his party and the government of Sri Lanka. . . .

For many years, he and his party has [*sic*] sought fulfillment of the legitimate rights and aspirations of the Tamil people of Sri Lanka within a united Sri Lanka, but failed to get any helpful response. On the contrary, the Tamils have been increasingly harassed, and the latest outrages against them have left them totally without confidence in negotiations. However, he feels that as a result of India's efforts, the picture has changed and, although differences between the two sides remains [*sic*] deep, there might now be some possibility of a solution.[24]

The critically important sentence in the last paragraph of the extract quoted above is the one where she states that the Tamil people had failed to get any helpful response to their demands for fulfillment of their legitimate rights and aspirations. We confront a harsh dilemma in that seemingly bland statement. If Mrs. Gandhi actually believed what she said on that occasion, she was displaying a level of ignorance of Sri Lankan affairs that was totally unfair to the Jayewardene government; if she did not believe it but merely expressed it for such political effect as it may have had on her listeners in the Indian parliament, those who read that sentence in Sri Lanka were entitled to believe that hers was a cynical and calculated exercise in political propaganda.

Mrs. Gandhi concluded her speech with an appeal for calm and restraint, a theme which External Affairs Minister P. V. Narasimha Rao expanded on when it came to his turn to speak. There he emphasized the need for caution: "Caution capital 'C', perhaps, all the letters in capital," he urged, was the need of the hour.[25]

Narasimha Rao's two speeches of 16 and 18 August, the former in the Rajya Sabha and the latter in the Lok Sabha, were simply an extended gloss on the prime minister's speeches which had preceded his. In the introductory paragraph of his speech in the Rajya Sabha he thanked

> the 20 hon. members who have participated in the debate and given us their views and the benefit of their views. There have been several levels of emotion, but I am glad to say the objectives have been the same, the trend has been the same, the spirit has been the same. The Prime Minister, while making her statement, brief but pointedly, put the whole thing in the correct perspective when she said that what we say or do should have only one criterion, one consideration in view, whether it is going to be helpful or harmful to our Tamil brethren in Sri Lanka.[26]

Indira Gandhi had put it in much the same terms when she urged members of the Rajya Sabha to

> understand that however strong our feelings the government has to show greater restrain [*sic*], not because we are hesitant or reluctant, but because at every step we have to consider whether our words and actions will help or harm the Sri Lankan Tamils. . . .
>
> The agony of our brothers and sisters in Tamil Nadu and of Tamils everywhere is also ours.[27]

She was to repeat that last sentence virtually in the same form two days later in the Lok Sabha.

In neither the Rajya Sabha nor the Lok Sabha did she encourage those who called for direct military intervention in Sri Lanka. Implicit in her call for restraint and caution was a repudiation of such adventures. But she would not explicitly repudiate them either. Nor was there one single word of criticism of the rhetorical excesses of the anti-American speeches she had listened to.

The Regional and International Background

For Mrs. Gandhi and the Delhi bureaucracy's South Block the intervention in Sri Lanka was a matter less of conflict resolution than of conflict management. It was a purposeful bid to use the leverage available through the mediation to persuade, if not compel, the Sri Lankan government to pay more heed to India's perception of her own security interests in the conduct of Sri Lanka's foreign relations. In short, it was an attempt to get Sri Lanka's president to synchronize his foreign policy with India's, to move the country away from what India saw was its pro-Western (and, in particular, its pro-United States) orientation.

To say that the leaders of the two countries distrusted each other would be saying nothing more than the plain truth. They had conflicting, if not diametrically opposed, security concerns. Indira Gandhi was an accomplished exponent of the *realpolitik* of the *raj* and in her zealous commitment to maintaining the security traditions of the *raj*, she was the heiress of Dalhousie and Curzon. The fundamental weakness of her position was that India had only the resources of a poor South Asian state with which to play the demanding role of the legatee of the *raj*. But although the cards in her hand were not the most advantageous for the game she was intent on playing, they were more than adequate, at that time, to deal with her Sri Lankan counterpart whose hand was even less advantageous.

Jayewardene's aim was to check the intrusion of Indian power in the Indian Ocean region, by joining other small states in a bid to use the rivalries of the superpowers as a countervailing force against the emerging regional power. But every attempt to do this only increased the sense of insecurity in the minds of Indira Gandhi and her advisers.

How much the mistrust of each other's strategic visions was due to their penchant—Mrs. Gandhi's and that of the South Block in particular—for that fundamental exercise in diplomacy, to create doubts about one's intentions, it is difficult to say. But the doubts did exist, independent of any process of manufacture, and were exacerbated by the intrusion of superpower rivalries in the region, and India's fears of her great Asian rival, China.

It was not clearly understood by Jayewardene that the Indians were not really happy with the presence of Soviet forces in Afghanistan. But the Indians, despite this, never saw the Soviet Union as a threat to their interest in becoming the security manager of the subcontinent, and were convinced that except in Afghanistan Moscow would continue to accept Indian predominance in the region. Their main complaint about the arrival of the Soviet army in Afghanistan was that it led to the renewal of the U.S.-Pakistani security tie which, for them, was much worse than the Soviet presence on the borders of South Asia. Jayewardene's main concern was this latter.

Again, although China was intent on improving relations with India, the former's conflict with Vietnam revived unpleasant memories for most Indians. The similarity of China's "teaching a lesson" to Vietnam in 1979 with her "teaching a lesson" to India in 1962 was particularly painful, not least to the Janatha party foreign minister Atul Behari Vajpayee, who was visiting China at the time (and promptly curtailed his trip). Indian support of Vietnam was thus as much an instinctive reaction as it was a carefully calculated gesture of support of China's traditional enemy. Jayewardene's concern, however, was with Vietnam's invasion of Kampuchea and India's lukewarm attitude on this, in which he saw a parallel to India's response to the Soviet invasion of and presence in Afghanistan.

Sri Lankan diplomats in New Delhi in the early 1980s recalled that there seemed to be a breakdown in communications between the two countries at the highest levels. The mandarins of New Delhi's South Block often accused Sri Lanka of disregarding India's security concerns in the conduct of Sri Lanka's foreign policy. These accusations were conveyed obliquely, sometimes by and through pliant journalists like G. K. Reddy, well known as a spokesman for the South Block.

Sri Lanka's futile attempt to secure membership in the Association of Southeast Asian Nations (ASEAN) late in 1980 was treated as one such example. This was regarded as proof of the Sri Lankan government's general pro-Western if not pro-United States attitude. Despite the failure of this initiative, Indian officials generally believed that Sri Lanka had not really given up this effort and that there were groups in ASEAN who would welcome Sri Lanka, first as an observer and later on as a member. Further evidence of pro-U.S. attitudes was presumably provided when expanded facilities were granted to the United States for its Voice of America (VOA) relay station in the island, and also in the choice of a consortium consisting of Oroleum (Pvt) Ltd., Singapore Oil Tanking, West Germany, and Tradinaft, Switzerland to restore to commercial use a complex of oil tanks in the vicinity of the strategically important port of Trincomalee.

As regards the first of these, the purpose was to expand the very obsolete civilian shortwave broadcast facility of the VOA, which had been operating in Sri Lanka since the 1950s to receive and rebroadcast VOA programs—news, music, sports, English language lessons, and the like. Sri Lanka's central location in the Indian Ocean gave it unusual utility. Because of its advantageous location and atmospheric conditions, one could reach well into central Asia, East Africa, western China, even Korea, with an improved broadcast power (now five hundred thousand watts each) and only one radio bounce. Howard Wriggins recalls that when he was U.S. ambassador in Sri Lanka (1977–80), a key objective of the VOA was to reach listeners in central Asia, Afghanistan, and western China, areas that were then out of reach of the VOA from relay stations in the Philippines or Cyprus. He was skeptical about its usefulness and wondered whether it made any difference to the fate of the United States whether VOA broadcasts reached these areas, but the VOA and United States Information Agency (USIA) people thought it important, and the State Department went along.[28]

The VOA station in Sri Lanka did not have any intelligence function, nor was it a communications relay station such as the one the United States had at Asmara in Ethiopia. Indeed, it did not have any communications function. All it did was receive programs (prepared mainly in Washington by USIA/VOA) and rebroadcast them on civilian shortwave accessible to anyone with a shortwave set.

Originally there was some idea of one of the transmitters being made available to the Sri Lanka Broadcasting Corporation (SLBC) to continue broadcasts overseas, particularly for India, where foreign exchange was earned by advertising on behalf of Indian entrepreneurs. (Until the new facility starts working that arrangement is still in effect for the old transmitters as it has been for a long time.) But that idea was dropped for the future, since the Japanese provided the SLBC with a transmitter that can serve that purpose. The United States provides a cash fee instead for use of the land and broadcasting channels.

When plans for expansion of the VOA station were originally prepared, the U.S. engineers asked for one thousand to fourteen hundred acres, to accommodate ten to twelve transmitters. This was a large amount of land by local standards, but U.S. government specifications made it necessary. Regulations in the United States require some fifteen hundred feet from a tower to the perimeter fence; thus the more transmission towers, the more space routinely called for. The United States is more rigorous about radio frequency radiation than any other country.

A number of safeguards were incorporated in the agreement entered into by the Sri Lankan government and the VOA in December 1983, beginning with paragraph 4, which stipulated that the U.S. government would retain "for 30 days records of the programmes of the VOA relayed from [Sri Lanka]" and that these would be made available to the Sri

Lankan government on request. Two other paragraphs, 5 and 22, were devised to provide additional protection. They read as follows:

> **Paragraph 5:** Out of respect for the concerns expressed by the Government of Sri Lanka the Government of the USA shall use its best endeavours not to broadcast programmes detrimental to the national interests of Sri Lanka.
>
> **Paragraph 22:** At any time during the operation of the Agreement either Party shall have the right to request a review of the provisions of the Agreement, which review shall take place forthwith.[29]

The Indian government was kept informed of these negotiations and External Affairs Minister Narasimha Rao was provided with a draft of the agreement for scrutiny.[30] Despite all this, Indian suspicions remained as we shall see in later chapters.

The original land tentatively assigned to the project in Chilaw by the Sri Lankan government was not sufficient and there were efforts to acquire additional adjacent private land. But that proved difficult and the negotiators examined a site in Puttalam. Puttalam was less desirable for the staff, since it was far from Colombo, but there was more space available. A new agreement was signed. In the meantime, however, the U.S. Bureau of the Budget argued that the whole project was too big and too expensive. There was a reduction in the scale of the operation, from the ten or twelve transmitters originally contemplated to just three. As a result it was possible to house the transmitters and building on the 350 to 500 acres available in the Chilaw site. The agreement was renegotiated and signed, and construction began in 1993(!).[31]

One of the problems was that the project disturbed the Soviet Union leaders, who feared that the installation would be used to guide nuclear submarines in the Indian Ocean and were busy spreading rumors to that effect; they also suspected that it was part of the naval satellite navigation system in the Indian Ocean linked to Diego Garcia. The VOA project in Sri Lanka had no connection whatever with Diego Garcia. The latter was a military service facility; it could receive spare parts by air for a naval task force that might be passing through the Indian Ocean. (A number of pre-positioned supply ships stationed there for emergencies were pulled over to the Persian Gulf during the Gulf War.) As for communications, Diego Garcia is not now used for navigational purposes since ground stations are of little use and ship guidance is mostly done by satellites.

The Soviet Union was, at one time, very worried about U.S. use of strategic nuclear submarines to patrol the Indian Ocean as a floating base for nuclear missiles, a troublesome part of the U.S. deterrent. But during the naval limitation talks with the Carter administration, in the late 1970s negotiators were able to give reassurances that it made no sense to station such submarines so far from the United States when they could be just as much of a deterrent from nearer home. The Soviet Union stopped worrying after that, but the Indians kept up their professed worries, despite the fact that copies of the VOA agreement were shown to the Indian government by Sri Lanka and that the United States had fully briefed India about the VOA expansion. Moreover, it can be assumed that Indian intelligence agencies were also aware of the strict limits to the facility's operations.

The oil tank farm at Trincomalee had been built by the British for use during the Second World War. This complex of about one hundred tanks fell into disuse after the British handed over the Trincomalee base to Sri Lanka around 1957. Interest in it was revived after 1979 in the wake of the second oil price hike of the 1970s, which hit Sri Lanka very hard in terms of steeply rising prices for oil, but equally important was a growing sense of insecurity in the supply of oil in a disturbed market. One of the objectives in restoring the oil tank farm to commercial use was to gain a measure of security in the access to oil, since it was expected that some of the oil stored there would be for the use of Sri Lanka.[32] The corporations that sought to operate it were interested in storing oil for the Japanese market. There were plans also for a second oil refinery for Sri Lanka based on this complex, if the venture succeeded.

From the outset, the transaction aroused Indian suspicions. They believed that the consortium of companies seeking to restore the oil tank farm to an economic asset—or constituent elements of that consortium— had covert links with the U.S. armed services, and that therefore the project as a whole had concealed political and strategic interests. The contract incorporated provisions making it incumbent on the joint venture to comply with all directions issued by the government of Sri Lanka in the interests of national security, defense, and foreign policy. In addition the joint venture was prohibited from storing or selling oil for military purposes.

The state-owned Indian oil corporation submitted a bid to run this oil tank farm. The bid was unsuccessful, partly because, just as India was suspicious of the consortium that won the contract, there were fears in Sri

Lanka about letting a state-owned Indian enterprise secure a bridgehead in a part of the island Indian strategists coveted.

Eventually the attempt to revive the oil tank farm failed. Once again the factors at work were purely commercial ones. The venture was only viable if oil prices remained as high as they were in 1979–80 (around U.S.$30 to $35 a barrel). If they dropped substantially below that, which is what happened after 1981, there would once again be a glut of oil. There was no possibility of running the tank farm at a profit in the changed circumstances. As for a second oil refinery for Sri Lanka, the economics of such a venture were now clearly unfavorable.

The controversy on this continued till the end of the 1980s. Even as late as 1987 India was intent on securing entry to the project in the form of a joint venture with Sri Lanka's state-owned oil refining and distribution corporation. From beginning to end India's interest in the venture was strategic, not commercial.

The Making of a Diplomatic Quadrilateral

Mrs. Gandhi and the Indian government's deep concern about Tamil Nadu sentiment resulted in the evolution of a unique combination of forces in the negotiating process on Sri Lanka's ethnic conflict, at its most benign a quartet, or when the situation deteriorated, from Sri Lanka's point of view, a quadrilateral. Ranged on one side were the Indian government, the state government and opposition parties in Tamil Nadu, and representatives of Sri Lankan Tamil opinion. The fourth side of the quadrilateral was the Sri Lankan government. This arrangement of forces first developed by Mrs. Gandhi and her advisers survived for the better part of six years and left little room for maneuver for President Jayewardene. From the outset he was negotiating from a position of unusual weakness, and it required a great deal of political and diplomatic skill, and indeed sheer guile, to keep this quadrilateral from evolving into a triangle of forces ranged against the Sri Lankan government.

Just as Mrs. Gandhi had picked a close confidant of hers and her father's to handle the negotiations with Sri Lanka, thus keeping these under the control of the prime minister's office rather than the Ministry of External Affairs, Jayewardene also looked beyond his cabinet and diplomatic service to find a negotiator. He picked his younger (by ten years) brother, H. W. Jayewardene, a well-known lawyer, for this purpose. From early August 1983 to the end of August 1985 and even beyond, H. W. Jayewardene served as Sri Lanka's principal negotiator, very often holding the status of special envoy, if not ambassador plenipotentiary. His first set of negotiations with India was with Mrs. Gandhi herself in early August 1983. Thus, for most of the period from August 1983 to July 1987, the negotiations with India were kept within the president's office. Very little use was made of the Ministry of Foreign Affairs, except to the extent that Sri Lanka's high commissioner in Delhi served as a diplomatic channel for the transmission of messages or documents.

With Sri Lanka's principal friends the United States and the United Kingdom tacitly acknowledging India's "right" to mediate in the Sri Lankan conflict, the weakness of Sri Lanka's position vis-à-vis Mrs. Gandhi's India was underlined. In an almost desperate search for understanding, if not support, H. W. Jayewardene was dispatched on a ten-nation Asian tour in September 1983. The countries visited included the ASEAN states and Japan, South Korea, the People's Republic of China, and Burma.[33] This was an essential piece of diplomatic fence-mending and a morale booster.

President Jayewardene was thus confronted with an uncomfortable new political reality: the riots gave a fresh impetus to the internationalization of Sri Lanka's ethnic conflict. One part of this process was already causing him and his defense advisers deep concern, namely, support from Tamil Nadu for the Tamil separatist cause. As we shall see, the Indian factor in the internationalization process became more pronounced.

The new feature of the process of internationalization was the response—one of shock and dismay—of the European democracies and the United States at this patent failure of Sri Lanka's political system in the management of her ethnic problems. In their humanitarian concern at the plight of Sri Lanka's Tamil minorities, swift measures were taken—in Canada, Australia, and the United Kingdom in particular—to accommodate substantial numbers of Tamils as political refugees, thus increasing the numbers of Tamil diaspora groups living in these countries. These latter groups now found greater leeway for their political activities in their adopted homes.

Neither the United States nor the United Kingdom was willing to consider military assistance—by way of training facilities and the supply of matériel—to Sri Lanka. To do so would have ensured Indian displeasure at the best of times; in the aftermath of the July 1983 riots where the negligence, partisanship, and worse of the Sri Lankan security forces had been revealed for all to see, there was even greater reluctance. Eventually the Sri Lankan government had to resort to less orthodox allies— Israel and shadowy private organizations that employed British mercenaries—for the training of its security forces. By this time they were under greater pressure than ever before by Tamil separatist guerrillas, who had the advantage of training facilities and bases in Tamil Nadu, and a regular supply of arms.[34] The People's Republic of China and Pakistan, India's main Asian rivals, became in time the principal suppliers of arms to Sri Lankan security forces.

In August 1983 Parathasarathy traveled from Delhi to Colombo seeking to devise a set of proposals that would be acceptable to the three parties involved—the Tamils of Sri Lanka primarily, the Sri Lankan government, and the Indian government. As Mrs. Gandhi's special representative he negotiated directly with the Sri Lankan president. In addition, he established close links with the TULF, with the objective of winning its support for a scheme of devolution of power and other safeguards that would be an acceptable alternative to a separate state in the north and east of the island for the Tamils of Sri Lanka. Many of the Tamil groups, including the TULF, were now advocating this. In time Parathasarathy's closeness to the TULF eroded the confidence President Jayewardene and the Sri Lankan government originally had in him and he came to be regarded as an advocate of TULF policies.

Apart from the close links they had established with G. Parathasarathy, the TULF leadership were in constant touch with senior Indian officials in Delhi dealing with Sri Lankan affairs, and on occasion they met with Mrs. Gandhi herself. Thus the TULF was able to reopen the debate on the devolution of power in Sri Lanka with the assurance of a sympathetic understanding and support of their views at the highest levels of the Indian government. With Parathasarathy's approval they formally withdrew their support for the district development councils established in 1981, claiming that these were inadequate in meeting the needs of the Tamil minority in Sri Lanka as they perceived it in the context of the changed situation. They staked a claim for a system of provincial councils as the second tier of the governmental structure in Sri Lanka. Their main aim was to secure the establishment of a large regional council encompassing the Northern and Eastern Provinces, where the Tamils would be a dominant if not overwhelming majority, something they had advocated since the 1950s (through the Federal Party, the core of the TULF established in the late 1970s).

From the very outset of Parathasarathy's mediation there was, in effect, a triangle of forces operating in unison—the Indian government, the Tamil Nadu government and opposition, and TULF—in negotiations with the Sri Lankan government. Parathasarathy himself was at once a mediator between this triangle of forces and the Sri Lankan government and an advocate of the TULF proposals. Within a few weeks of commencement of his negotiations, the blurring of the role of negotiator and advocate led to widespread criticisms of his initiatives both within the government of Sri Lanka and among critics of the latter. There was a ground swell of opposition to Parathasarathy, which President Jayewardene had to cope with.

Notes

1. Sinha Ratnatunga, *Politics of Terrorism: The Sri Lankan Experience* (Canberra: International Fellowship for Social and Economic Development, 1988), 105–26, 130–38.

2. James Laue, "The Conflict Resolution Field: An Overview and Some Critical Questions," in *Dialogues on Conflict Resolution: Bridging Theory and Practice* (Washington, D.C.: United States Institute of Peace, 1993), 24.

3. Ibid, 25.

4. Shankar Bajpai, interview with the author, December 1992.

5. See the *Daily News,* 21 and 22 July 1983 for the official Sri Lankan reaction, and the *Hindu,* 22 and 23 July for the Indian defense of its position on this issue.

6. Shankar Bajpai, interview with the author, December 1992.

7. Dom Moraes, *Mrs Gandhi* (London: Jonathan Cape, 1980), xv-xvi.

8. Ibid.

9. Ibid.

10. Sheik Mohammad Abdullah, *Flames of the Chinar: An Autobiography,* trans. Khushwant Singh (New Delhi: Viking, 1993), 164–65.

11. Ibid., 164.

12. For Parathasarathy's political orientation, see "The 25 Most Powerful People in India," *Imprint* 25, no. 1 (April 1985): 19. By the time this article appeared he had lost most of his influence and power.

13. For discussions of this theme, see K. M. de Silva, "Decentralization and Regionalization in the Management of Sri Lanka's Ethnic Conflict," *International Journal of Group Tensions* 14, no. 4 (1989): 317–18.

14. See the *Hindu,* 27 July 1983.

15. As reported in the *Hindu,* 1 August 1983.

16. Ibid.

17. See the report in the *Hindu,* 28 July 1983.

18. *Hansard* [Rajya Sabha], 16 August 1983, cols. 358–59.

19. Ibid., col. 347.

20. Ibid., col. 346.

21. *Hansard* [Lok Sabha], 18 August 1983, col. 413.

22. Ibid., col. 414.

23. *Hansard* [Rajya Sabha], Prime Minister Indira Gandhi's speech of 16 August 1983, cols. 330–32. Most of this short speech was devoted to fulsome praise of Amirthalingam.

She expressed (col. 330) her "admiration for the statesmanship which Mr Amirthalingam has shown."

24. *Hansard* [Lok Sabha], 18 August 1983, cols. 412–14.
25. Ibid., col. 468.
26. *Hansard* [Rajya Sabha], 16 August 1983, col. 416.
27. Ibid., cols. 330–31.
28. Communication from Howard Wriggins, 14 July 1993.
29. I had access to a copy of the draft agreement through Lalith Athulathmudali sometime in 1984.
30. Ernest Corea, interview with the author, 20 May 1992. Corea was Sri Lanka's ambassador in Washington at the time the negotiations commenced.
31. The project remains a matter of controversy even today. The people living in the vicinity have been staging protests against it, led by the Roman Catholic clergy in the area (which is largely Roman Catholic).
32. Sri Lanka was experiencing a serious power shortage at this time during the period of February to May. There were power cuts ranging from two to five hours a day.
33. Ratnatunga, *Politics of Terrorism*, 105–26, 130–38.
34. Ibid., 162–66, for the background to the developments.

7

Confronting Indian Pressure, September 1983–November 1984

The Parathasarathy Initiative

AN UNEASY CALM had settled on Sri Lanka in the wake of the ethnic tension of late July and early August. By mid-August, very slowly, but with increasing confidence, the government regained control, and with that law and order were effectively restored. As for a political settlement with the Tamils the position, so far as one could discern it, was that Jayewardene and the government were taking a deliberate "wait and see" policy. There was no anxiety to hasten things and thus endanger the brittle peace that prevailed.

In the meantime his main effort seemed to be directed at achieving a consensus among the principal Sinhalese parties on the essential features of a viable political settlement with the Tamils. There were informal talks on this including secret discussions with Mrs. Bandaranaike herself[1] through intermediaries. During this period Jayewardene seemed more inclined to gauge the limits others would tolerate than to shape a concept they could be persuaded to accept. In assessing the responses that reached him the Sri Lankan president came to the conclusion that the current situation was still fraught with dangers. Most persons he consulted were insistent that on no account must differences among the Sinhalese be permitted to result in any threat to the unitary political structure of the country; and that above all else India must not be allowed to interfere in the island's internal affairs through exploitation of the current ethnic tensions or through the Tamil United Liberation Front (TULF).

More to the point, the majority of Jayewardene's cabinet colleagues advised him that a settlement should be worked out, if possible, without

Indian initiatives. Indeed, he realized that there was so much Sinhalese resentment against India and Indian initiatives in the country that he felt it necessary to play down Parathasarathy's role as mediator. This was one reason why the decision was taken to ask him to postpone his second visit—his first had been in August. Furthermore, by the time Parathasarathy was scheduled to return, the president's brother and special envoy would have come back from his visit to the Association of Southeast Asian Nations (ASEAN) countries and the Far East.

Mrs. Gandhi's special envoy was expected back in the island by mid-October to resume the postponed mission. Jayewardene was hoping that by then two things would have happened: that a consensus would have emerged among the Sinhalese parties as to the maximum that could be conceded to the Tamils by way of a settlement; and also that the more extremist Tamil political groups and the TULF itself would have realized that there was neither Indian nor, much less, international support for the establishment of a separate Tamil state in the north and east of Sri Lanka.

At this point, he had doubts about the usefulness of Parathasarathy's mediatory efforts, for a number of reasons. The lack of support for this Indian mediation in the country at large was being reflected in both the cabinet and the government Parliamentary Party. Part of the problem was the general Sinhalese perception of the TULF as Indian surrogates and their wariness of the TULF's close links with Parathasarathy. To make matters worse the government was in possession of a letter dated 6 October written by Amirthalingam's son Ravi, incriminating as regards the TULF's links with extremist and terrorist groups in Tamil Nadu.[2]

The government published the letter a few days later,[3] in the hope, no doubt, that it would damage the TULF cause abroad. To his closest associates Jayewardene indicated that much would depend on talks he hoped to have in New Delhi with Mrs. Gandhi in November at the Commonwealth Heads of Government meeting.

The riots of July 1983 had upset Jayewardene's plans for a comprehensive reshuffle of his cabinet and a more systematic reorganization of the government's departmental structure. There was the real danger that if he fired anyone from the cabinet at this stage—mid-October 1983—the person so dismissed could pose as a "Sinhalese nationalist" who had been driven from office because he had taken a stand on behalf of the Sinhalese against the president and his closest advisers.[4] Jayewardene's own past, especially his sweeping rejection by the electorate in that first landmark election in 1956 and the long years he had spent putting it all behind him, was like a wound that had not really healed. The riots of 1983 seemed to rub the scab off that wound, and it would take a year or so before it would heal again. During the early months when the country was recovering from the effects of the riots, Jayewardene was unusually anxious to protect his electoral base, and extraordinarily sensitive to the need to reassure the Sinhalese majority that he was concerned about their interests.

His own position within the political system was weaker at this stage than it had been before the riots. The balancing act he was called on to perform to rectify the situation had two conflicting aspects. To ensure a return to normality he needed to keep the concerns of the Sinhalese Buddhist pressure groups very much in mind in whatever he did. At the same time he had to ensure that his government would take effective measures to regain the confidence of the Tamil minority both as an end in itself and as a means of reestablishing political stability in the country. Thus in mid-October he was reflecting on the fact that some cabinet ministers were talking, or seemed to be talking, at cross purposes on the rehabilitation process after the riots and on the minority problem in general. He had asked Cyril Mathew, the most outspoken advocate of Sinhalese Buddhist causes, to refrain from making any public pronouncements, a warning of firm action in case of any serious breach of conventions on statements on government policy by cabinet ministers, and Mathew took it to heart at least for a while.

Two weeks later there was a change of policy in regard to Parathasarathy. It was announced that he would be visiting the island at the beginning of November. This decision had been taken largely because of S. Thondaman's persuasive arguments at the last cabinet meeting for October 1983. Some of those who were present at the meeting[5] described Thondaman's performance as a tour de force not so much because of his eloquence, but because of the plain speaking he indulged in.

In addressing the cabinet Thondaman made the point that he had joined the government because of his confidence in Jayewardene. He assured his colleagues that he still retained that confidence and felt more certain than ever before that only the president could formulate a policy for settlement of the ethnic problem. He pointed out that India and even Tamil Nadu were eager to reach an agreement with Sri Lanka on this issue and that it would be sensible, at this stage, to use India's expressions of goodwill for this purpose. Thondaman urged that Parathasarathy be asked to come to Sri Lanka for discussions *before* the president left for India in mid-November for the Commonwealth Heads of Government meeting. In the course of his brief speech he turned on some of his critics in the cabinet—he was referring to men like Mathew—and pointed out that all efforts to reach an agreement among the Sinhalese parties had failed so far.

Jayewardene's mood had thus changed from the previous week as regards India and Tamil Nadu. He himself attributed his decision to invite Parathasarathy to Colombo in early November largely to the work done by Thondaman during his recent visit to India.[6] He had come to the view that it was necessary to *talk* to someone now that the round-table conference idea had fizzled out. He seemed more assured now about Indian intentions, and was ready to negotiate a settlement of the Tamil problem through the good offices of the Indian government. In a new mood of realism, he asserted that no settlement would be possible without Tamil Nadu being brought into it; after all, Tamil Nadu was only twenty miles away from the Jaffna peninsula and Tamil separatist activists could easily slip in and out of their hideouts there. The central government could be friendly to Sri Lanka, or neutral, or could even back Tamil Nadu. Just at this stage the central government was formally friendly but verging on an attitude of neutrality. That was better, Jayewardene thought, than opposition, direct or indirect.

There had been some criticism of Thondaman prior to this cabinet meeting. The Sri Lankan press carried unfavorable reports of discussions he had had with one of the most prominent Sri Lankan Tamil separatist leaders, Uma Maheswaran, in India. The basic theme of these reports was that cabinet ministers should not be talking to Sri Lankan separatists in India. It was recognized that the talks had been on Thondaman's initiative and that the president had not been consulted. The latter, however, stood by Thondaman even though he had not secured prior permission for this. Jayewardene felt that it was necessary for someone to talk to the separatist activists and if possible bring them into any discussions on a settlement. Without their support no settlement would be effective; certainly the TULF on its own could not make a settlement stick. Maheswaran had assured Thondaman that he was ready to accept a negotiated political settlement. At this stage President Jayewardene was willing to consider an amnesty for the separatist activists accused of serious breaches of the law, as he had done, in 1977, for the Janatha Vimukthi Peramuna (JVP) activists who now had gone underground.[7] In time, as we shall see, Jayewardene would change his mind about discussions with separatist activists, especially when their sporadic attacks increased in ferocity and frequency as did clashes with the police and security forces. With Parathasarathy's visit to the island in November 1983, and President Jayewardene's to Delhi later that month, a momentous phase in Indo–Sri Lankan relations would begin, and with it also a new phase in the internationalization of Sri Lanka's ethnic conflict. The meeting between Mrs. Gandhi and President Jayewardene got off to a better than expected start. A substantial measure of cordiality was established. Nevertheless, Jayewardene's visit to India on this occasion served to underline the weakness of his position in parleys with the Indian government on the resolution of the political crisis in Sri Lanka stemming from its ethnic conflict. The negotiations Parathasarathy had begun in Colombo were resumed in Delhi, where the Sri Lankan president was on his own, without access to his advisers, most of whom had remained in Colombo on the assumption that there would be no systematic negotiations on this occasion beyond a discussion of basic principles. Instead, he found Parathasarathy more than ordinarily persistent, and pressing him for an agreement on a framework of a settlement. The document which embodied this came to be known as "Annexure C" (see Appendix Document III). It was in the main Parathasarathy's distillation of the TULF demands. In presenting this to him for scrutiny and possible approval, Parathasarathy was hoping that the Sri Lankan president would be more amenable to his suggestions in Delhi than he would be in Colombo. To make it even easier for himself, he contrived to keep the final touches, the definition of terms used, and the refining of the structure of the settlement to a meeting between himself and President Jayewardene alone. The result was that the final version of "Annexure C," the framework of a settlement with the TULF and other Tamil groups, included the merger of the Northern and Eastern Provinces into a single Tamil ethno-region (see Appendix Document III). This was something that Sinhalese opinion had steadfastly refused to accept as a politically viable proposition and President Jayewardene himself had strongly opposed it when it was first proposed in 1957–58. Now the same proposition was elevated to the position of a cardinal principle of a political settlement between the Sinhalese and the Tamils.

The Challenge of Separatist Violence

With the riots of 1983 there was a closing of ranks within the cabinet, on the surface at least. This continued for the rest of 1983 and the early part of 1984. But the deteriorating security situation emerging from a new militancy among Tamil separatist groups, who were making forays against the security forces and Sinhalese villages in the border areas from camps and other havens in Tamil Nadu, compelled the government to adopt a more comprehensive security system. The focus of attention was on the Tamil Nadu connection.

By the end of 1983 the Sri Lankan government faced a formidable challenge from Tamil separatist forces within and without the country. As their attacks became more daring in scope and destructive in impact, the government responded with a new institutional structure and new policies. One of these was the establishment in March of a Ministry of National Security, to coordinate the activities of the security forces and the police in organizing counterinsurgency and counterterrorist activities.

Jayewardene's dilemma, like that of any government dealing with a well-organized and determined secessionist movement, was to find the appropriate blend of policies of accommodation to win the moderate elements away from the extremists while hitting hard at the more violent elements. It was a difficult balancing act; there were frequent incidents that drew popular sympathy—among the Tamils—toward the extremists. On 23 March 1984 Lalith Athulathmudali took his oaths as minister of national security and deputy minister of defense, a new post with a wide range of responsibilities and one which placed him in the public eye to a far greater extent than as minister of trade.[8] Again, for the first time since independence, a very urgent need was felt for a rapid increase in the numbers of armed services and police personnel as well as modernization of their equipment to match those of the Tamil separatists.

Another of the new institutional devices created was the Security Council,[9] which met every Monday morning, with additional meetings at other times if they were needed. President Jayewardene presided over it; the other members were Lalith Athulathmudali as minister of national security; Ravi Jayewardene, the president's son, who became security adviser to his father in the wake of the riots of 1983; W. M. P. B. Menikdiwela, the president's secretary; the secretary of the Ministry of Defence; and the service chiefs as well as the inspector general of police. Lalith Athulathmudali recalled that, at the beginning particularly, there were problems of coordination. Often it took a while for the service chiefs to explain themselves to the president and Athulathmudali. There were delays until, by trial and error, the mechanisms began working more smoothly.[10]

Whether by deliberate choice of his own or because of Jayewardene's preference, the prime minister did not play any significant part in the new defense program and policy, apart of course from whatever views he may have expressed in the cabinet when these issues were discussed. Just as Athulathmudali became the principal spokesman of the government on these issues, so also, because of the salience of defense issues in foreign policy at this time, he was one of the principal spokesmen of the government in the exposition of foreign policy, enjoying the president's confidence to a much greater degree than Foreign Minister Hameed.

Political observers agreed on two points. First, it was clear that the creation of a Ministry of National Security had improved the government's political standing in the country at large because of the belief that at last there would be coherent policy on meeting the challenge posed by Tamil separatist activists. Thus, despite all the violence in the north of the country, the rest of the country remained quite undisturbed. Part of the problem in July 1983 would appear to have been a feeling that the government had done little about the law-and-order situation in Jaffna, and that the Tamil separatist activists were allowed to get away unscathed despite the violence they indulged in against persons and state property.

Second, there was, at this stage, a great deal of confidence in Lalith Athulathmudali and his style of dealing with the problems he faced—a mixture of firmness and conciliation based on a *policy* of action. At the village level and in the urban areas, all reports indicated a remarkable upsurge of support for him at a *personal* level. The result was that he was quite clearly seen as the number-three man in the government; indeed many believed that if he succeeded in bringing the situation in Jaffna under control he was likely to be challenger to the prime minister's position as number two. In brief he was seen already as a potential presidential candidate for 1988–89. Much could happen between 1984 and then, but quite clearly he had upstaged Gamini Dissanayake, another aspirant for the position of third in the government.

Within a few weeks of Athulathmudali's elevation to this new position, a correspondent on the prestigious British weekly, the *Economist,* was talking about the "undeclared battle for the succession" to Jayewardene and the boost that Athulathmudali's chances had received. The article stated:

Early this year when the government grip in the north and east appeared to be slipping, the president brought in the ablest man in the cabinet, a former Oxford Union President, Mr Lalith Athulathmudali, as minister of national security and deputy minister of defence. Mr Jayewardene himself, holds the defence portfolio. . . .

The appointment of Mr Athulathmudali was intended to impose a firmer grip on disaffected elements in the security forces. It proved also to be a catalyst for a political re-alignment.[11]

In fact, the phrase a "political re-alignment" was not an accurate description of the responses to the appointment within the government. There was, however, a great deal of truth in the contention of this correspondent that "The prime minister, Mr Ranasinghe Premadasa, rightly saw the promotion of his younger rival as a threat to his own prospects of succeeding Mr Jayewardene."

Athulathmudali's (and indeed Jayewardene's) freedom of action in regard to this upsurge of separatist violence in the north and east was constrained by the operation of external forces and influences, Indian in the main. For one, there was the mediation effort under Indian aegis which—as we shall see—took the form of an All Party Conference (APC). But more important, the Indian government had yet to concede that there were any training camps or bases for Tamil separatist activists in Tamil Nadu or elsewhere in India, much less take any effective measures to restrain such activities and still less to close down such camps and bases.

One of the problems President Jayewardene and the government faced was the widespread perception of the army, in Jaffna in particular, as a group or groups of ill-disciplined young men with a predilection for violence directed against civilians. This situation had emerged as a result of a confluence of a change in the ethnic and religious composition of the forces (they had become largely Sinhalese and Buddhist since the 1960s) and a fundamental change in the nature of the problem they confronted in their traditional role of the peacekeepers of last resort. In earlier phases in Sri Lanka's postindependence cycles of ethnic violence (in the mid- and late 1950s), army units had earned the plaudits of the Tamils as a tough and impartial peacekeeping force that cracked down hard on troublemakers and refused to be intimidated by politicians, however highly placed they may have been, when such persons sought to protect those who disturbed the peace.

The Tamil political activists chose at first to direct their attacks on the police, and not the army. The police presented a softer, more vulnerable target. In October 1981, for the first time, two soldiers were killed in the course of these attacks. The casualties in the past had all been policemen. Clashes between soldiers and Tamil activists became more frequent thereafter, and casualties on the side of the latter were often quite high. As a result the army was often accused of killing civilians either in the process of these operations or by deliberate and calculated choice. For their part the army spokesmen argued that in the sort of challenge they confronted in Jaffna and the Northern Province it was difficult to distinguish between political activists or terrorists and civilians because the former blended so imperceptibly with the latter. The problem was that the army's response to attacks was predictably tough, much tougher than that of the police.

The first serious acts of overreaction on the part of army units in the face of politicized youth agitation and terrorist acts came in 1983. One can identify three such occasions, beginning with an incident on 18 May 1983 at Kadaraman in Jaffna town, when an army unit retaliated against Tamil activists who had shot and killed two soldiers guarding a polling place during local government elections. The body of one of these soldiers had been dragged away by the attackers and publicly mutilated. In the army attack that ensued, several bystanders were killed in the crossfire. Next there was the overreaction of the soldiers when thirteen of their comrades were killed in the now wellknown and momentous ambush of 23 July at Tinnevelly in Jaffna. At least forty local residents were killed when vengeful soldiers went on a rampage that frightful night. Third, stemming from this but also in a sense a distinct episode or set of episodes, was the reaction of the army when anti-Tamil riots erupted in Colombo and other parts of the island a few days later. The army did little to help the police in restoring law and order. On the contrary, in a mindless demonstration of misplaced loyalty to dead colleagues they generally obstructed the police in the latter's efforts to prevent the riots from spreading. They failed, if not refused, to intervene when their intervention could have saved lives and protected property from looters and arsonists. Indeed, their willful neglect of duty helped the riots to spread and intensify, especially in the city of Colombo. A fourth incident occurred in Mannar in the northwest of the island in August 1984.

Morale and discipline among the small army units stationed in Jaffna had reached their nadir. Tamil publicity campaigns capitalized on these incidents, and used them—with the exaggerations and distortions that are inherent in successful propaganda campaigns—to evoke a sympathetic response abroad to their cause. Their campaigns benefited also from visiting Western journalists who sent back reports of the army's misdeeds.

Nevertheless, in the early part of 1984 the army was the only law enforcement agency left in Jaffna. The police had been driven out of their stations by a series of violent assaults. The attacks on the army increased, not indeed in the sense of frontal assaults, but generally through land mines and improvised explosive devices, which had as their base large amounts of gelignite buried under road surfaces or culverts. No vehicle— not even armed troop carriers—could withstand such blasts, which in fact were adequate to bring down huge concrete buildings. The technology had been learned in India, but the Sri Lanka Tamil activists quickly improved on the techniques taught by their Indian mentors. In time they would surprise them as they did the Sri Lankan forces.

These land mine blasts took a heavy toll of soldiers' lives throughout 1984, but with the exception of the incident at Mannar in August 1984 the army units affected reacted with restraint. Indeed, by the beginning of 1985 there was a distinct improvement in the discipline and morale of the army. Shortly after, General Cyril Ranatunga was recalled from retirement and appointed to the newly created post of general officer commanding the Joint Operations Command, in overall charge of all security forces. The new post was established in order to coordinate security operations, and was also necessitated by the enormous increase in the size of the armed forces. The army itself was more than doubled in numbers, and new special units were established for antiterrorist activity, the best known of which was a commando unit. There was also the Special Task Force of the Police, the proposal for the creation of this latter force coming from Jayewardene's son Ravi.

Foreign Policy

To an extraordinary extent Sri Lanka's foreign policy of this period was affected by the riots of 1983 and the internationalization of the country's ethnic conflict. Once India entered the scene as the mediator in the Sri Lankan ethnic conflict, relations with India were the primary diplomatic interest of the government as it attempted to repair the damage done to its image by the riots. The Western powers generally took the position that the Sri Lankan conflict could not be resolved without India's support. The corollary to this was the view—also expressed by the Western powers no less than by the People's Republic of China and Pakistan—that it was in Sri Lanka's interest to work out a settlement of the country's ethnic conflict through negotiations with India. Jayewardene found himself with little option but to acquiesce, but throughout the period covered by this chapter he endeavored to repudiate any suggestion of subservience to

India as the price to be paid for Indian mediation in the Sri Lankan conflict.

Almost as soon as the riots broke out, he sent a mission led by his brother H. W. Jayewardene to the ASEAN states and to the Far East seeking to explain his government's position in regard to the riots. Of the ten nations chosen for this exercise, five were considered vitally important: China, Japan, South Korea, Malaysia, and Singapore. An official who accompanied H. W. Jayewardene on this mission recalled that the Chinese leadership was both understanding and sympathetic and, more to the point, as a gesture of support had extended an invitation to President Jayewardene to visit China. The Japanese prime minister of that time, Yoshihiro Nakasone, seemed baffled by the ferocity of the riots. He confessed his inability to reconcile this violence with Sri Lanka's political culture as one of Asia's democracies, and her Buddhist heritage. Having raised these questions, however, Nakasone assured the government of continued support. There were no difficulties as regards South Korea, where the leadership lent a sympathetic ear and gave a positive assurance of support. The most positive assurance of support had come from Singapore and Malaysia. Lee Kuan Yew, who had built a warm friendship with Jayewardene, was disturbed by these events and the setback they meant for the island's economic regeneration. He was unhesitating in the offers of diplomatic support. Malaysian prime minister Dr. Mahathir Mohammed understood the nature of the problem, and especially India's role as part of it. Without being very explicit he drew a parallel with Malaysia's position vis-à-vis China. He told the Sri Lankan delegation that when the riots of July 1983 broke out in their country the Tamils in Malaysia had been agitated and expressed a desire to stage a protest march. Their leaders came to see him and, having listened to them, he told them there would be no official permission given for such a march. Indeed, he had told them, if you begin a march, you will have to march to the sea. There was no march![12] Thus the Sri Lankan president had very good reason to be satisfied with the results of this diplomatic mission.

Jayewardene was perturbed by the overt and covert support given by India and Tamil Nadu to the Tamil cause in the wake of the riots. There was, for instance, a speech by Mrs. Gandhi to the UN Correspondents Association in New York on 30 September, in which she had spoken about the Sri Lankan riots and the loss of lives and property they caused and had expressed India's concern at the situation in Sri Lanka.[13] At that session of the United Nations, the secretary general was presented with a petition with over one million signatures protesting against the riots. The Tamil Nadu government sponsored the petition, and one of its ministers—sent as a member of the Indian delegation—actually handed it over, ceremonially, at the United Nations.

Jayewardene regarded these as part of an overt attempt by the Indian prime minister and government to internationalize Sri Lanka's ethnic conflict, and more specifically to gain international support for India's mediatory role. But he realized too that they were, to some extent, reflections of Tamil Nadu internal politics as well as legitimate exercises in political pressure meant to influence Western opinion. More disturbing was the evidence the government had of training facilities being provided in Tamil Nadu and elsewhere in India to Tamil separatist activists. There was nothing very covert about these activities. Indeed, on 13 November 1983 a Sri Lankan newspaper reported a speech by a Liberation Tigers of Tamil Eelam (LTTE) spokesman in Madras, asserting that "[t]he fight for Eelam will be by bullets and not by words across the table. For this we are raising a national liberation army and we need Indian help. But right now the Indian government is riding the wrong horse. It has committed a serious diplomatic blunder."[14]

The "diplomatic blunder" referred to was perhaps the dispatch of Parathasarathy to Colombo and the continuation of the mediation effort, but what caught the attention of discerning readers in Sri Lanka was the first part of the statement.

Jayewardene decided to launch another diplomatic offensive, and this time to lead it himself, in an effort at searching for a countervailing force or forces against Indian pressure. In May and June 1984 he set out on extended tours beginning with the People's Republic of China. He was responding to the invitation sent to him when his brother was on a diplomatic mission to Southeast and East Asia in the aftermath of the ethnic disturbances of July. There were no outstanding issues between the two countries, and so the visit was very much in the nature of a goodwill visit. He met the Chinese president Li Xian Nian,[15] Prime Minister Zhao Zi Yang, and Deng Ziao Ping himself, and had discussions with all of them. From China he proceeded to South Korea, where he met President Chuan Doo Hwan on 28 May.

Although he was trying hard to play down the external political implications of the visits and to emphasize the goodwill aspects, New Delhi viewed them, particularly his visit to China, as a Machiavellian (or Kautilyan, to use the Indian equivalent) effort to strengthen ties with India's northern neighbor and rival, as well as part of a concerted attempt to win political support in the context of Sri Lanka's ethnic problems. The political implications were important for South Korea, too, since that country was building ties with friendly South and Southeast Asian states. For Jayewardene the economic aspects of the visit to Seoul were just as important as the political, especially in regard to investment in industry and agriculture here, and the shift of labor-intensive industry from South Korea to Sri Lanka.[16]

Next came Jayewardene's long-planned visit to the United States in June 1984. Suffice it to say that there was less effort to play down the significance of his visit to Washington than there had been with his visits to China and South Korea. Apart from his call on President Reagan at the White House, the customary speech on the south lawn—in the course of which he presented his host with a baby elephant—and the official dinner, the Sri Lankan president had business visits with a number of key officials and legislators. These included Vice President George Bush, Secretary of State George Shultz, and Treasury Secretary Donald Regan. He also met a number of key senators and representatives. One of the highlights of the visit, so far as Jayewardene was concerned, was a breakfast meeting at the *Washington Post* hosted by its influential and formidable publisher Katherine Graham. What he wanted from all of them was a sympathetic hearing at which he aired his views on the Sri Lankan situation and on India's role in the country's ethnic conflict. Jayewardene fielded their questions with his customary aplomb.

Coming as these visits did shortly after a bold diplomatic initiative in the establishment of an Israeli interest office in the U.S. mission in Colombo, India saw them as part of a continuing effort to draw away from the traditional nonaligned positions into closer links with the United States and the West. The opening to Israel was, of course, a calculated risk Jayewardene took, notwithstanding the danger of alienating the Muslim vote that had generally gone to the United National Party (UNP)[17] and the strong Muslim representation in the cabinet and in the UNP Parliamentary Party. But he thought that the urgent need to get professional training for the Sri Lankan army at a time when India was providing extensive training facilities for Tamil separatists from Sri Lanka made the risk worth taking. The disapproval that greeted this decision from Muslims in general, along with the denunciation from the opposition, did not result in any adverse repercussions for Jayewardene within the government. No Muslim cabinet minister or MP resigned. Some of them made their displeasure known to President Jayewardene, but their criticisms were muted and he was able to ride the storm.

In the meantime, the use of Tamil Nadu as a base by Tamil separatist activists and their terrorist groups increased. Occasionally their activities led to incidents that caused grave embarrassment to the Indian government. One of these was an incident that occurred on 2 August 1984, when a massive explosion destroyed part of the airport building at Madras Meenambakkam Airport, killing about thirty people (of whom twenty-four were Sri Lankans) in the transit lounge.[18] It transpired that the explosion had been caused by the accidental explosion of bombs hidden in two suitcases meant to be transferred to an Air Lanka[19] flight to Colombo for dispatch on Air Lanka flights to London and Paris. The bombs were planted by Sri Lankan Tamils. Some of the perpetrators of this outrage were arrested but a few of them escaped from India—with the connivance of Indian officials—and secured refugee status in London! A few years later K. Mohandas, the deputy inspector general of police (intelligence) of the Tamil Nadu police, revealed that "a senior policy maker" in Delhi had indicated to him "that we had a duty to protect the Sri Lankan militants and that, if we continued along the known lines of investigation in the airport blast case, the Sri Lanka Government would take advantage of it and proclaim to the world the existence of militant training camps in India which had "officially been denied" by New Delhi."[20]

Mohandas's revelation was published in 1992. Through most of 1984 the Indian government persisted in its denials of the existence of training camps and bases for Sri Lanka Tamil separatist activists in Tamil Nadu. The denials continued until the end of 1984, but generally stopped in the aftermath of a visit to Colombo and Delhi by General Vernon Walters, Washington's troubleshooter. Walters made two visits to Sri Lanka, dealt within greater detail later in this chapter. The point to be made here is that Walters had informed Sri Lanka that the United States had clear evidence of the existence of camps and bases for Sri Lankan Tamils in Tamil Nadu. Lalith Athulathmudali recalled that Walters had "told us that they had clear evidence [through] . . . satellite photos of Indian camps. He went on to Delhi to let them know that they had better stop denying the existence of training camps. The US had satellite photos that could be released. They [the Indians] stopped denying their existence after that."[21]

The All Party Conference

On his return to the island from Delhi in November 1983, President Jayewardene set about the business of gaining the support of as wide a range of political opinion in the country as possible for the terms of the settlement incorporated in "Annexure C" (see Appendix Document III).[22] He called a conference—the All Party Conference (APC)—to discuss this among other proposals. The discussions began in January 1984.[23] The UNP's election manifesto for the general election of 1977 had made reference to such a conference to seek a resolution of the island's ethnic conflicts, but once in office there was marked preference for bilateral negotiations with the TULF. Now the scope of participation was widened to include not merely political parties but representatives of religious groups as well, including representatives of the Buddhist order, the *sangha*. The latter were generally hard-line opponents of all schemes of devolution. The Sri Lanka Freedom Party (SLFP), the principal opposition party, could not be persuaded to participate in the discussions at the conference.

While the absence of the SLFP deprived the APC of some of its political credibility, the fact that all other parties, including the TULF and the Marxist parties, were participants encouraged hopes of reaching a compromise settlement the government and the Tamil leadership alike could accept. Parathasarathy was in the island during some of the discussions and was able to meet some of the delegates informally. He was encouraged to talk to the *sangha* representatives and did so, but was unable to dispel their suspicions of him and the proposals with which he was associated.

The discussions at the APC continued through most of 1984. Partly this was because a comprehensive discussion and review of policies was encouraged and attempted through committees that included officials, but it included an element of political calculation. President Jayewardene recalled that Mrs. Gandhi herself had informed him through Parathasarathy that it might be a good idea to stretch the negotiations until after the Indian elections she planned to hold by the end of the year or very early in 1985. In this way any decisions taken would not figure as controversial issues in the electoral campaigns in Tamil Nadu. However, when the TULF leader A. Amirthalingam complained to her about the delays that resulted from the long, drawn-out discussions at the APC, she blamed President Jayewardene for it.[24]

The lengthy discussions at the APC produced substantial results. A consensus was reached on the crucially important issue of the range of powers to be devolved to regional bodies. The *sangha* representatives accepted the need for a second tier of government, something they had been unwilling to do up to that time. Nevertheless they were still reluctant to commit themselves to a system of provincial councils. Moreover very substantial progress was achieved in regard to other issues such as language policy. Above all a detailed study was made of the distribution of state-owned land under major irrigation schemes, and a formula was evolved which combined a recognition of demographic factors and ethnic identity.[25] This formula remained the basis of future discussions on this controversial topic. The formula proved to be acceptable to all groups in the island. The government published an elaborate legislative framework based on the consensus reached at the APC—this included a scheme for a second chamber—as the basis of a settlement.

In the meantime that hardy perennial in Indo–Sri Lankan discord over the last five decades—the political status of Indians resident and working in Sri Lanka—was well on the way to amicable settlement in the post-1977 period through the operation of the democratic political process in Sri Lanka. One of the more fruitful results of the APC of 1984 was the decision that 94,000 stateless persons—Indian plantation workers—should be granted Sri Lankan citizenship. This recommendation was accepted in principle by the government. Legislation for this purpose was ready in 1986–87 and approved by Parliament (through the Grant of Citizenship to Stateless Persons Act No. 39 of 1988). With its adoption, plantation workers of Indian extraction fell into two clear categories: Sri Lankan citizens and those with Indian citizenship but resident in the island for the duration of their working lives.

These discussions on the mechanics of devolution took place against the backdrop of an increasing frequency of guerrilla attacks and terrorist incidents in the north of the island, and the extension of these into the eastern seaboard. The guerrilla forces were now much larger, much better trained (the training was largely in India), and much better equipped than before. The training and equipping of guerrilla forces in India with the active support of Tamil Nadu had begun in the early 1980s, well before the riots of July 1983, but there is no mistaking the intensification of these processes as a result of the violence inflicted on the Tamils in July 1983. Tamil Nadu had always been a ready haven for these guerrilla forces, but now the support they received was strengthened immeasurably, as was the extent of the protection they enjoyed. Their morale was stronger and their motivation keener after these riots than before, and by the end of 1983 they demonstrated a greater willingness to take risks and greater resourcefulness and daring in their attacks on the carefully chosen targets. Until about the end of 1985 they were in many ways better equipped than the small security services units stationed in the north of the island.

The first reports on these training camps and "bases" located in India appeared in Western newspapers in April 1984, at about the same time that comprehensive coverage of the camps and bases appeared in a prestigious Indian journal, *India Today*.[26] And if more solid evidence was required of the use of Indian soil by Sri Lankan guerrillas and terrorists, this had been the incident at the Madras International Airport on 2 August 1984 related earlier. The Indian government generally refused to acknowledge the existence of training camps and facilities for Sri Lankan Tamil guerrillas and terrorist groups on Indian soil. Instead it sought to divert attention from Sri Lankan charges and protests with counter-charges of human rights violations in Sri Lanka, attributing these quite explicitly to the lack of discipline among the Sri Lankan security forces. In so doing they met an embarrassing fact with a half truth.

The fact is that Sri Lankan Tamil guerrillas and terrorists operated in Tamil Nadu with a freedom and publicity for which the only parallel is the Palestine Liberation Organization (PLO) and its various factions in the Arab world. Quite apart from the public support they enjoyed in such large measure in Tamil Nadu, they engaged in fund-raising drives at public meetings in other parts of India as well, in particular Bombay.[27] There was a clear double standard on separatism and terrorism: to crush separatism ruthlessly when seen to pose a palpable threat to the Indian polity, as was done in 1984 in the Punjab through Operation Blue Star, to protest vigorously at the tolerance accorded to Indian extremists and terrorist groups operating in the Western world (the Sikhs in Britain, Canada, and the United States for instance), and yet to feign ignorance of the existence of training camps and "bases" for Tamil guerrillas and terrorist groups on Indian soil. This double standard was one of the great stumbling blocks to cordial relations between India and Sri Lanka during this period and on to 1987 or later.

India's policy in regard to the internationalization of Sri Lanka's ethnic conflict was a two-pronged affair. Discussions and negotiations with the Sri Lankan government on a settlement of differences between the government and the Tamil minority were proceeding, with India in her role of mediator. Yet India at the same time was using its formidable diplomatic resources through its high commissions and embassies in the West—in Ottawa, London, and Washington, in particular—to accuse the Sri Lankan government and its armed forces of violations of human rights in attacks on Tamil civilians, in the course of or in the wake of security operations in the north and east of the island. At the United Nations General Assembly, Indian delegates—generally a Tamil Nadu politician (a Tamil Nadu minister in 1983)—would raise the Sri Lankan issue in the course of debates.[28] The situation was even more favorable to this diplomatic offensive at the United Nations office in Geneva and the sessions of the Human Rights Commission there. The Indian representative would either raise the Sri Lankan issue on his own, or more often would support countries such as Argentina (smarting under Sri Lanka's support of Britain in the Falklands War) and Norway in raising the issue officially. Since some of the Western nations—the United States and Great Britain—were represented on the commission by nongovernmental organizations, and there was in addition the conspicuous presence of human rights groups, Sri Lanka was under much greater pressure in Geneva than in New York.[29]

In the meantime the TULF leadership was living in self-imposed exile in Madras as guests of the Tamil Nadu government. This was quite apart from more radical Tamil activists who also lived in Madras and conducted their clandestine operations (including a lucrative trade in narcotics to Europe) and political campaigns through Madras and India, linking with well-funded diaspora groups living in the West. These latter groups sought and received political support from Indian embassies and high commissions in Washington, D.C., and Ottawa, not to mention London.

Then again, while persistently ignoring the provision of training facilities to Tamil activists in Tamil Nadu (and elsewhere in India) and the transfer of weapons from India to Jaffna, the Indian government under Indira Gandhi used pressure on Western powers to prevent the sale of sophisticated weaponry to the Sri Lankan forces. Fortunately for Sri Lanka, Pakistan and the People's Republic of China lay beyond the range of India's diplomatic pressure. As we have seen, Sri Lanka was able to purchase weapons from Pakistan and the People's Republic of China. Pakistan also provided much of the military training, and Sri Lanka also turned to Israel for assistance for this purpose.

One of the key issues so far as the Sri Lankan government was concerned had to do with the ease with which Sri Lankan Tamil activists and terrorist groups operated in Tamil Nadu and moved to and from there. The Sri Lankan government called for joint patrols of the Palk Strait by the two navies—Indian and Sri Lankan—to curb this, as well as the flourishing smuggling trade with its close links with Tamil separatist activists. Far from agreeing to discuss this, the Indian government would not even concede that such a problem existed.

Facing a purposeful challenge from the Tamil separatist guerrillas, and with their attacks becoming more daring in scope and powerful in impact, the government responded with the new institutional structure and new policies discussed earlier in this chapter. Of the new policies, two are of special importance to our discussion here: the attempt to check the easy flood of men and arms to and from Jaffna to Tamil Nadu by establishing a surveillance zone and a marked increase in expenditure on the armed services. The concept of a surveillance zone covering most of the north and northwest coastal region seemed simple enough, but its implementation, which began in the last week of November 1984, was not so rigorously imposed as it might have been. It was evident that much greater resources in naval craft and trained personnel than Sri Lanka's diminutive navy possessed were called for to make this policy really effective.

The establishment of a surveillance zone did not bring any significant reduction in the number of guerrilla attacks within Sri Lanka; on the contrary, these attacks assumed a greater intensity and took on a new dimension. For the first time they were directed against Sinhalese peasants living in the Vanni regions on the southern and southeastern boundary of the Northern Province. Two attacks, which took place on 30 November 1984 and 19 December 1984 respectively in Mullaitivu and in a traditional Sinhalese fishing village (the villagers were mainly Roman Catholics) on the northeast coast, were designed to cause panic in those regions and to get the people to flee to other parts of the country.

One unexpected result of the establishment of a surveillance zone was a new wave of refugees to Tamil Nadu, generally fisherfolk who had lost their livelihood. This later phase in the influx of refugees to Tamil Nadu was, in its initial stages, voluntary, but soon pressure was used, by separatist activists, on the fishing population in the surveillance zone to flee to Tamil Nadu in large numbers in hopes of aggravating the refugee situation there. In this campaign the TULF and their more activist and violent rivals worked together.

The All Party Conference—The Final Phase

In the last quarter of 1984 the discussions at the APC were reaching their final stages. A draft ordinance incorporating a system of revitalized district councils, empowered to link together where necessary on a wider basis, was brought to the table for discussion at the APC on 30 September. Critics focused attention on the latter feature and declined to support the draft bill. The TULF declared its opposition to it, as did the SLFP (which had refused to participate in the discussions of the conference); the one because it did not go far enough in the direction of provincial autonomy, and the other because it went too far in undermining the country's unitary structure. Despite this setback the negotiations continued.

At this point U.S. envoy Vernon Walters made a second visit to Sri Lanka, this time on the invitation of the Sri Lankan government. (The first had been in the previous year on the initiative of the U.S. government.) Although some of the local newspapers reported that he was expected to discuss the question of military assistance in the form of weapons and training, his visit was arranged on the understanding that this would not figure at all in the discussions. The Sri Lankan government was looking on Walters as a sort of sounding board. Its main aim was to explain to Walters the current state of negotiations with the TULF on the basis of the APC talks, and to indicate to him what the government had in mind with regard to proposals to meet the demands of the Tamils. It was hoped that he would convey this information to New Delhi, on the assumption that he would be a more reliable transmitter of the Sri Lankan government's intentions than almost anyone else. As on the previous occasion, Walters saw President Jayewardene alone. He listened. He warned the Sri Lankan president that there was a very real prospect of an Indian invasion, and that he would do well to find a resolution to the conflict. This second warning was more direct than the first.[30]

On his visit to New Delhi, Walters urged the Indians that they really should not attempt to invade Sri Lanka to impose their will on that country, and he also told them, as he had done on his previous visit in late 1983, that the United States had photographs of the training camps for Tamil separatists, as well as addresses of the main separatist groups in Tamil Nadu. Walters recalled that the Indian officials he met were quite paranoid about the alleged U.S. interest in the old British base at Trincomalee. He found P. C. Alexander "very hard," and he described Parathasarathy as "everything that makes Indians difficult to deal with." Walters believed that they had been victims of systematic Soviet disinformation, and that they were quite persuaded that the United States had serious ambitions regarding Trincomalee and thought they had solid evidence for it.[31] If the Walters visit was expected by the Sri Lankan government to soften India's attitude to Sri Lanka, there is very little evidence that it did.

On 31 October came Mrs. Gandhi's assassination. Indeed, over much of 1984 her attention and that of her government had been directed at the tumultuous affairs of the Punjab where her attempts at exploiting divisions within the ranks of the principal Sikh separatist groups culminated in unprecedented violence associated with the storming of the Golden Temple by the Indian army and the bloody carnage that flowed from it. She was the most prominent victim of Punjab's burgeoning separatist violence.

As for the immediate consequences of her death on Sri Lanka, it inevitably resulted in some postponement of the discussions at the APC, where the government of Sri Lanka was known to be preparing a fresh set of proposals. For the Sri Lankan government and President Jayewardene, the likelihood that Rajiv Gandhi would head a new government after the next general election was regarded with some relief. He believed—at this stage—that Rajiv Gandhi was more likely to follow the example of his grandfather rather than his imperious mother.[32] For the TULF and other Tamil separatist groups, Mrs. Gandhi's assassination was a staggering blow. The TULF leadership's poignant assertion that her death left them orphaned was at once a terse and accurate description of their predicament, so accustomed had they grown to the protective shield she had thrown around them.

To accommodate the wishes of the TULF, two draft bills were placed before the APC for its final sessions in November and December 1984, one of which was a draft district and provincial council bill. The immediate response of the TULF leadership seemed encouraging. Some of them conceded that these proposals came as near as possible to the proposals in Annexure C (see Appendix Document III), which had emerged from discussions between President Jayewardene and the Indian government, and which the Tamil groups generally regarded as a major breakthrough. Up to 21 December the TULF, after a careful consideration of the APC proposals, concluded that they formed the basis of an acceptable settlement.[33]

By 23 December, however, the TULF had rejected the proposals, and in so doing they undermined the viability of the consensus reached at the

APC. The government had expected the SLFP to reject the proposals; they also expected opposition from some of the monks, and they felt that this could be overcome by an appeal to the people. But once the TULF rejected them there was nothing left to do save abandon them.

Thus at the cabinet meeting of 26 December it was decided to drop the proposals. The rejection was recommended by President Jayewardene himself. There was much speculation in the country on the TULF's about-face on these proposals. One theory held that the more radical and activist groups had compelled them to scuttle the proposals. The TULF's position vis-à-vis these groups had always been an ambivalent one. It had never been more ambivalent than it was at the end of 1984. Since the TULF was based in Madras, its members, including its leadership, were more vulnerable to their threats and pressures, especially where these were sent through Tamil Nadu intermediaries. Others thought it was the result of an assumption that the process of negotiations could begin afresh, after the Indian elections, and with a new government in power. This latter assumption was one they shared with the Sri Lankan government. The TULF hoped, no doubt, that the triangular relationship that left the Sri Lankan government an isolated fourth party, as it had been for the most part with Mrs. Gandhi in control in New Delhi, would continue, while the Sri Lankan government believed that there would be a quadrilateral of forces which would give it greater maneuverability than under Mrs. Gandhi.

The TULF leadership, as we have seen, had been living in exile in Tamil Nadu as guests of the state government there since the outbreak of the riots of July 1983. Now with the collapse of the APC they appeared to be more receptive than before the presumed attractions of Indian intervention on behalf of the Tamils of the north, on the Bangladesh model. This pressure for Indian intervention received little encouragement from New Delhi. The firm assurances to Sri Lanka that India contemplated no such intervention did not dampen the enthusiasm of Tamil separatist groups who kept up a steady barrage of propaganda on the need for Indian intervention.

Notes

1. Mrs. Bandaranaike had lost her civic rights for a period of seven years, from October 1980. She nevertheless kept her position as head of the SLFP despite all efforts to persuade her to step down in favor of her deputy.

2. In the letter it transpired that his group claimed responsibility for the assassination of the UNP parliamentary candidate for the Vavuniya constituency in the Northern Province,

Pulendran. Reference was also made to the purchase of land in southern India for the purpose of training separatist activists.

3. The letter was published by the government under the title *Tale the Letter Tells* (Colombo: n.d. [early October 1983]).

4. J. R. Jayewardene, interview with the author, 14 October 1983.

5. Among those who spoke about this to the author were Lalith Athulathmudali and J. R. Jayewardene.

6. J. R. Jayewardene, interview with the author, 28 October 1983.

7. Ibid.

8. *Economist,* 14 July 1984.

9. W. M. P. B. Menikdiwela, interview with the author, 5 July 1990; Lalith Athulathmudali, interview with the author, 9 July 1990.

10. Lalith Athulathmudali, interview with the author, 9 July 1990.

11. *Economist,* 14 July 1984.

12. This summary of the mission's discussions is based on the recollections of C. Mahendran, a senior Sri Lankan diplomat, who spoke to me about the mission on two occasions, one very close to the event, and again at much greater length at an interview I had with him in Tokyo (where he was Sri Lanka's ambassador) on 3 August 1992.

13. *Weekend Sun,* 2 October 1983.

14. *Weekend Sun,* 13 November 1983.

15. The meeting with the Chinese president was on 20 May.

16. J. R. Jayewardene, interview with the author, early May 1984.

17. See the article entitled "Sri Lanka: The Israel Imbroglio," *India Today,* 30 June 1984.

18. On this event see Sinha Ratnatunga, *Politics of Terrorism: The Sri Lankan Experience* (Canberra: International Fellowship for Social and Economic Development, 1988), 100–102.

19. Air Lanka is the national airline.

20. K. Mohandas, *MGR: The Man and the Myth* (Bangalore: Panther Publishers, 1992), 118.

21. Lalith Athulathmudali, interview with the author, 9 July 1990.

22. On the negotiations that led to the drafting of "Annexure C," see Ratnatunga, *Politics of Terrorism,* 322–29. N. Tiruchelvam has reviewed G. Parathasarathy's role as a mediator in the Sri Lankan ethnic conflict in two short articles in the *Asian Wall Street Journal,* 6 August 1987, and the *Hindu,* 5 August 1989.

23. The most comprehensive account of the discussion at the APC is in Ratnatunga, *Politics of Terrorism,* 331–57.

24. J. R. Jayewardene, interview with the author, January 1985.

25. The principal elements of the formula were that land under major irrigation schemes such as the Mahavali would be distributed on an ethnic basis (74 percent for the Sinhalese and 26 percent for the minorities) while land under village irrigation schemes would be distributed on the basis of ethnic composition of the local population.

26. See *India Today,* 31 March 1984, 84–99, particularly the essay in investigative reporting entitled "Sri Lanka Rebels: An Ominous Presence in Tamil Nadu;" *Sunday Times* (London), 1 April 1984; and Reuter reports on these bases published in Sri Lanka in the *Sun,* 23 May 1984, and the *Island,* 25 May 1984. See also the London-based journal *South: The Third World Magazine,* March 1985, 14–15, and *Time International,* 3 April 1989, 10–11 for a later account.

27. There is a large Tamil population in Bombay and its suburbs, and this has been the source of support to the Tamil cause. One of the key figures in this was an underworld boss, Mudaliyar, a Tamil. Sri Lankan Tamils are now very prominent in Bombay's under-

world, especially its drug trade. See the Indian journal *Sunday,* 31 July–6 August 1988, which carried an article entitled "Sri Lankan Tamils in Bombay's Underworld."

28. One of the Indian delegates to the UN General Assembly was S. Ramachandran, a minister of the Tamil Nadu state government. On 21 October 1983 he addressed the special political committee and raised the question of Sri Lankan refugees in Tamil Nadu. See the official publication issued by the Indian Mission to the United Nations, *Indian News,* 21 October 1983. Ramachandran's speech was on Agenda Item 74: International Cooperation to Avert New Flows of Refugees. On 27 September 1984, Mr. Mirdha, an Indian delegate, made much the same points in a statement on behalf of his country at a general debate at the thirty-ninth Session of the UN General Assembly.

29. Official records of the UN Geneva office show that in 1983, 1984, and 1985 Indian delegates raised the issue of human rights violations in Sri Lanka at meetings of the UN Commission on Human Rights and the Subcommission on Prevention of Discrimination and Protection of Minorities. Of particular interest in this regard is the speech of M. C. Bandhare, a member of the subcommission, in Geneva, 21 August 1984.

30. General Walters, interview with Howard Wriggins, 13 April 1992; and the author's interview with Ernest Corea, 20 May 1992. Corea, as Sri Lanka's ambassador in Washington, had arranged Walters's visit and had traveled to Colombo to brief President Jayewardene on it. Corea had informed President Jayewardene on this occasion that the U.S. government had not changed its policy with regard to the supply of arms to Sri Lanka and that it would be both inappropriate and fruitless to raise the issue with Walters.

31. General Walters, interview with Howard Wriggins, 13 April 1992; Ernest Corea, interview with the author, 20 May 1992.

32. President Jayewardene, interview with the author, early November 1984.

33. President Jayewardene, interview with the author, early January 1985. See also Sinha Ratnatunga, *Politics of Terrorism,* 350–57.

8

The Thimpu Discussions and the Delhi Accord, July–August 1985

Rajiv Gandhi's Overtures

AS SOON as he took over from his mother, Rajiv Gandhi conducted his first political campaign as leader of the party. He won the most decisive electoral victory that any Indian prime minister had secured up to that time. In the early months of 1985 he was basking in the sunshine of his huge victory and very real popularity—this was the springtime of his prime ministership. Treating his massive victory as a mandate for fresh initiatives and dramatic changes, he picked two of the thorniest issues he had inherited from his mother for early resolution—Punjab and Assam. The Punjab crisis, quite naturally, took greater priority, and he began negotiations with the Akali Dal leadership in the Punjab.

He also made overtures to the Sri Lankan government through the Sri Lankan high commissioner in Delhi, Bernard Tillakaratne, just three days after he became prime minister. His first words to Tillakaratne, the latter recalled, were, "I want to do everything I can to see that this thing is settled. I want to help if I can. I do not know much about your country but whatever I can do I will."[1] The gist of what he said, so far as Jayewardene understood it, was as follows. The new Indian prime minister was anxious to make a fresh start in the Indian mediation effort, and there was a hint, if not a promise, of a more evenhanded approach to the problem than there had been under his mother.

In February 1985 Jayewardene dispatched Minister of National Security Lalith Athulathmudali for discussions with Rajiv Gandhi. The devolution package then being considered by the Sri Lankan government was

147

naturally the central theme of the talks, which took place on 9 February. In addition, Athulathmudali was asked by the Sri Lankan president to emphasize two other issues. The first, the one he treated as a matter of very great urgency, was to secure the establishment of joint Indo–Sri Lankan naval patrols of the Palk Strait. The second was to press for a firm understanding from the Indian prime minister that India would not give in to pressure from Tamil groups in Madras for direct interference in Sri Lankan affairs.

Athulathmudali reported[2] on his return from Delhi that the talks he had with Rajiv Gandhi had been both friendly and very fruitful. He found that the latter had a much clearer understanding than his mother of the limits of political concessions on regional autonomy possible in Sri Lanka. Rajiv Gandhi himself had commented that there was no need for districts to be linked together to form a region—thus seemingly endorsing the Sri Lankan government's own policy on devolution and also repudiating Parathasarathy's position on this. Both sides agreed that more power should be conceded to districts. Lalith Athulathmudali was delighted to find that Rajiv Gandhi himself believed that law and order should not, in any way, be conceded to the districts. That, he said, was the mistake India had made with regard to the Punjab.

Describing the Tamil United Liberation Front (TULF) as a separatist group at heart, Sri Lanka's version of the Akali Dal, he assured Athulathmudali that there would be limits placed on the TULF's hitherto free and easy access to the government and senior officers in New Delhi. He urged the Sri Lankan government to begin discussions with the state government of Tamil Nadu in an effort to reduce subcontinental tensions. The general feeling was that with M. G. Ramachandran's party back in power constructive discussions could commence soon.

The Indian prime minister stated that he was deeply interested in establishing good and friendly relations with all his South Asian neighbors, including and especially Pakistan. He was anxious that the role of the superpowers in South Asia be limited. Athulathmudali carried away the impression that the Soviet Union's role in South Asia and India would be more restricted than it had been with Mrs. Gandhi. For his part, Athulathmudali assured Rajiv Gandhi that Sri Lanka was not eager to get the United States involved in Sri Lankan affairs either on its own or through its allies or surrogates. Rajiv Gandhi told Athulathmudali that he was very anxious for President Jayewardene to pay a visit to India as soon as it was convenient for him to do so.

Very shortly after Athulathmudali's return to the island from his discussions with the Indian prime minister, President Jayewardene wrote a personal letter to Rajiv Gandhi on 1 March 1985.[3] Addressing the Indian Prime Minister as "My dear Rajiv," Jayewardene began by reminding the former that he was the third generation of the Nehru family with whom he [Jayewardene] would be associated in an official capacity.

> I need hardly mention that it is not only as the President of Sri Lanka that I am writing to the Prime Minister of India, I am also writing as a friend of the Nehru family, you being the third generation that I have known since I became acquainted with your grandfather when I entertained him at my home in Sri Lanka in 1939. He was one of my heroes, together with the other great leaders of India who led the Freedom Movement, cherishing Truth and Non-Violence as their guiding principles. I still try to follow those ideals.
>
> I was his guest for a few days at his home in Allahabad when I attended the Ramgarh Sessions of the Congress in 1941. I later corresponded with him when he was in jail. I have sent copies of those letters to the Nehru Archives and I wish to present one to you whenever I have a chance to do so.

He proceeded to the difficulties that now existed in relations between the two countries.

> Unfortunately, relations between our two countries have been affected recently by difficulties which we are both aware of. This has weighed heavily on my mind for some time and I hope that it will be possible to set this right soon.
>
> In this context, I am specially appreciative of the hearing which you gave my Minister a few weeks ago. His report of conversations in Delhi have [*sic*] encouraged me to make a new effort to break the kind of deadlock we now face.
>
> In order to do this, I would very much like to meet you personally for further discussions. However, before such a meeting, I think it would be most useful if you could send one of your senior officials to meet me here. I would welcome such a visit as it will be helpful to enable me to arrive at an understanding of your present thinking. This will help me to formulate a common approach to some of the problems that now exist.

In the second page of the letter he referred to the work done at the APC.

> I have in my speech [to Parliament on 20 February] referred to the All Party Conference at pages 3–6. It was only on two matters viz., the joining of the two provinces, North and East, in one Council; and the Second Chamber that there was no agreement with the TULF. I had agreed to the proposals outlined in Annexures A, B & C which visualised Provincial (Regional) Councils within a Province. I had also expressed my desire to continue discussions with the TULF with regard to decentralisation of powers and functions to Provincial Councils, thus continuing the commitment to a political solution.

He turned next to his principal concern and asked for India's help in that regard.

> I ask of you very little. Let us forget the issue of training camps; the existence of Sri Lanka terrorists in South India; their plotting and planning. I ask you to help me to prevent them coming here with arms. At the same time could we not also prevent Sri Lankans from seeking refuge in your country?
>
> If we can agree on a common scheme to do this, by some form of mutual or combined surveillance, it will enable me to withdraw the Armed Services from combat; to suspend the operation of the Terrorist Act; and to help the North and East of Sri Lanka to return to normalcy.
>
> Surely you can take this step forward which will help stop this taking of life and damage to property, and the resumption of civilised life in your most friendly neighbour.
>
> We are both representatives of the people, both having received massive majorities at elections, where over half the electorates voted for us and enjoying in our Parliaments a 5/6th majority.
>
> Cross-border terrorism threatens the very fabric of this democracy. It is an issue on which all major political parties in Sri Lanka agree and is the single most important impediment to a solution of our ethnic tension.
>
> Do please understand our problem, which is now yours too, and help.

An Early Setback

The flow of arms from India to the Tamil separatist activists continued unabated. In an interview with the Sri Lankan newspaper, the *Island*, on 18 April, Lalith Athulathmudali revealed that there were two main arms dumps in Tamil Nadu from which the Sri Lankan Tamil groups were supplied—at Rameswaran and Vedarabayam. He complained that even after the suspension of aerial bombings on the hideouts of the separatist activists in the north of Sri Lanka, a signal of the government's decision to search for a political solution, there had been no reduction in the flow of arms from Tamil Nadu.

Rajiv Gandhi and the Indian government had been critical of the Sri Lankan government for the hard measures, such as aerial attacks, that had to be taken in these circumstances. S. Thondaman, the Ceylon Workers Congress (CWC) representative in the Sri Lankan cabinet, in an interview with the *Hindu* on 13 April, stated that President Jayewardene and the people of Sri Lanka, for their part, seemed to be losing faith in Rajiv Gandhi. They asked, he said,

> Does Mr Gandhi really mean business when he says that his Government will never support or encourage Eelam for the Indian Government firmly believes in the solidarity of Sri Lanka?
> [I]f Mr Gandhi's policy was "No Eelam", then what were the constraints that stood in his way to clinch the issue with Sri Lanka Tamil youth, militants and leaders of other organizations to whom the Indian Government had given asylum and shelter?

On 17 April the Sri Lankan government handed over to Rajiv Gandhi a set of proposals for a resolution of the Sri Lankan conflict. These were brought by A. C. S. Hameed, the foreign minister who was in Delhi for a meeting of the Coordinating Bureau of Non-Aligned Countries. The proposals were based on the consensus reached at the All Party Conference (APC).

At much the same time, President Jayewardene gave an interview to the Australian Broadcasting Corporation complaining of India's double standards with respect to Sri Lanka and stating that Sri Lanka regarded Pakistan as a better friend. The full text of his interview was carried in the *Hindu* of 18 April. Asked who was Sri Lanka's better friend, "India which is trying to bring about a peaceful settlement, or Pakistan which is supplying military assistance," Jayewardene's candid response was

"Pakistan is a better friend . . . my relations with India are always above board, [with] Pakistan they are above board. If India does not help us and helps the terrorists, it is not helping us. They have double standards: so we cannot be friendly with a person with double standards."

Jayewardene's forthright comments earned a quick riposte from the Indian government by way of an official statement in the Lok Sabha on 29 April by Khursheed Alam Khan, minister of state for external affairs.[4] Alam Khan had spoken from a written text. There had been a clash between Tamils and Muslims in the east of the island. The minister's interpretation of the event caused dismay in Sri Lanka. For one thing, he described the Muslims as Tamils, merely because they spoke Tamil, a misidentification Sri Lankan Muslims had always rejected. For another, he claimed that there was a "hidden hand" behind the riots[5] implying that the Sri Lankan government had encouraged the Muslims to resist. His statement read as follows:

It is a fact that this new element of [a] Muslim dimension is a very dangerous thing because it is an old rule of divide and rule; and actually we feel that the Muslims are also Tamils; they speak the Tamil language and therefore there is no difference between the two. But, surely there is a hidden hand which is trying to divide the two. I hope better sense will prevail amongst the Muslims in Sri Lanka and they will see through this game and they will not be caught in this game. It is also a fact that this is a definite and calculated instigation. This is a notorious old game, as I said, but, we earnestly hope that people will realise, particularly the Muslims of Sri Lanka, will realise that it is their cause also which is being fought by other Tamils.[6]

Alam Khan castigated the Sri Lankan government for permitting the "intrusion of foreign agencies in Sri Lanka."

We are aware about the intrusion of foreign agencies in Sri Lanka. This is a very serious thing because we do not want any foreign agencies so near our country and particularly the SAS which is providing training to the commandos or the Mossad which is a notorious agency like the CIA. Therefore, we never want that these agencies should be allowed to come into Sri Lanka. We have made this very clear to the Sri Lankan government. Similarly, we do not appreciate that they have allowed a broadcasting station of the

Voice of America to be installed there; it will not be in the interest of this region and we want that this region should be free from all such agencies. Just as we want that the Indian ocean should be a zone of peace, similarly, we don't want any kind of intrusion into our region.

He proceeded to an explanation of why the Indian government would not agree to a joint patrol of the seas separating the two countries, and a defense of India against the allegation that she was encouraging terrorism in Sri Lanka.[7]

Quite a few members were anxious to ask as to what we have tried and what we have told the Sri Lankan government. There also I would like to say that personalities do not count, really it is a question of achieving the objective; who goes there, who talks to them and how many times, who has gone, the personalities are not very relevant. It is the objective that we want to achieve. And the objective that we have suggested to them has been withdrawal of troops from Tamil areas—and they should be sent back to the barracks, the civil administration should take over; the keeping in abeyance the policy of settlement of 30,000 Sinhalese families in the pre-dominant areas of Tamils; withdrawal of the sixth amendment to the Constitution, removal of restrictions from restricted and prohibited surveillance zone; the intrusion of a foreign agency in our region is a matter of great concern to us; we do not want this in this region. That was the reason also that we had refused their proposal of joint patrolling by two Navies. We said that this could not be done in isolation. If a solution is to be found, it has to be found in totality. By just having joint patrolling there will be no solution.

One hon. Member said about 7500 people had been killed. To tell you frankly, there are no authentic figures available about the number of people killed or the number of people who are imprisoned, because they have not furnished any such figures. It is only through newspapers or whatever the source of information of the hon. Members that this information is available.

I have already said that the allegation that terrorism is encouraged in India is totally baseless and false. Whatever propaganda they are doing, I can assure you that steps will certainly be taken to ensure that this baseless propaganda is contradicted. But we will do it in a dignified manner and not in the manner that they are doing.

SHRI KOLANDAIVELU: What about recognition of [the] liberation movement?

SHRI KHURSHEED ALAM KHAN: I think, this question is quite complicated and it may not be possible for me to say anything about it at this moment.

The Sri Lankan government was mystified by many of the statements in Khursheed Alam Khan's speech in the Lok Sabha. They seemed to contradict much of what the new Indian prime minister had told Sri Lanka's minister of national security, Lalith Athulathmudali, a few weeks earlier when the latter had met him. The general assumption in the Sri Lankan government was that India's bureaucracy—the well-known South Block in Delhi—was still continuing Mrs. Gandhi's practices. It took deft diplomacy on the part of the Indian prime minister to convince the Sri Lankan president to ignore this outburst and to accept his (Rajiv Gandhi's) invitation to him to visit Delhi for talks. The new Indian foreign secretary, Romesh Bhandari, was a key figure in this, and in seeking to convince his Sri Lankan counterpart, and the Sri Lankan high commissioner in Delhi, that he was intent on a fresh start.

Rajiv Gandhi, so much less dependent on a southern Indian political base than his mother, and intent on taking a more evenhanded approach than her to the problems posed by Sri Lanka's ethnic conflicts, found his options for leverage more limited than he would have liked them to be. The constraint lay in the ethnic politics of Tamil Nadu and the public support the Sri Lankan Tamils enjoyed there. The Tamil guerrillas and terrorist groups continued to have training facilities and bases in Tamil Nadu and ready access to sophisticated weapons and money.

Among the most prominent of the regional political notables in the interplay of forces in India on the Sri Lankan issue was the charismatic old film actor, M. G. Ramachandran, the chief minister of Tamil Nadu. By 1983–84 the health of this enormously popular political figure was visibly failing, and his associates and aides had begun to take decisions on his behalf. After 1984–85, his health broke down to the point where he could hardly speak (his critics in New Delhi dubbed him the "unspeakable" chief minister of Tamil Nadu). His entourage, male and female, interpreted his wishes through lipreading and movements of his eyes (and sometimes his eyelids) and hands.

The Tamil separatist groups in Sri Lanka all had their supporters among the political parties of Tamil Nadu, the government and opposition parties alike. None of the Tamil Nadu political parties was able to keep the peace among the rival Sri Lankan Tamil groups, whose internecine warfare was by now a prominent feature of the politics of the Tamils of Sri Lanka. In addition, the support given from Tamil Nadu was essential in sustaining the Tamil separatist activities operating in the north and east of the island against the Sri Lankan security forces.

Guerrilla and terrorist attacks against the security forces were generally repulsed. Most of these attacks, however, were now directed against unarmed Sinhalese civilians in an attempt to demoralize the civilian population in the remoter areas of the country in the north central and eastern regions. The most ferocious of such attacks had occurred on 14 May 1985, when a heavily armed group of terrorists made a surprise raid on Anuradhapura, killing nearly 150 civilians. It included an attack on the precincts of the sacred bodhi tree there, one of the most venerated sites of the Buddhist world. Attacks on civilians became more frequent thereafter. A new pattern was perceptible in these attacks. Sinhalese peasants in the east of the island were the targets of raids by Liberation Tigers of Tamil Eelam (LTTE) hit squads especially during religious festivals or on full moon days, when the villagers were most vulnerable to surprise attacks. Scores of men, women, and children were killed in these raids.

By this time Tamil separatist groups had become a formidable guerrilla force, much stronger than their Indian mentors had believed they would ever be. The Sri Lankan government for its part was compelled to divert a steadily increasing proportion of its annual budget to the expansion and equipping of its armed forces. Military action against these Tamil separatist groups in the north and east was escalated. Equipped with arms purchased from Pakistan and China, and trained either in Pakistan or in Sri Lanka by Israeli and British mercenaries, the Sri Lankan armed services were becoming more impressive fighting units than they had ever been before.

As clashes between these groups and the security forces became more frequent and casualties increased, there was a return to the policy initiated by Indira Gandhi of a diplomatic offensive against Sri Lanka. Propaganda campaigns conducted through its embassies and high commissions abroad accusing the government of human rights violations in its military campaigns against Tamil separatists were resumed, all part of a policy of "moral" sanctions aimed at persuading Sri Lanka to return to the bargaining table. The Indian embassy in Washington and the Indian high commissions in Ottawa and London, in the meantime, continued to be centers of support for Tamil separatist groups operating in those countries. Indian newspapers, led by the *Hindu,* gave their support to this government-inspired campaign. At a different level, the Sri Lankan government found traditional Western arms suppliers reluctant to sell arms to Sri Lankan forces, and most of the Western powers were unwilling also to provide training facilities on any large scale for them. All of them were anxious not to give offense to India.

Romesh Bhandari and a Fresh Start

The new man Sri Lankan politicians and diplomats had to deal with in New Delhi, Romesh Bhandari, provided a contrast in style, substance, and outlook to his predecessor. In an interview he gave a well-known Indian journal in April 1986—after he had left office—Bhandari stated that "early in the new administration" it was decided to give high priority to developing a neighborhood policy, "and a new thrust in good neighbourliness."[8] He had tried to force the pace of Indian diplomacy to accomplish in "one year what should normally have taken three years. . . . New initiatives particularly towards the neighbours had to be telescoped in[to] a span of 200 days." These bold foreign policy initiatives were designed to project an image of Rajiv Gandhi as "a great conciliator," on a regional basis no less than within the country.[9] The formulation of foreign policy moved from the Ministry of External Affairs to Bhandari and a circle of advisers around Gandhi in the prime minister's office and elsewhere. The policy planning committee Parathasarathy headed, and Parathasarathy himself, were edged out of the decision-making process.

Bhandari was closely identified with these new policies, including the ones on Sri Lanka we discuss in this chapter. At the time he took over as India's principal negotiator on Sri Lankan affairs, relations between the two countries had been soured by misunderstandings and misapprehensions on both sides. On the Indian side there was the feeling that Jayewardene had not tried hard enough to win support in Sri Lanka for the agreements between him and the Indian government negotiated through G. Parathasarathy over the last months of 1983. As for Sri Lanka, Mrs. Gandhi was seen, and known, to be encouraging and manipulating Tamil separatist activists living in India to further India's strategic advantage in its quest for regional dominance. In particular, her, Parathasarathy's, and other Indian officials' refusal to acknowledge the existence of "bases" and training facilities for Sri Lankan Tamil separatists in Tamil Nadu and elsewhere—indeed she expressly denied the existence of such "bases and facilities"—was viewed as a cynical exploitation of separatist agitation in a neighboring country when a diametrically opposite policy of harsh measures was being pursued in the Punjab against Sikh separatists. Suspicion of her objectives in her mediation in the Sri Lankan conflict was compounded by Parathasarathy's patent failure to distance himself adequately from the importunate TULF to give greater credibility to his role as mediator.

Thus when Jayewardene traveled to Delhi to meet Rajiv Gandhi in June 1985 he went with great expectations. He naturally assumed that the assassination of Mrs. Gandhi had brought home to the Indian establishment, in the most unmistakable manner, the dangers inherent in the encouragement of separatism and separatists. He dismissed Kursheed Alam Khan's outburst as an aberration and preferred to rely on the discussions Rajiv Gandhi had with Lalith Athulathmudali and the new Indian prime minister's assurance that he was intent on a fresh start and on a more conciliatory policy toward India's neighbors than his imperious mother. Above all he believed that the level of political support that the young Rajiv Gandhi enjoyed in the country and within the Indian parliament was so high that he could initiate changes of policy without meeting any overt obstruction from those associated with India's Sri Lankan policy under his mother.

Rajiv Gandhi was at the height of his personal popularity at this stage. The warmth of his welcome to Jayewardene was quite a contrast to the cool if correct attitude of his mother. He found Sonia Gandhi a gracious hostess. Thus their official discussions took place in a greatly improved atmosphere. The Sri Lankan president, in fact, was touched by Rajiv Gandhi's informality and readily agreed to join him in a quick visit by helicopter to Bangladesh to view the flood damage in that country.

Jayewardene had set himself the task of explaining that Sri Lanka's ethnic conflict had two aspects, external and internal. India was directly involved in the first through the support—moral, financial, and in arms and military training—afforded to Sri Lankan Tamils on Indian soil; she was also involved in the internal aspect but only to the extent that the Tamil parties looked to India's mediation on their behalf to reach a settlement they could accept. While Mrs. Gandhi had insisted on India and India alone taking on a mediatory role in India's ethnic conflict, she had contrived to avoid discussion of the external factor, and especially India's involvement in it, in all her negotiations with Jayewardene and his government. It was too much to expect that this aspect of India's Sri Lankan policy would change immediately, but the Sri Lankan president succeeded in bringing it into the discussion with Rajiv Gandhi indirectly and subtly. Expressing a willingness to curb the activities of Sri Lankan Tamil separatists, especially their terrorist groups operating from Tamil Nadu, Rajiv Gandhi responded to Jayewardene's proposals much more positively than the latter had reason to expect given the well-established Indian policy of denying the existence of such groups operating from Indian soil. Jayewardene persisted with his proposal for joint patrols of the Palk Strait by the two navies. Rajiv Gandhi offered, instead, to step up Indian patrols off the Tamil Nadu coast.

Details of a possible political settlement came up for discussion. Jayewardene urged that the consensus reached at the abortive APC, which had concluded its sessions in December 1984, be treated as the starting point. Because of the far-reaching constitutional issues involved in the resolution of the Sri Lanka conflict the two heads of government agreed that a Sri Lankan team led by the president's brother, H. W. Jayewardene, and an Indian team led by K. Paskaran, the Indian attorney general, and including some officials from the Ministry of External Affairs should meet to examine these in some detail.

Shortly after Jayewardene returned home, Bhandari arrived in Colombo for talks with the Sri Lankan president. These resulted in a major breakthrough when Bhandari persuaded the Sri Lankan president to let his government begin talks with the several Tamil separatist groups, who were engaged in violent confrontations with the Sri Lankan security forces. Hitherto the government had negotiated only with the TULF, and had refused to talk to the separatist activists on the grounds that doing so would give the latter a legitimacy they were not entitled to have. The fact was that the TULF was rapidly losing ground to its younger and more radical rivals, and the decision to engage in discussions with them was, in fact, a belated recognition of political realities.

Romesh Bhandari's arrival coincided, more or less, with that of a new Indian high commissioner to Sri Lanka, Jyotindra Nath Dixit. The latter was in his late forties at the time of his appointment to Sri Lanka. A short, stocky, and enormously self-confident man, he had served in two very sensitive posts prior to his arrival in Colombo. His previous posting had been to Afghanistan as Indian ambassador, where he was known to be a staunch supporter of Mrs. Gandhi's soft line on the Soviet invasion of that country. But more important in view of Sri Lanka's own internal divisions and ethnic conflicts was his role in the dismemberment of Pakistan in the early 1970s. It was not known in Colombo at the time of Dixit's arrival that he had been directly involved in fashioning the administrative mechanisms for channeling Indian assistance to the resistance groups in the then East Pakistan in their opposition to the Pakistani military regime. Once the Indian intervention succeeded in its objectives and Bangladesh came into existence, he had been sent to Dhaka as deputy chief of mission but it was known in Dhaka that it was Dixit in combination with the first secretary (a woman named Arundathy Ghosh) and not the high commissioner (the aging Subimal Dutt[10]) who made the decisions. In short, he had been present at the creation of Bangladesh, the only successful separatist agitation in the postcolonial world up to very recent times.

Dixit proved to be one of the most astute diplomats India has ever sent to Sri Lanka. Apart from the Indian high commissioner's traditional contacts with Tamil groups on the island, he endeavored to influence Sri Lankan government policy in the Indian interest by cultivating a wider range of government politicians than his predecessors had attempted. Indeed, few if any of the latter had so great an influence on the making and implementation of Indian policy on Sri Lanka as he had. His influence increased with every passing month until it reached its peak in 1987 and 1988.

Bhandari quite deliberately set out to win the trust of the Sri Lankan president and his colleagues by demonstrating a sensitive understanding of their difficulties. The fresh start he had in mind would begin with a change of emphasis: Parathasarathy's policy of treating the TULF as the main spokesmen of Sri Lankan Tamil interests was to be abandoned, and talks would begin with the other Tamil separatist activist groups who by now had far greater influence in Tamil politics in the island. This innovation in the negotiation process required very careful preparatory diplomacy. Bhandari himself recognized the strength of the Sri Lankan government's arguments against it. Jayewardene had initially raised objections. He had asked Bhandari whether the Indian government would have negotiated with similar separatist groups in his own country, especially where some of the leaders of these separatist groups were terrorists wanted by the police for a wide range of charges, from gang robbery to responsibility for the 1975 killing of the then mayor of Jaffna, a fellow Tamil and a senior politician of the governing Sri Lanka Freedom Party

(SLFP). (A year later, the well-known Indian journal *India Today* in its issue of 30 June 1986 carried a prominent profile of Prabhakaran and an interview with him in which he proclaimed the killing of Mayor Durayappa as his first "military operation.") Jayewardene had asked him whether any government would consent to speak on equal terms to such individuals and groups.[11]

Bhandari won Jayewardene over by emphasizing the need for pragmatism in Sri Lanka's own national interest. He recalled spending several evenings talking things over with the president until at last he agreed to the proposal that representatives of the Sri Lankan government should meet Tamil separatist activists for discussions. Bhandari's confidence-building exercises thus resulted in a major breakthrough, when the Sri Lankan government agreed, officially, to begin negotiations with all the main—and competing—Tamil separatist groups, in addition to the TULF, something it had hitherto refused to do on the grounds that this would give these armed separatist groups a legitimacy they were not entitled to have.

Reflecting on these discussions in April 1991, Bhandari felt that his greatest achievement in the early weeks of his negotiations in Sri Lanka lay in thus persuading the Sri Lankan president to change his—and his government's—policy of refusing to talk with these groups. In making this change, Bhandari conceded, the Sri Lankan political leadership was taking a tremendous risk, something many Indian officials and politicians did not fully recognize.[12]

The increasing number of spokesmen for the Tamil minority that followed from this discussion had some predictable consequences, beginning naturally enough with a struggle among them for dominance and a quest for the position of sole spokesman. The TULF, the most moderate of the Tamil groups, found itself edged out of any position of influence. Instead the lead went at various stages to other groups with a bewildering range of acronyms: the People's Liberation Army of Tamil Eelam (PLOTE), the Tamil Eelam Liberation Organization (TELO), the Liberation Tigers of Tamil Eelam (LTTE), and Eelam People's Revolutionary Liberation Front (EPRLF). These were all assiduously cultivated by the Research and Analysis Wing, which, nominally a branch of the Cabinet Secretariat, was actually very much a part of the Indian prime minister's office. Better known by its acronym RAW, it was the Indian equivalent of the U.S. Central Intelligence Agency (CIA). RAW provided Tamil groups located in India with arms and arms training with the knowledge, if not under the aegis, of the Indian government. The TELO group was a special favorite of the RAW. The LTTE eventually pushed ahead to a position of dominance largely because of its strong and expanding base in Jaffna. The three leaders of the strongest of these groups, Prabhakaran, Uma Maheswaran, and Sri Sabaratnam, were soon engaged in a bitter and increasingly violent rivalry for the position of principal speaker for the Tamil cause. Prabhakaran eventually won the day. But that is another story.

The Talks at Thimpu

Because of the far-reaching constitutional issues involved in the resolution of Sri Lanka's ethnic conflicts, discussions were arranged between a Sri Lankan team led by H. W. Jayewardene and an Indian team led by K. Paskaran, the Indian attorney general. Jayewardene's team included other lawyers and officials, as did the Indian team, with the difference that the latter also had some officials from the Ministry of External Affairs. Starting around August 1983, H. W. Jayewardene had traveled as a special envoy to several countries in Asia (including India). He was now entrusted with the task of explaining to the Indian attorney general and his team how the nature of Sri Lanka's Constitution imposed limits on legislation devised to resolve the island's ethnic conflict.

This meeting, held at Hyderabad House, Delhi, on 15 and 16 June, was an exploratory discussion at which the nature of the Sri Lankan Constitution, and the difficulties it appeared to pose in regard to accommodating a second tier of government with a wider territorial range and greater power than the district councils established in 1981, were reviewed in considerable detail. The Sri Lankan side cautioned their Indian counterparts about the formidable problems posed by the entrenched clauses of the Constitution which sought to guarantee its unitary nature and protect the sovereignty of the people in fashioning the structure and power of such councils. One of the specific issues, raised avowedly at the request of the TULF, was whether a chief minister of a provincial council (established by the amalgamation of two or more contiguous districts) should of necessity be a member of Parliament (MP). The Indian delegation argued that one need not be an MP, while the Sri Lankan delegation insisted that a careful reading of the relevant portions of the Constitution would show that it would require a referendum if someone other than an MP were to be appointed a chief minister. The talks ended with the two sides agreeing to disagree. The constitutional issues that needed to be addressed at political discussions between the Sri Lankan government and representatives of Tamil opinion, to be held under Indian aegis, had been clarified.

Once the decision was made to hold talks between the Sri Lankan government and the various Tamil political groups involved in the conflict, the question of a venue arose. Bhandari's anxiety that the talks be as wide-ranging as possible was accompanied by a concern to protect their confidentiality. The decision to hold the talks in Thimpu in Bhutan was made because the venue would be as isolated a place as one could get in South Asia. While special telegraph lines were available between Thimpu and Delhi, no journalists would be permitted entry to Bhutan to cover the talks.

The "cessation of hostilities" announced on 18 June was planned as the first of a four-stage negotiation process that included a stoppage or substantial reduction in violence, to be followed by talks leading to a possible settlement. All this was expected to take eight weeks. The two governments felt, however, that speed was essential if the momentum generated by the announcement of 18 June was to be sustained. The decision was taken to hold the talks in Thimpu in the second week of July, at least a month ahead of schedule.

There has been as yet no coherent account of what happened at Thimpu, except for references to the four demands put forward by the Tamil groups during discussions there. These demands have received considerable publicity in journals and newspapers sympathetic to the Tamil cause. The discussion in this chapter is not meant to be an exhaustive review of the Thimpu negotiations, but to the extent that this is the first account, brief though it may be, based on a study of the official minutes kept by the Sri Lankan delegation, it will fill a gap in our knowledge of the Indo–Sri Lankan negotiations of the mid-1980s.[13]

The minutes reveal that Bhutanese foreign minister Lyon po Dawa Tsering proposed at the very outset that the discussions should be informal, and that in order to ensure this there should be no chairman. We are not aware whether this decision was made in consultation with the Indian or the Sri Lankan government, or both, or on his own. While this decision reduced if not eliminated time-consuming wrangling on seating arrangements and a formal agenda, the lack of an agenda proved to be a great drawback in conducting the negotiations. This was because the Tamil groups represented at the talks were reluctant participants. It would appear that most of these groups, with the possible exception of the TULF, had not been consulted about advancing the date of the discussions and they seemed to have been offended by this. Very likely they suspected that the two governments had agreed on a deal at their expense and that the new timetable reflected what amounted to a new political reality. This may explain why none of the more important leaders of the separatist groups decided to attend the talks. Except in the case of the TULF, which sent its most senior members, the Tamil groups were represented by persons who ranked very low in the party hierarchy. Thus the mood of the Tamil groups was, from the outset, one of distrust and noncooperation. They were aware that public rallies were being held in Jaffna protesting against the talks—the rallies were led by the LTTE and its allies—and taking their cue from this they indulged in a concerted campaign of obstruction, making repeated protests about alleged breaches of the "cessation of hostilities" by the Sri Lankan security forces and the police. From the beginning it was evident that the TULF had been reduced in status among the competing claimants to the title of representatives of Tamil opinion. Symbolic of this loss of precedence was the relegation of the TULF leaders to the less prominent seats at the conference table. They did not initiate the acts of obstruction indulged in by their younger rivals but they thought it politic, nevertheless, to support these latter in these tactics.

Once it was known that the Tamil representation—so far as the more dynamic and politically credible groups were concerned—would be at a second- or third-string level, none of the senior politicians of the government showed any desire to join, much less lead, Sri Lanka's official delegation. Thus H. W. Jayewardene was chosen to lead what appeared to be a "nonpolitical" team consisting of lawyers and senior officials.

When the talks began it was evident that the absence of an agenda had only served to push time-consuming obstructive tactics to the formal discussion stage rather than to the preliminary phases of the talks. There was very little serious discussion of substantive issues on the first day. On the second day (9 July), H. W. Jayewardene began his presentation of the government's proposals, but he had hardly completed this when the issue of alleged violations of the "cessation of hostilities" was raised and he was asked for an assurance—as the government's spokesman—from Colombo that these would cease. Much time was taken up on this matter and, even after a conciliatory official statement was issued, the discussions still concentrated on these charges rather than on the government's proposals. The discussions on 9 July set the pattern for the delibera-tions over the next three days.

Jayewardene did outline the government's proposals: a strengthening of the powers of district councils and the establishment of a provincial council for the areas of the north and east where the Tamils lived. This offer, which was meant to be the prelude to a process of political bar-gaining, naturally fell far short of the demands of most of the Tamil groups, the TULF included. It was left to the TULF, in fact, to respond to the government's proposals, made on this occasion. They were in no position, however, to concentrate on these to the exclusion of discussions on alleged violations of the "cessation of hostilities" which the other Tamil groups persisted in raising at every available opportunity. Over the next two days Jayewardene, supported by H. L. de Silva (himself an eminent lawyer), would emphasize the significance of the changes in policy embodied in the proposals they submitted, but there was no effort on the part of the Tamil representatives to treat these as they should have been treated, as the early stages in a process of political bargaining. When a formal response was eventually made (on 13 July) it came in the form of four demands which were described as their irreducible minimum. This response, which had been drafted by the lawyers who were serving as advisers to the Tamil groups, read as follows:

It is our considered view that any meaningful solution to the national question of the island must be based on the following four cardinal principles:
1. Recognition of the Tamils of Sri Lanka as a distinct nationality;
2. Recognition of an identified Tamil homeland and the guarantee of its territorial integrity;
3. Based on the above, recognition of the inalienable right of self-determination of the Tamil nation;
4. Recognition of the right to full citizenship and other fundamental democratic rights of all Tamils, who look upon the Island as their country.[14]

The discussion on 13 July ended on an inconclusive note as the last three paragraphs of the minutes kept by the Sri Lankan delegation would show:

Mr Amirthalingam stated that the 6 delegations on his side had spoken with one voice and placed before the S[ri] L[ankan] delegation the basic principles on which a solution acceptable to them should be based. The major youth groups had been represented at the conference. For the first time the voice of the Tamil youth had been heard. They would take back to their organizations the proposals made and discuss them further at the next meeting, which will be fixed on a date convenient to both sides. He said that the S[ri] L[anka] delegation had heard the unanimous voice of the Tamil nation and they awaited a response to their united voice.

A general discussion ensued thereafter about a likely date for the continuation of the meeting.

After consulting the Hon. Foreign Minister of Bhutan, the next conference was fixed to commence on Monday, August 12, 1985 at Thimpu.

In the meantime the confidentiality of the talks had been breached when the Madras-based *Hindu* carried detailed accounts of the discussions in its issue of 13 July. The leak could have been from any one of the Tamil groups. All of them had contacts in the Indian press, especially the *Hindu*. Given the nature of the persons involved in these discussions, it would have been impossible to maintain the sort of secrecy Bhandari had hoped for.

When the talks resumed on 12 August, H. W. Jayewardene read out the government's response to the four demands set out by the Tamil groups on 13 July. The ten-page document sought "to explain the relevance of the Government's proposals to the four principles."

Firstly, we wish to observe that there is a wide range of meanings that can attach to the concepts and ideas embodied in the four principles and our response to them would accordingly depend on the meaning and significance that is sought to be applied to them. *Secondly* we must state emphatically that if the first three principles are to be taken at their face value and given their accepted legal meaning they are wholly unacceptable to the government. They must be rejected for the reason that they constitute a negation of the sovereignty and territorial integrity of Sri Lanka; they are detrimental to a united Sri Lanka and are inimical to the interests of the several communities, ethnic and religious, in our country.

But in so far as these ideas and concepts can be given a meaning and construction which does not entail the creation of a separate state, or a structure of government that is indistinguishable from a separate state, we do believe that there is room for a fruitful exchange of views which can result in a settlement of the problems that beset us. . . .

[W]e do not acknowledge the right or status of any persons present here to represent or negotiate on behalf of all Tamils living in Sri Lanka. Those of the Tamil community of recent Indian origin who are commonly referred to as Indian Tamils have their own accredited representatives and the Government had reached certain understandings with them in regard to their problems and these do not need to be discussed here.

Despite the firm rejection of the first three principles in the form in which they had been presented on 13 July, the official statement indicated that there were alternative meanings to these which the Sri Lankan government would be able "to accept and recognize."

Any hopes that the opening offered by this statement could serve as a point of departure for a discussion of mutually acceptable forms of devolution of power were soon dashed when the Tamil delegates insisted on adjournment of the discussions until the evening of 13 August. They proceeded to spend the whole of the sessions of 13 August and nearly two hours of 14 August on a dogged reiteration of their original demands of 13 July, describing them as the irreducible minimum. In addition, objection was taken to a sentence in the official statement of 12 August in which the six Tamil delegations were described as "the six groups representing interests of certain Tamil groups in Sri Lanka." This, they argued, was a calculated denial of the legitimacy of the status of the six Tamil delegations, who in their view were indeed the sole representatives of all Tamils in Sri Lanka. They insisted that the discussions be held up until the Sri Lankan government formally "accepted the legitimacy of the six Tamil delegations as the sole representatives of the Tamil Eelam or the Tamil nation." Since it was almost certain that the Sri Lankan government would not accept the right of these groups to speak on behalf of the Indian Tamils, whose leadership were political allies of the government, there was very little hope of the talks continuing. On 16 August, even before they received a response to their demand of 14 August, the Tamil groups walked out of the conference, on the grounds that there had been a serious breach of the "cessation of hostilities" in the north of Sri Lanka on 16 August.

The talks had collapsed by 17 August. Nevertheless Bhandari was loath to concede failure and he persuaded the Sri Lankan delegation to remain behind in Thimpu for a few more days in the hope that he could get the talks resumed.[15] When he found the Tamil delegations still in an obstructive mood, an exasperated Bhandari ordered the expulsion of a London-based Tamil lawyer who had come to Thimpu to advise the LTTE group and their allies; in addition the Indian government canceled the visas of two other advisers to the Tamil groups, two men who were living in self-imposed exile in Tamil Nadu. The eventual failure of the attempt to expel them from India exposed the narrowness of the limits within which even the Indian government could operate given the depth of the support these men enjoyed in Tamil Nadu. Thus Bhandari's first exercise in personal diplomacy had ended in deadlock. But he was unwilling to leave it at that.

The Delhi Accord

He kept up the momentum begun by the Thimpu talks. First, he persuaded the Sri Lankan government to allow the "cessation of hostilities" negotiated prior to the discussions, originally for a period of three months, to be extended again. It had been scheduled to expire in the middle of September. Next the Sri Lankan delegation to Thimpu was urged to stay behind in Delhi for further discussions. While Bhandari preferred to deal with the TULF alone as the principal representatives of moderate Tamil opinion, negotiations with the other Tamil groups were continued and he was in communication with them throughout the discussions he had in Delhi in the latter part of August with the Sri Lankan delegation led by H. W. Jayewardene. These talks proved to be much more fruitful than the Thimpu discussions, in the sense that they yielded a framework for a realistic devolution of power in Sri Lanka that would meet some of the Tamil demands. They were based on the detailed proposals sent to Delhi on 17 April through Foreign Minister Hameed, and on modifications and additions to these decided upon in the course of Bhandari's negotiations in Colombo in May 1985.

One of the most significant features of this meticulously crafted agreement was that the unit of devolution was to be a province (there are nine provinces in Sri Lanka), no longer a district (of which there were 25). Also, the powers to be devolved on these provincial units were much wider than those offered earlier by the Sri Lankan government in discussions with Indian mediators and Tamil representatives. The complex new structures agreed upon constituted a major concession on the part of the Sri Lankan government to the demands of Tamils of the north and east of the island. The draft accord, which came to be known in official circles as the Delhi Accord of August 1985, was based on the consensus reached during the discussions Bhandari conducted in Delhi on that occasion, mediating between the official Sri Lankan delegation and the representatives of the Tamil groups in India. Initialed on 30 August, this draft accord became the basis of all future negotiations between them on Sri Lanka's ethnic problems insofar as these concerned the Tamil minority.[16]

The actual signing of the accord that Bhandari hoped would crown his mediatory efforts confronted a major obstacle in the reluctance if not refusal of most Tamil groups who were represented at Thimpu to give their consent once it became known that the LTTE was opposed to it. The longer they held out, the more difficult it became for the TULF to commit itself publicly to an agreement in the formulation of which they, among others, had been consulted and to which they had given their concurrence in Delhi.

Rajiv Gandhi's Peace Accords

The political settlement Bhandari was negotiating in Sri Lanka on behalf of the Indian government was the third in a series initiated by Rajiv Gandhi in the early months of his prime ministership. Discussions had begun with the political leadership of the separatist groups in the Punjab and in Assam, with Rajiv Gandhi himself as the principal negotiator.[17] By 25 July, Rajiv Gandhi had signed an accord aimed at healing the Punjab's suppurating political crisis.[18] Less than three weeks later he signed another on Assam,[19] and chose the occasion of the celebration of India's independence on 15 April 1985 to announce this.[20]

Rajiv Gandhi was on the crest of a wave of popularity. The euphoria of those early weeks of his honeymoon with the electorate did not last long. The assassination of Sant Harchand Singh Longowal, his cosignatory on the Punjab Accord, coming as it did less than a month after its signing, should have shattered any illusions he may have had on bringing peace to strife-torn Punjab. He refused to let this grim reminder of the pervasiveness of Punjab's political violence turn him back to any early return to the policies his mother had followed. A general election was held in Punjab, where, despite attempts by extremist groups to disrupt the polls (as had happened in Assam two years earlier), two-thirds of the registered voters went to the polls and gave the Longowal group of the Akali Dal a resounding victory. Congress I (the main Congress faction calling itself the Indira Congress) suffered a setback. Although early signs were propitious, the promises made in the accord were not fulfilled, and the situation drifted to a state of political paralysis accompanied by a reversion to the preaccord cycle of violence and repression in which thousands of lives were lost. In Assam, however, Rajiv Gandhi's peace accord achieved some success in giving that isolated state a measure of political stability, and the people at large more peace, than they had enjoyed for some time. The opposition groups that won power at the general election of 1985 succeeded in holding on although they had only a plurality at the polls.[21] More important, unlike the case in the Punjab, no attempt was made to undermine its position in order to build a coalition around the Congress I.

As for Sri Lanka, there was a qualitative difference in that Rajiv Gandhi was negotiating an agreement between two sovereign states on an ethnic conflict in one of them (Sri Lanka) involving a minority (the Tamils), which had affective links with the people of a state of the other, the Indian union (Tamil Nadu). From the resumption of talks with the Sri Lankan government in the second quarter of 1985, his objective, very clearly, was the drafting and signing of yet another peace accord. He very nearly succeeded in this objective less than two months after the signing of the Punjab Accord. His principal negotiator had succeeded in gaining the agreement of representatives of the Sri Lankan government to a framework of proposals for a resolution of the ethnic conflict in the island, the draft accord that came to be known in official circles as the Delhi Accord, initialed on 30 August by representatives of the two governments.

The signing of the accord was expected to take a few weeks, a month or two at most, but it became evident soon enough that representatives of the Tamil minority were reluctant to do so. The LTTE, the group with greater political support and by far the most violent, refused to endorse it. The TULF, which had been consulted—along with the others—in the framing of the Delhi Accord and had given its concurrence to it, was unwilling to take the risks involved in ignoring the wishes of the LTTE on this matter. The kidnapping and killing of two TULF stalwarts, both former MPs resident in the principal town in the Tamil-dominated Jaffna peninsula of Sri Lanka's northern province, Jaffna, between 1 and 3 September 1985 by the LTTE, was a clear reminder of the perils involved in disregarding their views. Coming as it did so soon after the assassination of Longowal in Punjab, it ensured that Tamil representatives would not sign the Delhi Accord.

As we shall see in later chapters of this book, the peace accord Rajiv Gandhi had in mind for Sri Lanka in 1985 came two years later and after tortuous negotiations between the two governments, and with representatives of Tamil interests in Sri Lanka. The two-year gap between the signing of the first of the accords, the Punjab Accord, and the third, the Indo–Sri Lanka Accord, should have provided time for reflection on the strengths and weaknesses of this mode of peacemaking. There is very little evidence to suggest anything of the sort was done in New Delhi, or for that matter in Sri Lanka.

Notes

1. Bernard Tillakaratne, interview with the author, 2 February 1987.
2. Lalith Athulathmudali, interview with the author, February 1985.
3. A copy of this letter is available in the J. R. Jayewardene MSS.
4. For Khursheed Alam Khan's speech, see *Hansard* [Lok Sabha], official record, 29 April 1985, cols. 362–71.
5. The Indian newspaper *New Today*, reporting this debate in the Lok Sabha in its issue of 30 April 1985, stated that "Khan strayed out of the prepared text to make a reference to the clashes between Muslims and Tamils in the Eastern Province."
6. *Hansard* [Lok Sabha], official record (debate), 29 April 1985, col. 365.
7. Ibid., cols. 368–69.
8. "Interview with Romesh Bhandari," *Illustrated Weekly of India*, 13 April 1986.
9. Ibid.
10. Subimal Dutt joined the Indian Foreign Ministry as secretary of the Commonwealth Relations Department in July 1947 and served in that capacity until April 1952. He then went to Bonn as India's first ambassador to the Federal German Republic; returning to Delhi in 1954, he served as foreign secretary until April 1961. He left the Foreign Ministry in April 1961 on appointment as Indian ambassador to the Soviet Union.
11. Romesh Bhandari, interview with the author, Delhi, 29 April 1991.
12. Ibid.
13. The following discussion is based on the minutes of the discussions, a copy of which was lent to me by Mr. H. L. de Silva, P. C. I am deeply grateful to him for this kind gesture.
14. For a comprehensive statement of the Tamil viewpoint at Thimpu, see N. Satyendra, "Thimpu Declaration: The Path of Reason," *Tamil Times*, 6(4), February 1987, 11–14.
15. Romesh Bhandari, interview with the author, 29 April 1991.
16. The draft framework of the terms of accord and understanding was initialed on 30 August 1985, by R. Mathai for the Indian side and by E. F. Dias Abeysinghe, secretary of the Sri Lankan delegation. The Sri Lankan delegation had further talks with senior

officials of the Indian Ministry of External Affairs on 10–13 September 1985 on conditions of implementation of this accord and on issues relating to the means of restoring normal civilian administration.

17. The negotiations on the Punjab Accord are reviewed in three short articles in the *Indian Express*, "The Punjab Accord I, Impasse was broken in April"; "The Punjab Accord II, Territorial issue most pertinent"; "The Punjab Accord III, Why Dal seeks poll postponement." *Indian Express*, 15, 16, 17 August 1985.

18. For the text of the Punjab Accord see *Indian Express*, Chandigarh, 25 July 1985.

19. On the problems of Assam, see M. Weiner, *Sons of the Soil: Migration and Ethnic Conflict in India* (Princeton, N.J.: Princeton University Press, 1978); S. Baruah, "Immigration, Ethnic Conflict and Political Turmoil in Assam, 1979–1985," *Asian Survey* 26, no. 11 (November 1986); and Jaswant Singh, "Assam's Crisis of Leadership," *Asian Survey* 24, no. 10 (October 1984).

20. See *Indian Express*, 16 August 1985, which also carried the text of the Assam Accord. An official statement on the Assam Accord was made in the Lok Sabha on the same day by S. B. Chavan, the home minister, who read the text of the Assam Accord into the official record of the Lok Sabha. See Lok Sabha, official record, 16 August 1985, cols. 296–300.

21. The Assam elections of December 1985 are reviewed in S. Baruah, "Lessons of Assam," *Economic and Political Weekly*, 15 February 1986; see also *India Today*, 15 January 1986, 22–35.

9

Refining the Delhi Accord, 1986–87

Bhandari's Retirement

RELATIONS BETWEEN Sri Lanka and India had deteriorated once again in the last quarter of 1985. The overt support given to Tamil separatists in Sri Lanka by all the major political groups in Tamil Nadu continued to be the main issue. In locking themselves into the politics of Sri Lankan Tamil separatist agitation, they were also drawn into the fierce factionalism that was part of the Sri Lankan Tamil political scene. Tamil Nadu continued to serve three indispensable purposes for the Sri Lankan Tamil separatist groups, as a sanctuary, base for training and supply of arms, and source of funds. Thanks in large part to the support they had in and from Tamil Nadu, the Tamil separatist groups, especially the Liberation Tigers of Tamil Eelam (LTTE) and its ally the Eelam Revolutionary Organization of Students, became a formidable guerrilla force, much stronger than their Indian mentors thought they would ever be.

The LTTE was also helped by a decision taken by the Sri Lankan government in July 1985, as part of an understanding reached with India prior to the Thimpu talks, that its forces in the Jaffna peninsula would be kept within their barracks or camps. Originally intended to last for two months, this arrangement was later extended, in response to Indian pressure, for three more months. The LTTE took advantage of this to mine all the roads leading out of the camps and proceeded thereafter to barricade them. Soon makeshift barricades were converted into concrete bunkers. The result was that the LTTE established effective control over the town of Jaffna if not the Jaffna peninsula itself, since the Sri Lankan army's movements were seriously hampered thereafter by these barricades. The units of the Sri Lankan army stationed in the fort of Jaffna could only be supplied by air.

The LTTE was emboldened by this shift in the military balance to embark on vigorous attacks in a hit-and-run campaign against the Sri Lankan forces, while attacks on softer targets, Sinhalese peasants in isolated settlements, became more frequent; simultaneously there was a ruthless program of eliminating its Tamil rivals. Sinhalese peasants in the remoter areas of the north central and eastern regions were among the principal targets. Such attacks became a serious political embarrassment to the Sri Lankan government, whose domestic critics regarded them as a demonstration of the futility of negotiations with India so long as the Indian government was unwilling to reciprocate by taking firm action against Sri Lankan Tamil separatist activists using Tamil Nadu as a base.

In addition, an increasing proportion of Sri Lanka's annual budget was diverted to the expansion and equipping of the armed services. Defense expenditure as a percentage of total government expenditure rose from 3.0 percent in 1982 to 3.80 percent, 4.8 percent, and 9.77 percent in 1983, 1984, and 1985. Along with it there was an escalation of military action against the Tamil separatist groups in the north and east of the island.[1] The Sri Lankan armed forces were now better equipped and better trained than before, with much of the training being done in Pakistan, while small groups of Israelis and British mercenaries honed the skills of special counterterrorist units in the army and police.

As clashes between the security forces and the Tamil separatist activists became more frequent and casualties, especially civilians, increased in number, the Indian government returned to the Indira Gandhi policy of a diplomatic offensive against Sri Lanka;[2] thus a propaganda campaign was launched through its embassies and high commissions abroad as well as Indian newspapers,[3] accusing the government of Sri Lanka of human rights violations, all part of a policy of "moral" sanctions aimed at persuading Sri Lanka to return to the bargaining table. Sri Lankan and Indian diplomats clashed at the United Nations in New York and Geneva. The Indian embassy in Washington and the high commissions in Ottawa and London, in the meantime, continued to be centers of support for Tamil separatist groups operating in those countries. In this regard the change from Indira Gandhi's time had made little or no difference.

Had the Indian government been more sensitive to the Sri Lankan government's difficulties, and made some unambiguous and noticeable effort to stop the use of Indian territory by the LTTE and others for their military activities, it would certainly have strengthened President Jayewardene's hand in his efforts to secure greater political support within Sri Lanka for a resumption of negotiations with the Tamil groups, or greater readiness to stop military action against the LTTE. In initialing the Delhi Accord on 30 August 1985, the Sri Lankan government had hoped that the Indians would be able to persuade the Tamil separatist groups to accept this as a significant step forward in the negotiating process. Also initialed, at the same time as the Delhi Accord, were the Conditions of Implementation of the Accord. These were designed to provide mechanisms for restoring normal civilian administration in the disturbed areas of the north and east. Neither the several separatist activist groups nor the more moderate Tamil United Liberation Front (TULF) had responded positively to the proposals in the Delhi Accord.

A Commonwealth Heads of Government meeting in the Bahamas gave President Jayewardene and the Indian prime minister the opportunity of reviewing the state of the Indian mediation in Sri Lanka. Aware that very little progress had been made since the initialing of the Delhi Accord on 30 August, Rajiv Gandhi returned to the familiar Indian policy of urging that more concessions be made by the Sri Lankan government, within the framework of the Delhi Accord, to make it more acceptable to the Tamils. The Sri Lankan president was not convinced that this would be very useful. For his part, he persisted with his proposal that the Indian government give serious consideration to a joint naval patrol to prevent the free flow of arms from India to Sri Lanka. Gandhi would make no promise on this score. Thus the deadlock continued.

The discussions in the Bahamas were also notable for a proposal for a Commonwealth mediatory initiative. Whether this came from Jayewardene himself, or whether he merely supported it when the head of the Commonwealth Secretariat, Sridath Ramphal,[5] suggested it, we do not know. We do know that Jayewardene sought to win Rajiv Gandhi's support for it. The latter, of course, was not interested, and said so to both Jayewardene and Ramphal, but the rejection was not so firm that Jayewardene felt he needed to drop the idea.[6] For a few more months he did cling to it, until a firmer rejection—by Gandhi and by others[7] in India as well—compelled him to abandon it altogether. Jayewardene was also thinking of secret talks with the Tamil groups in a new location away from India.

In the meantime the TULF leaders had had regular discussions with Indian officials, including Bhandari, and on occasion they were able to meet the prime minister himself. No amount of cajoling by the Indian government would persuade them to endorse the Delhi Accord. The TULF's repudiation of the Delhi Accord took the form of a memorandum dated 1 December, which the TULF leadership in Madras sent to the Indian prime minister.[8] The proposals incorporated in that document went back to the first three demands made at Thimpu on 13 July. The centerpiece of the document was a constitutional framework for Sri Lanka, overtly federal in character and incorporating the concept of a Tamil ethno-region encompassing the Northern and Eastern Provinces, a political manifestation of the demand for the traditional homelands of the Tamils. For the first time their case—such as it was—for treating the concept of the traditional homelands of the Tamils as a political demand based on "historical" data, discussed earlier, was introduced into the negotiations between the two countries.[9] Equally important, the federal system outlined in great detail in that document envisaged a "central government" with very limited powers. Power would devolve on the "states" of the "union."

Bhandari was scheduled to visit Colombo in early February 1986 for another set of talks with the Sri Lankan government, but the visit was abruptly cancelled. Indeed, he had traveled as far south as Madras when the cancellation of the visit was announced as an indication of India's disapproval of Sri Lanka's policy of a military response against the Tamil separatists and their violence. Bhandari retired from office within a few weeks, but, as we shall see, he continued to be associated in the making and implementation of Indian policy on Sri Lanka till well into 1986. During his brief spell as foreign secretary he had achieved a great deal in putting India's relations with Sri Lanka on a more constructive basis. Despite the failure to have the Delhi Accord signed, he was recognized in the island as an unusual man among Indian diplomats and administrators, someone who had endeavored to be as close as one could get to a neutral arbiter.

An Indian Model

Bhandari's successor as foreign secretary, A. P. Venkateswaran, was a southern Indian Brahmin who had much less rapport with Rajiv Gandhi, and greater sympathy for the Tamil activists of Sri Lanka. From the outset he contrived to return policy formulation to the Ministry of External Affairs, where it had been before Bhandari moved it to the prime minister's office. He also placed his trust in the TULF and virtually pushed them into taking the lead in negotiations with the Sri Lankan government. The TULF leaders, living in exile in Madras, were not unwilling to play the role Venkateswaran had devised for them. They were justifiably terrified at the prospect of antagonizing the more aggressive Tamil groups. Venkateswaran called representatives of these latter to Delhi and persuaded them to let the TULF take the lead in the discussions with the Sri Lankan government scheduled to be held in Colombo later in the year.[10]

The structure and details of the devolution package drawn up under Bhandari were reviewed through Venkateswaran's initiatives, and modifications were introduced to make the package more attractive to the Tamil representatives. As we have seen, the latter had been decidedly unenthusiastic about the framework of devolution negotiated between the two governments in 1985. Venkateswaran hit upon the idea of giving the Delhi Accord greater acceptability to the Tamils by using the Indian system as a model for Sri Lanka's devolutionary schemes. He believed that this subtle but very significant transformation—through the direct use of an Indian model—of the devolution package negotiated by Bhandari would appeal to the TULF because it was based on the Indian federal system, while it would be acceptable to President Jayewardene and his advisers because the central government in India was far more powerful than in most federations. The Indian system was often referred to as a quasi-federal rather than genuine federal structure. Besides, there was sufficient ambiguity in the new proposals to allow for bargaining and give and take, and for more compromise.[11]

Despite Venkateswaran's obvious sympathy for the Sri Lankan Tamils it took several weeks of negotiations with them before the Indian government could send an official delegation to Sri Lanka once more, to initiate further discussions on possible adjustments and modifications of the Delhi Accord. The new delegation was led by a minister of state not in the cabinet, P. Chidambaram, a young (forty) Tamil who aspired to a Congress-based leadership of Tamil Nadu, and K. Natwar Singh, Rajiv Gandhi's minister of state for external affairs. The key figure in the delegation was Chidambaram rather than the sauve and erudite Natwar Singh. Chidambaram's prominence in the negotiations, in combination with the replacement of Bhandari by Venkateswaran, gave the Indian negotiation process in Sri Lanka a distinctly southern Indian and Tamil flavor.[12]

The Chidambaram delegation arrived in Colombo on 30 April 1986 and held very intensive talks over the next five days. For the first time since Indian mediation had begun in late 1983, the principal negotiators for the Indian government were politicians and not bureaucrats or diplomats. Their arrival coincided with the LTTE massacre of the Tamil Eelam Liberation Organization (TELO) cadres and the killing of the TELO leader, Sri Sabaratnam, in the course of this clash. With Sri Sabaratnam's death, only two of the original triumvirate of Tamil separatist leaders were left, Prabhakaran and Uma Maheswaran.[13] On 3 May, while the Indian delegation was in the island, a Tristar aircraft belonging to Air Lanka was blown up at Colombo's international airport. The death toll was far smaller than it might have been if the explosion had taken place when it was airborne. Thus a slight delay in the aircraft's departure had prevented a much greater loss of life. The political message in these violent incidents[14] was directed at the two governments—the futility of negotiations in which the LTTE was not treated as the principal representative of Tamil opinion.

Despite the background of violence and terrorism against which they were held, the discussions were generally fruitful. A set of proposals was agreed to. Published on 4 May 1986, these proposals had two separate notes annexed to them, one on "law and order and the scope of the powers devolved thereunder," and the other "on land settlement." This latter was the result of negotiations between Chidambaram and Gamini Dissanayake, minister of lands, land development, and Mahavali development. In regard to both of these as well as other matters agreed upon on 4 May 1986, the Sri Lankan government gave an assurance that "further negotiations are possible to arrive at [a] final agreement." Upon the Indian delegation's departure from the island, a communiqué announced that "The Sri Lanka government agreed to make further concessions beyond the terms of the Delhi Accord."

A memorandum to President Jayewardene by Bernard Tillakaratne, Sri Lanka's high commissioner in Delhi, dated 31 May 1986,[15] and entitled "Points for Consideration," gives us a glimpse of the changes—in personnel and style—in Delhi's Sri Lankan policy consequent on Bhandari's retirement. Tillakaratne informed Jayewardene that since his return from Colombo on 10 May he had met External Affairs Minister Shiv Shanker. Their meeting lasted an hour. Chidambaram, Romesh Bhandari, and Venkateswaran had been present on the occasion. Subsequently Tillakaratne had had two meetings each with Chidambaram, Bhandari, and Venkateswaran. In the memo, Tillakaratne explained that the new thinking in Delhi's South Block was to avoid direct involvement of the Indian Prime Minister in ethnic negotiations. [Venkateswaran had] stated informally that in the past [the Indian Prime Minister] had been needlessly involved *personally* in the negotiation process and the Foreign Office evaluations were often "unduly optimistic, imprecise and airy-fairy.

This latter, Tillakaratne believed, was a criticism of Bhandari's style of doing things.[16] While Shiv Shanker was now playing a more assertive role he was not yet fully conversant with all aspects of the problem. More important, however, was a new "political" group established to advise Rajiv Gandhi on Sri Lankan affairs. Chaired by P. V. Narasimha Rao (chosen presumably for his past experience), it included Shiv Shanker, G. Parathasarathy, Chidambaram, Bhandari, and Venkateswaran. The establishment of this group was described in the report as "significant." Tillakaratne added that Bhandari had told him that it did not reflect a comeback by Parathasarathy, as neither Rao nor Shiv Shanker liked him very much. Besides, Bhandari himself was openly and strongly opposed to him.

President Jayewardene's proposal for "secret" talks in a third country was still under consideration. Tillakaratne explained that in this regard much would depend on further clarifications from Sri Lanka on the law and order in aspects of the Delhi Accord and in expansion of the agreement reached in Colombo on 4 May. Bhandari, "in a *very personal* discussion" with Tillakaratne, had urged that

Even some "private" agreement on additional clarification will help. This can even be a confidential note to be used by India, if and when necessary, during negotiations. He said if these clarifications are given to India, then the onus is on India to actively pursue negotiations. (Chidambaram said the same thing but less positively). When asked by me whether LTTE would participate, he said he was not sure. At the moment, they could only think of the TULF. Centre has not addressed its mind to this aspect as yet.

When I mentioned the possibility of escalation of terrorist violence, by those who are against talks, he said his advice, on a very *private* basis, is that security on the ground should be maintained by us at all times. (I said [the Indian prime minister] himself had recognized this earlier), but to avoid bombings and naval shellings as far as possible as this would lead to unfavourable publicity.

He said we should avoid any personal references to Rajiv [Gandhi] as in the present setup, with the inclusion of "hawks" in the policy making/group, such references will be used to prejudice [Rajiv Gandhi's] mind and thus far, [Gandhi] has been very careful in his references to ethnic situation in S[ri] L[anka]. (Reference was, I think, to [B. R. Bhagat, the former Indian foreign minister's] outburst in Rajya Sabha[17] which showed that he is anxious to defend [Gandhi's] name in Parliament, no doubt to impress him). [Bhandari] added one could always blame Tamil Nadu or the Indian government without personal references.

Bhandari said India is for continuing negotiations with S[ri] L[anka]'s co-operation. Paramount need is to keep down violence and avoid adverse publicity during negotiation period. Bombing and naval shellings had been publicized not only in the Indian media but also in the world press and this is utilized by hawks here. I explained our problem. If terrorists gain the upper hand anywhere— even in Jaffna where vital camps are located—what would be the situation and what will happen to talks? Even [Gandhi] recognized the need for basic ground control by us in his discussions with [Lalith Athulathmudali].

Bhandari discussed [Dixit's] role. He was surprised to hear of a High Commissioner canvassing different Ministers. When I mentioned S[ri] L[anka] newspaper headlines based on [Indian high commission] press releases, he said Dixit should be asked to see only one Minister on ethnic matters.

Tillakaratne also conveyed the gist of *informal* discussions with Chidambaram on 30 May, at which the latter had stated that

(a) Complete clarifications on law and order would help him begin negotiations with Tamil parties. I feel he has already discussed our proposals with the TULF at least and further clarifications are being sought at their behest! We are aware of his meetings with [TULF spokesmen] in Colombo.

(b) I asked [Chidambaram] assuming some clarifications are given, would the TULF and other terrorist groups agree to negotiations. Could he give us an assurance?

(c) He replied that he could give us a "reasonable" assurance but progress would depend on further discussions between [the Sri Lankan government] and Tamil parties but the main pre-condition is absence of provocative action by [Sri Lankan] forces, such as bombing.

(d) I said that those groups that wish to block negotiations are capable of escalating at will, of violent incidents in Colombo, [and the Eastern Province] and threaten the few Government outposts in Jaffna itself, and the Government would have no option but to take defensive action, as has happened in the recent past, i.e. the bombing of the Air Lanka plane even while talks were taking place and recent LTTE attacks on Jaffna Fort etc. I added that bombing has no significance now as at least two of the terrorist groups are reported to have anti-aircraft guns.

(e) C. replied that he could understand if it was only "defensive action" and he informally inquired whether in cases where we anticipated increased terrorist action, whether we could not confidentially inform them in advance whenever possible, as the Indian Government would then be forewarned and perhaps some pressure could be brought on terrorist groups to desist from such action. This suggestion is worthy of consideration, I think.

(f) Other than matters already agreed on, he said we would have to go into greater detail on institutional arrangements between the two provinces, as some groups are bound to insist on linkage.

Tillakaratne warned the Sri Lankan president that negotiations would be, at best, a long, drawn-out process, particularly if the LTTE did not participate.

Unless Rajiv Gandhi is prepared to apply pressure, which seemed very unlikely in the foreseeable future considering his problems within the Congress Party and the situation in [Tamil Nadu]. Chidambaram told me candidly that the Indian Government must give primary consideration to its own political future in Tamil Nadu. It is also evident that the Indian Prime Minister is now avoiding direct involvement, quite unlike last year.

However, India cannot abandon negotiations, even for its own sake and evidently all aspects are being carefully considered. Appointment of new group reflects this.

Significant that Balasingham[18] paid an unpublicized visit last week to Delhi, reportedly to assure the Centre that they were not opposed to Indian Government peace initiatives, contrary to public posture. Uma Maheswaran is presently in New Delhi and he has been meeting [Bhandari] and others.

In the present situation, [the Sri Lankan government] must also discreetly if necessary, consider other measures to try to influence India to help find an early solution and restrain terrorists.

Earlier in the memorandum Tillakaratne had informed the Sri Lankan president that

India is not happy with the Commonwealth mediation idea (fearing exposure no doubt). [Gandhi] had earlier told Ramphal to this effect at CHOGM [Commonwealth Heads of Government meeting]— though earlier proposal was for a Commonwealth force to supervise ceasefire monitoring. Chidambaram has now confirmed this in exceptionally strong language. His reply is more significant than suggestion itself.

In Colombo, in the meantime, preparations were being made for yet another set of discussions, this time a follow-up on the negotiations conducted with the Chidambaram delegation. When J. N. Dixit, the Indian high commissioner in Colombo, called on President Jayewardene at his private residence on the morning of 9 June, he was asked to convey a message to Rajiv Gandhi on this matter. The message was handwritten and bore, besides the date, the time at which it was handed over, 10:30 A.M. It read as follows:

India has played its part and all issues raised by the Chidambaram delegation have been answered. I wish the proposals emanating from the several discussions over [the] last two years with India and the proposals of the APC [All Party Conference] of 1984, now to be made public; and the forum for discussion to be in Sri Lanka only, among its Political Parties and Parliament for better or worse.[19]

The message was meant to reassure the Indian government about a renewal of the political process on negotiations after the Chidambaram delegation's departure. The Indians asked for some clarifications, especially on whether the TULF could attend the discussions and on constitutional matters on which further concessions had been promised. The response came in the form of a letter handed over to Dixit the following day.

On 11 June President Jayewardene, in a letter to Dixit, urged him to convey the following message to Prime Minister Rajiv Gandhi:

My last message to you sent on Tuesday the tenth of June 1986 appears to have been misunderstood.

In a few days our High Commissioner will bring to India the clarification to the clauses on the devolution of Law and Order, and my suggestions, as regards,

(a) Institutional arrangements for discussion between Provinces; and

(b) the use of Tamil and English Languages.

The portfolio on constitutional Proposals will then be complete. The next stage is to place them before the Cabinet, the Political Party Conference and Parliament in draft legislative form. I intend to do so. The Tamil United Liberation Front as a registered and functioning political party will be invited to the Conference. They as well as all other invitees can then express their views on these proposals. They can suggest additions, subtractions and other amendments. The Indian Government and you yourself personally can help by persuading the TULF to attend the Conference.[19]

Refining the Delhi Agreement

These assurances helped the Indian government to persuade the TULF to begin direct negotiations with the Sri Lankan government for a further refinement of the agreements reached so far. By the time the TULF arrived in Colombo, President Jayewardene had embarked on a new political initiative, the Political Parties Conference (PPC). Eight political parties met him at the conference room of the cabinet office in the early afternoon (4 P.M.) of 25 June 1986. A delegation from the Sri Lanka Freedom Party (SLFP) met the president later that afternoon (6 P.M.) but it was evident from the very outset that they would play no part in the proceedings of the PPC. A series of discussions with a number of political parties was held between 2 and 12 July, following upon these preliminary discussions. On 9 July the proposals agreed to in Delhi in August 1985, with modifications and extensions decided upon in Colombo and Delhi thereafter, were published for discussion at the PPC.[20]

A TULF delegation led by A. Amirthalingam arrived in Sri Lanka from India, and met President Jayewardene for formal talks on 13 July 1986. They joined in the discussions at the PPC, but, even more important, the TULF had no fewer than thirty-seven formal meetings either with President Jayewardene or with him and some senior ministers of the government or senior ministers on their own, between 13 July and 29 August 1986. Among the cabinet ministers with whom the TULF had discussions were the minister of finance, Ronnie de Mel; the minister of national security, Lalith Athulathmudali; and Gamini Dissanayake, minister of lands, land development, and Mahavali development. They had four separate meetings with Gamini Dissanayake, between 23 July and 29 August 1986, for discussions on the distribution of state lands in the north and east, and especially in the areas covered by the gigantic multipurpose Mahavali development scheme. The principles and details of the settlement reached between Dissanayake and Chidambaram were subjected to very close scrutiny during these discussions. While some adjustment of the details was made, the principles remained unchanged.[21]

The negotiations between the government of Sri Lanka and the TULF and the discussions and debates within the conference continued over three months. While the SLFP boycotted it, all other parties (including the traditional left, not represented in Parliament) actively participated in the conference and in the work of its committees. In general the conference endorsed the proposals submitted for discussion by and through the committees, clarified some complex issues, and identified potential points of difficulty and ambiguity, all of which made it possible to widen the scope of the powers conceded to the provinces in the scheme of devolution submitted for discussion. These modifications and extensions were incorporated in the proposals sent to India in September 1986. Consisting of fifty printed pages in all, they included draft constitutional amendments, a draft Provincial Councils Bill, schedules setting out "the Reserved, Concurrent and Provincial Lists," as well as detailed memoranda dealing with law and order, land and land settlement, and education. The subjects of finance and administration were discussed in detail, but no final agreement was reached. An official statement issued by the Sri Lankan government on 26 November 1986 asserted that "apart from the subjects finalized, these proposals constituted a package which would have been a reasonable basis of settlement, fair to all sections of the people of Sri Lanka."

The outstanding difficulty was not finance and administration, on which agreement had still to be reached with the TULF, but the fact that the TULF and other Tamil separatist groups in general continued to press for the creation of a single regional unit encompassing the Northern and Eastern Provinces. The Sri Lankan government was unwilling to consider, much less concede, this, because of its political implications. The opposition from large and vocal sections of the Sinhalese would have resulted in an extensive erosion of the government's electoral base, leading in turn to a rapid undermining of its stability.

Although both the Indian and the Sri Lankan governments were eager to treat the TULF as the main representatives of Tamil opinion in Sri Lanka, it was evident that there was an element of unreality in giving them this status. By living in self-imposed exile in Tamil Nadu and elsewhere— largely because of fears of assassination by LTTE "hit squads"—they had cut themselves off from the Tamil people. To convert the position that had been conferred on them by Venkateswaran into a hard political reality, the TULF would have had to give up living in exile, and to face the deadly challenge posed by the separatist activist groups who had filled the vacuum caused by the TULF's absence. This the TULF were not inclined to do, and yet the longer they stayed away their chances of a political rehabilitation became more of a chimera than they already were. Thus the negotiations with them were an exercise in futility. Yet they were the only group who could understand the complexity of the devolution exercise and could negotiate the details in a spirit of give and take. Nevertheless they themselves were stuck with the concept of a Tamil ethno-region—a Tamil homeland—which had gained currency among the Tamils in the early 1950s through the efforts of the Federal Party (FP), the precursor of the TULF. The FP had abandoned this in the 1960s but the TULF revived it after 1976.[22]

The main Tamil separatist group, the LTTE, had established a position of primacy among the Tamils through their resistance to the Sri Lankan armed forces, as well as by a series of bloody internecine encounters in which they had eliminated their rivals. They were in no mood to accept anything short of a separate state. Nor were they inclined to respect the new status the two governments had devised for the TULF. On the contrary, they were intent on treating the artificially resuscitated TULF in the same way they had their other rivals, as an unacceptable threat— because of the Indian support to the TULF—to the supremacy they had so ruthlessly established among the Tamil political activists in the north and east of the island.

Deadlock over the Eastern Province

Throughout the second half of 1986, Indian mediators made a sustained effort to break the deadlock caused by the TULF's insistence on the creation of a Tamil ethno-region linking the Northern and Eastern Provinces. Venkateswaran came up with a proposal to divide the Eastern Province into three units, one Muslim, one Tamil, one Sinhalese, with the Tamil unit being linked to the Northern Province by a narrow land corridor. When this proposal won no support, least of all from the Tamils, the Indian negotiators prevailed upon the Sri Lankan government to consider the excision of the Sinhalese parliamentary electorate of Amparai from the Batticaloa district of the Eastern Province, so that the Tamil ethnic component in the province would reach a level of parity with the other ethnic groups there. Venkateswaran's proposal for the excision of Amparai from the Eastern Province continued to be official Indian policy until the end of the year,[23] and formed part of the 19 December 1986 formula the Indian government urged as the basis of further negotiations between the Sri Lankan government and the Tamils. The LTTE, however, rejected the formula as wholly unacceptable. Nor were the Muslim minority, who formed a substantial element (40 percent) of the population there, willing to accept it.

Agreement had been reached by the two governments on much if not most of the structure of the provincial system, including the crucially important issue of the role of the governor of a province. Venkateswaran had hoped to make the position of the governor of a province weaker than in the Indian system, but to his chagrin and that of other Indian officials the Sri Lankan negotiators had seen how important the governor was in the Indian system in protecting the interests of the central government and unhesitatingly opted for a governor on the Indian model. To the surprise of the Indians, the TULF conceded the point, without any reservations, leaving Venkateswaran and his advisers to suspect that the TULF fancied the prospect of a governorship for one of its members. There had apparently been another point of difference between Venkateswaran and the TULF: he had urged the TULF to stick to the district as the unit of devolution but the TULF was all for a provincial unit. Venkateswaran's argument was that the district was entrenched in the Constitution, while the province was barely mentioned in it. He believed that the problems of the Eastern Province—which became a matter of acute controversy later in 1986 and thereafter—may have been resolved more easily had the unit of devolution been the district and not the province. The Amparai district could have been left out of consideration, and an amalgamation of the Batticaloa and Trincomalee districts could have been sought.[24]

The proposals agreed to in September 1986 formed the basis of negotiations between President Jayewardene and Prime Minister Rajiv Gandhi when they met in Bangalore at the summit of the South Asian Association for Regional Co-operation (SAARC) on 17 and 18 November. Indian officials were generally unhappy at letting Rajiv Gandhi get involved in the minutiae of the negotiation process with the much more experienced Sri Lankan president, who understood the principles under discussion to a much greater degree than he. They had succeeded up to this point in keeping the negotiations under their control, but now they could only watch, apprehensively, as the two heads of government began and continued discussions on their own.[25] The Bangalore meeting gave Jayewardene an opportunity to renew his personal contact with Rajiv Gandhi. The cordiality that had been established in June 1985 had survived all that had happened since then, especially the disappointment on the part of Jayewardene that nothing had been done in the interval about preventing easy access to the Tamil Nadu coast for Tamil separatist activists from Sri Lanka.

These negotiations between heads of government were accompanied and followed by discussions at a ministerial level. Rajiv Gandhi and his advisers were also engaged in frenetic negotiations to bring the rival Tamil separatist groups, and in particular the LTTE, to accept the proposals that had emerged from several years of quiet diplomacy as the basis of a workable framework for an honorable peace in Sri Lanka. Most of these groups were willing to accept these proposals or at least to give them a try. At the end of the Bangalore conference it was announced that "[a]part from the subjects of finance and administration which were not clarified with the TULF, the matters which require further clarification, modification and agreement [were] . . . fully set out in [a] working paper on [the] Bangalore discussions, dated 18 [November] 1986."[26]

The LTTE alone adamantly refused to accept these proposals. At last the Indian government showed its displeasure by imposing restrictions on Sri Lankan Tamil activists operating from Indian territory.[27] This was the first time that such restrictions had been imposed although Rajiv Gandhi had promised to do this when he first met President Jayewardene in New Delhi. The initiatives of the Indian government in this regard were nullified by the Tamil Nadu government's patent reluctance to cooperate in these moves. The Indian government sought to prevent the LTTE leader Velupillai Prabhakaran, then operating from Tamil Nadu, from leaving India for Jaffna. They succeeded in this until the beginning of 1987, when Prabhakaran and the LTTE ideologue S. Balasingham slipped across the Palk Strait to the Jaffna peninsula, to continue to fight from there.

The progress made in the Bangalore discussions owed a great deal to the personal initiatives of the two heads of government. They agreed on a tentative timetable for the signing of an accord between the two countries. The first of the steps indicated was for the Sri Lankan government to give its final consideration to the proposals in the working paper prepared at Bangalore, as well as its response to the suggestions made by the TULF on the Sri Lankan paper, to the government of India by 25 November 1986, that is to say, within a week. The Indian government would then consult the Tamil groups and convey their responses to the Sri Lankan government before 2 December. A draft accord was then to be prepared by the Sri Lankan government and given to the government of India before 9 December, and the latter in turn was to secure acceptance of the draft accord before 16 December. The final stage, the signing of the accord, presumably by the two governments, was to take place as soon as possible thereafter, preferably in January 1987.[28]

When Chidambaram and Natwar Singh visited Colombo again—their second visit—on 24 November for discussions with President Jayewardene, it was evident that the timetable decided on at Bangalore needed adjustment. The political future of the Eastern Province remained the most intractable problem. No headway on its resolution was possible on this occasion either. President Jayewardene called a meeting of Muslim organizations on 11 December 1986. Their opposition to any merger of the two provinces, or an excision of the Amparai electorate, much less the Amparai district, was made abundantly clear.

Chidambaram and Natwar Singh visited Colombo for the third time on 17 December in one more attempt to break the deadlock. In association with Dixit and a team of Indian officials, they had prolonged discussions with Jayewardene and representatives of the Sri Lankan government. The Sri Lanka team included some of the senior ministers, Lalith Athulathmudali and Gamini Dissanayake in particular, and some members of the team that had been to Thimpu, H. W. Jayewardene and H. L. de Silva. While the technical aspects of the devolution package negotiated through

1985 and 1986 were among the points discussed,[29] the central issue was the Eastern Province. The Indian team as a whole were speaking to a brief. Their objective was to secure the establishment of a single unit for the Northern and Eastern Provinces. In that they were advocates of the Sri Lankan Tamil cause, none more doggedly so than Chidambaram. They believed that they could achieve that objective by excising either the Amparai district or the Amparai parliamentary electorate from the Eastern Province and reducing the numbers of the Sinhalese component in the population of the united Northern and Eastern Province. This contentious issue alone defied settlement.

President Jayewardene urged the Indian delegation to meet the MPs of the Eastern Province and to listen to their views. There latter included K. W. Devanayagam, a Tamil and senior cabinet minister; two Sinhalese MPs, one of whom (P. Dayaratne) was a deputy minister; and one Tamil MP, a woman. All of them were United National Party (UNP) MPs. There were also five Muslim MPs, one a deputy minister and two district ministers; all were UNP MPs. The Muslim MPs decided that they would meet the Indian delegation as a Muslim bloc, and so two meetings were arranged, one on 18 December where the Eastern Province delegation consisted of Tamils and Sinhalese, four in all, led by Devanayagam, and one on 19 December at which the Muslim MPs, five in all, met them.

A careful reading of the minutes of the discussions[30] at those two meetings reveals the weaknesses of the Indian mediatory process, two in particular. First, the Indian delegation, through its spokesman Chidambaram, revealed itself to be advocates of the Sri Lankan Tamil cause, in particular the views expressed by the activist groups and the TULF. Second, conflict resolution theorists who often speak of the difficulties of negotiating across cultures[31] would have found in the Indian negotiating process in Sri Lanka a splendid case study in the difficulties of negotiating *within* cultures. There was the easy assumption that the Indian experience was universally applicable in societies with cultures with an Indic base. And so we have Indian politicians, diplomats, and administrators (Venkateswaran being a good example), all assuming and insisting that Sri Lanka's Muslim minority were an integral part of a Tamil-speaking bloc, and indeed that they were Tamils. The Muslims of Sri Lanka always rejected that identification, but leaders of the Sri Lanka Tamils often made the claim despite their opposition.[32]

The exchange between Chidambaram and Devanayagam provides one example of the flaws in the Indian position. Indian advocacy of the TULF and Tamil activist position was maintained despite all the efforts of

Devanayagam, himself a Tamil and an elected MP from a constituency with Tamils and Muslims in the Eastern Province, to make him see the complexities of the historical and demographic realities of the region. A portion of the minutes of the meeting read:

> The Hon. P. Chidambaram explained broadly what he saw as the problems and the matters to be resolved. He said solutions had to be worked out—
>
> (1) to meet the aspirations and grievances of the Tamil speaking people, especially in the Northern and Eastern Provinces.
>
> (2) for constitutional and administrative arrangements to safeguard and satisfy their aspirations and grievances.
>
> The first problem required a political solution, and the second required legal and administrative steps. As far as legal and administrative steps were concerned, headway has been made after the previous discussions with the President and the Sri Lanka delegation last May. There were still some matters to be settled, but progress was on and difficulties could be ironed out.
>
> He explained that India was not in favour of Eelam and would not be supporting it. The unity and integrity of Sri Lanka had to be preserved. The Tamils had an accumulated sense of grievance and felt that their safety, security, culture and fundamental rights were in grave danger and wanted them secured.
>
> He said that the word "Homeland" has been used extensively by them but it should not be a source of worry for what they really wanted by it in actual terms was what was spelt out in the previous paragraph. He was aware that the Sinhalese did not support a "Homeland" theory not only because they accepted the unity of the country with no separate homelands for any parts of its people but were also suspicious that the recognition of a homeland would be a stepping stone to Eelam.
>
> *Minister Devanayagam* stated that the merger of the North and East could not be considered and that with the setting up of a Pradesheeya[33] Sabhas system of Devolved Government many of the fears and grievances of the Tamils would be considerably reduced as they would be part of a system of the Participatory Government of the country.
>
> *Hon. Chidambaram* of the Indian Delegation did not agree. His view was that Pradesheeya Sabhas would deal essentially with local

government functions and that in fact the Tamils would not get enough participation in a system of National Government through Pradesheeya Sabhas. He emphasized that the Tamils should not feel that they were second class citizens. He also went on to say that the patterns of settlement in the Eastern Province in recent years showed obvious strains of colonization. Steps should be taken to correct those demographic inaccuracies and imbalances. Colonization in the East must stop and the Eastern Province should go back to the pre-settlement demographic patterns.

Minister Devanayagam said that there were large areas in Bintenna Pattu and Wewagampattu which were never Tamil. They were Sinhalese and Kandyan for centuries. They could not ever be considered as Tamil homelands.

Mr. Chidambaram inquired whether it was not possible to recarve the Eastern Province leaving out the overwhelmingly Sinhala areas in Amparai. Seruwila is also Sinhala now as a result of recent Sinhala settlements. Some of the lands in Seruwila therefore necessarily should be for the Tamils. There has to be some co-relation between population and land. Population density in areas had to be considered.

Minister Devanayagam said that all the people (Sinhala, Tamil and Muslim) of the Eastern Province had lived together and should continue to live together in one Province. The Sinhalese necessarily had to be part of it.

Mrs. Pathmanathan, on the question of whether there should be a smaller Eastern Province consisting of Tamil speaking people to satisfy their aspirations, said that on this question the views of the Muslim [MPs] should also be ascertained for they too were part of the Eastern Province and Tamil speaking. If they were unwilling to sit together as one group with the [MPs] who had met the Ministers today, the Indian Minister could meet them separately and then perhaps they could meet together again as [MPs] of the Eastern Province if they were agreeable.

The Chidambaram delegation's discussions with the Muslim MPs of the Eastern Province are important for two reasons. First, they provide evidence of how difficult negotiating *within* cultures can be. Second, there is the theme of Chidambaram's tenacious advocacy of the cause of the TULF and other Tamil activist groups. The following extract from the minutes of the meeting with the Muslim MPs is particularly useful in illustrating this. The extract begins with Chidambaram's summary of the position as the Indian government saw it.

India agreed with Sri Lanka that there could not be a state of Eelam. The unity and integrity of the country had to be preserved. Consideration had therefore to be given to the pre-Bangalore position on this question. Tamils felt that they were being kept out of power and that they were being treated as second class citizens. There should be a sharing of power and a building up of confidence that Tamils were being fairly treated. There were charges of colonization and large scale settlements of Sinhalese people in these areas on more recent years. It would be necessary to go back in history to find reasons for these changes in demographic patterns. Were they natural and understandable or were they artificial? To his thinking there were three spells of colonization—1946 to 1953, 1956 to 1963 and 1970 to 1983. He asked for views of the deputation on this point.

There would be no fragmentation of the Eastern Province. In other words, the trifurcation of the Eastern Province which had been considered after the Bangalore meeting was not on and would not be pursued.

The minutes show that the Muslim MPs were not mollified by these assurances.

Deputy Minister Abdul Majeed stated emphatically that the Eastern Province was never a solely Tamil and Muslim area. Wewagampattu, Bintenna Pattu and Panama Pattu were Sinhala areas. They had been Sinhala areas for centuries. In fact their roots were Kandyan and the Kandyan Marriage Laws applied there. There was no question that these large tracts were Tamil homelands at any time.

He went on to say that the Federal Party and its successor the TULF gave up any pretence of being spokesman for the Tamil speaking people very early. The Muslims considered themselves a separate entity distinct from the Tamils and had to look after their interests as the Tamil political parties did not work for them. South of Batticaloa is essentially a Muslim area. The Muslims and Tamils in the Eastern Province have lived together for centuries with the Sinhalese. He reemphasized that the Muslims wanted to live together in the Eastern Province and that they would not be a hindrance to a peaceful settlement; but at the same time the Muslims should not be treated as a sacrificial lamb.

He added that the Eastern Province Tamils were treated badly and contemptuously by the Tamils of the North, almost as badly as the Muslims who were a poor and neglected community. They were essentially farmers and agriculturists. The Muslims were prepared to take a calculated risk to achieve a settlement as peace was so vital to them.

Mr. Chidambaram said that the Tamils spoke of enforced colonization. He inquired how the Eastern Province could have a dominant share of power.

He also raised another question namely whether Wewagampattu and Bintenna Pattu could not be added to Uva since they were essentially Sinhala areas. If this was done in [*sic*] demographic pattern could be adjusted and the Eastern Province would be a smaller province of essentially Tamil speaking people.

Mr. Majeed said that it would be necessary to take a calculated risk and stay as one Eastern Province. The Sinhalese were not an obstruction and the Eastern Province was not a Tamil homeland. It was important that peace be restored.

Mr. Sinnalebbe of Batticaloa supported him. The TULF in 1977 did not consider the Muslim community as a minority requiring representation in the election. They had put forward 2 Tamil candidates for this multi-member seat.

Mr. Majeed and the other [MPs] complained bitterly of the hardships that the Muslims were suffering at the hands of the militant groups. Banks were being robbed, Muslims were being killed and generally they were being terrorized by the militants. They had recently attacked the Technical College in Sammanturai which was built in an essentially Muslim area to serve the Tamil speaking people. How could that action be justified. Actions such as these hindered the development of a poor backward community.

In reply to a question from Mr. Chidambaram they said they were ready to have a dialogue with the militants if they wished it. The Sinhalese were part of the Eastern Province and the Muslims lived in amity with them.

He stated emphatically that peace had to be restored and it could be done only during the Presidency of Mr. J. R. Jayewardene. After him there could be a completely different point of view. The power of the Maha Sangha too might make a solution difficult.

An official statement issued after the 19 December meeting held later in the evening made the following points:

President J. R. Jayewardene and the two (2) Indian Ministers discussed further ideas in continuation of the discussions held in the past. At the end of the discussions the following proposals emerged:

(i) The present territory comprising the Eastern province minus the Amparai Electoral District may constitute the new Eastern province.

(ii) A Provincial Council will be established for the new Eastern province.

(iii) The institutional linkages between the Northern province and the Eastern province discussed earlier will be further refined in order to make it more acceptable to the parties concerned.

(iv) The Sri Lanka Government will be willing to consider a proposal for a second stage of constitutional development providing for the Northern province and the new Eastern province coming together subject to modalities being agreed upon for ascertaining the wishes of the people comprised in the Northern province and the Eastern province separately.

(v) The Sri Lanka Government is willing to consider the creation of an office of Vice President to be appointed by the President for a specified term.

(vi) The five (5) Muslim M.P.[s] of the Eastern province may be invited to visit India and to discuss matters of mutual concern with the Tamil side under the auspices of the Government of India.

Bangalore and After: Deadlock

The Sri Lankan government's discussions with the Chidambaram delegation ended on an indecisive note. Only one thing was certain, namely, that the proposal to divide the Eastern Province into three, which the Indians had adumbrated and which had been discussed in some detail at Bangalore during the meeting between the Indian prime minister and the Sri Lankan president and their respective teams, was now abandoned as unviable politically. It meant therefore that the deadlock over the fate of the Eastern Province continued and there was no headway possible on the implementation of the constitutional proposals agreed upon at Bangalore. The timetable for its implementation fell behind schedule.

For President Jayewardene there was some comfort from the Bangalore discussions, or the prelude to them to be more exact, in the restraints placed on the LTTE and other Tamil separatist groups in Tamil Nadu in response to pressure from the Indian government. The seizure of LTTE and other separatist arms caches, as well as their telecommunication equipment, provided hard evidence of the use of Indian territory to conduct raids—if not wage war—on a friendly neighbor. This matériel was usually transported to the Jaffna coast for use in attacks on the Sri Lankan forces. True, the LTTE leadership and their allies kept under house arrest were released much sooner than the Sri Lankan government had reason to expect given the size of the arms caches seized, but it was a small step in the right direction. Nevertheless the Sri Lankan government was acutely conscious of the fact that even the initiative taken to keep the leadership of the LTTE and their allies under house arrest and thereafter under surveillance, and the seizure of large arms caches, only revealed the limits of the Indian government's freedom of movement in this regard. The period of house arrest was too short to serve anything but a symbolic purpose, and so far as the Sri Lankan government was concerned there was no reason to believe that the arms seized would not be returned to the LTTE and others.

President Jayewardene's insistence on joint patrols of the Palk Strait by the navies of the two countries was based on one very significant fact. The LTTE and other allies operating from India were the only separatist group in South Asia with direct access to the sea. As long as they had their bases and safe havens in Tamil Nadu, there was little the hard-pressed and diminutive Sri Lankan navy could do to prevent easy entry to the Sri Lankan coasts to boats sailing from Tamil Nadu unless the Indian navy cooperated in preventing such boats from leaving India's territorial waters. Despite all the advances made in the discussions at Bangalore, there was no assurance forthcoming from Rajiv Gandhi on a more active role by the Indian navy in the interdiction of vessels engaged in the shipment of arms from Tamil Nadu to Sri Lanka, let alone joint patrols by the navies on the seas separating the Indian landmass from Sri Lanka's northern coast.

In every calculation that Sri Lanka's defense establishment, such as it was, made of the essentials of the island's security in the face of the vigorous challenge posed by the Tamil separatist forces, the Tamil Nadu factor had to be treated as an essential element. The response to the Tamil Nadu factor and the training and arms available to the Tamil separatist activists was a steady increase in defense expenditure in Sri Lanka from 1984 onward. We have seen how defense expenditure as a percentage of the government's expenditure as a whole had more than trebled (from 3.09 percent in 1982 to 9.77 percent in 1985). By 1986 it had risen to 15.56 percent, and even as the two countries conducted their negotiations at Bangalore the budgetary provisions for 1987 were based on the assumption that the levels would rise above the 1986 level merely to keep up with inflation. In fact they reached 16.79 percent in 1987.

These grim statistics were very much in the minds of President Jayewardene and the Sri Lanka delegation in their negotiations at Bangalore. Their sense of disappointment was all the greater, therefore, because nothing that happened at Bangalore, or as a prelude to the meeting there, held out the prospect of any early reduction in Sri Lanka's defense expenditure. The LTTE remained a serious threat to the political stability and territorial integrity of the country.

Notes

1. For discussion of this in greater detail, see K. M. de Silva, ed., *Sri Lanka: Problems of Governance* (Delhi, 1993), 361–69.

2. See the statement made by G. S. Dhillon, leader of the Indian delegation to the forty-second session of the UN Commission on Human Rights, under agenda item 12, on 5 March 1986. This brief statement was in response to a very comprehensive one made by H. W. Jayewardene, leading the Sri Lankan delegation on 4 March 1986, setting out in detail the negotiations conducted between the two governments, and also details of attacks by Tamil separatist groups on civilians, and clashes between the Sri Lankan security forces and Tamil separatist groups.

3. And not only Indian newspapers. Indian officials in New Delhi were talking to Western journalists based in New Delhi. See, for example, Steven R. Weisman, "India Shows Impatience with Sri Lanka Talks," *New York Times,* 27 December 1985.

4. This paragraph is based on information derived from Sri Lankan diplomats and other officials present on this occasion. I am particularly grateful for an account of it given me by Ernest Corea, then Sri Lanka's ambassador in Washington, a few weeks after this meeting.

5. Ramphal is a Guyanese of Indian extraction. He had been foreign minister of his country before he joined the Commonwealth Secretariat as its administrative head.

6. Several expatriate Sri Lankans living in the United States and United Kingdom were mentioned as possible participants in this enterprise. Ramphal himself had initiated a search for possible members of the commission or committee he had in mind.

7. See Bernard Tillakaratne's memorandum to J. R. Jayewardene, 31 May 1986 in the J. R. Jayewardene MSS.

8. A copy of this memorandum is available in the J. R. Jayewardene MSS.

9. On the problems of the Eastern Province and its links with the concept of a traditional homeland of the Tamils, see Gerald H. Peiris, "An Appraisal of the Concept of a Traditional Homeland in Sri Lanka," *Ethnic Studies Report, 9*, no. 1 (January 1991): 13–39; K. M. de Silva, *The "Traditional Homelands" of the Tamils—Separatist Ideology in Sri Lanka: A Historical Appraisal,* Occasional Paper no. 4 (Kandy: International Centre for Ethnic Studies, 1994).

10. A. P. Venkateswaran, interview with the author, 24 April 1990.

11. Ibid.

12. On Chidambaram's arrival in Colombo a local newspaper, the *Sun,* published a photograph reproduced from the *Hindu* in Madras, showing him engaged in street demonstrations in Madras condemning the Sri Lankan government and President Jayewardene himself for alleged atrocities against the Tamils of Sri Lanka.

13. For three days beginning on 29 April 1986, the LTTE turned their guns on their rivals, the Tamil Eelam Liberation Organization (TELO) and crushed them remorselessly. The TELO leader Sri Sabaratnam was among those killed on that occasion. For an account of what happened on that occasion see an article entitled "The Wounds of the People's Psyche are Deeper," in the *Hindu,* 13 May 1986.

14. These included a bomb set off in Colombo's Central Telegraph Office on 7 May. See the accounts in the *New York Times,* 8 and 11 May 1986.

15. This is available in the J. R. Jayewardene MSS.

16. During my interview with him on 24 April 1990, Venkateswaran made much the same point.

17. The reference is to Bhagat's speech in the Rajya Sabha, on 9 April 1986.

18. S. Balasingham, an expatriate Sri Lankan Tamil holding a British passport, married to an Australian, was regarded as the ideologue of the LTTE. Because Prabhakaran was not English speaking, he relied greatly on Balasingham for his negotiations abroad.

19. Copies of the message of 10 June and the letter of 11 June quoted are available in the J. R. Jayewardene MSS.

20. This paragraph is based on a reading of the files in the J. R. Jayewardene MSS relating to this theme.

21. Ibid.

22. See note 9 above.

23. A. P. Venkateswaran, interview with the author, 24 April 1990.

24. Ibid.

25. Ibid.

26. J. R. Jayewardene MSS. Notes prepared at Bangalore.

27. On 8 November 1986 over 500 Sri Lankan Tamil separatist activists were detained in Tamil Nadu; many of them (their leaders Prabhakaran and Balasingham included) had their fingerprints taken and were photographed for security purposes. They were released after a short while. Large quantities of communications equipment and a massive haul of arms were also seized. See the *Weekend Sun,* 7 December 1986, quoting the *Amrita Basaar Patrika;* for information on the arrest of the Tamil separatist groups and their leaders see the *Island,* 11 November 1986; the *Ceylon Daily News* of the same date carried much the same information but also included extracts from some of the leading Indian newspapers on the same subject.

28. This is extracted from paragraph 11 of "The Working Papers on the Bangalore Discussions," 18 November 1986.

29. I was an adviser to the Sri Lankan delegation on this occasion, summoned at very short notice, to speak on the history of the Eastern Province.

30. The official minutes of the meeting discussed here are available in the J. R. Jayewardene MSS, and the extracts quoted below are from there.

31. For an excellent introduction to this theme, see Raymond Cohen, *Negotiating Across Cultures: Communication Obstacles in International Diplomacy* (Washington, D.C.: United States Institute of Peace, 1991).

32. For discussions of the controversies on this issue, see K. M. de Silva, *Managing Ethnic Tensions in Multi-Ethnic Societies: Sri Lanka, 1880–1985* (Lanham, Md.: University Press of America, 1986), 114–23, 227–35.

33. These were rural councils.

Part III

10

Conflict and Coercion, January–July 1987

Introduction

FOR THE Liberation Tigers of Tamil Eelam (LTTE) as for the Sri Lankan government, the Bangalore discussions (between the governments of Sri Lanka and India) and the prelude to these had been a period of disappointment and confusion. The disappointment sprang from the house arrest imposed on its leadership prior to the Sri Lankan president's arrival in Bangalore, and from what the Tamil separatist activists regarded as the insulting treatment accorded to their leadership—the process of photographing them, taking their fingerprints, and other measures associated with police procedures for criminal activities. But all it required to secure their release, as well as the release of some of the communications equipment and—it would appear—most if not all the arms seized, was a brief campaign of moral pressure in the form of a hunger strike by the LTTE leadership. Even more satisfying to them was the summoning of the LTTE leader for backstage discussions at Bangalore. He had arrived in the company of his mentor, M. G. Ramachandran.

Although no direct discussions were held on that occasion between the Sri Lankan president and the LTTE, the latter was consulted by the Indian government and the Indian prime minister in regard to the proposals discussed by the two governments and subsequently agreed upon. Prabhakaran would not relent on his principal demand: a union of the Northern and Eastern Provinces as the minimum price for his support of the proposals. The Sri Lankan president, who had been under relentless pressure from the Indian government to make more concessions on the program agreed to earlier in the year, insisted that he could not agree to

201

this. It was in this context that the proposal for a division of the Eastern Province into three parts had been brought up by Indian officials.[1] The proposal had not been unacceptable to the Sri Lankan president, but he had insisted that it be tested on the elected representatives of that province before it was formally incorporated as part of the proposals to be implemented.

Prabhakaran would have nothing to do with that proposal, and had no hesitation in saying so. Rajiv Gandhi was struck by Prabhakaran's intransigence on this occasion, and this was to have considerable significance in determining his attitude toward him later on. On an earlier occasion (in 1985) Rajiv Gandhi had invited Prabhakaran to come up to Delhi to meet him,[2] but the latter had not acceded to this request, unusual behavior for a man living in exile on Indian territory.

There were, of course, advantages flowing to Prabhakaran from his presence at Bangalore. The LTTE was the only Tamil political group invited to the discussions, a tacit recognition of its position as the principal political party of the Sri Lankan Tamils. The Indian government was deviating from its practice of treating the moderate Tamil United Liberation Front (TULF) as the main representative of the Tamils, although its leaders were aware that the TULF had been superseded by more activist groups as the genuine representative of Tamil opinion.

Meanwhile, at the time the Tamil Nadu authorities, acting under pressure from the central government, had seized arms and telecommunications equipment held by the LTTE and other Tamil separatist groups, the Sri Lankan security forces had gone on the offensive. They regained control of three areas the LTTE had dominated for some time: Point Pedro and Valvetithurai, part of the smugglers' coast, Prabhakaran's home town, and Thondamanaru.[3] A few days later the Sri Lankan army conducted cordon and search operations in the Kilinochchi and Mullaitivu districts of the Northern Province, in which the LTTE had several well-constructed and well-protected camps.[4] Surprisingly, in all these campaigns, the security forces met with very little resistance.

In the early part of December there was a clash between Tamils and Muslims in Batticaloa in the Eastern Province, and on 14 December the LTTE and a rival group, the Eelam People's Revolutionary Liberation Front (EPRLF), were reported to be engaged in a bitter struggle. The LTTE responded by attacking sections of the Muslim population in Batticaloa on the grounds that they were aiding the security forces; the conflict with the EPRLF was viewed as part of the LTTE's persistent campaign to weaken its rivals militarily as a prelude to their complete elimination.

Just at this time an Indian newspaper based in Calcutta, the *Amrita Bazaar Patrika,* had revealed that the monetary value of the arms haul taken over from the LTTE had been as high as 40 crores (four hundred million Indian rupees or U.S.$25 million at the prevailing rate of exchange). The report described the haul in detail: five thousand AK-47 rifles, anti-tank guns, rocket-propelled grenades, machine guns, surface-to-air missiles, and sophisticated communications equipment.[5] These revelations set alarm bells ringing in Colombo. The magnitude of the arms haul was cause enough for serious disquiet, but even more serious was the fact that the arms seized were not effectively sealed off from the LTTE and their allies. Indeed, much if not most of that haul had been returned to them through the good offices of the Tamil Nadu government. There was also the suspicion in Sri Lanka that the weapons taken into custody temporarily were only part of the LTTE's armory, and that other caches of arms, on the Tamil Nadu coast close to the Jaffna peninsula, as large as those seized or even larger, had not been touched at all by the Tamil Nadu government.

On 15 December 1986 a Sri Lankan newspaper, the *Sun,* reported that the LTTE was planning to set up a Tamil state in the north and east of the island by 1 January 1987, a political initiative that would take the form of a unilateral declaration of independence. Coming as this did only a week after the same newspaper had carried a report based on the *Amrita Bazaar Patrika* revelations on the massive scale of the arms haul seized from the LTTE and other Tamil separatist activists in Tamil Nadu, the Sri Lankan government was greatly perturbed.

A unilateral declaration of independence would raise the separatist challenge several notches higher than it already was. It would pose a deadly threat to the fragile peace that had held in the Sinhalese areas of the country since 1984. The government was intent therefore on forestalling any such moves, and would use all the force at its disposal for that purpose. But just at the time the government was assessing the political risks involved in this new development, the LTTE, surprisingly, made an overture.

An LTTE Overture

A few days later, an LTTE group sent out a feeler for direct talks with the government. The intermediary in this instance was a United National Party (UNP) MP.[6] Although wary of the offer, the government decided to test the waters. A small delegation was sent for this purpose to Jaffna to hold secret talks with the second-tier LTTE leadership. The two groups met in the office of the town council at Kankesanthurai on 27 December 1986. Among those attending these unofficial and essentially exploratory discussions was a knowledgeable official, E. F. Dias Abeysinghe, who kept a record of what was said on this occasion. Dias Abeysinghe, who was the secretary to the Political Parties Conference and had served as secretary to the Sri Lankan delegations from the time of the Thimpu talks, had been associated with all the negotiations and discussions in India up to that time.

He noted that the LTTE group's chief spokesman[7] had begun by saying that "what we say is unofficial, our private views as ordinary citizens of Jaffna."[8] The LTTE spokesman "had made it evident that they were suspicious of the stand of the Indian government in the negotiations. India was using the situation for her political gain and her internal security." He disclosed the fact that

Even when a cease-fire had been arranged about the time of the Thimpu talks in 1985 India was supplying arms to all 5 Tamil groups. [The spokesman] stated emphatically that the LTTE would not be "puppets of the Indian Government." They would resist any invasion by Indian forces. They were the only Tamil group who were resisting them, but at the same time they would not break with them or act without their awareness and consent in their mediatory process.

They were distrustful of the S[ri] L[anka] Government too. [It] had always gone back on promises.

In inviting government representatives to informal talks, the LTTE clearly intended to drive a wedge between the governments of India and Sri Lanka at the very moment that an accord on the resolution of Sri Lanka's ethnic conflict seemed ready for signature. The LTTE spokesman suggested secret talks with the top LTTE leaders, Prabhakaran and Balasingham, who were then in India and (so the LTTE spokesman said) unable to get out. Clearly this was not possible for any government-sponsored delegates because of the need for visas to India. It would be impossible to maintain the secrecy required. (The LTTE, of course, had their own methods of illicit entry.) More to the point, the government spokesman stated quite categorically that "India has always played a mediatory role and was interested in helping S[ri] L[anka] to achieve a solution. We cannot distance ourselves so from India."

Even more important in view of future developments was the insistence of the LTTE representatives that they were not "puppets of the Indian government and would resist any invasion by Indian forces." So strong were the Sri Lankan officials' suspicions of the LTTE that these remarks passed without comment. Certainly very little credence would have been attached to them even if they had reached senior politicians. The latter would perhaps have found much more ominous the LTTE's reiteration of the position that they were the one group with whom the government should negotiate on issues relating to Sri Lanka's Tamil problem. There was no response to this latter point from the government spokesmen at this secret meeting but they did make particular note of it. Although there was wide-ranging discussion of the LTTE's political demands, it was evident that there was no real sign of any flexibility on them despite their claims of being prepared to "accept any practical solution" and their contention that, because the Tamils had been let down over the past thirty years, "we therefore decided to ask for the maximum, Eelam." One encouraging sign was that the LTTE spokesman expressed the wish that secret and informal talks would be followed by formal talks with the government at a future date. And, on a more piquant note, the spokesman asked the government representatives to ignore any bellicose comments uttered by the LTTE leadership from India.

Conflict

The LTTE's overtures of the last two weeks of December 1986 proved to be no more than diversionary tactics to gain time. Prabhakaran's return to the island early in January 1987 marked the beginning of a more activist and violent phase in the ongoing conflict between the Tamil separatist groups led by the LTTE and the Sri Lankan forces. It was evident that the LTTE was intent on scuttling the agreement that the two governments were on the verge of implementing. A unilateral declaration of independence in the north and east of the island was regarded as the most effective means of doing that. Once news of the plan leaked out, the LTTE began to call it merely "the establishment of an administration" in the north and east of the island to fill the gap caused by the collapse of the Sri Lankan government's administration there.

The Sri Lankan government's response was predictably tough. In an attempt to preempt a unilateral declaration of independence in any form whatever, the government sent troop reinforcements into the Eastern and

Northern Provinces with instructions to clear these areas of the LTTE and other separatist groups. Contrary to expectations, the LTTE forces did not put up much of a fight. Their retreat was anything but orderly. They fled to the Jaffna peninsula in considerable disarray.

The Indian government, much perturbed by this turn of events, returned once more to diplomatic and political pressure on the Sri Lankan government to abandon these military moves and to resume the search for a political solution. As we shall see, public expressions of displeasure from New Delhi strained relations between the two countries in February and March 1987.

In the meantime, on 20 January 1987, the unhappy relationship between Rajiv Gandhi and Indian foreign secretary A. P. Venkateswaran came to a head, and the latter was removed from his post in a blaze of unintended publicity. The humiliation inflicted on Venkateswaran had nothing to do with any differences of opinion on Sri Lankan policy. By the time Venkateswaran left office the principles and most of the details of that policy had been settled.[9] In time he would become a vigorous critic of Rajiv Gandhi's Sri Lanka policy, but that would be in 1988 and 1989.[10] Rajiv Gandhi took great pains to control the damage caused by the manner of Venkateswaran's dismissal. One of the measures taken was to choose yet another southerner to take over as foreign secretary, K. P. S. Menon, Jr. The latter's father had served in Sri Lanka as the agent of the government of India in Kandy, handling matters relating to Indian plantation workers in the island.

By the time Menon took over as foreign secretary, the Sri Lankan government had succeeded in confining the LTTE to parts of the Jaffna peninsula. The communications system in the north, constantly attacked by the LTTE, was now knocked out by the government. An economic blockade was imposed on the Jaffna peninsula in the hope that the local population would use pressure on the LTTE to abandon plans to set up an administration of their own for that area.

Démarche

There were soon a flurry of telegrams between the governments of India and Sri Lanka on this new situation. The Sri Lankan government's tough response to the LTTE's political initiative had been based on the grounds that the LTTE's projected unilateral declaration of independence in the north and east had radically altered the political situation and that the hard measures taken in January were justified by this.

The Indian government was not convinced by this argument and a message from Rajiv Gandhi to President Jayewardene on 9 February 1987 made this clear. It read as follows:

1. As far as the current military operations against Tamil civilians continue and other discriminatory measures like economic and communications blockade affecting civilians exist, India is not in a position to resume discussions with Tamil militants. While this is so for the present, India will remain willing to resume the peace process if and when these actions are withdrawn.
2. India is firmly of the view that the proposals which emerged on the 19th of December after Mr. Natwar Singh and Mr. Chidambaram's visit to Colombo, must clearly be affirmed by the Government of Sri Lanka as a basis and only a beginning point for further negotiations. India is also of the view that the final framework of a solution based on those proposals can only be forged when Sri Lankan Government and Tamil side come together again for negotiations.
3. If the Government of Sri Lanka continues the economic blockade and military operations against Tamils, prospects of violence will increase. India's assessment is that the conflict will be prolonged and will escalate.[11]

This message was treated in Colombo by President Jayewardene as well as members of his cabinet as evidence of Indian insensitivity to the dangers posed by the LTTE's decision to establish its own "administration" in the north of the island. The Eastern Province was under the effective control of the government. It was decided to publish this message in the hope of alerting the country at large to the pressures confronting the Sri Lankan government, and to extract as much public support as possible for the line of action that the government had embarked on. The economic blockade of the Jaffna peninsula was strengthened to the extent that the delivery of petroleum products to that area was severely restricted.

India responded to this virtual rejection of its message with a more forceful one on 10 February in which it threatened a démarche. India's good offices, that is to say its mediatory role, would be withdrawn unless three conditions were met. These latter were a reaffirmation by the Sri Lankan government of the 19 December proposals; the termination of the economic blockade of the Jaffna peninsula; and a suspension of the military campaign in the north of the island.[12]

The threat of a démarche by India did not result in either an immediate relaxation of the economic blockade or a halt to the military measures then being taken to consolidate the gains made by the security forces. A reaffirmation of a commitment to the 19 December proposals was made.

The response from Colombo dated 12 February was the work largely of the president's office, in association with Lalith Athulathmudali's Ministry of National Security.[13] The Sri Lankan government's response mixed conciliation with a firm reaffirmation of its intention to pursue the course of action it had embarked on unless the Tamil separatist activists "officially" withdrew their call for the establishment of a separate "administration" and ceased their military activities.

It was pointed out that the term "economic embargo" meant nothing more than restrictions on the supply of certain commodities (fuel, in particular) to the Jaffna peninsula. These restrictions would be lifted as soon as an announcement was made by the Tamil separatist activists that they had abandoned their plans for establishing a parallel administration, and ceased their military activity.

On a more conciliatory note, the message indicated the Sri Lankan government's readiness to negotiate with representatives of the LTTE in New Delhi with Indian representatives present as mediators. A general amnesty would be offered if the armed separatists would give up arms. All persons held in custody under the Prevention of Terrorism Act and against whom no charges had been filed would be released. The Sri Lankan government rejected the charge made by India that it was engaged in any military action against the civilian population of Jaffna.

The message reaffirmed the Sri Lankan government's commitment to the 19 December 1986 proposals and acknowledged continued reliance on the mediatory role of the Indian government in further negotiations, which could begin at an early date. There was also an insistence on India "underwriting" the implementation of any agreement reached.

The Indian government was not satisfied with the Sri Lankan government's message of 12 February, and High Commissioner Dixit called on Lalith Athulathmudali seeking clarification of certain points raised in the message. One of these had to do with the call for India to "underwrite" any settlement reached. What precisely did this mean? The term was fuzzy, and Athulathmudali's explanations were kept deliberately vague. One aspect of it was evident, namely that the mediator would have to serve as guarantor of the settlement negotiated. Lalith Athulathmudali would give no assurance about stopping the military campaign as a prelude to a revival of the negotiatory process. His instructions from President Jayewardene were clear enough: do not stop the campaign until a firm assurance was received that the LTTE was abandoning its plans for a parallel administration.

On 18 February another message came in from New Delhi, from "the Government of India to be conveyed to his Excellency President Jayewardene by High Commissioner Dixit." It read as follows:

> The Sri Lankan Government response to High Commissioner Dixit on 12th February 1987 is inadequate. The circumstances under which the response was conveyed cast doubt about its seriousness. The clarification offered by Minister Athulathmudali to High Commissioner Dixit does not carry conviction.
>
> The three principal requirements before India can resume its good offices have been conveyed to Sri Lankan Government on 10th February 1987. India shall not resume its good offices unless military operations are stopped immediately by the Sri Lankan Government. We expect any response to our demarche of 10th February 1987 to be conveyed directly to us by the Sri Lankan Government in clear and unambiguous terms.
>
> We trust that President Jayewardene will take due note of this message and not make any statement or take any action that will completely close the doors to the prospects of India resuming its good offices.[14]

President Jayewardene would give no assurance that the military campaign in the north of the island would stop. His response had been sent directly to the Indian prime minister on 13 February. It contained three points. First, the government of Sri Lanka was "[c]ommitted to the concept of devolution within the framework of a united Sri Lanka." Second, the government of Sri Lanka expected India to underwrite any settlement reached. Third, Tamil separatist activists should desist from creating a parallel administration.[15]

Thus the exchange of messages ended on an inconclusive note. The Sri Lankan government had not given way to Indian pressure. Instead, the pressure on the LTTE in Jaffna had succeeded in preventing it from establishing a parallel administration. In the process a great deal of hardship was imposed on the people of Jaffna, who were caught between the LTTE's ambitions and the Sri Lankan security forces intent on thwarting them.

Throughout this period the Sri Lankan government and the security forces were engaged in an assessment of the options for the campaign that was in progress and for the weeks ahead. Lalith Athulathmudali recalled that the Sri Lankan military leadership in Colombo was reluctant to engage in a bold advance into the territories controlled by the LTTE because they felt that the forces at their command were inadequate to take control of the territory abandoned by the LTTE in the Northern and Eastern Provinces and engage the LTTE in combat in the densely populated Jaffna peninsula. It took a great deal of pushing and prodding by the political leadership to persuade them to give this more aggressive policy a try.[16]

In the meantime, defense expenditure reached its peak in 1987, by which time the total number of security personnel (army, navy, air force, police, and paramilitary forces) had reached around seventy-five thousand. The police had developed its own paramilitary wing, the Special Task Force (STF), which combined police duties with security operations in the eastern region. A second paramilitary group was the home guards, armed peasants given the task of defending their villages in the periphery of the Tamil districts or within them from attacks by Tamil guerrilla bands. These armed incursions, in which unarmed civilians were the deliberately chosen victims, could not be checked in any other way.

Athulathmudali succeeded in convincing the military leadership in Colombo that they now had the men as well as the matériel for a more aggressive policy. There was a sharp difference of opinion between Athulathmudali and President Jayewardene on the tactics of the military campaign. Their strategic objective was clear enough—to break the military power of the LTTE. But they disagreed on how this was to be done, in particular, on whether or not an attempt should be made to take effective control of the town of Jaffna. Jayewardene was in favor of such a measure, if it was the only way of breaking the back of the LTTE and its hold on the people of the north. Athulathmudali argued that the principal objective could be achieved without actually taking physical control of the town of Jaffna; effective control of the coast could achieve that purpose, without the heavy loss of civilian life which an assault on Jaffna entailed.[17] He succeeded in persuading the president that the more limited exercise would provide all the advantages that an assault on the LTTE strongholds in Jaffna was expected to yield.

In the latter half of February and the early part of March the Sri Lankan forces were engaged in that exercise, taking control of the coastal towns and villages in an attempt to cut off the LTTE's regular supplies of matériel from Tamil Nadu and elsewhere. At no stage did Athulathmudali publicly indicate that the government was not committed to the reestablishment of its hold on the town of Jaffna. The aim was to keep the LTTE guessing as to what the government intended to do. While tactically sound, this policy carried the disadvantage that others, including the Indian government, were equally at a loss to understand what the aims of the Sri Lankan government's military exercise really were.

One of the most interesting features of the mechanics of the evolving relationship between India and Sri Lanka at this stage was the part played by India's dynamic high commissioner, J. N. Dixit. Taking full advantage of the informality that was a hallmark of President Jayewardene's style of government, Dixit established a cordial relationship with him. This gave easy access to the president in his office, an access that extended also to the latter's home. Many of the president's cabinet colleagues were resentful, regarding it as a fundamental error of judgment on his part, none more so than Lalith Athulathmudali, who believed that high commissioners and ambassadors should observe the conventions and rules governing their access to heads of government.

It would appear that Dixit was often shown the letters the president was in the process of drafting for dispatch to the Indian prime minister and government, even before Sri Lankan cabinet ministers saw the document themselves. One such occasion was at the end of February, when relations between the two countries were strained because of the Indian government's refusal to see the gravity of the LTTE's attempt to establish a parallel administration. The Indian journalist M. Ram[18] recalled a conversation between the Sri Lankan president and Dixit at the former's private residence which took place in Ram's presence. Dixit was shown a letter that Jayewardene was about to send the Indian prime minister. Having read it, he urged the president to soften its tone somewhat for fear that it would be unhelpful in improving relations between them and returning to the level of cordiality that had prevailed at Bangalore.

We shall turn to that letter presently, but one aspect of the discussion recalled by Ram was especially important. It related to the Sri Lankan president's insistence that India underwrite any settlement reached with the LTTE. That, Dixit had insisted, was something very new in the diplomatic bargaining between the two countries, and the Indian government had to reflect on its implications.[19] Dixit was being more than the cautious professional diplomat here, because the matter had come up for discussion at Bangalore, and K. Natwar Singh and A. C. S. Hameed had been asked to prepare a paper on it for the two heads of government.[20] It was one more example of how the Indian bureaucracy would often thwart the implementation of decisions taken by heads of government.

The Jayewardene manuscript files contain the draft of a letter to the Indian prime minister dated 25 February 1987. Whether this was the letter shown to Dixit we do not know. But it was an important document in helping us to understand President Jayewardene's views on the problems that confronted him at that time.[21]

The draft letter was addressed in more formal terms than "My dear Rajiv," with which he began his first letter to him. This time it was "My dear Prime Minister." Its first paragraph read thus:

> The attempts made over a period of ten years by me and my Government to find a political solution to the ethnic problem in Sri Lanka are well known to the Government of India, for they too have taken part in discussions since 1983. These steps have been outlined in detail in my address to Parliament in 1984, 1985 and 1986 with complete documentation.

The second paragraph was more significant, especially its last line:

> There is no ambiguity in the December 19th proposal. This proposal, when it emerged (it was not a proposal of mine) it was stated to be unobjectionable to, inter alia, the Moors (Muslims), living in the Eastern Province. Subsequently, I found out that this was not approved by the Muslims, all the Members of Parliament, Muslims and Tamils, saw me and said so. But as I have said repeatedly if the LTTE accept this idea as part of the total peace package, I shall do my best to persuade the cabinet, government, Muslim and other Eastern Province interests to accept the same as the prize [sic] of peace, if necessary by holding a referendum.

Here we have, for the first time, a reference to a referendum to be held in the Eastern Province to determine whether the people there wished to link themselves with the Tamil-dominated Northern Province. The next part of the letter was both a defense of the Sri Lankan government's policies and a criticism of policies of New Delhi and Tamil Nadu.

There is nothing more any Sri Lanka Government can offer, now or in the future, without violating the Independence, Integrity and Unity of Sri Lanka's Constitution.

The Indian Government has stated publicly to the Separatist groups that it does not support the merger of the Northern and Eastern Provinces, the concept of a Tamil Homeland, and the creation of a separate State. It is these three issues that supposedly keep these groups from accepting the proposals.

During these ten years, except the TULF, the other groups especially the LTTE have unleashed, a violent, terrorist campaign in which more than 4000 Security personnel, civilians, men, women and children, of all races have been killed, many more injured, rendered homeless and suffered immeasurable losses.

The latest atrocity committed a few weeks ago has been the killing of several Sinhala women and children, without provocation in the darkness of the night by the cutting of their throats. As far as we know no terrorist group in the World has been guilty of such inhuman behaviour.

India has experience of terrorism in several States, and particularly in the Punjab, where a separatist movement is using violence to achieve its goal.

The Sri Lanka Government, both politically and militarily has done nothing more or less than what any democratic Government, including the Indian Government, will do to deal with a terrorist problem. The military operations *are not*, repeat *not*, a move away from a political solution. We do not believe in the possibility of a military solution to this problem. On the contrary we have made and shall continue to make every effort to arrive at a political solution. All our efforts, yours and mine, have failed so far with the main terrorist group the LTTE. The LTTE has in recent weeks intensified their activities particularly killing of innocent citizens, including women, children and babies in arms. They have also moved in men and materials into Sri Lanka and were getting ready for a major strike against us. Can I or any government stand idly by? The moment the LTTE comes to the conference table and ceases hostile acts, there will be no need for military action. That is my earnest wish.

And what has the State of Tamil Nadu been doing during these ten years? It has given refuge to Tamil groups, including those using violence. The leader of the LTTE group, Prabhakaran who publicly says he murdered the Tamil Mayor of Jaffna, Mr. Durayappa[22] and many others, is entertained as a guest by the Chief Minister. Prabhakaran as well as others who direct violence in Sri Lanka, use a media centre against a lawfully elected democratic Government and self-governing local institutions, are supported and permitted to buy, possess arms and communication equipment, and conduct military exercises. They are permitted to come over to Sri Lanka with men and military material to wage war on an independent democratic Government.

Though promises have been made that all this will be stopped these promises have not been fulfilled. Because of open warfare between these groups a large quantity of arms and equipment was confiscated in Tamil Nadu. The communication equipment confiscated was returned. They are used to direct the war in Sri Lanka. The Central Government of India is aware of these facts.

The Government of Sri Lanka continues to be committed to make all efforts to arrive at a political solution. But it cannot ignore LTTE's and other acts, they kill their rivals, they kill and abduct Sinhala, Tamil and Muslims, innocent civilians, including women, children and babies in arms. Can the government of Sri Lanka or any Government stay idle in the face of such atrocities? While paving the path for a solution, we have to take steps to strengthen the preservation of law and order and free our citizens of all races from the attacks of a band of terrorists. While pursuing this policy it is entitled to use its power to persuade the terrorists that their efforts cannot succeed but will only cause hardships to the inhabitants living among them in parts of the Jaffna Peninsula. . . .

Summing up we state that our Government is committed to non-violence. If the terrorist groups give up violence and lay down their arms, the Government will immediately direct the Security Services to stay in their barracks. We will then implement the Provincial Councils scheme and hold elections so that together with the other 7 provinces the people of the Northern and Eastern provinces may elect their Councils, Members, Ministers, Chief Ministers and govern themselves in all the subjects and functions devolved on these Councils as discussed and decided with the TULF and the Indian Government. The Tamil groups can take part in these elections for they will be pardoned under an amnesty if they abandon violence.

All we ask of the Indian Government is, not to permit the soil of India to be used for violent activity against a friendly neighbour and not to permit such activities to be brought over to Sri Lanka in the form of men or arms. This Government's sole aim is to permit Democracy and the Rule of Law to flourish once again in the Northern and Eastern Provinces, as in the other provinces, under the administration of the elected representatives of the people living in them.

The Government of India should help us to achieve this goal and persuade the Government of Tamil Nadu to do the same.

The Vadamarachchi Campaign

The note of recrimination one observes in this draft letter suffused the exchange of diplomatic messages between the two governments in February 1987. Both governments were prisoners of their democratic electorates: the Sri Lankan president and his party could not be seen to buckle under pressure from the LTTE or the Indian government; the last named had to pay heed to Tamil Nadu opinion and the Sri Lankan Tamil groups supported by Tamil Nadu and working in association if not in tandem with it.

By the early part of March, with the Sri Lankan army seemingly intent on proceeding with its reestablishment of control over the Jaffna peninsula, the TULF made an appeal to Rajiv Gandhi, urging that the Sri Lankan government be restrained from proceeding with the course of military action it was engaged in. And of course there was pressure once more from Tamil Nadu.

In March the two governments made one more attempt to revive the stalled political process. On 14 March an Indian emissary, another minister of state, Dinesh Singh, arrived in Colombo with a message for discussion from the Indian prime minister. The basis for getting the negotiations started afresh was agreed upon. The Sri Lankan government stood by its policy outlines conveyed on 12 and 13 February. The Sri Lankan security services were asked to stop their offensive against the LTTE in order to get the negotiations started again. At the end of March the Sri Lankan government offered the Tamil separatist activists a cease-fire for the duration of the national holidays in April 1987. Although the LTTE made no response to this offer, the government nevertheless went ahead and announced a cessation of hostilities during the holiday period.

The LTTE spurned this offer and responded with the massacre of about 125 passengers traveling in buses on the road from Trincomalee to Colombo on Good Friday. The LTTE's allies, the Eelam Revolutionary Organization of Students (EROS) group, followed this up by exploding a bomb in Colombo's main bus station leaving over one hundred persons dead. The first incident might have been avoided had the army not stopped its patrols of the Colombo-Trincomalee road on the assumption that it was not necessary to do so because a cease-fire had been declared and the army had been instructed to remain in their barracks. They had relaxed their guard as the people at large prepared for a long week of national holidays—the Sinhalese-Tamil New Year, Good Friday, and Easter Sunday.

Faced with a serious erosion of political support as a result of these outrages,[23] the government revived its plans to regain control of the Jaffna peninsula. This time the government announced that it was seeking a military solution. The objective was to weaken the LTTE militarily, and to bring the Jaffna peninsula under the government's control. The strategy was to control the coasts of the Jaffna peninsula rather than to move into the town of Jaffna. In short it was Athulathmudali's rather than Jayewardene's strategy and tactics that were adopted.

"Operation Liberation," which began on 26 May in the Vadamarach-chi division in the northeastern part of the peninsula, was directed at preventing the hitherto easy movement of men and matériel from Tamil Nadu. It was also chosen as a target because Prabhakaran's hometown was located there. By the end of May, Sri Lankan forces had gained control of this area. The LTTE, the most formidable Tamil separatist group, had suffered a serious setback in a region they had dominated for a long time. This demonstration of the LTTE's failure as a fighting force triggered a chain of events that resulted eventually in Indian military intervention in Sri Lanka's ethnic conflict.[24]

At this point India moved swiftly to prevent the subjugation of the Jaffna peninsula by the Sri Lankan forces. High Commissioner J. N. Dixit pointedly informed Minister of National Security Lalith Athulathmudali that India would not permit the Sri Lankan army to take Jaffna.[25] That afternoon President Jayewardene had ceremonially opened the Bank of Ceylon's new headquarters building. In the course of his speech on that occasion he had dwelt at some length on the Vadamarachchi operation, and the government's intention to proceed with it until the LTTE forces were defeated. In the evening Dixit called on him at his home in Ward

Place and conveyed a message from the government of India. The gist of it was written by Dixit (on an envelope!). It read as follows:

1. Deeply disappointed and distressed.
2. Thousands of civilians killed since 1983 has aroused tremendous indignation.
3. Your latest offensive in Jaffna peninsula has altered the entire basis of our understanding.
4. We cannot accept genocide.
5. Please do not force us to review our policies.[26]

The "review of our policies" Dixit threatened on behalf of the Indian government came very quickly. There was first a well-publicized monetary grant of U.S.$3.2 million from the Tamil Nadu government to the LTTE and its allies. The Indian government, for its part, escalated the level of its own involvement in the Sri Lankan imbroglio when it announced that it would be sending shipments of food and petroleum products to Jaffna, which, it claimed, was facing a severe shortage of these items through the blockade by the Sri Lankan forces.

New Delhi's reaction to the Sri Lankan government's successful military campaign in the north of the island against the LTTE was a carefully orchestrated exercise in political pressure. The idea was to send food supplies and fuel, but in a flotilla of twenty Indian fishing boats rather than Indian navy ships. The fact is that there was really no shortage of food in Jaffna at this stage. Food trucks sent to Jaffna had been stopped by the LTTE at the strategically important Elephant Pass, the point of entry to the Jaffna peninsula, and to that extent any temporary shortage of food in some locations was the result of the LTTE's actions rather than of any deliberate policy on the part of the government. Nevertheless the Sri Lankan government went along with the Indians on this. A ceremonial welcome had been arranged for the boats and the principal government official in the north of the country, the government agent in Jaffna, and the Sri Lankan Red Cross were to receive the food and fuel on behalf of the government. The flotilla of boats—which had been arranged in Tamil Nadu—would go back with a cargo of gifts from the Sri Lankan government.[27]

But things went disastrously wrong as a result of an LTTE initiative. In Sri Lanka the government had decided to make a public show of welcoming the flotilla and had indicated this to the Indian government. On 2 June, however, an LTTE group waylaid a bus in the Batticaloa district and killed a group of 32 *bhikkhus* (members of the Buddhist order), most of them youths and boys undergoing training for ordination. Once the news of this massacre spread throughout the country, the Sri Lankan government was compelled to change its plans. Thus instead of giving an official welcome to the flotilla of boats, it decided to demonstrate that the boats were not welcome, and a young naval officer acting in conformity with his general instructions refused to allow the flotilla to enter Sri Lankan territorial waters. India had invested a great deal of publicity on this venture—the press had been alerted and were actually present in some of the boats—only to find that the flotilla was turned back by representatives of the Sri Lankan navy.

When this happened the Indian government decided on predictably stronger measures. The action resorted to came as a great shock to the Sri Lankan government. In a blatant violation of international law and of Sri Lankan airspace, five Indian Antonov-22 transport planes escorted by four Mirage-2,000 combat planes dropped food and medical supplies in Jaffna on the following day, thirty-two tons in all.[28] Sri Lanka's high commissioner in Delhi, Bernard Tillakaratne, was summoned to the Ministry of External Affairs and told about the airdrop. He was asked to inform Colombo that any aircraft attempting to intercept the Indian planes would be shot down. The Indian aircraft left for Sri Lanka almost as soon as the information on their departure was given to Tillakaratne. The Sri Lankan government had exactly thirty-five minutes in which to prepare for it. This violation of Sri Lankan air space was seen as an unmistakable demonstration of Indian support for the Tamil separatist movement in Sri Lanka. The Indian supply of food to Jaffna continued over the next few weeks by sea with the formal but clearly reluctant agreement of the Sri Lankan government. The result was that by the end of June Indo–Sri Lankan relations were mired in mutual recrimination and deep suspicion. And the island's ethnic conflict seemed headed for prolonged and debilitating deadlock.

The northeast coast of the Jaffna peninsula—the smugglers' coast— was under the control of the Sri Lankan army and navy, and the camps the army had newly established in that narrow strip of territory braced themselves to withstand the attacks the LTTE was certain to launch against them. The fact that the LTTE had been dislodged from the area came as a morale booster to the army. But the Tamils of the Jaffna peninsula had taken heart from the Indian intervention—the airdrop of food, and the more formally correct but equally unwelcome supply of food sent by ship. The message India appeared to be sending seemed clear enough: it would not permit either the military subjugation of Jaffna with the bloodshed it would cause or an economic blockade of the Jaffna peninsula to bring its people to their knees. The Indian high commission in Colombo, through its first secretary for political affairs H. S. Puri, figured very prominently in this food distribution campaign in Jaffna. The ecstatic welcome the Indians received in Jaffna—it was garlands and cheers all the way—was one of the most conspicuous features of this episode. Those who organized the distribution of food on this occasion were left with the illusion that they had Jaffna literally in the palms of their hands. They were to learn soon enough that nothing is so evanescent as the plaudits of a hard-pressed people in their first encounters with their presumed liberators.

This demonstration of Indian power against a small neighbor achieved a number of objectives those who planned these operations had set themselves. It had stopped any expansion of the Sri Lankan army's campaign in the Jaffna peninsula after the Vadamarachchi expedition; it saved the LTTE from any further weakening of its military strength; and above all it reduced the Sri Lankan government to political impotence in regard to its initiatives on the Tamil problem. In the rest of the country the mood was one of anxiety over a long war of attrition in the north (there was less anxiety about the eastern coast); among the people at large as well as among most sections of the intelligentsia an attitude to India ranged from atavistic fear to a helpless rage, an attitude Prime Minister R. Premadasa's speeches mirrored all too accurately.

Notes

1. Indian negotiators claimed that the idea came from President Jayewardene himself, but the fact is that it originated from Indian officials. A. P. Venkateswaran, interview with the author, 24 April 1990.

2. This information was provided by a number of persons, including Sri Lanka's then high commissioner in New Delhi, Bernard Tillakaratne, interview, 2 February 1988.

3. See the reports in the *Sun,* 11, 13, 16 November 1986.

4. *Sun,* 22 November 1986.

5. This report was carried in the *Weekend Sun,* 7 December 1986.

6. Vincent Perera, MP for Yatiyantota and later district minister for Amparai.

7. The extracts that follow are from Dias Abeysinghe's notes.

8. The LTTE spokesman on this occasion was Balasubramaniam Kanagaratnam, better known by his nom de guerre of Rahim; associated with him was Sathasivam Krishnakumar, or Kittu.

9. For discussion of the background to Venkateswaran's dismissal, see Nicholas Nugent, *Rajiv Gandhi: Son of a Dynasty* (London: BBC Books, 1990), 122–23, 172.

10. He became an active member of the World Federation of Tamils and participated in its propaganda campaigns. See, for instance, his chapter, "Indian Government Had Betrayed Its Own Culture" in N. Seevaratnam, ed., *The Tamil National Question and the Indo–Sri Lanka Accord* (New Delhi: Konark, 1989), 11–15. The paper had been presented at the first International Tamil Conference held in London in 1988.

11. A copy of this telegram is available in the J. R. Jayewardene MSS. A handwritten note at the bottom of the page states that it had been handed personally to President Jayewardene by Indian High Commissioner J. N. Dixit on 9 February 1987 at 11:15 A.M.

12. Available in the J. R. Jayewardene MSS.

13. Also available in the J. R. Jayewardene MSS.

14. The copy of this message in the J. R. Jayewardene MSS carries a note "Recd 9 p.m., 18. 2. 87."

15. There is a note on which this message was based in the J. R. Jayewardene MSS.

16. Lalith Athulathmudali made these points on several occasions in discussions with me. His views were endorsed by President Jayewardene himself.

17. Lalith Athulathmudali, interviews with the author, late 1987 and July 1991.

18. Ram, then deputy editor of the *Hindu*, is presently editor of the *Frontline*, a weekly of the *Hindu*. Interview with the author, 17 December 1991 in New Delhi.

19. At the 17 December 1991 interview M. Ram stated that Dixit was somewhat baffled by this proposal, and had told President Jayewardene as politely as possible that the Indian government was not ready for such a commitment.

20. A paper dated 17 November 1986 in the J. R. Jayewardene MSS outlines the main discussions at Bangalore; its second paragraph reads as follows: "India to underwrite the agreement. No third party. Natwar and Hameed to work out."

21. The letter quoted here is based on a copy in the J. R. Jayewardene MSS.

22. The reference was clearly to the interview with Prabhakaran, "Profile of a Tiger," published in the well-known Indian journal *India Today*, 20 June 1986, in which he stated that "I shot and killed the former Mayor of Jaffna, Alfred Durayappa."

23. For a description of the public anger over the incidents, see Sinha Ratnatunga, *The Politics of Terrorism: The Sri Lanka Experience* (Canberra: International Fellowship for Social and Economic Development, 1968), 363–64.

24. "Operation Liberation" is reviewed in Ratnatunga, *Politics of Terrorism,* 365–67.

25. Athulathmudali made this known to President Jayewardene and the cabinet on 12 August 1987. The same point was made by Gamini Dissanayake in my interview with him on 23 September 1989. Minutes of discussions at the cabinet meeting of 12 August 1987 are available in the J. R. Jayewardene MSS.

26. This note is now in the J. R. Jayewardene MSS. Whether the warning to Athulathmudali was conveyed prior to the delivery of this note is not clear.

27. This is based on information derived from discussions with Jayewardene at this time. The same point was made by Sri Lanka's high commissioner in Delhi, Bernard Tillakaratne, in an interview, 2 February 1988.

28. This information was gleaned from interviews with officials of Sri Lanka's Ministry of Foreign Affairs, including Bernard Tillakaratne.

11

The Making of the Indo–Sri Lanka Accord: The Final Phase, June–July 1987

A Changing of the Guard

ONE IMPORTANT DEVELOPMENT for Sri Lanka in the aftermath of the unusual but emphatic demonstration of Indian power seen in the airdrop by the Indian air force was a painful reappraisal of the options available to Sri Lanka in meeting the threat posed by the Liberation Tigers of Tamil Eelam (LTTE) to the peace and stability of the country. The military campaign against the LTTE had ground to a halt, and the most the army could do was hold on to the areas they had secured and to consolidate their position there. As for the political options available the official Indian attitude seemed to indicate that the only possible choice was to work within the framework of agreements reached so far under Indian aegis, that is to say, on the decisions taken at Bangalore in November 1987 and in Colombo on 18 and 19 December. But it was clearly too early to renew negotiations after the humiliation inflicted on Sri Lanka in early June.

Nevertheless there was a revival of the negotiation process within two weeks of the airdrop. It began tentatively at first and through the use of a private individual as the go-between. That private individual was the Indian journalist M. Ram, who used his access to a cabinet minister, Gamini Dissanayake, minister for lands, land development and Mahavali development for this purpose.[1] From the middle of June 1987 on, Dissanayake took over the role of principal negotiator for the Sri Lankan government with India on the resolution of Sri Lanka's ethnic conflict. In effect there was a suppression of Lalith Athulathmudali, who had played the leading role in these negotiations on behalf of the Sri Lankan government hitherto and had been its chief spokesman on matters relating to the negotiations in Parliament and elsewhere. As minister of national security and deputy minister of defense, he had given political leadership to the campaign against the LTTE up to that time. In an extraordinary development the negotiation process moved to Gamini Dissanayake and his office, and Lalith Athulathmudali was kept out of the negotiating process.

We need to remember that President Jayewardene was now eighty years old—he would be celebrating his eighty-first birthday on 17 September—and was expected to retire from office at the end of 1988, a mere eighteen months hence. Now the formulation of Sri Lanka's India policy was caught up in the jockeying for the succession to President Jayewardene, in which up to this time the front-runner had clearly been the prime minister, R. Premadasa. But eighteen months is a long time in politics, and there was the prospect that either Lalith Athulathmudali or Gamini Dissanayake could beat him to the tape. Or again, if R. Premadasa did secure the succession, the prime minister's post was available to either of these two contenders.

On a more practical basis, Athulathmudali had two difficulties, or rather one principal difficulty with two facets, as a result of the impasse in regard to India. He had been associated too closely with the enunciation and implementation of policies and measures in regard to the negotiation process, and in matters relating to security and defense, to escape the consequences of the events of late May and early June 1987. Besides, he was a firm critic of Dixit's style of diplomacy, and held him responsible for the hardening of the Indian attitude to Sri Lanka because of his insensitivity to the political difficulties the government faced from the LTTE's activities, especially those of its terrorist groups. Dissanayake, on the other hand, found it easier to work with Dixit. Over the next six weeks they worked together in a concerted attempt to draft the basis of an agreement between the two countries.

Dissanayake was very much an Indophile, as was evident in a memorandum (in the form of a long letter) dated 10 June 1985, which he submitted to President Jayewardene on the general theme of Indo–Sri Lankan relations. There he argued the case for paying greater heed than had hitherto been done to the geopolitical realities of Sri Lanka's situation. This memorandum had alerted the president to the need for a reappraisal of Sri Lanka's policies in regard to India.[2] One of its most significant features was its annexure in which he argued the case for the study of Finland's relations with the Soviet Union as a model on which to base Sri Lanka's relations with India.

It would be evident, in the light of this very thought-provoking document, that Dissanayake was a strong supporter of a policy of negotiations through Indian mediation. He had participated in the negotiations in Sri Lanka throughout the period 1984–86, and it was largely through his initiative that agreement was reached in 1984 on a formula for distribution of state-owned land. That formula was endorsed during the discussions that took place in 1986.

On 23 September 1989, Dissanayake recalled a confidential security briefing sometime late in 1986 or early in 1987, given to some members of the cabinet, at the request of President Jayewardene, by the heads of the security services including the police.[3] At that time the conflict with the LTTE was absorbing a great deal of expenditure and causing heavy casualties on both sides. In general the views expressed at the meeting were pessimistic. General Cyril Ranatunga, general officer of the Joint Operations Command, spoke of the extraordinary difficulties of fighting the LTTE in a situation where the latter had the support of the people of Jaffna, and where moreover no intelligence information on the LTTE could be secured.[4] Furthermore heavy casualties caused by land mines were affecting the morale of the troops. These officers had spoken of the need for political solutions and warned that a military solution was illusory. Even if such a solution could be achieved it would be a temporary one unless the political problems were handled effectively.

Dissanayake asserted that this was not the view the cabinet received through Lalith Athulathmudali, who exuded confidence in a military victory over the LTTE to the very end. The fact, however, is that this latter view was less than fair to Lalith Athulathmudali. He did know the views of the senior officers in Colombo, but was aware of a sharp difference of opinion between them and field officers in the Northern Province. The latter were far more confident of the possibility of weakening the LTTE militarily to the point of making them more amenable to a political solution within the framework of the settlements negotiated between July/August 1985 and the end of 1986.

The displacement of Lalith Athulathmudali from the negotiating process from mid-June 1987 on brought to an end the consensus of opinion within the cabinet on the negotiations and Indian mediation. From this point there were sections of the cabinet who had serious reservations about the strategy and tactics of the negotiating process, a theme we shall pursue later on in this chapter.

Early Initiatives, June 1987

What happened over the four weeks after the food drop by the Indian air force was a superb demonstration of the "art of ambivalence" the high priest of the extension of India's power, K. Subhramanyam, has spoken of in relation to Pakistan:

> The art of ambivalence is to let the people know that one has the capability, then to deny that the capability is backed by intention to do what one can, to drop hints that it may have to be done under certain contingencies, then more hints that such a course has been imposed upon the party by external circumstances, then again to deny the development, inspire those not in authority to disclose the possibility of it, allow discussions to take place on the general assumption of the capability, once again officially deny it, release some partial but inadequate information about the capability, carry out actions which tend to reinforce the suspicions, issue statements that confirm interest in dispelling any suspicion yet vehemently deny having embarked on the course of action.[5]

A renewal of the negotiating process in June 1987 led eventually to the belated signing of the accord the two governments had originally scheduled for January 1987. The main phases in this, outlined below, form a classic study in the demonstration of the limits of a small power's initiatives when it confronts a regional power intent on imposing its will on it. All the initiatives now lay with the regional power, India.

Within a fortnight of the Indian food drop there was talk once more of a negotiated settlement of the Sri Lankan conflict through Indian mediation. Those who had some inkling of these early moves would not take them too seriously. They had heard of peace moves so often and just as often these had come to naught. How was it possible to expect something more fruitful after the Indian humiliation of Sri Lanka, and the resultant bitter anti-Indian feeling in the country? The general belief was that Sri Lanka would be under tremendous pressure to make more concessions to the Tamil separatists.

On 12 June 1987 Gamini Dissanayake received what turned out to be the first of these feelers.[6] It came in the form of a letter from M. Ram, the influential deputy editor of the well-known Madras-based Indian newspaper, the *Hindu*. Dissanayake had come to know Ram during his visits to India as chairman of the Board of Control for Cricket in Sri Lanka. Ram and his newspaper had taken an active interest in Sri Lanka's Tamil problem ever since it had become a major divisive issue in the region, and had been in touch with many of the principal figures in the negotiations between the two countries, including President Jayewardene himself. Given Ram's easy access at that time to Rajiv Gandhi, the presumption was that the contents of the letter had been discussed with the Indian prime minister himself and had his approval. The letter outlined a set of proposals for a possible settlement of the Sri Lankan crisis through Indian mediation. First, the Sri Lankan government would not reopen military operations in the Jaffna peninsula; second, the Sri Lankan government would remove all restrictions then in force for the transport of food and other essentials to Jaffna, and would restore telecommunications facilities; third, the government and the LTTE should agree to begin negotiations for a political settlement. The talks could be held at any agreed venue. Some agreement should be reached about a broad recognition of Tamil rights in a pluralistic society and the devolution of authority to a Tamil-dominated ethnic area or areas, with appropriate safeguards for other ethnic groups living there. Most important, India would play a mediatory role in all discussions, and would underwrite the implementation of any agreement reached. The underlying assumption was that the resolution of the conflict would not affect Sri Lanka's independence or its territorial integrity.

Ram's initiative proved to be one of the important early steps in the train of events that led to the signing of the Indo–Sri Lanka Accord in July 1987. When the information it contained was transmitted to President Jayewardene he looked on it as a means of breaking through the political immobility that confronted him after the Indian airdrop. He also saw it as a means of using Indian power to check the LTTE's political ambitions in Sri Lanka. That was the only option available to him after Prime Minister Rajiv Gandhi had demonstrated India's perception of the permissible limits of Sri Lanka's military action in reimposing control over the Jaffna peninsula. The Indian high commissioner J. N. Dixit was given a mandate to begin negotiations within the framework of the principles enunciated in Ram's letter.

After these negotiations had commenced and were proceeding apace, a stiff official response from India to an announcement by the Sri Lankan government that local government elections would be held in Sri Lanka along with by-elections to sixteen vacant parliamentary seats in the Northern and Eastern Provinces brought to mind K. Subrahmanyam's "art of ambivalence." The TULF who held these seats had vacated them after the passage of the sixth Amendment to the Constitution in 1983, which placed a ban on the advocacy of separatism as a political objective and required all MPs to take an oath to uphold Sri Lanka's unitary Constitution.

While the local government elections could have gone ahead if the government had really persisted with them, it was unlikely that the by-elections could have been held in the Northern and Eastern Provinces in the situation prevailing there, with the LTTE riding high because of the newly established rapport with the Indian government and the Tamil United Liberation Front (TULF) unwilling to contest them in the face of the opposition of the LTTE and of the Indians. The Indian riposte on 1 July surprised President Jayewardene. It took the form of a personal and confidential message from Rajiv Gandhi to him, delivered by High Commissioner Dixit at the president's private residence in Ward Place at 7:30 in the evening.[7] It read as follows:

1. While there is no intention at all to interfere in the internal affairs of Sri Lanka, the Government of India has taken note of recent formal decisions taken by [*sic*] Sri Lankan government to hold bye-elections to 16 vacant Parliamentary seats from the North and the East of Sri Lanka and to hold elections to Municipal Councils, Urban Councils and Pradeshiya Sabhas [*sic*].

    It is the Government of India's assessment that going in for these elections without resolving the ethnic problem on the basis of a durable framework of compromises by peaceful means, will only prolong the ethnic crisis of Sri Lanka, including the violence which characterizes this crisis.

    To India this also implies that the processes that we have followed since 1983 to evolve a compromise are no longer valid. The Government of India has also taken note of the views expressed by all other important political Parties in Sri Lanka opposing these proposed elections. In this context, the President may carefully consider the implications of holding these elections unilaterally and then take a final decision.

2. India suggested that relief supplies to Jaffna may continue for some more time in response to genuine needs of the people there. The relief operations have also helped in bringing down the temperature and reducing violence in the peninsula. The time so gained can be utilized for positive purposes.

3. The Government of India believes that a peaceful political solution to the ethnic problem is possible if the Sri Lankan government evolves a genuine solution which would meet the basic concerns of the Tamils. If the Sri Lankan government has any further ideas in this regard, India would be willing to cooperate on the basis of such ideas to evolve a compromise with the Tamils. Prime Minister would like to have His Excellency President Jayewardene's reactions to this suggestion if any.

It was a blatant act of interference in Sri Lanka's internal affairs and it rattled President Jayewardene, who could not reconcile its tone and contents with the feeler sent through Ram, and the negotiations that had begun on that basis. On 2 July he gave an interview to Professor Edward Azar, the Lebanese-American head of the Center for International Development and Conflict Management at the University of Maryland, who was then on a brief visit to Sri Lanka. President Jayewardene was in a very thoughtful and reflective mood on that occasion, deeply disturbed by the very muted criticisms of the Indian actions from the Western powers, especially the United States. Naturally, Indo–Sri Lankan relations figured very prominently in the discussions, of which Azar kept a comprehensive record.[8] Two brief extracts from that document are quoted below. They have a particular poignancy and sadness in the light of later events— the assassination of Rajiv Gandhi by the LTTE.

India says the ball is in our court. However I am not sure to whom to throw it back. In this, India is engaged in threatening the future of Sri Lanka and perhaps the region. Unless India acts positively, the future of Sri Lanka will witness hard times but so will the future of India. You can not play with fire without worrying about the spread of it to beyond what you control.

The second extract read:

Sri Lanka wonders who is helping increase the level of victimization and violence. India may be weakening itself by helping those who would destabilize Sri Lanka.

The Sri Lankan government returned the ball to the Indian side of the court. It took the form of a telegram dated 6 July in which President Jayewardene explained Sri Lanka's views. This important note is quoted in full below.[10]

There is reference in your note about the elections we propose to hold in the North and East. These elections are necessary to enable people to express their views. These will in no way mitigate against a political settlement. Once a political settlement is arrived at, if necessary, these election results can be reviewed.

To postpone elections would be to continue the freeze placed on the democracy in the Northern Province. This is exactly what the LTTE/EROS [Eelam Revolutionary Organization of Students] wants to ensure.

We note that during the period of relief supplies the LTTE has activated their sea movements from India and consequent to that they have attacked our Army establishments. The LTTE have done this despite their own cessation of hostilities during the period of relief. Do you expect the Sri Lanka Government to remain inactive in the face of such threats [?]

We stand committed in making every effort to resolve this matter politically. We believe that the TULF and also the other terrorist groups which have lost their military power may want to do so but on our present information it is quite clear that the LTTE and probably the EROS do not want anything other than a Separate State.

Recent LTTE settlement [*sic*] confirm their intransigence. We are convinced that the LTTE will come for talks only when, like the other terrorists groups, their military power is sharply reduced. We seek your co-operation to do so.

However, we are prepared to discuss the following ideas to resolve the current problem within Sri Lanka:—

(a) Specific discussions regarding alleged grievances of the Tamil community covering the whole of Sri Lanka, particularly those matters referred to the UNP [United National Party] Manifesto of 1977.

(b) The establishment of Provincial Councils set out in June 1986 and the improvement and adjustment made thereafter.

(c) A setting up of the Boundary Commission to determine the boundaries of the Northern and Eastern Provinces in order to elevate [*sic*][9] the fears of all communities.

(d) Setting up of Inter Provincial Councils enabling cooperation between different Councils on any matter of the devolved subjects. We are prepared to discuss further details of the modalities of Inter Provincial Councils.

(e) The wishes of all the communities in the Northern and Eastern Provinces must be considered and there must be accommodation of their views.[10]

Throughout this period there appeared to be no sign of improvement in relations. Indeed, Sri Lanka was intent on boycotting a South Asian Association for Regional Co-operation (SAARC) ministerial meeting scheduled for early July in Delhi, and it required considerable persuasion from Pakistan and Bangladesh to get the Sri Lankan government to send Foreign Minister A. C. S. Hameed to attend this meeting. Yet a dramatic change occurred between 7 and 15 July 1987. What happened to bring about this change? One factor was probably President Jayewardene's note of 6 July. Also, it would appear that the Indians, and Dixit in particular, had received a signal from the LTTE just at this time offering to accept the 18/19 December 1986 proposals if an amalgamation of the Northern and Eastern Provinces was incorporated in them.[11] Once this "signal" was received, messages flashed between Colombo and New Delhi and both leaders felt that this would help break the deadlock.

President Jayewardene seized the opportunity to lay down his own conditions.[12] He indicated that the offer contained in his note of 6 July was "conditional to an acceptance of the Proposals from 4.5.86 to 19.12.86, and the relevant proposals finalized on 30.8.85 to 13.9.85." By this he meant a continuity of the negotiating process that had commenced with Bhandari's initiatives and had been interrupted by the Sri Lankan campaign against the LTTE in early 1987, and the Indian government's actions of early June 1987.

In addition to this he insisted that if any Tamil separatist group refused to accept this settlement

a) Government of India [would] co-operate directly with the Sri Lanka Government to implement these proposals;

b) . . . [and would] ensure that the Indian Navy co-operates with the Sri Lankan Navy in preventing Tamil separatist activities from affecting Sri Lanka.

c) . . . [would] deport from India, Sri Lanka citizens who are taking part in terrorist activities or advocate separatism.

d) . . . [and would] expedite the repatriation from Sri Lanka of Indian citizens to India who are resident here simultaneously with the return of Sri Lanka refugees from Tamil Nadu.

The fifth condition laid down by President Jayewardene was of special significance.

[If] the Sri Lanka Government requests the Government of India to afford it military assistance to implement these proposals, the Government of India will co-operate by giving such assistance as requested.[12]

Reactivating Negotiations, July 1987

The negotiations went on, with greater confidentiality than in the immediate past. Sometime after 9 July Rajiv Gandhi confirmed that India was intent on helping to break the deadlock in the negotiations on a settlement of Sri Lanka's ethnic conflict, and that he would force the Tamil separatists to accept a settlement on the basis of the agreements reached between the governments of India and Sri Lanka between May and December 1986. The gist of the offer was as follows. If the Sri Lankan government would agree to an amalgamation of the Northern and Eastern provinces on a *temporary* basis, India would impose a settlement on the Tamils. If the LTTE would not agree, the settlement would still go ahead, and they would be forced to comply.

To the skeptics in the government this offer was no more than a trap, one more humiliation Rajiv Gandhi seemed intent upon heaping on Sri Lanka. However, a small group within the government were inclined to consider the offer as an important breakthrough to a negotiated settlement. The leadership was taken, as usual, by President Jayewardene, and he had the support of Gamini Dissanayake and Minister of Finance Ronnie de Mel. The president came up with the suggestion that the *temporary* amalgamation should have a time limit, and that a referendum be held in the Eastern Province to decide whether the people there wished to continue the link with the Northern Province, a line of policy he himself had proposed to Rajiv Gandhi in his letter of 25 February. The Indians agreed to this suggestion with remarkable alacrity.

In agreeing to an amalgamation of the two provinces, even on a temporary basis, President Jayewardene was taking a calculated risk. He himself had gone on record in the past—as early as 1957—and frequently in the early 1980s as being strongly opposed to the concept of a Tamil ethno-region encompassing the Northern and Eastern Provinces. He was aware that neither the Sinhalese nor the Muslims, who together constitute 60 percent of the population of the Eastern Province, would willingly accept its merger with the overwhelmingly Tamil Northern Province. There was, of course, the escape clause of a referendum, which President Jayewardene hoped would mollify critics of this proposal within the government and in the country at large. As against this he saw what he thought were the great advantages of getting the Indian government to underwrite a settlement of the Sri Lankan dispute.

By mid-July the Indian government, through its envoy in Colombo, the masterful J. N. Dixit, indicated that they would indeed underwrite such a settlement. They requested as a quid pro quo an agreement between the two countries that would satisfy some of the foreign policy concerns of India in regard to Sri Lanka.

By now Rajiv Gandhi was tired of Prabhakaran and the LTTE and felt that it was time for a decisive move. He had made up his mind that he would proceed with implementation of any deal he would make with President Jayewardene, with the LTTE's acquiescence if possible, or without the LTTE if necessary. Indeed he had decided that he would impose it on the LTTE and use force for that purpose. He was therefore responsive to the last point in President Jayewardene's undated note, referred to earlier, which states that in case "the Sri Lanka Government requests the Government of India to afford it military assistance to implement these proposals, the Government of India will co-operate by giving such assistance as requested."

The Sri Lankan government then made a crucial decision in insisting that any agreement reached must be between the two governments, not between the Sri Lankan government and the LTTE. India readily agreed to this, and proceeded to add that if this were indeed to be so, then her own foreign policy interests must be part of the agreement. These were to include Trincomalee and other ports; foreign communications centers based on Sri Lankan soil;[13] the training of Sri Lankan troops; and the foreign military presence in Sri Lanka (Israelis and British mercenaries).

President Jayewardene was by then so deeply disappointed with the failure of the United States and other Western powers to condemn the Indian airdrop that he was willing to accept these restraints on Sri Lanka's freedom of action if it meant that Indian support could be secured to effectively curb the Tamil separatist movement.[14] The agreement that emerged was so framed, however, that the existing arrangements in regard to these issues would not be immediately disturbed.[15]

Once agreement was reached on the broad principles of the accord, both parties set to work on the details. These latter were hammered out in the course of discussions between Dixit and Gamini Dissanayake, with the president's approval and encouragement. Much of the drafting was done by Dixit and Gamini Dissanayake at the Bullers Road office of the Mahavali Development Authority in Colombo.[16] The president himself vetted each successive preliminary draft until agreement was reached on an acceptable final version.[17]

In preparing these drafts of an agreement, Gamini Dissanayake and the officials who helped him in this business ensured that the concept of a traditional homeland of the Tamils should not be endorsed. They hit on the phrase "historical habitations," intended to mean "where the Tamils had lived," and which they felt did not have the separatist political connotations of the term "traditional homelands."[18]

A draft of the accord was ready by 15 July for discussion by the cabinet at its meeting of 16 July. Dixit was invited to meet members of the cabinet on two occasions, 16 July and 27 July 1987, to explain the implications of the draft as the Indian government saw it and especially to explain the nature of India's commitment and her interests.[19] On both occasions the cabinet moved to the conference room of the old Senate building in Republic Square when Dixit spoke to its members. The discussions were not in the cabinet room proper.[20] Dixit recalled that on the first occasion—15 July—the most critical comments came from ministers Gamini Jayasuriya (Agriculture), M. H. Mohammed (Transport), and Ranjith Atapattu (Health). Lalith Athulathmudali (minister of national security) was skeptical about the agreement from the outset. However, despite these critical comments from important cabinet ministers there was no formal opposition from any of them, much less from the cabinet as a whole, to President Jayewardene proceeding with the negotiations.

Once Rajiv Gandhi secured support for the main outlines of the accord from the Sri Lankan president, he moved very swiftly. He proposed that the accord be signed in Colombo on 25 July (Saturday). Jayewardene had to hold him back until 29 July (Wednesday). The Sri Lankan president needed to gain the formal support for the accord from the cabinet, from the Executive Committee of the UNP, and above all from the prime minister, who was out of the island and was due to return on 25 July. The cabinet was due to meet again on 27 July. By then the news of the impending signing of an agreement between Sri Lanka and India had leaked out; several versions, generally garbled, of its contents were being spoken of in the press. The news that Rajiv Gandhi would be in the island to sign an agreement could not be kept a secret for long. When the cabinet met on 27 July, Dixit was called in once again for discussions, to answer questions relating to the proposed accord directed at him by its critics. This time the critics included Prime Minister R. Premadasa, who had just returned from an overseas visit. Lalith Athulathmudali remained the principal critic. Dixit recalled visiting Athulathmudali around 25 July intent on securing the latter's support for the agreement, but the latter remained skeptical. His main objection was that the accord seemed more concerned with Indo–Sri Lankan relations than with Sri Lanka's ethnic conflict.[21]

The cabinet meeting of 27 July took place against a general background of violent opposition to the accord led by the proscribed Janatha Vimukthi Peramuna (JVP), in association—willing or not—with the Sri Lanka Freedom Party (SLFP), and a large mass of *bhikkhus*. Indeed the signs seemed so unpropitious that even President Jayewardene began to worry about the situation. But in an extraordinary display of personal and political courage he went ahead with arrangements for the signing of the agreement. Although it was virtually impossible to put it off now that the Indian prime minister was scheduled to arrive in the island for the official signing the outbreak of violence in and around the city of Colombo and other parts of the country was fraught with so much danger that he would have been justified in postponing the signing till the government regained control over the situation. The ringing endorsement of the accord President Jayewardene hoped the cabinet would give him on 27 July was not forthcoming. Nevertheless the cabinet as a whole gave him authority to proceed with the signing of the accord on the scheduled date of 29 July.

Several factors were at work behind the pressure for signing an accord. First, for Gandhi the compelling force was the need to gain some political "triumph" to overcome the damaging effects of his many recent electoral failures. Second, there was the need to arrive at a settlement while the charismatic Tamil Nadu chief minister, M. G. Ramachandran, was still alive. Ramachandran's health was failing rapidly. In India as in Sri Lanka, the general belief at the time was that Ramachandran's death would leave a huge vacuum in Tamil Nadu politics, and that the struggle to fill it would lead to instability and chaos. Third, the Indian government was visibly tired of its mediatory role in the Sri Lankan Tamil problem, and wanted to get it over with by converting it into a Sri Lankan rather than an Indian or Tamil Nadu problem. Fourth, there was the need to reach a settlement while President Jayewardene was still in control of things in Sri Lanka. The Indians believed—with good reason—that neither Prime Minister R. Premadasa nor Mrs. Bandaranaike, as potential successors to President Jayewardene, would have the same strong commitment to the package of proposals for a settlement of Sri Lanka's ethnic conflict that had been negotiated through 1984 to 1987.

The Sri Lankan president for his part was just as anxious to reach an understanding with the Indian government. The next presidential election was scheduled for the period 4 December 1988 to 3 January 1989, while parliamentary elections could be held at any opportune moment up to August 1989. An agreement with the Indian government on the basis of the terms negotiated between the middle of 1985 and mid-July 1987 would give his government time to begin the reconstruction and rehabilitation of the Northern and Eastern Provinces and to stimulate economic growth in other parts of the island in time for the elections. Moreover, his principal military advisers in Colombo were urging the need for a political settlement. They argued that the successful Vadamarachchi expedition should not blind the government to the realities of the military situation—the manpower resources of the Sri Lankan forces were inadequate for the purpose of holding the areas recently recaptured from the LTTE in the Jaffna peninsula. Thus the options, as they saw it, were either an honorable settlement underwritten by India or damaging reverses at the hands of the LTTE in territory in which the latter held most of the advantages.[22]

The Accord and Its Annexure

The principal document and its appendix (referred to as an annexure) of the Indo–Sri Lanka Accord faithfully embodied the proposals agreed to between the two governments since the middle of 1985. They are included in full as Appendix Documents IV and V in this volume. India's security concerns were contained in a letter from the Indian prime minister to the Sri Lankan president and the latter's rather brief response to it, included in this volume as Appendix Documents VI and VII. The first clause and its five subclauses of the principal document were in the nature of a preamble about the nature of the Sri Lankan polity and its "multi-ethnic, multi-lingual, and multi-religious plural society." The substance of the accord lay in its second clause, with its eighteen subclauses, beginning with 2.1 to 2.7, which dealt with the temporary amalgamation of the Northern and Eastern Provinces, and the referendum that would be held in the Eastern Province.

Subclause 2.9 was also important. It read as follows:

The emergency will be lifted in the Eastern and Northern Provinces by August 15, 1987. A cessation of hostilities will come into effect all over the island within 48 hours of the signing of this Agreement. All arms presently held by militant groups will be surrendered in accordance with an agreed procedure to authorities to be designated by the Government of Sri Lanka.

Consequent to the cessation of hostilities and the surrender of arms by militant groups, the Army and other security personnel will be confined to barracks in camps as of 25 May 1987. The process of surrendering arms and the confining of security personnel moving back to barracks shall be completed within 72 hours of the cessation of hostilities coming into effect.

In subclause 2.14 the Indian government agreed "to underwrite and guarantee the resolutions, and co-operate in the implementation of the proposals." The next subclause, 2.15, stated:

These proposals are conditional to an acceptance of the proposals negotiated from 4.5.1986 to 19.12.1986. Residual matters not finalized during the above negotiations shall be resolved between India and Sri Lanka within a period of six weeks of signing this agreement. These proposals are also conditional to the Government of India co-operating directly with the Government of Sri Lanka in their implementation.

Next was the vitally important question, so far as the Sri Lankan government was concerned, of what would be done in case "any militant groups operating in Sri Lanka" did not accept the proposals in the accord. This was dealt with in subclause 2.16, which stated that "These proposals are also conditional to the Government of India taking the following actions if any militant groups in Sri Lanka do not accept this framework of proposals for a settlement." Five conditions were laid down, four of them based on those insisted upon by President Jayewardene in his telegram to Prime Minister Rajiv Gandhi on 6 July 1987. The subclause included the condition that

> In the event that the Government of Sri Lanka requests the Government of India to afford military assistance to implement the proposals the Government of India will co-operate by giving to the Government of Sri Lanka such military assistance as and when requested.

The annexure to the agreement had six clauses, all of which clarified issues dealt with in the main document. We need to focus attention on the sixth clause:

> The Prime Minister of India and the President of Sri Lanka also agree that in terms of paragraph 2.14 and paragraph 2.16(c) of the Agreement an Indian Peace Keeping contingent may be invited by the President of Sri Lanka to guarantee and enforce the cessation of hostilities, if so required.

India's security concerns were outlined in Prime Minister Rajiv Gandhi's letter to the Sri Lankan president. The latter's response to this letter was extraordinarily brief. It merely said: "This is to confirm that the above correctly sets out the understanding reached between us."[23]

The employment by Sri Lanka of foreign military and intelligence personnel was the first of these issues identified; it was followed by three others. India sought assurances that Trincomalee or any other port in Sri Lanka would not be made available for military use by any country in a manner prejudicial to India's interests; and that the restoration and operation of the Trincomalee oil tank farm would be undertaken as a joint venture between India and Sri Lanka. There was, finally, a call for a review of Sri Lanka's agreements with foreign broadcasting organizations to ensure that any facilities set up by them in Sri Lanka would be used solely as public broadcasting facilities and not for any military or intelligence gathering purposes.

Of these, the second was a restatement of an obvious Indian concern. Sri Lanka would not, at any cost, want to get involved in any military use of these ports by others, especially any military use directed against India. But the first of these directly concerned Sri Lanka's own interests and was seen by critics of the accord as a constraint on *its* choices in security. The references were directly to an Israeli presence in the island and to British mercenary groups engaged in training Sri Lankan forces. Resort to these was forced on Sri Lanka by Indian pressure on Great Britain and other countries likely to be of assistance to Sri Lanka not to establish training facilities for Sri Lankan forces in the island. The Indian offer to provide training facilities and military supplies for Sri Lankan security forces was regarded as one-sided when the threat to Sri Lankan security was, and still is, seen to come from India alone. Throughout this period Pakistan had provided both training facilities and matériel, and China was the main supplier of arms. A reading of the operative clause in the letter of the prime minister of India to the president of Sri Lanka dated 29 July 1987, clause 3(i), would show that it did not actually place an embargo on the provision of training facilities by other nations. This letter is included as Appendix Document V to this volume.

Opposition to the Accord

The opposition parties in the island and the JVP in particular sensed much more accurately than the government the public mood of hostility to an agreement with India so soon after the humiliation inflicted on Sri Lanka in early June. The accord ignited massive protests in the country in the last week of July. The intensity of the opposition was partly a reflection of an innate hostility to Indian pressure, partly a rejection of the more controversial features of the accord, such as the amalgamation of the Northern and Eastern Provinces and the provision for the entry of an Indian peacekeeping force. There was also antipathy if not antagonism to Rajiv Gandhi himself because of the violation of Sri Lankan airspace that had occurred just six weeks earlier.

Although the cabinet had approved the signing of the accord at its meeting of 27 July, the divisions in its ranks on this issue were public knowledge, especially the opposition of the prime minister and of Lalith Athulathmudali. Opponents of the accord outside the ranks of the government were greatly encouraged by this latter development, and sought to exploit it to their advantage in gathering support for the extraparliamentary agitation they were organizing. Sinhalese newspapers and pamphlets and leaflets gave extensive coverage to the divisions in the cabinet, and used it very effectively in whipping up opposition to the accord.

From 23 July or so there was mounting tension in the city of Colombo and its suburbs as *bhikkhus* gathered in force to protest against the accord. They had the support of the SLFP and other political groups as well as Buddhist lay organizations. As we have seen, the prime minister was out of the island on a visit to Britain and Japan—he had left the island on 9 July—and only returned on 25 July. Just as his absence during these critical negotiations with India fueled speculation about his own views on the accord, his arrival was anxiously awaited by opposition critics of the accord in the expectation that, given his general anti-Indian views, he would oppose the accord at the crucially important cabinet meeting scheduled for 27 July. The Sri Lankan cabinet usually met on Wednesday mornings, but because the Indian prime minister was expected to arrive in Colombo on 29 July to sign the accord—29 July was a Wednesday—the meeting was advanced to Monday 27 July. Even as the cabinet met, violence broke out in Colombo, when the police broke up an opposition rally held in one of the most crowded parts of the city— in close proximity to the main bus station and railway station. It soon spread into the suburbs and the main towns of the southwest of the island and developed into the worst antigovernment riots in the island's post-independence history. The government's thinly spread security forces and the police took three days to a week to quell the riots.

When Prime Minister Rajiv Gandhi arrived in the island on 29 July to sign the accord, the security services and police were still engaged in preventing the mobs from entering the city of Colombo intent on demonstrating their opposition to the accord. Never had a peace accord been signed in less propitious circumstances.

Several critics of the accord within the cabinet absented themselves from the signing ceremony at the president's house—the prime minister and Lalith Athulathmudali being among the more prominent among them—thus providing opponents of the accord further evidence of divided counsels at the highest levels of government. The former was absent also at all the social occasions associated with the Indian prime minister's visit, the latter on some. The signing ceremony took place in the afternoon, an unusual time of day for an important diplomatic occasion such as this.

Rajiv Gandhi himself narrowly escaped serious injury if not death when an enraged sailor swung his rifle butt at him at the guard of honor ceremony prior to his departure from Colombo on 30 July. Pictures of the assault on the Indian prime minister were flashed around the world in newspapers and television screens. One other picture, also flashed around the world but not on television screens, showed one of the more prominent critics of the accord, a lawyer and Buddhist activist, seeking to restrain a young *bhikkhu* in a violent mood, at a protest meeting in Colombo on 27 July. The two pictures together conveyed a vivid impression of the passions that tore the country apart that fateful week and nearly took the life of Rajiv Gandhi, four years before the LTTE succeeded in doing precisely that.

He left behind him a ghost city and an imperiled government.

Indian Negotiations with the LTTE: New Delhi, July 1987

Prior to Rajiv Gandhi's visit to Sri Lanka, leaders of the five main Tamil separatist groups had been flown to New Delhi for negotiations with the Indian government. The Indian high commission in Colombo, and in particular High Commissioner J. N. Dixit, arranged to get them from Jaffna to India expeditiously. The first stage was a helicopter flight to Palaly Airport (the Jaffna airport) from where they were whisked across to India. The Tamil groups were kept, heavily guarded, at the government-owned Ashok Hotel in New Delhi located near the diplomatic enclave there. The initial reaction of the separatist groups was hostile. A Reuter report carried by the government-controlled *Daily News* in Colombo on 28 July stated that the Tigers in particular refused to agree. Not that the others were more enthusiastic. The LTTE's main sticking point was at having to lay down arms within 72 hours of the signing of the accord.[24]

Gandhi summoned ailing Tamil Nadu chief minister M. G. Ramachandran to Delhi to talk to the LTTE. But he had not been able to persuade Prabhakaran to accept the accord by the time Rajiv Gandhi left for Colombo.

On his return to Delhi on 31 July, Rajiv Gandhi was informed that Prabhakaran had at last agreed to accept the accord. There was still considerable reluctance, but he had agreed. A telegram from a very relieved Gandhi informed President Jayewardene on 2 August 1987 of these new developments.[25] That document read as follows:

1. In light of offers conveyed through Dixit on 1st August about interim administrative arrangements in the North-Eastern Province to be created, and offers concerning employment of Tamil separatist cadres after they surrender their arms, Prabhakaran, leader of the LTTE has:

   (a) *agreed to participation in the implementation of the agreement;*
   (b) *agreed to the surrender of arms;* and

(c) Prabhakaran would like to be in Jaffna personally to organize surrender of arms.

2. In the interest of conciliation and peaceful implementation of the Accord, Prabhakaran will be air-dropped at Jaffna by the evening of today, 2nd of August. Prabhakaran has agreed to the following schedule for the surrender of arms, etc. as given by Government of India:—

August 2 evening - Arrive in Jaffna

August 3 noon   - Indian Army to fan out into all parts of the Jaffna peninsula, including Jaffna city. LTTE to publicly announce surrender of arms to the press on the same day.

August 4 & 5   - Surrender of arms by LTTE. Events to be witnessed by the Press and TV.

August 5   - President Jayewardene may kindly announce the decision, in principle, to set up an interim Administration in the North-Eastern Province before Provincial-Council elections. Details to be worked out in consultation with Government of India.

3. I would like to assure you that if Prabhakaran goes back on his word in any manner or fails to organize surrender of arms, *the Indian Army will move to disarm LTTE by force.*

4. In the light of the above, time limit for the surrender of *arms will have to be extended from 1530 hours of August 1 to the evening of August 5th: another 48 hours extension is envisaged.* Cease-fire will be maintained by the Indian forces.

5. *I request that no publicity should be given to these arrangements till the late afternoon of 3rd August. The above arrangements can be announced on the 3rd August afternoon.*

There was considerable speculation in Sri Lanka at this time and later about the reasons behind Prabhakaran's change of heart. There was little doubt that some arm-twisting had been done by the Indian government. But suspicions remained that there was something more shadowy, if not sinister—the payment of a large sum of money—suspicions that were confirmed through revelations made in the Indian Parliament, on 6 April 1988, about a payment of money to the LTTE.[26]

Clearly after all this hard bargaining and Rajiv Gandhi's message to President Jayewardene on 2 August, Gandhi would have had few illusions about the LTTE and the prospects of a peaceful implementation of the accord. His fears in this regard would have been strengthened by the initial reaction of the Indian high commission in Colombo and its senior officials as they read Prabhakaran's speech to the citizens of Jaffna at Sudamalai on 5 July as the text of it came in from Jaffna through the high commission telex in Colombo.[27] They realized at that time that he was intent on making trouble for both Sri Lanka and India, and advised the Indian government to take early action to restrain the LTTE, but Delhi was not inclined to take such firm measures so early.[28]

The cabinet meeting of 27 July had revealed deep fissures within that body on the Indo–Sri Lanka Accord. As we have seen, there was no enthusiastic general support for President Jayewardene on the accord, merely a general consensus that he could proceed to sign it under his executive authority. Perhaps as a gesture to mollify the opponents of the accord, he had invited members of the cabinet on that occasion to set down their views on it in writing for discussion at the next meeting. This latter took place on 12 August, a fortnight or so after the turmoil of late July, and the early, seemingly hopeful phase in the Indian Peace-Keeping Force (IPKF) mediation effort in Jaffna.

A cabinet subcommittee had been appointed to consider the views submitted by members. When that body met on 12 August, it had about ten memoranda to consider.[29] The president had invited General Cyril Ranatunga, general officer commanding the Joint Operations Command, to address the cabinet subcommittee on a number of crucially important issues: why he had advised the president, in February 1987, against moving on to capture Jaffna town; what difficulties the army had confronted during the Vadamarachchi campaign; whether the Indian troops were helpful in their mediation in Jaffna and elsewhere; when the Indian army could be asked to return home; and what security problems the country could face in the future.

Ranatunga appears to have been more forthcoming on the first two of these issues than on the others. His view was that the main constraint in moving on the capture of Jaffna town was simply that the number of troops available was quite inadequate for that task. Even if Jaffna town had been brought under its control, the Sri Lankan army would have been hard put to retain control given the limited number of troops available. Besides, there was the danger of heavy civilian casualties in the capture of Jaffna. Members of the cabinet were not aware that this assessment did not reflect the views of the field commanders in the Northern Province.[30]

Naturally the cabinet was anxious to know about the amount of arms surrendered by the Tamil separatist groups. The answer provided by General D. Sepala Attygalle, secretary to the Ministry of Defence, was hardly reassuring: of the 3,060 or so weapons believed to be in the hands of these groups (especially the LTTE) only 381 had been surrendered up to that point.

The main purpose of the meeting was to consider the memoranda submitted by members of the cabinet on the Indo–Sri Lanka Accord and its impact on the Sri Lankan polity. Not surprisingly, the memoranda reflected the divisions seen in the cabinet at its meeting of 27 July. The views ranged from enthusiastic support from S. Thondaman, to a more measured but still very positive endorsement from Gamini Dissanayake, to skeptical and conditional support from some (including Ranil Wickremasinghe, the young minister of education and of youth affairs and employment) and general support from the large majority of the others, to the critical views of Athulathmudali and Premadasa. Athulathmudali pulled no punches in his assessment that the accord had less to do with the resolution of Sri Lanka's ethnic conflict than with a concerted attempt to reduce Sri Lanka to the status of a Bhutan or Sikkim. Premadasa's criticisms ranged over a wide field, from a condemnation of the amalgamation of the Northern and Eastern Provinces on the ground that it could lead to further division of the country and to separatism, to the constitutionality of holding a referendum in a single province. He argued that the presence of Indian officials to oversee such a referendum could be "interpreted as an infringement of our independence and sovereignty."

On 8 September Gamini Jayasuriya, minister of agricultural development and research, sent a memorandum in which he stated that he entertained "grave doubts as to its viability as a long-term solution to the Tamil problem and as a sound basis for Peace in our country." He was opposed to the amalgamation of the Northern and Eastern Provinces. In principle, he was in agreement with the views of the prime minister and Athulathmudali. A few weeks later Jayasuriya resigned his cabinet portfolio as well as his seat in Parliament, the only dissident cabinet minister to do so in protest against the Indo–Sri Lanka Accord.

Notes

1. M. Ram, interview with the author, 17 December 1991 in New Delhi, and Gamini Dissanayake, interview with the author, 23 September 1989.

2. I am grateful to Gamini Dissanayake for giving me a copy of this document.

3. Gamini Dissanayake, interview with the author, 23 September 1989.

4. Brigadier Vijaya Wimalaratne, then commander, Security Force, Jaffna, in an interview with the author, 13 December 1991 in New Delhi, made this point very forcefully.

5. K. Subrahamanyam, "Pakistan's Nuclear Capability," in V. D. Chopra, ed., *Studies in Indo-Pak Relations* (New Delhi: Patriot Publishers, 1984), 132. I owe this reference to Howard Wriggins, who has used it in another context altogether.

6. Gamini Dissanayake, interview with the author, 23 September 1989.

7. This note is in the J. R. Jayewardene MSS.

8. A copy is available with the author, who was present throughout the interview with Azar.

9. An obvious mistake. It should have been "alleviate."

10. This document is in the J. R. Jayewardene MSS.

11. J. N. Dixit, interview with the author, 3 April 1989.

12. This document is in the J. R. Jayewardene MSS. The copy there does not bear a date. This message was probably relayed to New Delhi through Dixit.

13. The reference was clearly to the Voice of America relaying station. Negotiations had been concluded for an extension of the lease and an expansion of the facility.

14. President Jayewardene's deep disappointment with the West and the United States in particular was made clear in his interview with Edward Azar, referred to earlier. In an interview with Howard Wriggins, Ronnie de Mel, the former finance minister, made this point very strongly. Ronnie de Mel's interview was on 21 July 1990.

15. Dixit, interview with the author, 3 April 1989.

16. J. N. Dixit, interview with the author, 3 April 1989; Gamini Dissanayake, interview with the author, 23 September 1989.

17. There are several such preliminary drafts in the J. R. Jayewardene MSS.

18. Gamini Dissanayake, interview with the author, 23 September 1989.

19. Dixit, interview with the author, 3 April 1989.

20. Gamini Dissanayake, interview with the author, 23 September 1989.

21. Dixit, interview with the author, 3 April 1989.

22. This paragraph is based on several official documents in the J. R. Jayewardene MSS, including a report to the cabinet by General Cyril Ranatunga on 12 August 1987. Ranatunga was in overall charge of the operations against the LTTE forces.

23. This brief letter is included in Appendix Document IV to this volume.

24. Lalith Athulathmudali explained this to me on more than one occasion. He added that he had told Dixit on a later occasion that the surrender of arms would only succeed if Prabhakaran, who was then in Delhi, were kept there or elsewhere in India until arms were surrendered.

25. There is a copy of this important telegram in the J. R. Jayewardene MSS. The underlining of some of the passages in the text appears to have been done in Colombo at the president's office, very probably by President Jayewardene himself.

26. See discussion of this in chapter 12 of this volume.

27. Prabhakaran's speech (in an English translation) was carried in full in the *Hindu*, 6 August 1987.

28. Dixit, interview with the author, 3 April 1989.

29. This review of the discussions at this cabinet meeting is based on interviews I had in August and September 1987 with a number of cabinet ministers and President Jayewardene. The J. R. Jayewardene MSS contain a large file with all the memoranda submitted to him by his cabinet colleagues for the meeting held on 12 August.

30. Several senior army officers made this point in discussions with me. I need to make special mention of an interview I had on 13 December 1991 with Brigadier Vijaya Wimalaratne, then commander, Security Forces, Jaffna.

12

The Indian Peace-Keeping Force (IPKF) in Sri Lanka, August 1987–April 1988

Conflicting Illusions

THE INDIAN GOVERNMENT ASSUMED, naturally enough, that the enormous popularity Indians enjoyed in Jaffna in and after June 1987, in the aftermath of the Indian air force food drop, and the distribution of food under the aegis of the Indian high commission staff led by its first secretary for political affairs, H. S. Puri, would be the basis for extracting support for the compromise settlement incorporated in the Indo–Sri Lanka Accord, a settlement that called for sacrifices from all parties. This proved to be the first of several illusions that were soon to bedevil relations between the Indians and the people of Jaffna. With the entry of the Indian Peace-Keeping Force (IPKF), the Indians soon found that popularity and gratitude are the most ephemeral of political commodities, and—as with the Israelis in their disastrous Lebanese intervention of 1982—that intruding foreign armies are initially hailed as liberators, only to be denounced within a very short time as arrogant and bumbling invaders. It took much less time for the Indians to lose their popularity among the Tamils of Jaffna than for the Israelis among their clients and allies in Lebanon.

The second of the Indian illusions—and one they also shared with the Israelis in Lebanon—was that clients would inevitably do the bidding of their mentor even when, as in this instance, they were called on to do many things they found unacceptable and unpalatable. From this second illusion stemmed the most unrealistic part of the accord, the speed with which some of the most controversial issues were to have been settled. A cease-fire was to be in effect within forty-eight hours, and the process

245

of disarming the Tamil separatist groups, that is to say, the handing over of arms by them, was to be completed within seventy-two hours. As we have seen, this timetable was adjusted on the initiative of the Indian government through the Indian prime minister's telegram of 2 August to President Jayewardene. The delay asked for was one of two days, not two months or even two weeks! Just as unreal was the assumption that the completion of the political process involved in the passage through the Sri Lankan Parliament of the devolution package incorporated in the accord could be completed within about six months. The devolution package had to be transformed into detailed and complex legislation and then placed before the constitutional court (consisting of judges of the Supreme Court) to test its constitutionality, prior to its introduction for debate in Parliament. There were also several rounds of negotiations in India and Sri Lanka on some of the lacunae in the legislation to be introduced. After Parliament approved the legislation there was the hard campaigning for elections to the provincial councils, and followed thereafter by a difficult process of institution building.

Another illusion was one the Sri Lankan government shared with its Indian counterpart, at least to the extent of a naive belief that the Indian intervention would not merely underwrite a complex and controversial settlement, but also impose it speedily on the Tamil separatist groups should the latter decide to oppose it. Intelligence assessments made by the Research and Analysis Wing (RAW) assumed that it would take the Indian forces just a week or so to impose their will on the recalcitrant Liberation Tigers of Tamil Eelam (LTTE). The fundamental assumption under which President Jayewardene and the Sri Lankan cabinet consented to the accord was that the separatist groups were clients of India and would do what India told them to do. From the last quarter of 1986, the major premise of President Jayewardene's discussions with Indian negotiators was that India must underwrite any settlement reached with Sri Lanka's Tamil political activists. More than once emissaries sent by the U.S. government had urged him to reach an understanding on this issue with India. This was the sum and substance of the messages conveyed in November 1983 and December 1984 through Ambassador-at-Large General Vernon Walters. Thus President Jayewardene regarded a settlement underwritten by India as the only viable policy for him in his efforts to thwart the political ambitions of the LTTE. What precisely he meant by the term "underwrite" was left deliberately vague, but in agreeing to "underwrite" the agreement, as Prime Minister Rajiv Gandhi appears to have done by the last quarter of 1986, and more specifically after June

1987, India took a calculated risk. The fact is that Indian negotiators did not expect any serious challenge to their policy from the Tamil separatist groups, and generally assumed that should such a challenge emerge it would be dealt with easily and expeditiously.

For the Tamils in general, especially the Tamils in the north of the island, the illusion was that the Indian forces would be infinitely better as protectors of the civil population and as guardians of law and order than the Sri Lankan police and armed services had been. They had few if any objections to India's underwriting a settlement between them and the Sri Lankan government. On the contrary, most of them, with the possible exception of the LTTE, treated it as one of the positive advantages of such a settlement. They proceeded to give as euphoric a welcome to the IPKF when they landed in Jaffna in the last days of July and early August 1987, as they had done to the Indian high commission officials and others in June 1987. But when battles broke out between the IPKF and the LTTE in October 1987, the civilian population of Jaffna were caught in the cross fire and suffered heavy casualties, quite apart from the privations imposed on them in the temporary relocation centers to which they were sent by the IPKF. Their disenchantment was all the more poignant because illusions of the benign nature of the Indian force were being shattered. As we shall see, the IPKF became substantially larger in numbers than the Sri Lankan forces in Jaffna ever had been, and proved to be much more heavy-handed in their treatment of the people there than their Sri Lankan counterparts.

The various Tamil separatist groups, funded, protected, and nurtured by Tamil Nadu, infiltrated by Indian agents, and paid by RAW, had fewer illusions. All of them welcomed the withdrawal of the Sri Lankan police and security forces to their barracks and looked forward to political contests for seats in the provincial councils and in Parliament. The Tamil United Liberation Front (TULF) believed they could resume their political role as the mainstream Tamil moderates under the new system. The LTTE alone had no illusions. They had prevailed over their Tamil rivals despite all the efforts of RAW to prevent their success and they were intent on a continuation of this struggle despite the Indo–Sri Lanka Accord and the entry of the IPKF into Jaffna.

The Arrival of the IPKF

The dispatch of an Indian Peace-Keeping Force to the north of Sri Lanka, the main theater of fighting between Tamil separatist groups and the Sri

Lankan security forces, had been made explicit as part of the political agenda of the Indo–Sri Lanka Accord. The speed with which this force was dispatched and the scale of the operation were both affected by the eruption of widespread rioting against the accord in the Sinhalese areas of the country, especially in and around Colombo and on the southwest coast. Some of the crucially important decisions in regard to these issues were taken in Colombo by Rajiv Gandhi and J. R. Jayewardene on 29 July at President's House.[1]

Even as the ceremonies and discussions on the Indo–Sri Lanka Accord were taking place, Colombo had all the signs of a city under siege. More to the point, news was coming to the president and the Sri Lankan cabinet ministers present on the occasion that the security situation in Colombo and its suburbs gave cause for serious concern. These discussions took place in Rajiv Gandhi's presence and he naturally came to share these concerns. The main difficulty, as the inspector general of the police (IGP) informed the president, was that the manpower resources of the police were stretched almost to the breaking point because over four thousand policemen were in Kandy providing security for the annual *perahera,* the ritual procession associated with the Temple of the Tooth, which generally attracted enormous crowds. If a large number of the policemen were to be brought back to Colombo, the government would either have to ask the temple authorities to curtail the *perahera* or take the risk of conducting the ceremonial procession with very limited crowd protection resources. Both courses of action were unacceptable to the government. President Jayewardene recalled that Rajiv Gandhi, listening to his conversation with the IGP, had asked whether he could help in any way. The president had responded that the Indian prime minister could indeed help by bringing in the Indian troops assigned to the IPKF immediately, and by helping to transport some of the Sri Lankan army units then in Jaffna and the Jaffna peninsula to Colombo.[2] Rajiv Gandhi was asked whether this could be done at once, that is, on 29 July. The Indian prime minister was soon on the telephone to his officials and defense staff in Delhi, who informed him that the IPKF could be transported to Jaffna very quickly, but not until the following day at the very earliest. And so it was decided to bring the Indian troops into Jaffna by 30 July, and to arrange for the same transport planes, and Indian army helicopters, to ferry Sri Lankan troops from Jaffna to Colombo to relieve the pressure on the security forces there.[3]

Throughout the nights of 30 and 31 July, Indian army transport planes ferried half the Sri Lankan security force in the peninsula to Colombo.[4]

The army and especially detachments of the Special Task Force (STF) of the police beat back the mobs and brought the situation under control. The decision to ask for Indian assistance for the transport of over four thousand Sri Lankan soldiers from Jaffna and the Jaffna peninsula to Colombo stemmed from a recognition of the total inadequacy of resources within the Sri Lankan security forces for an exercise of this scale in which speed was essential.

Just after the accord was signed, President Jayewardene asked the United States through its ambassador in Colombo, James Spain, for some assistance in this regard.[5] Neither the U.S. nor the British representatives in Colombo were aware of the contents of the accord. At a first reading of the clauses of the accord both had indicated that they were pleased that a resolute decision had been taken and were generally optimistic about the outcome. Spain was not very disturbed by the clauses relating to security and defense issues, the annexures to the accord, and the letters. He felt that the clauses relating to security and defense issues as well as the reference to foreign broadcasts from Sri Lanka had been very cleverly drafted to ensure that existing arrangements were not disturbed. At the signing ceremony, he had handed over to President Jayewardene an envelope containing a letter from President Ronald Reagan expressing his satisfaction at the agreement reached between Sri Lanka and India on measures taken to resolve Sri Lanka's ethnic conflict.[5]

Ambassador Spain was surprised, however, when President Jayewardene requested of him, shortly after the signing ceremony, that the U.S. government provide some military assistance to Sri Lanka. He was told that similar appeals were being made to other friendly governments such as the United Kingdom, Pakistan, and the People's Republic of China. President Jayewardene seemed anxious to have even a token measure of military support to reassure his critics in Sri Lanka that the country was not totally dependent on India for defense. The United States was the only country to respond positively to this surprising request—surprising, in the context of the arrival of a group of Indian soldiers as part of what became the IPKF—and the response came within twenty-four hours, remarkable speed for the Washington bureaucracy.

Spain's undated note to President Jayewardene in response to this request sets out very clearly the narrowness of the limits within which U.S. support would be made available. The letter[6] is quoted here in full:

We wish to do whatever we can to support the agreement that you and Rajiv Gandhi reached to end the ethnic conflict in Sri

Lanka, and we realize that the disturbances you face are a direct outgrowth of the agreement.

We believe the most helpful thing we can do is assist you in increasing your air transport and reconnaissance capability, as requested by [Defense Secretary] General Attygalle.

Because of the urgent need to have these assets operational, we have focussed on aircraft which would be compatible with ones you already have. Unfortunately, we have not yet been able to locate any which are immediately available. We are continuing to look urgently.

Another approach would be to provide logistics support, e.g., spare parts, to increase the availability of aircraft which Sri Lanka already has. We would be prepared to assist in this effort if appropriate but need details.

We are prepared to provide immediately two million dollars in F[oreign] M[ilitary] S[upplies] credit for use in financing the purchase of logistics support and/or aircraft.

We would provide such assistance with the agreement and cooperation of India, which we will look to you in the first instance to obtain. We would also wish to raise the issue directly with the GOI [Government of India].

The last paragraph of this note is a reiteration of the central feature of U.S. policy to Sri Lanka in the 1980s, a reluctance to provide any military assistance because of Washington's sensitivity to Indian concerns regarding the supply of American arms to the smaller countries of South Asia. Thus the insistence on the prior approval of the Indian government even where very limited military assistance was being provided to a beleaguered government of a friendly country. Not only Sri Lanka but also Nepal and Bangladesh were interested in obtaining arms from the United States; their requests had generally been turned down.

The IPKF, as originally envisaged by the Indian government, was to have been rather small in numbers—between two thousand and four thousand troops—adequate for the limited purpose of disarming the Tamil separatist groups and keeping the peace among them, as well as between them and the Sri Lankan security forces, who, according to the terms of the accord, were to remain in their barracks. As it was, the dispatch of the IPKF to Jaffna was speeded up because of the security situation in Colombo and its suburbs, while the number of troops sent was larger than had been anticipated for the initial stages of this program.

The Sri Lankan armed services had not been consulted on the Indo–Sri Lanka Accord, and in particular on the entry of the IPKF to Sri Lanka, largely because things had moved too fast. Many of them regretted the fact that the army had not been allowed to finish the job it had begun so well in the last quarter of 1986 and the first half of 1987, when the LTTE had been expelled from many of its bases in the north and east of the island, and the army had waged the Vadamarachchi operation in May 1987.

The LTTE had not put up much of a fight against the army during these encounters and seemed completely demoralized. The army leadership in Jaffna believed the LTTE could have been decisively defeated at that stage if the Indians had not intervened. The decision that the Sri Lankan security forces in the north and east of the island should be "confined to barracks" was seen as poor recompense for the sacrifices made by the soldiers. In military parlance "confined to barracks" was a punishment. Nor could they see the need to send the IPKF into the Eastern Province with its multiethnic population. The Sri Lankan security forces had established control over the region and the LTTE was not a force to be reckoned with there.[7]

Indeed, the decision to send the IPKF to the Eastern Province took the Sri Lankan defense establishment by surprise. It would appear from Rajiv Gandhi's early pronouncements that the dispatch of sections of the IPKF to Trincomalee and Batticaloa was somewhat of an afterthought, one more ad hoc decision taken in response to a developing situation. In the Eastern Province, unlike Jaffna, the large Sinhalese and Muslim sections of the population were acutely unhappy about the entry of Indian soldiers to their villages and bazaar towns, and regarded this decision as something that undermined their own security vis-à-vis the Tamil separatist groups.

The Sri Lankan forces in Jaffna had not the slightest doubt that the LTTE would not cooperate in the surrender of arms or in keeping the peace. For that reason the senior officers of the army in Jaffna urged that the security forces be "confined to barracks" only *after* the IPKF and the Sri Lankan government were satisfied that a substantial quantity of weapons had been surrendered by the Tamil separatist forces. They argued that their reading of the terms of the accord entitled them to believe that this was the intention of those who drafted those particular clauses. When they raised this issue with the Sri Lankan government they were persuaded by President Jayewardene not to insist on this strict reading of the terms of the accord.

In the euphoria of the enthusiastic reception that the IPKF received in Jaffna in late July and early August 1987, the Indian army leaders in Jaffna were remarkably optimistic about their ability to sort things out very quickly. They scarcely concealed their contempt for the LTTE—and the Sri Lankan armed forces as well—as they set about the business of imposing themselves between the warring factions in Jaffna in implementing the terms of the accord signed between the two governments.

If the officer corps of the IPKF were excessively self-confident about their ability to sort things out, they shared some of their soldiers' astonishment at what they saw in Jaffna.

When they arrived in Ceylon [Sri Lanka], they had a vague idea that they had come to protect Tamils from the Sri Lankan army. They had also expected to see a pitifully downtrodden population. But what they saw in Jaffna was contrary to expectations. Instead of uniform unrelieved poverty, there was a fairly large well-to-do middle class. Most people dressed well and lived in reasonable comfort. Unlike in India where each village may have just one television set, every other house in Jaffna had colour television. Shops were stocked with modern Japanese goods.

[Indeed] . . . the shops reminded them of what is said about Singapore. For the first few weeks the IPKF was pre-occupied with the shops at Kasturiar road. The officers bought Japanese TV sets, video recorders and 3-in-1's. The Jawans [soldiers] looked for radio-cassettes, pen torches and ball point pens. As the weeks went by, some Jawans told civilians: "We thought we came to protect you from the Sinhalese. But all we see is your boys killing each other. We do not see any Sinhalese."[8]

We have seen in the previous chapter how the early signs of a successful implementation of the accord had seemed encouraging. The timetable set for the surrender of weapons and the disarming of the warring factions among the Tamil separatist groups in the accord had been adjusted slightly in response to a report from the Indian prime minister, but the delay had been a matter of a few days. The delay was in fact the result of continuing negotiations between the Indian government and the LTTE leadership in New Delhi. Once Prabhakaran returned from New Delhi, the LTTE began a symbolic—although visibly reluctant—handing over of arms. The smaller Tamil separatist groups handed over their arms in much larger quantities than the LTTE, relative to the weapons in their possession. The Sri Lankan security forces in the Northern and Eastern Provinces returned to their barracks and the paramilitary forces there were disarmed as part of the Sri Lankan government's obligations under the accord.

The IPKF, like their political mentors in New Delhi, banked on a speedy disarming of the Tamil separatist activists, including the LTTE. Rajiv Gandhi and his advisers had planned on an early departure of the IPKF, by the end of 1987 or early 1988 at the latest. In the early part of August it looked as though this timetable was not so unrealistic.

The problem, as we have seen, was the LTTE. Their leader Velupillai Prabhakaran and a few of his close associates had been flown to India by helicopter from Jaffna and on a special flight thereafter to Delhi a few days before the signing of the accord. There they had been housed in the state-owned Ashok Hotel located near New Delhi's diplomatic enclave. Generally when the LTTE came to Delhi, or were invited to Delhi, to meet Indian officials or politicians, they had traveled by train (in the crowded third-class carriages) and were accommodated in cheap lodgings or nondescript hotels.[9] While the accommodations were vastly superior on this occasion, it could hardly be said that the LTTE were treated as honored guests. In fact they were treated as more or less wayward and fractious dependents summoned to meet their mentors, the Indian prime minister and others, and to sign on the dotted line. M. G. Ramachandran, the chief minister of Tamil Nadu, and some of his aides had been flown in from Madras to help persuade the LTTE to accept the Indo–Sri Lanka Accord as an honorable settlement. Ramachandran was one of the LTTE's principal benefactors and it was expected that he would be able to influence the LTTE in a way that nobody else could.

Prabhakaran would not yield to these pressures. He preferred to wait until he had met the Indian prime minister in person to make up his mind. The meeting with Rajiv Gandhi took place on 31 July on the latter's return to Delhi after signing the accord in Colombo. After several hours of hard bargaining, Prabhakaran agreed to support the accord. Rajiv Gandhi announced this to President Jayewardene on 2 August. As we shall see later in this book, it was revealed—in April 1988—that the Indian government had indeed agreed to provide the LTTE with a substantial sum of money on this occasion in return for their support for the accord. Only the first installment was ever paid, because within three months of the signing of the accord the IPKF was at war with the LTTE in Jaffna.[10]

Rajiv Gandhi emerged from this meeting with Prabhakaran with the feeling that the latter would continue to be difficult and, as his telegram of 2 August to President Jayewardene would show, already convinced that India would have to use force against an intractable Prabhakaran in the event of his resisting pressure to surrender a substantial portion of the weapons in the possession of his organization, or to refrain from using violence against his rivals. It was an impression shared by J. N. Dixit, the Indian high commissioner in Colombo, whose task it was to engage in negotiations with the LTTE to get them to honor the promises made by their leadership to support the accord during their meetings with the Indian prime minister and his advisers.

The Implementation of the Accord: The Early Stages

Although many risks were expected in any progress toward the stabilization of the accord (given the opposition of the Sri Lanka Freedom Party (SLFP), the proscribed but nevertheless powerful Janatha Vimukthi Peramuna (JVP), and a section of the government), the early indications seemed encouraging. True, the original timetable for the surrender of weapons and the disarming of the warring factions was not adhered to, but at least the LTTE had begun to hand over arms, if only in small numbers. As we have seen, the smaller separatist groups joined the process less reluctantly.

The Sri Lankan security forces in the Northern and Eastern Provinces returned to their barracks and the paramilitary forces there were disarmed as part of the Sri Lankan government's obligations under the accord. Although the Indian intervention prevented the completion of the campaign of sealing off of the coast of the Jaffna peninsula, which had begun in late May 1987 with the Vadamarachchi campaign, the Sri Lankan security forces were willing supporters of the political settlement set out in the Indo–Sri Lanka Accord. The final stages of the negotiations on the latter had been conducted with so much secrecy and at such speed that the military aspects of the implementation of the accord had not been given adequate consideration. As it turned out, the accord gave the Sri Lankan forces in the north and east of the island little or no role to play. Indeed, senior Sri Lankan officials in the civil administration believed that, in the early stages of the IPKF's arrival in the island, the Indians were more concerned with the business of restricting the Sri Lankan forces in the north and east of the island—confining them to barracks— than with curbing the activities of the LTTE.

Rajiv Gandhi and his advisers had banked on a speedy disarming of the Tamil separatists, including the LTTE, and a speedy departure of the IPKF.[11] Their hidden timetable for a departure by the end of 1987 or early 1988 was based on intelligence assessments provided by RAW.[12] These latter proved to be fundamentally flawed, but the information was all the Indian government had for its contingency planning. When things began to go wrong, and they went disastrously wrong within a few weeks, the IPKF was confronted with a task for which it was ill prepared because neither political objectives nor the chain of command were really clarified for purposes of a long military campaign against a defiant LTTE.

The information at Rajiv Gandhi's disposal when he embarked on his Sri Lankan intervention was clearly defective. First, he was, he stated in 1990, quite insistent from the outset that the IPKF would not be sent to Sinhalese areas. Was he unaware that the Trincomalee district had a substantial Sinhalese population, as did the Amparai district? Moreover, the IPKF had necessarily to go through the Sinhalese districts of the North Central Province in traveling from the Northern Province to the Eastern Province. Second, many of the senior officials in Delhi's South Block persisted in regarding the Muslims as Tamils merely because they spoke Tamil. This was based on southern Indian experience, and they did not know, or ignored the fact, that the Sri Lankan situation was totally different. Third, although the RAW had armed and financed various groups and individuals among the Tamil separatists, they had neglected to keep essential data on their protégés, with the result that when the IPKF really needed to crack down on the more recalcitrant among them the information at their disposal was very inadequate. The deficiencies in the material at the IPKF's disposal were best illustrated by the fact that they were using 1937 ordinance maps of Jaffna, when any self-respecting intelligence operative could easily have secured more up-to-date maps in Colombo.[13] No wonder Rajiv Gandhi, for one, reflecting on these events in 1990 as leader of the opposition, was bitterly critical of the RAW and its role in Sri Lanka.

The problem, however, was the LTTE. For most of August 1987 the Indian high commission in Colombo, and the dynamic J. N. Dixit who was by now both high commissioner de jure and proconsul de facto, were engaged in exasperating and long, drawn-out negotiations with the LTTE to get them to stick to the promise extracted from them in Delhi to support the accord. From the outset both Rajiv Gandhi and Dixit realized that this was a very difficult task. Once he was back in Sri Lanka Prabhakaran shifted ground. The LTTE leadership did not change their basic aim, which was to secure recognition of the claim to be the sole spokesmen for the Tamils of Sri Lanka. And they regarded the Indo–Sri Lanka Accord as essentially an obstacle to their objective of establishing a separate state.

The LTTE kept up the pressure on their Tamil rivals in the north and east of the island. The bloody encounters with them became more frequent. No amount of cajoling by the Indian high commissioner and his staff could bring the LTTE to an acceptance of the need to accommodate their rivals in political activity rather than to turn their guns on them.

More important was the complex question of the interim administration of the amalgamated Northern and Eastern Provinces, on the setting up of which the Indian government had extracted a promise from its Sri Lankan counterpart. Although the composition of the proposed Interim Council for the Northern and Eastern Provinces had not been settled before the accord was signed, its establishment was treated as an essential and urgent necessity for the effective implementation of the accord. There were two problems here: the relative strength of the Tamil groups within it and the question of council leadership.

While the Sri Lankan government was committed to the principle of such an Interim Council, it was also intent on seeing that the LTTE would not have a majority on it, and that there would be a balance between representation for the Northern and Eastern Provinces. While the latter did not present any great difficulties from the LTTE, the first clearly did; they were intent on securing not merely an influential position but a numerical majority and a clearly dominant position.

By the first week of September the handing in of arms by the Tamil separatist groups, and in particular by the LTTE, had become more sporadic. It was clear that only a fraction of the arms in LTTE possession had been surrendered. The LTTE had already clashed with the IPKF, who were inclined to ignore the incident in the name of a peaceful settlement. The implementation of the accord was impeded by further and bitter factional fighting among the Tamil separatist groups (involving the LTTE in particular). The LTTE turned their guns on their Tamil rivals once more and killed over 150 of them, while the IPKF did little or nothing to check these killings.

The Indian government, for its part, seemed intent on moving slowly in collecting weapons from the Tamil activist groups, and above all else was anxious to get the LTTE to enter the arena of democratic politics. On 20 September the Indian government sent President Jayewardene a note on the composition of the Interim Council. Its principal feature was that it gave the LTTE a majority (seven out of twelve) in that body as well as a say in the nomination to the post of chief administrator. Although this was a clear departure from the understanding reached with him, President Jayewardene gave his consent to this new arrangement on 25 September. The document[14] read as follows.

1. On the basis of latest discussions with the LTTE and other Tamil groups, the Government of India puts forward the following proposals for the composition of the Interim Administrative Council:—The Council may consist of:
   - Chief Administrator - 1 (one of the nominees of the LTTE)
   - LTTE members - 5
   - TULF members - 2
   - Muslims - 2 (one of the Muslims may be LTTE nominee)
   - Sinhalese - 2
2. The Chief Administrator and the 5 LTTE nominees may be chosen out of a list of nominees already available in the President's Secretariat.
3. Mr. Soosaithasan and Mr. Sampanthan may be nominated as TULF members of the Council.[15]
4. Out of the two Muslims, President may kindly choose one of the Muslim nominees of the LTTE. The second Muslim may be chosen in discretion.
5. The two Sinhalese may be nominated in discretion (Mr. Lionel Fernando is acceptable to the Tamils).[16]
6. President may kindly consider giving up the idea of nominating Co-Administrator initially.
7. In the orders detailing the terms of reference of the Interim Administrative Council, President may consider transferring power envisaged in paragraphs 10.1 and 10.2 of the Bangalore proposals.

In the meanwhile, the Government of India is immediately approaching the LTTE to simultaneously fall in line on various matters step-by-step. The Interim Administrative Council may be announced, if possible, in the coming 24 to 36 hours, so that it politically neutralizes attempts of the LTTE to misinform the Tamil population about various developments. It is the Government of India's assessment that either the LTTE will join the Interim Government and give a momentum to the peace process or if they do not join after the announcement of the Interim Government by His Excellency, it will start the process of their political marginalization.

It is important to remember that the word "may" as used in this document meant "must" or "should," not "might" or "could" as would be the case in the British and American usage.

The official announcement of the Sri Lankan government's acceptance of this new arrangement was made on 28 September. The government had made yet another concession under Indian pressure. But every concession led to more demands by the LTTE.

By the middle of September it was very evident that the LTTE was looking for an opportunity for a dramatic demonstration of their opposition to the Indo–Sri Lanka Accord and a confrontation with the Indians. On 15 September Amirthalingam Thileepan, a prominent LTTE activist— he was chief of the LTTE's political wing in Jaffna—began what he called a fast unto death. He put up five demands, two of which dealt with the settlement of Sinhalese peasants in the Eastern Province and release of prisoners. At first the fast was regarded as a ploy to divert attention from the LTTE's attack on other Tamil groups in Batticaloa, which took place two days earlier.[17] But Thileepan was in earnest, and did fast to death.

His death was soon overshadowed by a more significant event that gave the LTTE the opportunity it was looking for. On 4 October the Sri Lankan navy intercepted a boat carrying a group of LTTE men off Point Pedro. It contained seventeen men, including some of the most prominent LTTE leaders. One of them was Pulendran, who had led the group that had butchered over 125 men, women, and children in the Good Friday bus massacre of 1986, at a time when the government had declared a unilateral cessation of hostilities. In addition, the boat carried arms in contravention of the accord. The Sri Lankan government insisted that the captured men be brought to Colombo for interrogation. Dixit was not in Sri Lanka at this point. The IPKF man on the spot in Jaffna and the Sri Lankan army representative were working at cross-purposes. The latter insisted on carrying out his instructions to take the group to Colombo, the former on preventing that from happening. At the time of their capture these young men did not have the cyanide capsules for which the LTTE is well known. But while in custody these capsules were apparently smuggled in to them. They preferred to commit suicide by swallowing them rather than face interrogation in Colombo.[18] Some died immediately; others lingered on to die a slow death. The death toll from this mass suicide attempt was twelve. Their deaths gave the LTTE the excuse to do what they had always intended to do. They turned their guns on the Sinhalese in Jaffna (the few who remained) and in the Batticaloa and Trincomalee districts, in a deliberate attempt to destabilize the Eastern Province.

The LTTE's aim was to drive the Sinhalese out of the Trincomalee district, and to cause so much confusion and panic that the Sinhalese in the Eastern Province would flee to the south of the island. They had in mind the referendum to be held to decide whether the amalgamation of the Northern and Eastern Provinces would be made permanent, and they were intent on reducing the number of Sinhalese voters. The LTTE caused enormous damage to Sinhalese property in the town, apart of course from killing a large number of men, women, and children.

The IPKF contributed to this process of destabilization in two ways. First, they committed a serious blunder in sending a Madrasi regiment to Trincomalee, who, being largely Tamils, fraternized with the LTTE; second, and even more important, they made no attempt to intervene when the peace was broken. Indeed there is evidence that some of the IPKF soldiers participated in the burning and looting of houses and the harassment of the beleaguered Sinhalese.

The attacks on the Sinhalese in Trincomalee town and district and elsewhere in the Eastern Province created a potentially dangerous political problem for the government. Fleeing refugees wended their way to towns in the north central and central regions, and some even took trains to Colombo. There was for a few days the prospect of a Sinhalese backlash in the rest of the island. The JVP and SLFP either singly or in concert were fanning the flames of discontent.

The massacre of about two hundred Sinhalese eventually led to a toughening of the Indian attitude. On 4 October President Jayewardene announced that he would be compelled to order the IPKF out of Trincomalee, if law and order were not restored immediately, and to call on Sri Lankan forces to keep order there.

The LTTE had hoped for a clash between the IPKF and the Sri Lankan armed forces in Trincomalee. Such a conflict might have erupted if the Madrasi regiment had not been ordered out of Trincomalee, and if the IPKF had not begun to check the LTTE's depredations. Fortunately for both countries the clash did not take place.

In the meantime urgent discussions between President Jayewardene and Prime Minister Gandhi brought into force part of the hidden agenda of the peace accord, that Indian troops would eventually be used against the LTTE. The Indian defense minister, K. C. Pant, and the Indian army chief of staff, General Krishnakumar Sunderji, were dispatched to Colombo. General Sunderji, one of the principal exponents, in the Indian defense establishment, of an aggressive extension of Indian power in the South Asian region and elsewhere, was yet another case of a southern Indian Tamil wielding decisive influence on India's Sri Lankan policy at a critical moment in its evolution.

With practically worldwide condemnation of the LTTE, and a chorus of criticism of India—also worldwide—for its failure to maintain the peace, the Indian government through Pant and Sunderji decided to implement part of the hidden agenda of the Indo–Sri Lanka Accord, to disarm the LTTE and if necessary weaken if not destroy it as a military force. There was thus an ultimate irony. The Indian government forces that had intervened to prevent the destruction of the LTTE by the Sri Lankan army earlier in the year were doing it themselves; the Indian government leaders that objected to the Sri Lankan army taking Jaffna city were doing it themselves, and in that process inflicting much heavier casualties and far greater hardships on the people of the Jaffna peninsula than anything done so far by the Sri Lankan security forces. The Indian government that accused the Sri Lankan forces of violation of human rights in their confrontation with the Tamil separatist groups now found itself facing similar charges and with even greater frequency.

India's national pride was at stake through this defiance of India by the forces of Tamil separatism in Sri Lanka, and so the LTTE had to be brought to heel. The LTTE now represented a threat not merely for Sri Lanka but for India as well. A once ragtag band trained and supplied in India and perceived—by the Indian defense establishment—as an instrument of India's national interest now represented a formidable separatist force.

Accordingly, the IPKF now moved in to disarm the LTTE and, when faced with resistance from the latter, launched a frontal assault on the LTTE strongholds in the Jaffna town and peninsula in the second week of October. Despite stiff resistance from the LTTE, which necessitated the deployment of thousands of reinforcements, the LTTE's hold on the peninsula was eventually broken. Both parties, the Indian army and the LTTE, suffered heavy casualties, but those who suffered most were the people of Jaffna and the Jaffna peninsula as the Indian army set about its business of defeating the LTTE with a heavy-handed professionalism. There was no Indian coup de grâce either. The LTTE survived a bruising defeat. Their harried forces escaped, or were allowed by the IPKF to escape, to the jungles south of the Jaffna peninsula.[19] From there they continued their resistance against the Indian forces for more than two years. The short, sharp campaign Rajiv Gandhi had planned turned out to be India's longest war.[20]

The IPKF as Combatant

The events leading to the outbreak of hostilities between the IPKF and the LTTE have been outlined and analyzed earlier in this chapter. We need to look now at the IPKF at the point when its original role of peacekeeper was quickly transformed to the very unusual one of combatant in Sri Lanka's ethnic conflicts. Never before had an intermediary and peacemaker turned combatant against groups of the very minority in whose interests it had originally intervened.

The change in the nature of the IPKF role was the result of a political decision taken with little or no consultation with the Indian armed services. Indeed, all the evidence would suggest that they were not adequately prepared for this new role,[21] and the man chosen to lead the attack, Lieutenant General Depinder Singh, had serious doubts about the wisdom of the course of action to which the IPKF was being committed by the Indian prime minister. M. Ram recalled how Depinder Singh had called on him on the eve of his departure to Sri Lanka and expressed his fears about the conflict between the IPKF and LTTE—as representatives of the Tamil separatist movement—becoming a long, drawn-out one, a thirty-year war, in fact.[22]

Depinder Singh was an exception in this assessment that the LTTE would engage the IPKF in a prolonged conflict. Generally the Indian officers of the IPKF had a disdainful attitude toward the LTTE, at least in the initial stages, and they moved into battle in the firm belief that they could swiftly crush the LTTE's resistance. The LTTE operatives with whom they came in contact looked and behaved like rather simple young men. Apart from their leadership, they were mostly sarong clad and wore *chappals* (sandals) rather than shoes. The Indian officers believed that this "rabble" did not amount to very much. In coming to this conclusion the Indians were making the same sort of mistake the U.S. forces made with regard to the Vietcong in Vietnam.[23] Thus, when the LTTE hit back so ferociously in the earliest encounters with the IPKF in the latter's Jaffna campaign,[24] the complacency of the Indian officers was rudely shattered. It took them some time to understand the true nature of their opponents, who were skilled guerrilla fighters, trained ironically enough in India and equipped with the most modern automatic weapons.[25]

Despite the LTTE's poor performance against the Sri Lankan army, especially at Vadamarachchi, the Sri Lankan forces respected the LTTE's fighting skills, especially their expertise in the manufacture and use of improvised explosive devices (IEDs), a skill in which they had been origi-nally trained by their Indian mentors. When warned by Sri Lankan army officers about the deadly effectiveness of these IEDs, the Indians tended to dismiss these as exaggerations, at least in the early stages. In any event they did not believe that the LTTE could manufacture the sort of IEDs the Sri Lankan army had to cope with, and were inclined to believe they had been obtained in the international arms market. But once they confronted the same homemade IEDs and saw how lethal they were, the Indians were anxious to learn from the experience of the Sri Lankan forces.[26]

Just as the IPKF had been contemptuous of the LTTE and the Sri Lankan forces, the people of Jaffna and the Sri Lankan forces stationed there were generally unimpressed with the IPKF. The Sri Lankan officers had been surprised by the obsolete weapons the IPKF soldiers carried. They had mostly World War II vintage self-loading rifles (SLRs) that the Sri Lankan army had abandoned because they were too cumbersome and slow for the sort of fighting encounters with the LTTE entailed. The LTTE and other Tamil groups the Indians had trained carried much better and more modern weapons (especially the semiautomatic weapons, the ubiquitous AK-47s). The Indians were to learn at great cost how ineffec-tive SLRs were against the LTTE's AK-47s.[27] In addition, the Indian soldiers were generally badly turned out by way of uniforms and footwear in contrast to the Sri Lankan soldiers, who were also much better paid.

The Indian soldiers generally created a very poor impression in Jaffna and elsewhere because of their unsanitary habits and the frequency with which they would loot houses and shops, even for such ordinary items as soap.

Once the hostilities with the LTTE began there was a rapid increase in the number of soldiers in the IPKF. They went up from seven thousand in August 1987 to twenty thousand during the IPKF's first attack on the LTTE in October 1987, code-named Operation Pawan. By early 1988 there were seventy thousand IPKF troops in the north and east of the island.

Despite the early setbacks, the IPKF eventually broke the back of the LTTE resistance. Indian casualties were higher than expected, largely because of the successful use of IEDs by the LTTE. While the LTTE suffered much heavier casualties than the IPKF, those who suffered most were Jaffna's civilian population. Estimates of civilian deaths in the IPKF "capture" of the Jaffna peninsula have varied from two thousand to five thousand. With seventy thousand soldiers—three-quarters of the size of the Soviet army in Afghanistan—concentrated in the north and east of the island, the civilian population were bound to be under greater pressure from the military presence than they had ever been before.

The rapid increase of the size of the IPKF to these massive proportions stemmed from the Indian army's reliance on a "saturation" policy, the stationing of large numbers of troops in troubled and troublesome villages to control the situation by the sheer force of numbers. This strategy had worked well in the northeast frontier regions of India in Nagaland and Assam, where separatist agitation posed a serious challenge to the Indian state. The rapid and huge increase in the size of the IPKF could be explained as an attempt to replicate these tactics in a totally different environment.[28]

The Sri Lankan army officers in Jaffna were surprised when the Indians brought in tanks (the latest Soviet models) and heavy artillery to be used in Jaffna. The Sri Lankan officers could not see the need for tanks in built-up areas where they were ponderously inefficient and very vulnerable to destruction by the LTTE's IEDs. The tanks would have been far more effective had the Indians decided to go "cross-country" and not use the heavily mined roads of Jaffna, but surprisingly the Indians never did that. The heavy artillery was used against LTTE concentrations.[29]

The Indian army made a number of tactical mistakes that helped the battered LTTE forces to regroup. The latter were allowed—or able—to escape from the Jaffna peninsula to precisely those areas of the Northern Province from which the small Sri Lankan army had driven them out earlier in the year. The LTTE leadership established themselves in well-fortified and skillfully concealed hideouts in the Mullaitivu forests; Prabhakaran made this area his headquarters and remained there for nearly four years (1988–91). They were also permitted to establish themselves in the Trincomalee district of the Eastern Province, in which up to that time they had not much more than a foothold.

A number of questions arise from the LTTE's survival in the forests of the Northern Province against the massive presence of the Indian army—the number of Indian soldiers in the IPKF rose in the course of 1988 to a peak of over one hundred thousand. Why was it that the Indian army, despite its commitment to a "saturation" policy that worked well for them in Assam and the northeast frontier of India, was unable to deliver a coup de grâce to the LTTE? Was this a result of a reluctance based on political purposes linked to the byzantine politics of Tamil Nadu? Or was it because the LTTE's far superior knowledge of the terrain they were operating in, relative to that of the Indians, helped them to survive? The answer is that there was some validity in both these elements.

The saturation policy had been effective in the northeast of India because the Indian army operated on Indian soil, where the time constraint was not so important a factor as it was in Sri Lanka. They could go on for years—as they did—until they broke the back of the insurgency. The situation in the north and east of Sri Lanka was rather different, and there was always a time constraint. There was no systematic attempt to saturate the villages in Mullaitivu, Vavuniya, and elsewhere in the Northern and Eastern Provinces close to the LTTE camps and settlements in the forests. Nor did the saturation policy work well even in the urban areas of Jaffna and Batticaloa, where LTTE cadres survived underground and continued to impose their will on the people.

Again, the Indians never succeeded in preventing supplies of arms from coming in to the LTTE from Tamil Nadu and elsewhere. The much larger and better equipped Indian navy did not fare better in this regard than did the Sri Lankan navy. The LTTE's small and swift boats were more suited to the peculiar features of the Sri Lankan coast than the ships of the Indian navy. Besides, the LTTE—with a long tradition of smuggling behind them—knew every inch of the coast, and easily outwitted the Indians. Throughout their stay in the island the IPKF never improvised measures to deal with this threat to their own security. The LTTE were able to send their wounded across to Tamil Nadu for treatment with impunity.

The LTTE maintained a not very inconspicuous presence in Madras, through which it channeled its official "messages" to various parts of India and from there to the rest of the world, much to the discomfiture of the Indian government. This tolerance of the LTTE "office" in Madras was regarded in Sri Lanka as a concession to Tamil Nadu sentiment.

Although the IPKF was never seen outside the north and east of the country (except in the North Central Province on the way from the north to the east) its shadow lay across the country's political landscape. Its presence was exploited against the government, by the SLFP and the JVP acting together or separately.

Notes

1. This paragraph is based on the author's interviews with Rajiv Gandhi, 23 April 1990, and with J. R. Jayewardene, July and August 1991.

2. Ibid.

3. Rajiv Gandhi, interview with the author, 23 April 1990.

4. J. R. Jayewardene MSS, undated secret document entitled "Deployment of Troops," where it is stated that 4,265 out of a total of 9,903 troops in the north of the island had been withdrawn to Colombo immediately after 29 July 1987.

5. James Spain, interview with the author, 22 February 1993. The point about not disturbing the existing arrangements was also made by Indian High Commissioner J. N. Dixit in his interview of 3 April 1989.

6. This letter is in the J. R. Jayewardene MSS.

7. This paragraph and the two following it are based on discussions the author had with some senior officers of the Sri Lankan armed forces. They did not wish their identity to be revealed.

8. This extract is from a study by a group of Sri Lankan Tamil academics based in Jaffna, Rajan Hoole et al., *The Broken Palmyra: The Tamil Crisis in Sri Lanka—An Inside Account* (Claremont, Calif.: Sri Lanka Studies Institute, rev. ed., 1990), 169–70.

9. Manoj Joshi, special (defense) correspondent of the *Hindu* and *Frontline,* interview with the author, 18 December 1991 in New Delhi. Joshi identified one of these hotels as the Ranjith in Connaught Circle.

10. See chapter 14 for discussion of this.

11. Rajiv Gandhi, interview with the author, 23 April 1990.

12. Ibid.

13. See Shankar Bhaduri and Afsir Karim, *The Sri Lankan Crisis,* Lancer Paper 1 (New Delhi: Lancer International, 1990), 65 for a discussion of this.

14. This document is in the J. R. Jayewardene MSS.

15. Soosaithasan and Sampanthan had been TULF MPs for Mannar and Trincomalee respectively in the period 1977–83. They were widely regarded as moderates.

16. Lionel Fernando had been a very popular government agent (chief administrative officer) of Jaffna in the early 1980s.

17. Lalith Athulathmudali as minister of national security made the decision to bring the captives to Colombo and, despite some initial hesitation, President Jayewardene backed

him on it. One of the most comprehensive and objective accounts of politics in Jaffna during this period is provided in Hoole et al., *The Broken Palmyra*. The Thileepan fast is discussed on 170–74.

18. Ibid., 187–94.

19. These were the areas from which they had been driven out by the Sri Lankan army earlier in the year.

20. See his comment, "It should be a short, sharp exercise and our boys should be back home soon," *Far Eastern Economic Review* 31 (August 1987). He made the same point in his interview with the author, 23 April 1990.

21. See particularly Bhaduri and Karim, *The Sri Lanka Crisis;* see also Depinder Singh, *The IPKF in Sri Lanka* (New Delhi: Trishul, 1991); S. C. Sardespande, *Assignment Jaffna* (New Delhi: Lancer Publishers, 1991).

22. M. Ram, interview with the author, New Delhi, 17 December 1991.

23. Manoj Joshi, interview with the author, 18 December 1991.

24. The early setbacks of the IPKF in Jaffna are discussed in Bruce Mathews, "Sri Lanka: An End to the Violence?" *Current Affairs* (Sydney, Australia) (November 1988): 11–17; Steven Weisman, "Sri Lanka: A Nation Disintegrates," *New York Times,* Sunday Magazine, 13 December 1987. There are more comprehensive reviews in Bhaduri and Karim, *The Sri Lanka Crisis* and Rajesh Kadian, *India's Sri Lanka Fiasco: Peace Keepers at War* (New Delhi: Vision Books, 1991).

25. Shekar Gupta, "Jawans Learn War Lessons in Lanka," *India Today,* 22 October 1989. Much the same points were made to me by senior Sri Lankan army officers.

26. This information is based on discussions with some senior Sri Lankan army officers.

27. Ibid. See also Shekar Gupta, "Jawans Learn War Lessons"; Kadian, *India's Sri Lanka Fiasco,* 103.

28. Manoj Joshi, interview with the author, 18 December 1991.

29. Information derived from discussions with some senior Sri Lankan army officers.

13

President Jayewardene: The Politics of Survival, September 1987–April 1988

The Government under Severe Pressure

FOR A WEEK or two after the signing of the Indo–Sri Lanka Accord, things seemed to augur well for its success. Indeed, in the ranks of the supporters of the accord within the government, President Jayewardene included, there was an air of euphoria about the prospects of an early restoration of peace. Several ambassadors of Western countries had called at the Ministry of Foreign Affairs to congratulate Sri Lanka on taking the bold step of signing the accord, and pledged support for reconstruction efforts, which they hoped and believed could begin soon.[1] Returning home after a visit to the United Nations and to Europe, Foreign Minister Hameed was ruminating on his meetings with his counterparts from a number of Western countries, all of whom had expressed satisfaction at the onset of peace through the accord.[2] More to the point, all of them expressed some concern about the presence of the Indian army in the north and east of the island, and some expressed fears that this army would not go away so easily. To Hameed this seemed a hypocritical attitude because, if these governments had shown the same concern earlier on India's role in the Sri Lankan ethnic conflict and had been willing to give public expression to it, Sri Lanka might not have had to concede some of the more controversial terms embodied in the accord, and the resort to an Indian Peace-Keeping Force (IPKF) might not have been necessary if the Western powers had been willing to criticize India for its support of Sri Lankan Tamil separatism. Yet he found all the Western countries, without exception, unwilling to give public expression to these fears because of a general reluctance to cause offense to India.

267

The euphoria about the accord reached its peak when Stephen Solarz, the influential chairman of the Asian-Pacific Subcommittee of the Foreign Affairs Committee of the U.S. House of Representatives, an enthusiastic Indophile, announced that he would be nominating Prime Minister Rajiv Gandhi and President Jayewardene for the Nobel Peace Prize for their statesmanship in formulating and signing the accord. In London the *Economist* in an editorial comment stated that

> The two leaders have set out on the right path. They will deserve great praise if they stick to it. Mr Jayewardene will have saved his country. Mr Gandhi will have exercised powers of statesmanship and decision that seemed to have deserted him.[3]

Others took a decidedly more cautious attitude to the accord. Pakistan was disappointed at the turn of events that led to the signing of the accord, and so was China. There were no comments from either Beijing or Islamabad on the accord itself, only a deep silence.[4] Bangladeshi diplomats, like their Nepali counterparts, had grave misgivings about the accord and were distressed at this ruthless demonstration of the extension of Indian power in the region.[5]

In the Sinhalese areas of the country the opprobrium attached to the Indo–Sri Lanka Accord was focused on its architects within the government, principally J. R. Jayewardene himself. For his part, the Sri Lankan president had no option but to go ahead with its signing. He placed his trust in Rajiv Gandhi's assurances—which proved, in the end, to be far too optimistic—that the Indian army could sort things out and impose peace in the north and east of the island.

The Janatha Vimukthi Peramuna (JVP), the most vocal, violent, and persistent critics of the accord, called for his assassination through handwritten posters and inflammatory pamphlets and speeches (transmitted through cassettes). The slogan "Kill JR" was painted on public highways throughout the island, and on walls in public places—in the universities, for example—a reminder of how dangerous the situation was for him and the government. On 18 August 1987, the JVP very nearly succeeded in assassinating him within the parliamentary complex when the whole government parliamentary group, including the cabinet, were gathered to discuss the implementation of the accord. Two grenades were lobbed into the room and onto the table at which Jayewardene was seated. They rolled off the table onto the carpeted floor and a short distance from him before they exploded. The ensuing explosion killed one district minister, and several others, including some cabinet ministers, were seriously injured. The one who suffered the most serious injuries was Lalith Athulathmudali. (One MP had been killed on 31 July by the JVP in the violence that broke out in the wake of the signing of the accord.) Jayewardene himself had a miraculous escape. There was not a scratch on him, but the hearing in one ear was impaired as a result of the explosion, and he took to wearing a hearing aid thereafter.

The Accord: Indo–Sri Lankan Discussions

As an indication of the confidence in New Delhi about the progress made in putting the accord into effect, a group of senior officials from India were in Colombo for discussions on residual matters relating to the accord just over a fortnight after Rajiv Gandhi's departure for India from Colombo. They were in the island from 19 August (only one day after the attempted assassination of President Jayewardene and the botched plan to kill a large number of ministers and government party MPs) to 21 August. They returned to the island for the same purpose on 17 September for four days of talks, and a delegation of Sri Lankan officials led by W. M. P. B. Menikdiwela, President Jayewardene's secretary, visited New Delhi from 1 to 5 September to continue the talks with their Indian counterparts.

The object of this exercise in continued discussions was to resolve the residual matters referred to in Article 2.15 of the Indo–Sri Lanka Accord, which stipulated that these should be resolved between the two governments within six weeks of the agreement being signed. From the outset the two sides approached the problem differently. The Sri Lankan officials' understanding of the situation and the instructions given them by their government were that residual matters were strictly limited by the terms of the discussions in Bangalore in November 1986; the Indian side was pressing for a more expansive interpretation which included constitutional matters as well. An exchange of letters between J. N. Dixit and H. W. (Harry) Jayewardene in October 1987 focused attention on this difference of interpretation.[6]

Harry Jayewardene's opinions on these matters were not merely his own, but reflected the views of the government led by his brother.

In early November, President Jayewardene was in New Delhi for further discussions with the Indian government. A bland communiqué issued on 7 November 1987 with the signatures of J. R. Jayewardene and Rajiv

Gandhi was, for once, a concise and accurate summary of the differences in the views of the two governments on the implementation of the accord. It read as follows:

> The visit of President J. R. Jayewardene to Delhi provided an opportunity to the two sides to review the progress of the implementation of the Indo–Sri Lanka Agreement.
>
> The Indian side pointed out to the Sri Lankan Government the imperative need to incorporate some additional provisions into the proposed legislation in order to make the functioning of the Provincial Councils, and the devolution more meaningful, adequate and self-contained. The Sri Lankan side pointed out that if the draft legislation now before Parliament is not passed into law as approved by the Supreme Court, and the Provincial Councils are not immediately set up in their present proposed form, the process of implementation will be avoidably delayed. On the establishment of the Provincial Councils, the legislation creating them and their functioning as referred to at the discussions will be given the most serious and urgent consideration and steps will be taken to include such changes as are mutually deemed necessary for more effective devolution, better functioning of the proposed Provincial Councils and for the complete implementation of the Indo–Sri Lanka Agreement.[7]

A list of some of the matters referred to in this document showed that they went well beyond the residual matters referred to in Article 2.15 of the Indo–Sri Lanka Accord. Indeed ten of these were identified as having been discussed as well as an eleventh—"any other matters by mutual agreement."[8] The Sri Lankan president had refused to commit his government to anything beyond the matters identified at Bangalore in November 1986.

The Establishment of Provincial Councils

In the first week of October, as the Sinhalese inhabitants of the Eastern Province fled their homes by train, bus, van, lorry, and other forms of improvised transport in search of security in other parts of the island, the Sri Lankan government seemed more imperiled than it had been at any time since the riots of July. The buses that brought these refugees to the towns of the Central Province—to Kandy in particular—were covered with anti-Jayewardene and anti-government slogans in black and red. Huge posters written in black and red covered the space not occupied by graffiti painted directly on the bodies of the vehicles. Some of the refugees reached Colombo by train in the hope of seeking refuge with their kinfolk in the Southern Province. Black flags flew over shops and temples, some put up voluntarily and some under pressure from the JVP.

The deteriorating situation in the Eastern Province, to which these hundreds of refugees living in makeshift camps, or more prominently in temples in the city of Colombo, offered such distressing evidence, served to provide those opposed to the IPKF's presence in the island with more political ammunition to use against the government. Much of the criticism was directed against the president himself and the ministers associated with him in the negotiation and signing of the accord, especially Gamini Dissanayake and Ronnie de Mel. Their lives were seen to be in imminent danger and their homes were provided with very tight and conspicuous security. They traveled with armed guards and very often in bulletproof cars.

Those who met President Jayewardene at this time came back with the feeling that, despite all that had happened since the signing of the peace accord and the arrival of the IPKF, he still believed that the IPKF could and would sort things out in the north and east. Taking a very practical view of the situation, he argued that, while the IPKF may have failed in its endeavor to disarm the Tamil separatist activists within five days, the decision to fight the Liberation Tigers of Tamil Eelam (LTTE) and the move against them in Jaffna and the Jaffna peninsula were more than adequate compensation. The burden of fighting the LTTE had been assumed by the IPKF and—more to the point—the heavy expenses involved was being borne by the Indian government.[9] Few people in the country saw the situation in the same way as he did. Indeed very few people took the same dispassionate view of the IPKF's role and India's assumption of the responsibility of defeating the LTTE and bearing all the expenses.

The Sri Lankan government, for its part, had fulfilled its obligations by keeping its forces in the north and east in their barracks. Most of the home guard units had been disbanded. Now the president's attention was focused on the most significant part of his obligations, namely to introduce legislation in Parliament for the establishment of provincial councils and eventually the merger on a temporary basis of the Northern and Eastern Provinces.

The legislation had been ready for some time. Its basis lay in the Delhi Accord signed in August 1985 and its refinement, amendment, and expansion over the next two years. This process was continuing as late as

September 1987, when at last President Jayewardene and the government decided that the time had come to introduce it for debate in Parliament. In doing so he confronted a number of difficulties involving the extent of support his cabinet colleagues and MPs would give him at this time of crisis. Both were under severe threat from the JVP, which had launched a campaign of terror against the United National Party (UNP). They had killed one MP in the wake of the signing of the accord in July, and a district minister on 18 August during the attack on the government parliamentary group in Parliament. As we had seen, President Jayewardene himself had a very narrow escape from death on that occasion. The JVP threat was the most serious but not the only one the president had to take into consideration in assessing the political risks involved in getting parliamentary approval of this controversial legislation. There was the question of Prime Minister R. Premadasa and his attitude to the bill and to the president. Relations between the two were severely strained as a result of Premadasa's conspicuous failure to join in signing the accord and his refusal to participate in any of the social occasions associated with Rajiv Gandhi's visit. Over the next two months—August and September—Premadasa maintained a studied ambivalence on matters relating to the accord and the legislation that would flow from it. He had played no role at all in the preparation of that legislation, although it would be his duty—as leader of the house—to introduce it for debate in Parliament.

President Jayewardene and his prime minister barely maintained the civilities of their relationship at that stage. There was a very real danger of a breach between them, and in all the former's calculations at that time that possibility was part of the equation. Premadasa for his part was anxious not to precipitate a break with his leader. Thus the president was relieved when Premadasa made it known to him that he would support the bill and pilot it through Parliament once the Supreme Court had delivered its verdict on the constitutionality of the draft bill.[10] It all depended now on the Supreme Court's verdict.

The Provincial Councils Bill did not really need a constitutional amendment but because of the perennially controversial nature of schemes of devolution in Sri Lankan politics and because of Indian pressure (see chapter 5 of this volume), the government thought it appropriate to incorporate the new scheme in the Constitution. It was also meant to be a gesture of reassurance and conciliation directed toward the Tamil minority.

President Jayewardene knew as well as Premadasa did that the real danger to the government at this stage came not so much from the political opposition as from the Supreme Court. The constitutionality of the two bills—the Provincial Councils Bill and the Thirteenth Amendment to the Constitution—was challenged by a disparate collection of political groups and individuals: the Sri Lanka Freedom Party (SLFP) and other Sinhalese opposition parties, representatives of Buddhist opinion, and some extreme nationalists among the Sinhalese. Their contention was that the two bills sought to make such fundamental changes in the constitutional and political structure of the country that, in addition to the requirement of a two-thirds majority of all MPs, there should also be the approval of the people at a referendum.

President Jayewardene had no serious difficulty commanding the support of the great majority of his parliamentary group on this legislation and he knew he could always get a two-thirds majority. But his greatest fear was that the court might well insist on a referendum in addition to the two-thirds majority in Parliament. He was certain that the bills would be overwhelmingly defeated at such a referendum, and the country would then face a political crisis of the gravest order. Quite apart from the fact that such a decision would have been construed—rightly—as a rejection of the government by the people at large, and a tremendous morale booster for the opposition forces ranged against the bill and the Indo–Sri Lankan peace accord, it would have meant a triumph of some of the most reactionary forces in the country. Above all, the prospects of peace would have been slimmer than they were at that time.

Like most politically conscious people in the country, the president was awaiting the verdict of the Supreme Court with great anxiety. No one was more relieved than he when the Supreme Court held that the bills required a two-thirds majority of MPs but not a referendum. Nevertheless, while he was thankful that the worst had not happened, he was concerned by the narrow margin of this decision. Indeed, the decision in favor had been the narrowest possible, five to four. Jayewardene noted that of the six Sinhalese judges of the Supreme Court, four had voted in favor of the referendum. It was a narrow escape from a situation for which he, for once, had no contingency plan—to get the electorate as a whole to vote in favor of the Indo–Sri Lanka Accord.

Once the verdict of the Supreme Court was in, the political battle shifted to Parliament and the cabinet. President Jayewardene himself and his ministers and MPs were now under immense pressure in the form of threats of assassination from the JVP, the objective being to prevent them from actually getting to Parliament for the debate and vote scheduled for 13 November. He was relieved to find that only one minister, Gamini Jayasuriya, refused to support the two bills. He was opposed to even a temporary amalgamation of the Northern and Eastern Provinces. The president did his best to persuade Jayasuriya to change his mind, but the latter would not do so. He resigned from the government and his seat.[11]

As for his MPs he realized that they did face great danger, at least in some parts of the country, and so he devised a very practical solution. He got them to Colombo a week or so ahead of the vote and housed them in one of Colombo's five-star hotels, where they were provided with security of a sort they could not have had in their hometowns or in houses in Colombo. They would travel thence to Parliament in a convoy of heavily guarded buses. Parliament itself was converted into a virtual fortress, so rigorous was the security introduced for the occasion.

The passage of these two bills through Parliament on 13 November 1987 was a triumph for President Jayewardene, one in which he prevailed against the heaviest of odds. The JVP led the extraparliamentary agitation against it, while within Parliament the SLFP voted against the Thirteenth Amendment.

In the meantime, the JVP's violence took a deadly toll of local UNP cadres. Although the killings appeared to be random, there was a steadily intensifying campaign designed to break the morale of the UNP and to undermine the party's loyalty to the leader. But this pressure only strengthened the president's hold on the party. When the debate began, every MP was present for the vote; only two MPs, both from the Southern Province, abstained from voting on the second reading of the Provincial Councils Bill. President Jayewardene responded by announcing that he would initiate measures for their expulsion from the party, but he relented when they eventually voted in favor of the bill during its third reading.

Thus the JVP's campaign of threats and violence failed to keep the UNP MPs from voting for the bill. The JVP and the SLFP expected that there would be violence on the scale that rocked the country in late July when the Indo–Sri Lankan peace accord was signed. The main opposition came from the university students—a reflection of the JVP's hold on the universities—but even in the universities there was no violence. Nor did the student demonstrations spill over into the streets. In the country at large the acts of sabotage were much fewer than expected. They were mainly in the Southern Province, where there was sabotage of electrical transmission lines and street demonstrations in some of the remote towns. These latter were mainly of school children who were cajoled into taking to the streets by JVP cadres.

President Jayewardene: A Visit to India, January 1988

President Jayewardene was invited to India as the guest of honor at the Republic Day celebrations in Delhi on 26 January. Under normal circumstances the invitation and the visit would have been an unalloyed honor and pleasure, but against the background of India's current role in Sri Lanka that was not to be. At the time he prepared for the visit, he had made up his mind that he would retire at the end of his current term, that is to say by 3 January 1989 at the latest. Apart from the ceremonial aspects of the visit there was much unfinished business. The visit would give him the opportunity for a review of the problems that lay ahead in the implementation of the political agenda of the Indo–Sri Lanka Accord. Then there were the questions being raised in the island about the IPKF's role. After some initial success in its campaigns against the LTTE in Jaffna and the Jaffna peninsula, the IPKF seemed unable—the government's critics would say unwilling—to break the LTTE's grip on the north and east of the island. Above all, the president was anxious to have the Indian government's assessment of the impact of the death of M. G. Ramachandran, long-time chief minister of Tamil Nadu, on the tripartite relationship of India, Tamil Nadu, and Sri Lanka.

Ramachandran was a singularly Indian phenomenon, a film star who captivated the masses, and turned that immense popularity into a political asset he successfully parlayed to dominate the politics of a region of India. He played several mythic roles, secular and "godly," always the embodiment of good, and always the protector of the poor against the enemies of the poor. Soon the poor began to see in M. G. R., as he was called, the embodiment of the virtues he portrayed, and they gave him loyal support that went far beyond the normal bounds of political response. The emotional scenes that followed his death were also characteristically Indian, but nothing on this same scale had been seen before in Indian politics at the passing away of a purely regional figure.[12]

Ramachandran was Indira Gandhi's—and Rajiv Gandhi's—staunch supporter. So as long as he was alive the central government in New Delhi had little to fear about Tamil Nadu. This was extremely important because every other region in southern India had voted heavily against the Indira Congress and had a non-Congress party in power.

Born on a plantation in Sri Lanka (near Kandy), Ramachandran never really lost interest in its affairs, especially as a champion of the Tamil cause—first the Indian plantation workers, later the Sri Lankan Tamil separatist forces. As regards the separatist movement, he provided a refuge for Tamil activists and terrorists, supported them with money, and helped them with their training programs. But as regards the various factions among the Tamil separatists, he was never consistent in favoring one or other among them over the rest. Originally opposed to the LTTE, he later became its main supporter.

However, there was one cardinal principle in all this: he was always willing to adjust or modify his policies on Tamil separatism in Sri Lanka to suit the needs of New Delhi. Thus, although he was a supporter of the LTTE he backed the Indo–Sri Lankan peace accord, and his support had been essential to Rajiv Gandhi in containing opposition within Tamil Nadu to the IPKF's campaigns against the LTTE in Jaffna and the Eastern Provinces of Sri Lanka.

In both New Delhi and Colombo the question being asked was what impact his death would have on the future of the peace accord. The speed with which Rajiv Gandhi changed his policy on Sri Lanka in early July 1987 was based, partly at least, on the belief that it was absolutely essential to get the accord signed while Ramachandran was alive. He had been ailing late in 1986. In fact, arrangements had been made to fly him to the United States for treatment. The U.S. consulate in Madras had been asked to approve visas for forty persons to fly Ramachandran and his entourage to the United States! The trip was planned and canceled several times in 1987.

President Jayewardene was afraid that Ramachandran's death could seriously weaken New Delhi's position in Tamil Nadu, and that it introduced another element of instability into Indian policy regarding Sri Lanka. But senior officials in his own Foreign Ministry believed that the death of Ramachandran would benefit both New Delhi and Sri Lanka, because nobody in Tamil Nadu would be able to dominate politics in that region as Ramachandran had. Ramachandran was a cult figure; everybody else was a mere politician. And people of that sort would be easier to handle than Ramachandran. In that sense—they believed and argued—the peace accord would not be seriously affected.

Moreover, the Sri Lankan Tamil separatist cause had suffered a setback in Tamil Nadu, not less than in other parts of India, by the recent behavior of the LTTE. The people of Tamil Nadu were becoming tired of them whether as refugees or political exiles, and seemed less likely, at this stage, to extend unconditional support to anyone who wished to patronize or encourage the LTTE.

President Jayewardene returned from his Indian visit on 31 January 1988 in a more ebullient mood than when he went. There were several reasons for this. For one thing, Rajiv Gandhi understood his concern about a potential recovery of the LTTE's military strength. Indeed, he assured him that India was anxious to deliver a coup de grâce, to the LTTE and by so doing to bring the IPKF back by the middle of 1988. He was told that instructions would be issued to the high commission in Colombo and the IPKF to make a special effort to capture the LTTE leadership.[13] The Indian government's principal interest at this stage was for an early holding of the provincial council elections, culminating in elections to the unified North Eastern Council. President Jayewardene agreed to advance the first set of elections to April/May from June/July, which his officials had indicated to him as the earliest possible given all the difficulties they faced. He had decided on that well before he set out for India.[14]

He had hinted to Rajiv Gandhi about his plans for retirement from politics at the end of his present term. The latter was taken aback by this, and sought to persuade him to change his plans in the interest of the peace process in Sri Lanka, and the successful completion of the political agenda envisaged in the Indo–Sri Lankan peace accord. The successful holding of elections to the provincial councils was only one part of this; the more important aspect was the nurturing of these councils during their early and formative months and years. Jayewardene's continuation in office beyond 1989 was seen as essential for this. Gandhi's arguments helped to change his mind; he came back intent on trying for a third term.[15]

Questions about the IPKF

With the IPKF still unable to make a final breakthrough to the defeat of the LTTE, now holed up in the north of the island, persons close to President Jayewardene were ready to talk to the LTTE for the first time about a possible settlement. Two initiatives were attempted in February 1988. The opening move was by Gamini Dissanayake and the intermediary was Kumar Ponnambalam, leader of the Tamil Congress. That approach failed because the Indians were opposed to it. Then a second attempt was made, this time at the insistance of National Security Minister Lalith Athulathmudali. It would seem that the Indians gave their blessings to this enterprise.[16] The intermediary, a U.S.-based Tamil academic, was in Colombo during the last weekend of February, having spent some days in Madras.[17] The aim in these negotiations was to get the LTTE to agree to a political settlement whereby their own position in the Northern Province as the main spokesmen of the Tamils would be recognized, while they would have to abandon a similar claim to the Eastern Province. There was a great deal of anti-Indian feeling among the Tamils, especially in the north of the island, and the idea behind these secret negotiations was to seek to exploit that feeling to the advantage of Sri Lanka.

The Indian government was generally unhappy about the negotiations initiated by Athulathmudali, but its leaders themselves were unable to object openly because of their lack of success in capturing the LTTE leader and his associates and destroying the LTTE as a political organization. Under pressure from Rajiv Gandhi, the Indian high commission in Colombo and the IPKF were intent on eliminating the leadership of the LTTE. The IPKF were insistent that they had the LTTE on the run and would be able to break its resistance by the end of March 1988. The president remained steadfast in his demand—which the Indians supported—of an unconditional surrender of the LTTE, but he was willing to support these secret negotiations.

No accurate information was available about the precise size of the IPKF in Sri Lanka as of March 1988. The estimate provided by the Indian government at that stage was fifty to sixty thousand. If so, the IPKF was larger than the British element in the Indian army had been in India during the heyday of the *raj*, and half as large as the Soviet forces then in Afghanistan.

Questions were being raised in Sri Lanka with regard to the tactics and objectives of the IPKF. Why was it, that with such a large force, the IPKF had been unable to defeat the LTTE decisively or capture its leader? The answer given by Indian official circles was that the Jaffna peninsula had been cleared of the LTTE, who had moved to the jungles of the Vavuniya, Kilinochchi, and Mullaitivu districts of the Northern Province. The area was large and offered great opportunity for concealment. The Indians sought to saturate the area with their troops, who would eventually encircle and destroy the LTTE and its leadership. Many of the forces engaged in the campaign had experience in dealing with guerrillas in the northeast of India, where these tactics had proved successful. In brief, the Indians were intent on using sheer numbers in their campaign against the LTTE.

But the IPKF had their critics in Sri Lanka—Lalith Athulathmudali, for one—who compared their performance with similar campaigns in other parts of the world and began to question the whole basis of this strategy. Their contention was that a campaign based on sheer numbers was slow and cumbersome. They pointed out that the British and their Malay forces had cracked the Communist rebellion in postwar Malaysia using a totally different strategy. The ratio of British/Malay forces to those of the Communists was much smaller than the current ratio of Indian forces to those of the LTTE yet the British/Malay forces were able to win through. The British forces in Malaya had a sound knowledge of the people and the terrain in which they fought. The IPKF was lacking in the knowledge of both, and without the active support of the Sri Lankan forces they would not acquire them. The Sri Lankan forces did give information to the IPKF, but it was clearly not adequate to overcome the IPKF handicaps of ignorance of the people and the terrain.

While the IPKF had some sort of control in the Northern Province, by March 1988 they had proved to be a disastrous failure in the Eastern Province, where the Tamils were a minority and there were large Sinhalese and Muslim populations. They failed abysmally in affording protection to the Sinhalese and Muslims in Trincomalee, Batticaloa, and Amparai. In March a large LTTE force had moved away from the Northern Province and were roaming the Eastern Province killing Sinhalese and Muslim peasants, and the IPKF had been quite unable to check them. President Jayewardene had decided that as of the end of March Sri Lankan forces and the police would be used to protect Sinhalese and Muslim villages, something the IPKF had singularly failed in doing. The Indian government had been persuaded to accept this.

All in all, the Indian performance through the IPKF had tarnished the reputation of the world's fourth largest army. They had been held at bay by a small group of ruthless and clever guerrillas. The old theory that the Indian army worked on, that they could conquer the whole of Sri Lanka in twenty-four hours, had been shown to be no more than an idle boast.

The president had been assured that the IPKF would start moving out of the island sometime in April, having broken the back of the LTTE resistance in the meantime. He was inclined to believe that Indians would want to get the IPKF away from Sri Lanka as early as they could because recent events in Afghanistan were seen as an ominous warning about the political dangers inherent in foreign forces operating against local guerrillas. The Indians would want to make a less precipitate departure from Sri Lanka than the Russians in Afghanistan, and to complete their self-imposed assignment before world opinion turned hostile to them.

Notes

1. This information is based on discussions with Foreign Ministry officials.
2. A. C. S. Hameed, interview with the author, September 1987.
3. The *Economist,* 1 August 1987.
4. A. C. S. Hameed, interview with the author, September 1987.
5. This information is based on discussions with Sri Lankan diplomats at the United Nations in New York and officials at the Ministry of Foreign Affairs in Colombo.
6. See Dixit's letter of 10 October 1987 to Harry Jayewardene and Jayewardene's response, J. R. Jayewardene MSS.
7. A copy of this communiqué is available in the J. R. Jayewardene MSS.
8. The themes discussed were "Size of the Provincial Councils, size of the Board of Ministers, Governor's discretionary powers, Parliament's powers to amend the devolution package, Parliament's powers to legislate on subjects in the Provincial List, matters relating to the Interim Provision (Section 37), Emergency Provisions, imposition of President's rule on the ground of failure of Governor to comply with directives, Provincial Council List, problems with regard to land and land settlement, and any other matters by mutual agreement."
9. These points were made by President Jayewardene in conversation with the author at this time; there were others including local and foreign journalists to whom he spoke on much the same lines.
10. J. R. Jayewardene, interview with the author, October 1987.
11. Gamini Jayasuriya resigned his seat on 11 November 1987.
12. On Ramachandran, see K. Mohandas, *MGR: The Man and the Myth* (Bangalore: Panther, 1992); see particularly 165–68.
13. J. R. Jayewardene, interview with the author, 10 January 1988.
14. On 13 January 1988 J. N. Dixit had conveyed a message to President Jayewardene from Rajiv Gandhi setting out five points for his consideration, all relating to the establishment of the provincial councils. The first of them is relevant for our purposes here. It reads: "President may consider holding elections to Provincial Councils including in the North and East, around May. . . ." To this J. R. Jayewardene's laconic reply of 18 January had been: "Approved, even earlier." The note is available in the J. R. Jayewardene MSS.
15. J. R. Jayewardene, interview with the author, 10 January 1988. See the *Daily News* of 9 May 1988, where it was reported that a committee of legal experts had been appointed to examine whether it was possible for President Jayewardene to run for the office a third time under the terms of the Constitution. The committee had reached the conclusion that this would require an amendment of Articles 31(2) and 160 of the Constitution.
16. This claim is based on information obtained in discussions with Gamini Dissanayake and Lalith Athulathmudali.
17. This was a Dr. Selvakumar, then an associate professor at Carnegie-Mellon University.

14

Implementing the Accord: The Last Phase, April 1988–January 1989

Provincial Council Elections

THE FIRST SET of provincial council elections, four in all, were scheduled for 28 April 1988.[1] The decision of the Sri Lanka Freedom Party (SLFP) to boycott these elections deprived them of much of the drama that usually revolves round electoral conflicts between the two main political rivals of Sri Lanka, the United National Party (UNP) and the SLFP. One consequence of all this, most political observers expected, would be a very low voter turnout, around 30 to 35 percent of the electorate. Generally there was a lower turnout at local government elections in Sri Lanka than at parliamentary elections, but this time there were two other factors operating to keep voters away from the polls. One was the fear of Janatha Vimukthi Peramuna (JVP) violence. The JVP had announced its intention to disrupt the polls and had passed sentence of death on all potential candidates. The second was that there was no general understanding of the nature of these provincial councils, and much suspicion about them because they were seen to be part of an imposition that emerged with the Indo–Sri Lanka Accord of July 1987.

Nevertheless the provincial councils would mark a major change in Sri Lanka's political structure. One of President Jayewardene's important contributions to the country was to establish a second tier of government between the national legislature and executive branch and the local government institutions, the first and third tiers. He had introduced the district councils system in 1980–81, and now in 1987 provincial councils were established. He believed that devolution of power would have a powerful impact on the nature of political relationships and of political

281

parties in the island. As a prelude to the provincial council elections, he announced the names of persons he had chosen as governors. Four were to be appointed by 27 April to the four provinces in which elections were scheduled to take place on 28 April. The recently retired chief justice, S. Sharvananda, was chosen as the governor for the Western Province in which the capital city of Colombo/Kotte is located; a Muslim, Bakeer Markar, then minister without portfolio and a one-time speaker for the Southern Province; another cabinet minister, E. L. B. Hurulle, minister of cultural affairs, for the Central Province; and for Sabaragamuva N. Wimalasena, one-time deputy minister of finance (1965–70) and after 1978 deputy chief of the Greater Colombo Economic Commission, which ran the island's free trade zones. In choosing persons of experience and standing for these posts, the Sri Lankan president was clearly intent on establishing the governor's position as a prestigious and influential one, something that would give the new system the good start that it badly needed.

Behind it all there was another important consideration: the establishment of these councils in May and June was expected to ensure that a substantial portion of the Indian Peace-Keeping Force (IPKF) would be leaving the island. The understanding between the two governments was that the troop reduction would start in late May/early June 1988 and be completed by July 1988.

In making these plans for elections to the provincial councils the president had little or no support from Prime Minister R. Premadasa, who continued to be one of the most intriguing puzzles in Sri Lanka's politics at that time. He had been away in Britain and Japan during most of July 1987, when the Indo–Sri Lankan negotiations that led to the signing of the accord of 29 July were being conducted. He was able to steer clear of any positive endorsement of its main principles, and he was free of any of the odium attached to it. Short of resignation he could not have expressed his attitude to the accord more unambiguously. He did support the concept of provincial councils in Parliament, but in April he announced that he would be away for a month on an extended visit to India and Nepal during the campaign for the first set of elections to provincial councils. The visit to India was to deliver the keynote address to the UN Commission on Human Settlements (HABITAT) in New Delhi, but when this was over in early April he stayed in India and then went to Nepal. He returned home just as the campaign was officially over.

With the first set of provincial council elections over, President Jayewardene was deservedly confident and optimistic about the second, scheduled for 2 June (the Western and Central Provinces) and 9 June (the Southern Province). None of his closest supporters really believed that the results of the elections held at the end of April and in June would yield such beneficial results. Indeed, most people felt that the voter turnout would be very low, and that the UNP would struggle to get a majority against a weak "left" wing opposition. Most assessments had it that the SLFP's boycott campaign and the JVP's threats would keep the bulk of the electors at home. But at every stage the president was confident that over 50 percent of the people would vote and that the voters would give the government substantial support. In the event he was proved right and all his critics wrong. The UNP had a majority in all the provincial councils. For the first time since May 1987—a year earlier—he was really in control of events and had demonstrated once more a sure touch in assessing the public mood.

His own assessment of the political consequences flowing from the holding of the provincial council elections was that the UNP base in the country remained very solid. The elections had revealed its weaknesses as well as its strengths, and he felt he now had time to devote to strengthening the party in areas in which the performance fell below expectations. Moreover, the provincial councils the party now controlled would provide an excellent base for the presidential and parliamentary elections.

India, the IPKF, and the LTTE

One way or another, it seemed impossible for J. R. Jayewardene to prevent the affairs of the IPKF and the Liberation Tigers of Tamil Eelam (LTTE) from causing problems for him and the government, and at the most unexpected moments. There had always been a suspicion that a reluctant LTTE had been cajoled into accepting the Indo–Sri Lanka Accord in late July–early August 1987 through some secret deal. Now in April 1988 it was revealed[2] that the Indian government had agreed to provide the LTTE with a substantial amount of money on that occasion in return for its support for the accord. An embarrassed Indian government felt compelled to make an official statement on this in the Indian Parliament through Natwar Singh, minister of state for external affairs, baring the details about the negotiations between the Indian government and Velupillai

Prabhakaran during the time he was in India at the end of July 1987. His argument was that

> In order to help [the] LTTE make the difficult transition from military to peaceful democratic policies, it was agreed to extend some interim financial relief to [the] LTTE on the understanding that such relief would only cover the period till the rehabilitation of its cadres. . . .
>
> I would like to categorically refute . . . the misleading newspaper reports that this payment was made to persuade Shri Prabhakaran to accept the Indo–Sri Lanka Agreement. This kind of aspersion is beyond contempt. As I have said Prabhakaran had already accepted the agreement. But he had explained certain practical problems in respect of his cadres during the transition. The financial assistance was intended to help [the] LTTE overcome these problems.[3]

Natwar Singh was protesting too much and too hard. The fact is that the LTTE had extracted a monetary payment from the Indian government before its leaders expressed their willingness to accept the Indo–Sri Lanka Accord as a political reality. Eventually only the first installment was paid, but that was because within three months of the signing of the accord the IPKF was at war with the LTTE in Jaffna.

Needless to say, the opposition in Sri Lanka gleefully exploited the advantage this revelation gave them to embarrass the Sri Lankan government. A question was raised in Parliament about the *Observer* report, by Lakshman Jayakody, its principal foreign affairs spokesman, on 8 April. Lalith Athulathmudali responded: "Our position is we are making enquiries about this matter. So far we have no knowledge of it other than public statements made elsewhere. Once we get a fuller report, we will give a further answer."[4]

Natwar Singh's statement in the Lok Sabha, on 6 April, was published in full by the Indian high commission in Colombo in an effort at damage control. From the time of the exhumation of this embarrassing episode, the LTTE moved in to exploit the situation to its advantage. Peace feelers were sent to the Indian government by the LTTE, and it would appear that these were being assessed by both the IPKF and the Indian government. Was the LTTE ready to lay down arms? Would it accept the Indo–Sri Lanka Accord? These were among the key questions being considered in this assessment.

This revelation was more of a shock to the Sri Lankan public than to the government because the latter had had its suspicions on this score for some time. But the more intriguing question was the source of the leak, and its timing. The evidence seemed to indicate that it came through the Indian high commission in Colombo, with J. N. Dixit's knowledge and connivance.[5] The timing had a great deal to do with a new initiative on a revival of the peace process in which the Research and Analysis Wing (RAW) took the lead. In that sense the leak was an attempt to muddy the waters for RAW, which was then engaged in negotiations with the LTTE through its cadres still operating in Tamil Nadu. This RAW initiative was being conducted on behalf of the Indian government.

The leak of information on the monetary payment to the LTTE was intended to embarrass both the LTTE and RAW. Its unintended result was to embarrass the Indian government as well.

Anand Verma, the head of RAW, had been sent on a secret mission to Colombo—in the course of which he met President Jayewardene himself—to test the reaction of the Sri Lankan government to the proposals for a settlement the LTTE negotiators had outlined to RAW. On 27 April 1988, M. Gunaratne, a senior Sri Lankan police officer with the rank of deputy inspector general of police, who was conducting negotiations with RAW, reported to President Jayewardene that he

> had a discussion with Sunil [the code name for Verma] today morning. It appears that his visit is to meet your Excellency in order to obtain certain assurances if possible since he is the main negotiator with the LTTE in Madras. It is also significant that his return to Delhi is through Madras.[6]

The evidence we have suggests that Dixit and the Indian high commission in Colombo were not consulted on these delicate negotiations. More to the point, the RAW operatives actually informed the Sri Lankan authorities that the Indian prime minister had lost confidence in Dixit.

In an appendix to Gunaratne's report, marked "Top Secret," President Jayewardene was informed that the

> I[ndian] H[igh] C[ommissioner]—Mr Dixit is not held in favour by Indian P[rime] M[inister] and therefore does not play any significant role in the process of negotiations. The reasons for his loss of influence are:
> —Public disclosures of payments made to LTTE on the eve of the Accord.

—"arrogant and overbearing" [Sunil's words]

—by his conduct and actions, is growing increasingly unpopular with Sinhalese and Tamils. . . .

All groups agreeable to enter political process; LTTE also keen to do so, subject to certain conditions being satisfied.

SUNIL feels that if certain conditions are satisfied, the LTTE would respond by:

(a) surrendering 700 of the estimated 1000 big weapons LTTE have in their possession; they want to retain 300 weapons for their security.

(b) with the surrender, a ceasefire would be announced. The LTTE would thereafter publicly support the Accord. The balance weapons would be released gradually thereafter, once the LTTE felt assured that a climate of security has descended on the North and East."

President Jayewardene was told that Sunil "requested that the fact of his negotiations with Kittu [Sathasivam Krishnakumar, a senior LTTE leader], and the lines of negotiations, be not disclosed to anyone in the Indian High Commission."

The visit of the head of RAW to Sri Lanka and his discussions with President Jayewardene, coming as they did in the wake of Natwar Singh's statement in the Lok Sabha, were seen by the Sri Lankan president as evidence of divided opinions within the Indian government. Whether President Jayewardene disclosed the fact that he was conducting negotiations with RAW to Dixit we do not know. But certainly he kept the Indian prime minister informed of the nature of the discussions.

On 30 May, K. C. Pant, the Indian defense minister, accompanied by senior officials of the Indian army and the Ministries of Defence and External Affairs, arrived in Colombo for two days of talks at the invitation of the Sri Lankan government. President Jayewardene was eager to see how far the Indians would go to accommodate the LTTE if the latter were genuine in their offers of peace, and he used the opportunity provided by Pant's visit to indicate his own views on the terms to be offered to the LTTE.

The seventh, eighth, and nineth paragraphs of the joint communiqué issued at the end of Pant's visit on 1 June reflected the Sri Lankan president's principal concerns at this time. These read as follows:

The government of Sri Lanka reiterated that if the Tamil militants would lay down arms and support the Indo–Sri Lankan Agreement, the detainees will be released and all Tamil militant groups would be granted general amnesty and would be allowed to return to the mainstream of the democratic process envisaged in the Indo–Sri Lanka Agreement and the latest amendments to the Sri Lankan Constitution.

The Sri Lankan side explained the process in the setting up of Provincial Councils under the new scheme of devolution of powers to the Provinces. President Jayewardene indicated that suitable changes and improvements in the devolution package will be brought about in the coming months after Provincial Council elections are over in all Provinces.

Both sides agreed that the strength of the IPKF in Sri Lanka will be determined by joint consultations between the two Governments within the framework of the Indo–Sri Lanka Agreement. As the situation in the Northern and Eastern Provinces continues to improve, the IPKF force levels will be reviewed, depending on operational requirements and the situation on the ground. In view of the encouraging situation in the North and East, the Indian side conveyed that forces not required would return to India in the near future. The two sides agreed to consult each other from time to time in this regard.[7]

In the meantime, negotiations between the Indian government and the LTTE, conducted through intermediaries continued, and appeared to be making some headway.

On 14 June an aide-mémoire issued by the Indian high commission in Colombo revealed the nature of the discussions being conducted by the two governments. It read as follows:

Points conveyed by High Commissioner Dixit to His Excellency the President of the Democratic Socialist Republic of Sri Lanka at a meeting on 14 June, 1988 at 12.00 noon at President's Office, Old Parliament Building:—
1. Merger.
2. Appointment of one High Court for North-Eastern Province.
3. Appointment of Governor for North-Eastern Province.

4. Amendment to 1956 Official Languages Act to make Tamil official language operationally.
5. Announcement for recruitment of Tamils for Armed Forces, Police, Civil Administration.
6. Change of G[overnment] A[gent] in Vavuniya and Jaffna.
7. Ensuring that Pradeshiya Sabhas and District Councils do not dilute role of Provincial Council and Provincial Government.
8. Finance Commission.
9. Refugees to be directly sent to Trincomalee to Clapenburg Camp.
10. Application of amnesty to Tamil militants should not be only up to October 1987. It should apply to all who lay down arms and abide by the Indo–Sri Lanka Agreement up to date.
11. Recognition of Tamil political parties.[8]

A letter marked "Top Secret" and dated 24 June 1988 from President Jayewardene to Prime Minister Rajiv Gandhi is the most comprehensive account of the negotiations between the two governments at this stage that we have. It is quoted at length below.

1. The Head of RAW, in a communique to my Intelligence Official on 23.06.88, has indicated as follows:
"The salient points of my discussions with the President on April 28th and on June 19th, had been communicated to my Prime Minister, including the assurance which had been furnished during these meetings. Therefore it is embarrassing to inform the Prime Minister that these assurances have been changed."

The impression I gather from the above is that you may be informed that I am not standing by certain assurances given. I would like to point out that the three public announcements requested from me (i.e. election to one Provincial Council, release of balance detenues, and adoption of the 1982 Electoral Register for North and East) were to be made by me, on an assurance that the LTTE would be totally disarmed. In fact, Defence Minister Pant had explicitly stated that a Ceasefire will take effect if the LTTE is totally disarmed.

In certain documents purported to have been prepared by the LTTE, the following disturbing features were clearly evident:—

(a) LTTE would hand over only 700 "usable small arms." (This would totally exclude half the number of small arms we know to be in their possession, heavy weaponry, all explosives, grenades and communication equipment.)

(b) Even the surrender of 700 weapons was to be made over a period of five months, but the Government of India had insisted on five weeks, which in my opinion is too long. The surrender of arms and entering of the political process being a voluntary effort, and knowing the logistical efficiency of the LTTE, a shorter period such as two weeks would be more than adequate. In fact, the LTTE were given only three days according to the conditions governing the Accord of July 87, to surrender all weapons.

(c) I informed your Intelligence Official on 19.06.88 that the LTTE must agree to surrender all weapons, explosives, and communication equipment in their possession. My Officials have not received an adequate reply to this as yet.

(d) According to the document prepared by the LTTE, they have requested the Indian Authorities to disarm all other militant groups fully, but not themselves. This naturally would give rise to dangerous consequences if implemented.

2. Therefore, without an assurance that the LTTE would be fully disarmed, (i.e. weapons, explosives and communication equipment) it would not be possible for me to justify making the three expected public announcements. There should be an explicit demonstration of their willingness to be disarmed totally, as has been the understanding at all times.

May I point out that it would be totally unrealistic to expect peace to be achieved, if the LTTE were to retain a quantity of small arms, all their heavy weaponry, their explosives and communications equipment. We know from Intelligence sources that the LTTE have collected polythene bags, oil and grease, to pack and bury their weapons and explosives. There is a strong possibility that the LTTE are most anxious to retain a large quantity of their arsenal for one or more of the following reasons:

(a) Resort to violence during the pre-election, election and post-election periods against their rivals, security forces, Police and the civil administration.

(b) Renew the campaign of violence for separation, if and when most of the IPKF troops are withdrawn.

3. My military and Intelligence authorities are convinced that the LTTE are presently under severe pressure. In fact, the present overtures for peace by the LTTE, are backed by a large number of public demonstrations in the North, orchestrated by the LTTE themselves. 4. This is the best time to put the required degree of diplomatic pressure on the LTTE, to bring them round to a just, reasonable and meaningful settlement, since they are in a state of disarray, in the wake of the successful campaign by the IPKF.[9]

Gamini Dissanayake, now the principal spokesman for the Sri Lankan government had written to Rajiv Gandhi on 21 June 1988 explaining President Jayewardene's anxieties on these negotiations.

Our President has requested that I convey to you directly his views on the situation prevailing in the North.

He would welcome a ceasefire in the North, provided the LTTE makes a total surrender of all arms and communication equipment. This surrender can be monitored by the IPKF and the Joint Operations Command of Sri Lanka. The President is of the distinct view that there are some elements who are in favour of allowing the LTTE to keep some arms. This should not be so. Defence Minister Pant has gone on record as saying that a ceasefire will take effect only if the LTTE is totally disarmed. In the discussions with the Indian officers the LTTE is insisting that the other groups must be totally disarmed. In this context, the LTTE should not be permitted to retain arms. There is a fear in other Tamil groups which is genuine that these arms will be used against them. Therefore it is imperative that there should be an unconditional surrender amongst other things to safeguard the reputation and the stature of the IPKF, who have performed well in Sri Lanka with a death toll of nearly 500 and serious injuries to 1,500.[10]

Later in the letter Dissanayake referred to the disbursement of funds to the LTTE. "The President has no objection in relation to the disbursement of funds to the LTTE to rehabilitate their cadres, but he stresses that such funding should be channelled through the Sri Lanka government according to a procedure in which the LTTE and the government of India can be represented." Rajiv Gandhi responded to these messages with an assurance that "we are committed to disarming the LTTE and bringing them into the political process."[11] He went on to explain that

[W]e share your assessment that the LTTE is under serious pressure. You are also aware that the negotiating process has not involved any relaxation of this pressure. The IPKF operations have effectively undermined the capacity of the LTTE to undertake organized military activity. The LTTE have lost a very large number of their cadres. Their command structure has been eroded and their communications system is in disarray. Their weapons and ammunition manufacturing capacity has been neutralized. Large quantities of their arms, ammunition and explosives have been seized. . . . It is our assessment that we must not be too concerned about the number of weapons to be surrendered. We have effectively reduced their armed strength to manageable levels. The surrender of all heavy weapons, explosives, and communications equipment are within the ambit of the arms surrender.

3. So far as the time table for laying down arms is concerned, we are trying to reduce this period to a reasonable time-frame, taking to account the dispersal of LTTE cadres and the breakdown of their command structures and communications equipment.

The last paragraph of his message was meant as a reassurance to the Sri Lankan president.

7. [I]f the LTTE reneges on the agreements arrived at the conclusion of the present negotiating process, we will nevertheless ensure the full implementation of the Indo–Sri Lanka Agreement.

As a quid pro quo the president was expected to announce "elections to a single Provincial Council [of the North Eastern Province], release of detainees and adopting the 1982 electoral register," all vital parts of a program of political pressure to be exerted over the LTTE.

These negotiations with the LTTE made no progress at all. The IPKF resumed its operations against the LTTE.

Seizing the Electoral Initiative

Even as President Jayewardene proceeded with his negotiations with Rajiv Gandhi on the fate of the LTTE, he continued with his plans for four by-elections to parliamentary seats scheduled for July. The fact that over 50 percent of the voters had braved JVP threats—and actual killing of campaign workers and voters—to go to the polls to elect the provincial councils encouraged him no end. That the UNP had won a majority and control over all seven councils was even more satisfying.

Above all he took great pleasure at the metamorphosis of the new secretary of the UNP, Ranjan Wijeratne,[12] from a technocrat into a first-rate party manager who had succeeded in instilling a sense of confidence into party candidates and workers in an atmosphere of unprecedented physical danger. Jayewardene realized that his own task in leading the campaign at the elections to the provincial councils would have been nearly impossible without the support of Wijeratne, and without the comforting thought that he was there to share the responsibility and risks. In January 1989 Wijeratne became foreign minister and minister of state for defense, and was given charge of negotiations with India and the LTTE.

In May 1988, shortly after the UNP's victory at the provincial council elections of 28 April, the president had announced that there would be by-elections to four seats rendered vacant by UNP MPs who had resigned to run for seats in the provincial councils. The elections were held on 14 July. From the day of the nominations to the seats, the UNP candidates were under grave threat from the JVP. Their close supporters were killed in droves. Of the twelve young men who had accompanied the candidate for the Welimada seat to the secretariat to hand in his nomination papers, no fewer than ten were killed by the JVP. Yet the campaign went on, led by President Jayewardene himself, Premadasa, and some of their cabinet colleagues, Lalith Athulathmudali and Gamini Dissanayake in particular, and a few others. Behind them all was Ranjan Wijeratne, helping the candidates in organizational work, disbursing funds for their campaign, and—along with the president—helping to keep their spirits high.

The UNP won three of the four seats contested, thus demonstrating afresh that Jayewardene's confidence in the party's continued hold on the electorate was justified. Despite the extraordinary difficulties the party faced from the brutal violence directed against it by the JVP, President Jayewardene and Wijeratne together had kept the party's electoral machinery in good order at a time it could well have collapsed. They now proceeded with their plans for the provincial council elections in August.

There was indeed a renewal of hope for his party, but not for himself personally, for President Jayewardene had decided by the middle of July that he would not run in the presidential election due later that year. This came as a surprise to a great many people. Up to the early part of July he had been making preparations to run again, and had been encouraged to do so by almost all members of the cabinet, other senior parliamentarians, and other members of the UNP. In addition a wide range of political leaders from outside the country, including Rajiv Gandhi and Prime Minister Lee Kuan Yew of Singapore, urged him to seek another term in office.

To the very close friends and confidants to whom he revealed his decision, he explained that he was tired and at eighty-two was beginning to feel his age. Although he did not make much of it publicly, it was known that his wife Elina was anxious that he should retire from politics at the end of the year. He argued that his age would be a factor at the next election, and that in fact he would personally be the main issue. The country's politics needed a younger person to handle them, someone who could bring a fresh outlook and new methods to deal with them.

Indo–Sri Lankan Relations

The announcement of President Jayewardene's impending retirement presented India with a number of difficult political problems. Neither Prime Minister R. Premadasa nor Sirimavo Bandaranaike (the two candidates for the presidency) was enthusiastic about the Indo—Sri Lankan agreement signed in July 1987. On the contrary, both had announced that they would, if elected, begin negotiations to have it replaced with a treaty more acceptable to Sri Lanka's interests. Indeed Premadasa had stated quite categorically that he would prefer a friendship treaty on the lines of the Indo-Soviet treaty of 1971. Mrs. Bandaranaike had not been quite so specific.

There were two related and interconnected problems—the IPKF and the provincial council system. Both had committed themselves to insisting on a speedy departure of the IPKF from Sri Lanka. Mrs. Bandaranaike was insistent that this should happen forthwith; Premadasa had not committed himself to any deadline, but was on record as saying that he would like the IPKF to go home as early as possible.

On the provincial councils the two presidential candidates held diametrically opposed views. Despite his early ambivalence toward them, Premadasa came out in support of the councils, and the UNP's election manifesto also expressed strong commitment for them. Mrs. Bandaranaike's attitude was more ambiguous. Members of her party, including her son Anura, had declared that the councils would be abolished if the SLFP won the presidential election. Mrs. Bandaranaike had not endorsed those views, but she had not repudiated them either. She was aware of the Indian interest in the councils, and was aware also that her chances of securing a speedy removal of the IPKF could be jeopardized by a declaration of opposition to them. As the Indians saw it, the chances were that—if elected—she would accept the councils. She might dissolve them and call for fresh elections, but that course of action too had its own dangers, because it would demonstrate how vulnerable the councils were to pressure from the central government, something the Indians would not want demonstrated to the Sri Lankan Tamils. The Indians, for their part, were certain to use a great deal of diplomatic pressure to keep the councils going.

These, however, were hypothetical issues. For the duration of J. R. Jayewardene's presidency the Indo–Sri Lanka Accord and the IPKF were very much his problems. He proceeded to deal with them as he thought best in the wider national interest and with little or no concern for the views of the two presidential candidates. As he saw it, there was much unfinished business and he had to attend to that.

One of the unforeseen consequences of the IPKF's military struggle against the LTTE was its direct involvement in the administration of the Northern and Eastern Provinces, in which, willingly or not, it took over the functions of the civilian government in the maintenance of law and order and the distribution of essentials of life—water, electricity, and on occasion food as well. Sri Lankan public officials, and officials in the state-owned banks, functioned under the protection if not supervision of the IPKF.[13] But the LTTE always maintained a shadowy existence and compelled an adherence to its dictates through its cadres who still moved about even in areas "pacified" by the IPKF.

The IPKF was drawn into the vortex of Tamil politics in Sri Lanka. Despite its continued military pressure on the LTTE—especially through the use of special counterinsurgency units brought in to supplement the IPKF's military resources—the Indian government felt compelled to resort to negotiations with the LTTE, especially because the latter made sporadic but well-publicized offers to talk to the Indians. Thus in April 1988, after the Indian government revealed the details of the negotiations conducted in New Delhi with Prabhakaran in late July and early August 1987, the LTTE, in a clever and well-timed attempt to exploit the embarrassment this caused the Indians, offered to resume negotiations. The LTTE laid down one prior condition: that the IPKF should withdraw to the positions it held in Jaffna prior to October 1987. This the Indians refused to concede, just as the LTTE would not accept the Indian demand that they lay down arms before negotiations could begin. These offers and counter-offers were public relations exercises, directed at international opinion and Tamil Nadu.[14] The IPKF had won the support of some of the smaller Tamil separatist groups—especially the Eelam People's Revolutionary Liberation Front (EPRLF)—and in turn patronized them and used them, where possible, against the LTTE. Even so, none of these groups ever succeeded in replacing the latter in its position of primacy, especially in the north of the island.

The political role of the IPKF became more apparent once the provincial council system was established after the passage of the Thirteenth Amendment to the Sri Lankan Constitution on 13 November 1987. As we have seen, elections to seven of the councils were held between 28 April and 9 June 1988 against the background of a violent campaign conducted by the JVP against the setting up of these councils. On 7 September 1988 President Jayewardene officially authorized the merger of the Northern and Eastern Provinces into a single North Eastern Province, in terms of the Indo–Sri Lanka Accord, a decision intended to be the precursor to the holding of elections to the council of the new province.

Since June 1988 there had been an exchange of telegrams between the two governments on the subject of the merger and the holding of elections to the provincial councils of the new province. The Indian government pressed hard to have these held within a few weeks of the merger. President Jayewardene adhered to the timetable agreed to with the Indian prime minister, in the face of the opposition of those within the Sri Lankan government and the Sri Lankan security services, who argued against holding the election so soon because such an election could not be free and fair so long as the IPKF was present in those regions.[15] These elections were held on 19 November 1988, and the timing had a great deal to do with the politics of Tamil Nadu. The Indian government was anxious that they be held before the elections to the Tamil Nadu state legislature. It had its way, but Congress I, or the Indira Congress, and its allies, whom this decision was intended to benefit, lost the Tamil Nadu election anyway, and a group favorable to the LTTE took control of the Tamil Nadu state government.

The provincial council elections for the North East Provincial Council concluded in November led to the emergence of a pro-Indian political group, the EPRLF, which not only supported the Indo–Sri Lanka Accord, but was seen to have won an election in the Eastern Province despite

LTTE threats against candidates, voters, and elections in general. In the old Northern Province the EPRLF and its supporters were returned uncontested; in the Eastern Province, where there was a high voter turnout, they captured most of the seats. It was alleged that the election and the voting there had been manipulated for the EPRLF by the IPKF. The IPKF played a role in holding these elections, and the mediator was, in this instance, accused of being a ballot rigger.[16] Other proaccord and pro-Indian groups, such as the Eelam National Democratic Liberation Front and the newly established Sri Lanka Muslim Congress also performed very well at this election. The EPRLF nominated a regional ministry in November 1988 to administer the new province.

Both governments were relieved that an election had been held and a provincial government formed. Thus the swearing in at President's House, Colombo, of the chief minister of the North Eastern Province on 9 December was given a great deal of publicity in the media. For one thing, a group of former separatist activists were seen to be pledging allegiance to the Sri Lankan state, and committing themselves to entering the national political system. Furthermore, for the retiring Sri Lankan president and his government it marked the completion of an important stage of a controversial experiment in the devolution of power.

From the outset the EPRLF were seen as creatures of India and the IPKF, and never succeeded in establishing themselves as an independent political entity. The Indian government and the IPKF now found themselves saddled with a puppet regional administration that they needed to sustain and protect against the LTTE. These problems became even more difficult once President Jayewardene decided that he would not run in the presidential election scheduled for late 1988.

This sudden change in the Sri Lankan political situation had an immediate impact on the affairs of the IPKF. With Jayewardene's impending departure from office, the commitment to the Indo–Sri Lanka Accord at the highest levels of the Sri Lankan government was certain to ebb. As we have seen, both of his potential successors, the UNP's R. Premadasa or the SLFP's Mrs. Bandaranaike, were strongly critical of it, and were opposed to the IPKF's presence in the island.

Notes

1. All the preliminary legal work involved in setting up a provincial council administration had been completed by the end of February 1988. A Ministry of Provincial Councils

had been established, and a senior diplomat with a great deal of experience in negotiations with the Tamil separatists, Tissa Jayakody, had been appointed secretary.

2. See the *Observer* (London), 3 April 1988.

3. The text of Natwar Singh's speech was released by the Indian high commission in Colombo on 6 April 1988. PR/23 of 6 April 1988, issued by the Information Service of India. The extracts quoted above are from this document.

4. Athulathmudali's response to Lakshman Jayakody, along with a reference to a telephone conversation between Dixit and President Jayewardene, was published along with the text of Natwar Singh's speech.

5. This charge was made by a number of Dixit's critics including Indian journalists. See particularly P. S. Suriyanarayana, *The Peace Trap: An Indo–Sri Lankan Political Crisis* (New Delhi: Affiliated East-West Press, 1988), 90, where he states that "Rather curiously Dixit, at this delicate stage, made a controversial 'leak' about a money deal between India and Prabhakaran. The secret deal had been struck on the eve of the July Accord. Letting the cat out of the diplomatic bag in early April 1988, Dixit broke the belated news of July 1987. Talking to a few Western journalists in Colombo, he said that a monetary transaction had been finalized on the eve of the July peace pact. This revelation raised a furor in both India and Sri Lanka."

6. This letter and its appendixes are in the J. R. Jayewardene MSS.

7. A copy of the communiqué is available in the J. R. Jayewardene MSS.

8. This aide-mémoire is in the J. R. Jayewardene MSS.

9. This letter is in the J. R. Jayewardene MSS.

10. J. R. Jayewardene MSS, Gamini Dissanayake to Rajiv Gandhi, 21 June 1988.

11. J. R. Jayewardene MSS, "Top Secret" message from Rajiv Gandhi delivered by hand to President Jayewardene by J. N. Dixit, 27 June 1988.

12. The president of the UNP was assassinated by the JVP in late December 1987 and the secretary of the party in March 1988. Wijeratne took over as president and secretary of the UNP, two posts no one wanted because of the JVP threats.

13. For discussion see Lt. Gen. Depinder Singh, *IPKF in Sri Lanka* (New Delhi: Trishul, 1992), and Lt. Gen. S. C. Sardeshpande, *Assignment Jaffna* (New Delhi: Lancer, 1991).

14. See the press statement issued by the U.K. branch of the LTTE on 9 July 1988.

15. The Indian government began expressing its concern about the holding of elections to provincial councils from the beginning of January 1988, but the exchange of telegrams on the subject became more marked after 24 June, after the first set of elections had been completed and the way seemed open for elections in the north and east. Two telegrams sent to J. R. Jayewardene by Rajiv Gandhi on 28 August and 13 September dealt with the need for expediting the merger of the two provinces, and for holding elections to the North Eastern Provincial Council. These telegrams are in the J. R. Jayewardene MSS.

16. See M. S. S. Pandian, "The Election that Was Not," *Economic and Provincial Weekly,* 3 December 1988.

15

The IPKF in Sri Lanka, 1989–90: Negotiating Its Departure

A Change in Leadership

THE VIOLENCE AND TURMOIL in the last few months of President Jayewardene's period of office were, if anything, on a more fearful and more widespread scale than the riots of 27 July to 2 or 3 August 1987 in the wake of the signing of the Indo–Sri Lanka Accord. They were also sustained over a longer period of time and were more difficult to contain. The source of the trouble was the same: Sinhalese intransigents, led and manipulated this time by the Jonatha Vimukthi Peramuna (JVP) in association with the Sri Lanka Freedom Party (SLFP). The Sinhalese areas of the country were convulsed by violence directed by the JVP against supporters of the United National Party (UNP), in which hundreds were killed. In the first two weeks of November a series of politically inspired strikes and disturbances organized by the JVP sought to bring the government down. By this time the JVP had made yet another change of policy: after agitating for over a year for presidential and parliamentary elections, they now demanded that the elections be postponed until the Indian Peace-Keeping Force (IPKF) had left the island. The JVP violence was directed at all political parties (including their newfound ally, the SLFP) participating in the elections. It required President Jayewardene's skillful use of the unwavering support the security services and the police gave him—although he was a lame-duck president—to hold the government and administration together in the face of the JVP's campaign of violence. The presidential election of December 1988 was perhaps the most violent ever held in a democracy, and most unusual compared to violent elections elsewhere, such as the national elections in Jamaica in the 1980s, because those who indulged in violence were not the supporters of the three candidates. In fact, those engaged in the campaign became the victims of terror directed by a group who wished to see the elections postponed.

The JVP was persisting in its policy of using the presence of the IPKF as an emotionally divisive issue in its national campaign. The Indian government was now on the defensive because both principal candidates in the Sri Lankan presidential election, R. Premadasa of the UNP and Sirimavo Bandaranaike of the SLFP, had gone on record as being opposed to the IPKF presence in the island. In an effort at damage control, the Indian high commissioner J. N. Dixit was sent to meet the two candidates with a message from New Delhi that the IPKF would be withdrawn soon. Both candidates were given the Indian government's views on the mechanics and timing of the withdrawal. They were urged to tone down public criticisms of the IPKF, as these would hamper the Indian government's efforts to prepare public opinion in India for the withdrawal.[1] R. Premadasa paid heed to this appeal and his criticisms of the IPKF presence became more subdued. Nevertheless he stuck to his claim that he would persuade the IPKF to leave as soon as he came to office. Indeed, he began to speak of a phased withdrawal of the IPKF, unlike the SLFP leader Sirimavo Bandaranaike, who held on to her original theme—"out as soon as possible."

The outcome of the election gave the Indians great satisfaction. They had good reason to claim—as some officials of the Indian high commission did claim at that time—that the IPKF's presence in the north and east, (especially the east) of the island, made the difference between defeat and victory, given the wafer-thin margin Premadasa secured over Mrs. Bandaranaike. Had people in the Eastern Province not voted in such large numbers, the election could have gone to Mrs. Bandaranaike. Indeed, some political observers believed—and they too had good reason to do so—that the IPKF had done more than that on Premadasa's behalf, that they had brought voters to the polling stations with the knowledge that this would help his cause.

Once the election was over and the UNP candidate had won, Dixit met President Premadasa just after he had been sworn in. Apart from the conventional good wishes of his government Dixit conveyed what he thought would be the message the new president really wanted, that is to say, when the withdrawal of the IPKF would begin.[2] The Indian government's message, that the first batch of IPKF soldiers would return to India in January 1989, should have delighted the new president. Instead,

Premadasa urged that the process be delayed, that the IPKF should remain in the north and east of the island during the election campaign for seats in parliament so that people there would feel secure enough to go out to vote. This surprising request, from a man who had opposed the entry of the IPKF to Sri Lanka and had pushed for their early return to India, left Dixit more than a little surprised. He returned from the meeting rather bemused but very satisfied at the prospect of what he saw was a more friendly attitude to India from the new president.

President Premadasa's narrow victory over Mrs. Bandaranaike did not lead to anything more than a temporary relaxation of the JVP's violence. It was resumed before the end of January 1989—around 20 January, to be more exact—and continued beyond the parliamentary elections of February 1989. The parliamentary elections, the first under proportional representation in Sri Lanka, saw the UNP winning 125 seats out of 225, while the SLFP, who obtained 30 percent of the votes, secured 66. The renewal of the UNP's mandate did not ensure a return to political stability. Instead the new president confronted a challenge from the JVP, which continued its career of terror, ruthlessly and relentlessly, and showed no signs of a change of attitude to the government despite the policy of conciliation he initiated and pursued. As part of this policy, he relaxed the state of emergency and released the JVP activists taken into custody on suspicion of involvement in the violence. The decision to release the latter was taken in the face of the reluctance of the police and security services to endorse such a policy. The JVP spurned this attitude of forbearance and continued its attacks on the government supporters. This wave of JVP violence that began around 20 January left over two thousand UNP members and supporters, as well as members of their families, dead. One of the principal demands of the JVP was the immediate departure of the IPKF. They were intent on setting the priorities in the political agenda for the new president.

New Men and New Policies

The Indian government's reading of the political situation in Sri Lanka was both somber and realistic. As they saw it, the government was reeling in the face of the JVP's attacks. The IPKF's continued presence was being used by the JVP as an excuse for its brutal campaign of violence directed against the new government and its supporters. However, because personal contacts between the two heads of government, President Premadasa and Prime Minister Rajiv Gandhi, were minimal, neither was aware of the other's concerns and attitudes in this volatile atmosphere.

The new president placed no trust in either Gamini Dissanayake or Lalith Athulathmudali, both of whom had been involved—the latter in particular—in previous negotiations with the Indian government under President Jayewardene. Instead, the new foreign minister, Ranjan Wijeratne, was given charge of the negotiations, such as they were. Because he was also minister of state for defense, the IPKF's "de-induction," the technical term used during these negotiations for the removal of the IPKF's soldiers to India, was assigned to him. Thus his responsibilities were more onerous, particularly because President Premadasa deviated from his predecessor's practice in deciding not to preside at meetings of Sri Lanka's Security Council, the meeting of the defense and police chiefs and senior officials involved in national security matters. Wijeratne carried this responsibility as well.

The first phase of the negotiations commenced in March 1989, when the mechanics of the "de-induction" process were discussed between the Indian and Sri Lankan foreign ministers, P. V. Narasimha Rao and Ranjan Wijeratne. Under the proposals set before Wijeratne by his Indian counterpart, the departure of the IPKF would begin almost immediately, that is to say, in March or April. The plan envisaged the withdrawal of at least half of the IPKF in June and July 1989, leaving around 25,000 to be withdrawn in batches of fifteen hundred or so a week until all of them were out of the island by the end of December. The Indian elections expected in early 1990 figured prominently in the calculations of the Indian government. The advantage of this projected timetable for the departure of the IPKF was that, even if the elections were held late in 1989, the great majority of the IPKF troops would have been withdrawn. This would ensure, or so the Congress I leadership believed, that the IPKF's continued presence in Sri Lanka would not become an election issue to be used against them. There was no way of guaranteeing this, for there were too many unanswered questions about the dispatch of the IPKF to Sri Lanka, too much controversy about its performance as both peacekeepers and combatants, and too many Indian lives lost, too many Indian soldiers crippled, for Gandhi's opponents to remain silent on the issue. The fact is that by February 1989 Indian newspapers were beginning to call for a swift withdrawal of the IPKF.[3]

In March it was announced that J. N. Dixit would be leaving Sri Lanka to take up duties as the Indian envoy in Pakistan. Thus the virtual coauthor of the Indo–Sri Lanka Accord and the man who gave political and administrative leadership to the IPKF operation would be leaving the country before the IPKF itself departed from its shores.

J. N. Dixit

Four years earlier J. N. Dixit had arrived in Colombo from Kabul, leaving one trouble spot for another. He was no run-of-the-mill diplomat; he was one of India's best, and in choosing him for the Colombo post in 1985 Delhi was acknowledging the need for a man of unusual ability to handle matters there for India. In a profile of Dixit entitled "Trouble Shooter," published in October 1987, a leading Indian weekly paid him a handsome tribute:

> Kissingerian activism is a commodity rarely seen these days in the realms of Indian diplomacy. The country's envoys are content with implementing the nuts and bolts of policy rather than creating it. With one startling exception, of course.
>
> **Jyotindra Nath Dixit. India's High Commissioner to Sri Lanka**
> Volatile situations are not unknown to the 51-year old diplomat. Dixit has served several years at the front. First in 1971, when he was appointed the first head of mission [*sic*] in Dacca, soon after the liberation of Bangladesh. The posting required considerable diplomatic and political finesse as Dixit had to oversee both the reconstruction of a battle-scared [*sic*] country and the consolidation of Indian interests.[4]

Very few people in Sri Lanka were really aware of Dixit's role in the creation of Bangladesh in 1971–72. He was a young man of thirty-seven at that time. Beginning as an important middle-rung officer in New Delhi (in charge of coordinating Indian assistance to the East Pakistani resistance in Delhi) and later on operating actively in the border between West Bengal and India and troubled East Pakistan, he made an important contribution to the success of the Indian exercise in subversion.[5] Once the new state was created, he was sent to Dhaka as deputy high commissioner. In describing him as head of mission, the Indian weekly quoted above was making a mistake of fact but not of substance. Subimal Dutt, the Indian high commissioner in Dhaka, an elderly Bengali long past the age of retirement, was only a figurehead chosen for his familiarity with the former East Pakistan. The effective head was Dixit, who had a direct link to the prime minister's office, reporting to one of her most trusted senior officials, D. P. Dhar.

Dixit's task, as the Indian weekly put it, was to "oversee the reconstruction of [the country] . . . and the consolidation of Indian interests." Bangladeshis who remembered Dixit during his Dhaka days believe that he paid more attention to the latter role than to the former. He earned the trust and respect of the victorious Indian army in Bangladesh for his political and diplomatic skills, and again in Sri Lanka after the IPKF came in. Along with his political officer—the first secretary—in Dhaka, a woman by the name of Arundathy Ghosh, Dixit built a network of political links that took him to the Bangladeshi cabinet itself. In retrospect one sees an amazing parallel with what happened later in Sri Lanka, where this policy was repeated, with the difference that as high commissioner he did not need the assistance of a political officer or first secretary. His influence with some members of the Bangladeshi cabinet became legendary and resulted eventually in unpopularity, for Dixit himself as well as for the Bangladeshi cabinet ministers associated with him, who were seen as Indian puppets.[6]

In yet another parallel, the Indians hailed as liberators in Bangladesh—as the IPKF were in the initial stages in Jaffna—soon became unpopular. There were a number of reasons why India and the Indians became unpopular in Bangladesh so soon, despite the swift return of the Indian army to their bases in India. Bangladeshis realized very quickly that India was too poor to finance the reconstruction of their country, and that Indian businessmen were seeking to establish a grip on the Bangladeshi economy.[7]

The simmering discontent with the Indians erupted to the surface in June 1974 during the visit of Pakistani prime minister Zulfiqar Ali Bhutto, who had been invited to Bangladesh in an obvious gesture of reconciliation.[8] To the amazement of practically everybody in Bangladesh, Bhutto was given a tumultuous welcome in a country that not so long ago had risen in revolt against the Pakistani establishment. Bangladeshi academics remembered this occasion as one on which anti-Indian feeling bubbled to the surface. Bhutto mistakenly thought the jubilant crowds were hailing him as a friend. This was only partly true. The mood of the crowd was more complex than that. Their effusive welcome to Bhutto was more an anti-Indian demonstration than a pro-Pakistani one, as Dixit himself learned to his dismay. His car was caught in a traffic jam as vehicles endeavored to make their way through the massive crowds returning to their homes after the reception for Bhutto. Trapped in his car, a stunned

Dixit watched in pained disconcertment as a section of the crowd, recognizing the vehicle as one belonging to the Indian high commission, began pelting it with shoes and sandals, the ultimate gesture of insult in Bangladesh.[9]

Dixit was one of the few links between India's Bangladeshi and Sri Lankan interventions. In both instances Dixit was closely linked to a military exercise; in both his mission ultimately failed. In Bangladesh that aspect of the Indian venture was a pronounced success, but the equally important political aspects of the enterprise were a dismal failure. The memory of that successful military intervention no doubt encouraged its use in Sri Lanka, although the circumstances were very different.

There were very few precedents in international politics for the decision to use an army in an attempt to resolve an ethnic conflict in a neighboring state. The Indian intervention in East Pakistan that led to the creation of Bangladesh was, of course, the classic case in recent years. There was also the Turkish intervention in Cyprus. Both were unilateral decisions of the governments involved. The contrast between these and the use of the Indian army, in the north and east of Sri Lanka, has been referred to earlier (see chapter 12), in particular the acquiescence if not support of the Sri Lankan government and of its president at that time, J. R. Jayewardene. This latter point brings us to one of Dixit's major achievements, discussed in earlier chapters, the forging of a cordial working relationship with the Sri Lankan president.[10]

In Sri Lanka as in Bangladesh, the Indian army was used in a calculated demonstration of military power to impose the will of the Indian government in support of what were seen to be India's national and strategic interests. The difference was that the tactics and strategy were so dissimilar: in Bangladesh the aim was to dismember Pakistan and ensure the triumph of Bangladeshi separatism; in Sri Lanka the objective was to prevent the success of separatism but at the same time to ensure a dominant voice for India in the affairs of the island. In the first instance, the Indian army did help achieve that objective; in the second, it did little to resolve the conflict. On the contrary the consequences were nearly disastrous for India's own national interest. Thus Dixit presided over a failed Indian enterprise in Sri Lanka, and while there were no sandals and shoes to dramatize it and to speed him on his way, Dixit must have had a sense of déjà vu as he left Sri Lanka and remembered his departure from Bangladesh fifteen years earlier.

In a farewell interview he gave the government-controlled *Daily News,* he said he was leaving the island "with a sense of satisfaction of having played the role of a catalyst in preserving the unity and territorial integrity of Sri Lanka and safeguarding India's interests."

Describing his stint in Colombo as the most challenging in his twenty-eight-year diplomatic life, he claimed that the Indo–Sri Lanka Accord

> had met the aspirations of the Sinhalese, Tamils and India. The Sinhalese wanted the preservation of the unity and territorial integrity of Sri Lanka. That has been served. The Tamils wanted to live in peace and security in the areas they traditionally lived in and an arrangement to manage their own affairs. India wanted a stable, democratic Sri Lanka.[11]

Even the friends he made in Sri Lanka would have agreed that he was putting the best possible gloss on a failed enterprise. A few weeks earlier, on 10 March to be exact, he gave a more comprehensive and forthright defense of India's intervention in Sri Lanka. The setting was Delhi's elite United Service Institution, where he addressed a gathering of high-ranking bureaucrats and an array of senior and middle-rung representatives of the defense services. At first glance the speech, which was subsequently published in the journal of that institute,[12] seemed unusual for an Indian diplomat—for its candor and for being delivered at all given the sensitive nature of the subject, especially because he was still high commissioner in Sri Lanka. But a careful reading shows that it was a skillful exposition of the essentials of Indian policy on Sri Lanka as the Indian government and New Delhi's South Block wished the world to see it. The extracts quoted below are from that journal.

The opening paragraph set the tone for the evening, initially somewhat defensive, but leading to a self-confident defense of Indian policy.

> I am slightly overawed by the audience because I see people whom I viewed from the lower and middle levels of the bureaucracy like General Candeth and I see a number of colleagues with whom I was associated during my assignment in Bangladesh and then Sri Lanka. I have not brought a written text but had I known that it would be such an august audience, I would have been prepared for a more structured presentation.

Our interest in this speech lies in the reasons he gave for the Indian intervention. The exposition was as notable for its mixture of truth with half-truth and, occasionally, downright invention, as it was for the clarity with which *realpolitik* was identified and defended as the essence of Indian policy.

[The] first reason why we went into Sri Lanka was the interest to preserve our unity: to ensure the success of a very difficult experiment that we have been carrying out ourselves. We claim to be the largest functioning democracy in the world. . . . Let us not forget that the first voice of secessionism in the Indian Republic was raised in Tamil-Nadu in the mid-sixties. . . . So, in a manner, our interest in the Tamil issue in Sri Lanka, Tamil aspirations in Sri Lanka was based on maintaining our own unity, our own integrity, our own identity in the manner in which we have been trying to build our own society.

The second reason why we went in was to counter the Sri Lankan government over its reactions to the rising Tamil militancy since 1972. . . .

In the period, between 1978 and 1986 the strength of the Sri Lankan Army was raised from approximately 12,000 to 35,000. The overall strength of the Sri Lankan Armed Forces rose approximately from 15,000 to 17,000 [*sic*] if we include the homeguards and paramilitary units. Sri Lanka signed informal confidential agreements with the governments of United States and United Kingdom to bring their warships into Colombo, Trincomalee and the Gulf. The frequency of visits by the navies of these countries showed a quantum jump between 1982–83 and 1987. Sri Lanka invited British mercenaries (Keenee-Weenee Services) into its Intelligence services. Sri Lanka invited Shinbeth and Mossad, the two most effective and influential intelligence agencies of Israel. Sri Lanka sought assistance from Pakistan to train its Home Guards, and its Navy, Sri Lanka offered broadcasting facilities to the Voice of America, which would have enabled the United States to install highly sophisticated monitoring equipment on Sri Lanka soil which could have affected our security in terms of their capacity to monitor our sensitive information for their own interests. Sri Lanka bought arms from countries with whom our relations have been difficult. So, the second reason, why we had to be actively involved in Sri Lanka was to counter, to the extent possible, this trend. The third reason, why we went to Sri Lanka was an important domestic political factor, and here I would preface what I am going to say by inculcating a premise that while morality and absolute norms should govern politics, in actuality it is not so. It cannot so happen, because the human conditions, remain imperfect. The Chemistry of power, the motivations which affect the interplay of power between societies are not governed by absolute morality. Of course, Lord Buddha, Mahatma Gandhi, who, once in a while came to enthuse this, and make a very tremendous impact on societies and people. But normally it is not.

Having said that, I would like to elaborate that we have to respect the sentiments of the 50 million Tamil citizens of India. They felt that if we did not rise, in support of the Tamil cause in Sri Lanka, we are not standing by our own Tamils and if that is so, then in the Tamil psyche, Tamil sub-conscious the question arose; is there any relevance or validity of our being part of a large Indian political identity, if our very deeply felt sentiments are not respected? So, it was a compulsion. It was not a rationalized motivation, but it was a compulsion which could not be avoided by any elected Government in this country. So that was a third reason [sic].

Dixit's audience may have found his recounting of the growth of Sri Lanka's security forces in the 1980s no more than an innocuous statement of facts. But this recounting lost any claims to objectivity without a reference to the Indian support for the Tamil separatist cause through training facilities and bases that had made the Sri Lankan defense expansion necessary. A great deal of what he said on that occasion about Sri Lanka's new defense capability was at least partly inaccurate. But there was one section that was wholly so. This was the statement that "Sri Lanka signed informal confidential agreements with the governments of [the] United States and [the] United Kingdom to bring their warships into Colombo, Trincomalee and the Gulf."

Sri Lanka did not sign any agreements, "informal," "confidential," or public, with either of these two governments for these purposes at this time. The reference to the gulf is mystifying in this context unless it was to the Gulf of Mannar, hardly an appropriate place for the entry of warships given the shallowness of its waters!

We turn next to his apologia for the IPKF operations in Sri Lanka.

I think the IPKF is several things in Sri Lanka. It is an affirmation of our commitment to the unity and territorial integrity of a small neighboring country. It is an external projection of our influence to tell our neighbors that if, because of your compulsions or your aberrations, you pose a threat to us, we are capable of, or we have a political will to project ourselves within your territorial jurisdiction for the limited purpose of bringing you back. Sounds slightly arrogant! It is not arrogant. It is real-politik and it brings you back to the path of detachment and non-alignment where you don't endanger our security.

The IPKF has been a catalyst for reviving democratic institutions in Sri Lanka after a gap of eleven years. Very few people remember that the last series of general elections were held in Sri Lanka in 1977. And what triggered off Elections, which were held between November 1988 and January '89 was the successful management of the elections to the Eastern Provinces by the IPKF. The credit entirely goes to our armed forces.

We have projected our Armed forces, therefore, not only in a peacekeeping role, but in a political role. Secondly, we are undoubtedly a factor against insurgency and mayhem in Sri Lanka. The worst critic of the IPKF in Jaffna, if asked, shall we withdraw immediately, says no, for God's sake, don't. Please don't. And what is interesting now that view is shared by the Foreign Minister and the new President of Sri Lanka, which gives us perhaps the capacity to negotiate from the position of strength and detachment because, I know that Indian Public opinion and our own good sense, impels us to say that you must not be in a foreign country for a very long time. We must move out, and, I think that is because it is a good approach and that is my view too. But the fact that despite performing a highly complex and at times unpalatable role, IPKF is being considered a necessity in a foreign country where there are so many complexes against India is a symptom of two things. First, that you are a factor of stability. Second, that whatever tasks have been assigned to us, we have done them with a sense of fair play and detachment regardless of minor criticisms here or there.

Finally, we must remember the special context in which Dixit's speech was delivered on 10 March 1989. It came at a time when he was still high commissioner in Sri Lanka, and well before an unorthodox political initiative by President Premadasa brought the two countries once more into an acrimonious dispute, on this occasion over the timing of the departure of the IPKF from Sri Lanka.

President Premadasa's New Initiatives

L. L. Mehrotra arrived in Sri Lanka to replace Dixit as India's new high commissioner only to face the difficulties that stemmed from a surprisingly new initiative taken by President Premadasa, a rapprochement between the government of Sri Lanka and the Liberation Tigers of Tamil Eelam (LTTE). The expectation that the animosities and hostilities of a decade could be overcome through negotiations conducted against the background of a common opposition to the IPKF was unrealistic except as part of a public relations exercise. Actually the LTTE was responding to appeals, which the government aimed primarily at the JVP, for discussions instead of violent confrontation. While the JVP contemptuously rejected this conciliatory gesture, the LTTE seized the opportunity to escape from the noose the IPKF had placed around them. Once the *apertura a LTTE* was announced, there was little the Indian government could do but acquiesce in an obvious awkward development. In the early stages the talks were of a purely explorative nature; indeed they never became anything more than that although they went on for over fourteen months.

The initiative now lay with the LTTE rather than the Sri Lankan government, and it made the most of the opportunities that had come so unexpectedly. The major premise of the new president's thinking was that no lasting peace settlement could be made with the Tamil minority if it did not include the LTTE as part of the peace process. He did not share his predecessor's antipathy to and mistrust of the LTTE, nor did he have his experience of dealing with them over a long period of time. Apart from that he was full of admiration for the LTTE leader's military prowess and for his and the LTTE's dogged resistance to the Indian army;[13] besides, he took the view that neither the Indian nor the Sri Lankan army had been able to crush the LTTE. Some of his senior advisers—civilian and military—took an even gloomier view of the situation; they argued that the LTTE would prevail over all other forces in the north and east of the island, and that it was politic therefore to come to terms with it sooner rather than later.[14] In coming to this latter conclusion they ignored two important facts: that it was the Indian government that had prevented the Sri Lankan army from crushing the LTTE in May–July 1987, and that the Indians had weakened the LTTE to the point where they had turned in desperation to negotiations with the Sri Lankan government. He was also impressed by the strong and enthusiastic support the LTTE enjoyed from and among the overseas Tamils, who had evolved in time into a very vocal and politically effective lobby in Western countries. There was another and more practical reason given for opening talks with the LTTE. Because of the enmity between the Indian government and the LTTE, there seemed to be much less chance than ever before of the triumph of Tamil separatism and the establishment of a Tamil state in the north and east of the island—Eelam. It seemed prudent therefore for the Sri Lankan government to continue with its negotiations with the LTTE, which seemed much more restrained and moderate at that time than before.

Not many people outside the government shared President Premadasa's confidence in the moderation and good sense of the LTTE. Certainly there were individuals, if not groups, in the cabinet (Ranjan Wijeratne in particular) and the government parliamentary group who were skeptical. Given the turmoil and violence generated by the JVP, those critics remained silent lest they be accused of pro-Indian sentiments. President Premadasa deputed Ranjan Wijeratne, the foreign minister and minister of state for defense, to lead the Sri Lankan delegation to the talks with the LTTE, the first of which was held on 12 May. Wijeratne was assisted by A. C. S. Hameed, the former foreign minister, a Muslim who had the advantage of being able to speak Tamil fluently. Other cabinet ministers were brought in when it was thought necessary to do so, but the crucially important fact is that none of them had any previous experience of negotiating with the LTTE.

The announcement of the commencement of negotiations between the Premadasa government and the LTTE had an immediate impact on informed opinion in India in strengthening the groups who were calling for a withdrawal of IPKF as expeditiously as possible. One by one the major Indian newspapers began urging the government to cut its losses and to bring the troops back. Left of center weeklies such as *Mainstream,* which had been skeptical about Rajiv Gandhi's Sri Lankan policy from the outset, became more outspoken in their criticisms.

The foreign ministers of the two countries met for the second time, in Zimbabwe in the last week of May. This was the highest level of contact between India and Sri Lanka since the new president had assumed office. At this meeting the Indian foreign minister confirmed the Indian government's commitment to the decisions arrived at between him and his Sri Lankan counterpart at their previous meeting in March, on the mechanics and timetable of the IPKF's departure to India. Ranjan Wijeratne concurred in this, and so by 25 and 26 May the two sides had agreed to a common approach to the thorny problem of the IPKF's departure to India.[15]

Ranjan Wijeratne arrived in Colombo from Harare, after his discussions with his Indian counterpart, with what he believed was a mutually acceptable timetable for the withdrawal of the IPKF, only to find the situation changing dramatically when President Premadasa dropped a verbal bombshell in a speech on 1 June, made at a temple at Battaramulla, a suburb of Colombo. In that speech he insisted that the IPKF should leave Sri Lanka by 29 July 1989, two years after they first arrived. The Indian government, taken aback as much by the manner in which the demand was made as the demand itself, treated it as an affront and a deliberate aggravation. While it was true that the decisions taken at the discussions between the foreign ministers in March and May 1989 had not been formally approved at the heads-of-government level, nevertheless there was no official indication given to the Indian government that Sri Lanka had rejected the timetable proposed in early March and confirmed only a few days before the president's speech. Ranjan Wijeratne himself was appalled by all this but remained silent.

President Premadasa's unorthodox diplomatic intervention can only be understood in the context of his own, and his government's, deteriorating political position. The government was reeling under the relentless pressure of the JVP, who had just announced a campaign to boycott Indian goods, a decision they were intent on enforcing on the people through their usual mixture of bluster, intimidation, and selective violence against random victims among persons who ignored or defied instructions issued by JVP cadres. But there was more to it than a mere wish to preempt the JVP, or to outdo them, in anti-Indian rhetoric. One needs to emphasize President Premadasa's deep-rooted distrust of the Indian leadership and visceral dislike of Rajiv Gandhi. Premadasa's astonishing diplomatic initiative could be attributed to his strong conviction that, unless some unorthodox measures were adopted to force the issue, the IPKF's departure would be delayed to conform to the political imperatives confronting the Indian government in an election year, while ignoring his own desperate need to stabilize his government against the pressures from the JVP. He placed no trust in the Indian government's assurances or the timetable they had committed themselves to. And this was despite his own initial requests conveyed through Dixit that the departure of the IPKF should be delayed. Again it is likely that he was seeking to reassure the LTTE, with whom his government had begun discussions about the strength of his commitment to the removal of the IPKF. He decided, therefore, on a public announcement of a timetable set by him, unilaterally, for the IPKF's departure from Sri Lanka.

Whatever the motive, once the speech was made the IPKF's departure became a major, and very acrimonious, diplomatic issue between the two countries. The result was to delay the process rather than hasten it. President Premadasa followed his speech of 1 June with another on 9 June at Mahiyangana in Uva, the site that year of the annual village reawakening ceremony—the *gam udava*, as it is called. On this latter occasion he not only reiterated his demand for withdrawal of the IPKF by July 29, but suggested in addition that if the Indian government was unable to withdraw all troops from Sri Lanka by that date, those left behind could be "confined to barracks" until the process of bringing them back to India was completed. This was seen as a gratuitous insult to the Indians and was treated as such by Rajiv Gandhi.

To the beleaguered Rajiv Gandhi, already under a cloud because of the Bofors scandal (involving the acceptance of alleged commissions—kickbacks—from the Swedish company, Bofors, which had won a huge contract to supply weapons to the Indian army), and facing a difficult election, President Premadasa's calculated conversion of the IPKF's departure into a divisive political issue, despite India's efforts to withdraw the IPKF on a timetable mutually agreed to, came as a wholly unexpected setback in the course of delicate negotiations for a return of the IPKF to India. To yield to the Sri Lankan president's unilateral demands was to risk a further and perhaps precipitous erosion of political support for him as well as for his party in the forthcoming elections. Besides, there was the need to make some arrangements for the protection of the Eelam People's Revolutionary Liberation Front (EPRLF), whose position had now been rendered hopelessly vulnerable by the rapprochement between the Premadasa government and the LTTE.

Gandhi responded to Premadasa with the claim that, since the Indo–Sri Lanka Accord was a bilateral agreement and India had underwritten it, the IPKF's withdrawal would have to be "conditional . . . a joint, parallel and linked exercise along with the devolution process so that the Tamils and the provincial council [of the North Eastern Province] can look after their security."[16]

He described the Sri Lankan president's demand that the IPKF be withdrawn on a timetable set by him as "unrealistic" because it was "unilateral." Thus the Indians were insisting on a mutually agreed upon timetable, which was a continuation of a policy outlined in March 1989, but in linking the phased withdrawal to certain conditions such as an improvement in the security situation in the North Eastern Province, and an effective devolution of power, they were going well beyond the scope of the obligations assumed by them as signatories of the accord. He made the point that "as the Indo-Sri Lanka agreements get progressively implemented, and as the mischief-making potential of extremist elements opposed to the agreement are reduced, further withdrawals will be made in consultation with the Sri Lankan government." Thus Rajiv Gandhi had introduced a new element into the negotiations on the transfer of the IPKF to India.[18]

The practical effect of this controversy, however, was that the plan to send half the Indian troops back to India by the end of July was shelved. No troops left the island until 29 July. Instead, there followed an exchange of letters between the two heads of government and the unilateral publication of the letters by the Sri Lankan government. The Indian government sent its foreign secretary to Sri Lanka in an attempt to break the deadlock. The first set of discussions proved to be a failure. As the deadline of 29 July approached and no IPKF soldiers had left the island, the Sri Lankan government faced a dual threat, one a diplomatic impasse with the Indians, who were in no mood to yield to pressure to withdraw their troops by 29 July, or even to begin to do so, and the other a three-day island-wide strike called by the JVP to coincide with the second anniversary of the arrival of the IPKF in Sri Lanka, a strike intended to underline their opposition to the continued presence of the IPKF in Sri Lanka.

The mounting tensions between India and Sri Lanka were abated when the Indian government agreed to receive a delegation from Sri Lanka to discuss the withdrawal of the IPKF. The delegation left the island for Delhi on 28 July. On 29 July, in a deliberate attempt to lessen the dissonance between the two countries, India withdrew six hundred troops. Once the negotiations were completed on 5 August, the departure of the Indian soldiers from Sri Lanka was resumed. Within three days of the completion of negotiations, over 1,500 soldiers departed to India.

The Sri Lankan delegation that left for Delhi on this occasion was led by Ranjan Wijeratne and included A. C. S. Hameed. Considering the acrimony that followed President Premadasa's speeches of 1 and 9 June, and the exchange and publication of the correspondence between the two heads of government, the negotiations in Delhi were surprisingly cordial.[19] It was clear to the Sri Lankans that the Indians were anxious to get the IPKF back, and were not inclined to leave any of their soldiers in the island. What they sought was a face-saving exit for the IPKF, without any semblance of departure under pressure. This was stressed at all levels.

The Indians stated that all troops would be removed from the island before the end of February 1990, that is, at the rate of 1,500 per week beginning in August 1989. The Sri Lankan delegation wished that this process be completed much earlier, if possible by September 1989, but it was evident that the Indians, their eyes set on the forthcoming general elections, did not want to hasten the withdrawal to a point which could be construed in India, and especially in Tamil Nadu, as a precipitate surrender to Sri Lankan pressure. In his correspondence with President Premadasa, Prime Minister Rajiv Gandhi had sought to link the departure of the IPKF—or at least the speed of its departure—with the effectiveness of the actual devolution of power to the provinces. At the discussions in Delhi, the Indians dropped their insistence on such a linkage.

The Indians expressed great concern about the need to plan ahead for the deployment of Sri Lankan troops to the north and east of the island, and to reestablish law enforcement authorities there to take control of the areas evacuated by the IPKF. They were anxious also about the safety (even survival) of the EPRLF ministry in the North Eastern Province, a concern and anxiety that was both natural and inevitable. Prime Minister Rajiv Gandhi made particular mention of these two points in his discussions with the two Sri Lankan ministers, a discussion that took over six hours and from which all officials, Indian and Sri Lankan, were excluded.[20]

The Indian representatives would not agree to the Sri Lankan government's request that the IPKF stop its offensive operations against the LTTE. Indeed the Indians stressed the need for the LTTE to surrender their arms before the IPKF would consider a cease-fire. The Sri Lankans came away with the impression that the Indians seemed intent on weakening the LTTE further before the IPKF left.[21]

An agreement between the two governments was reached on 18 September 1989, based on the discussions held in Delhi in July and August and subsequently through diplomatic channels. Under the terms of the agreement, India would withdraw between fifteen hundred and sixteen hundred soldiers each week until March 1990, when the "de-induction" process would be completed. There would be no linkage between the withdrawal of the IPKF and the implementation of the devolution proposals in the Indo–Sri Lanka Accord. The agreement incorporated proposals for security in the north and east with the withdrawal of the Indian forces.

The two sides agreed that the Sri Lankan army and police would move into the areas evacuated by the IPKF. At the insistence of the Indians, an elaborate security system was devised for the transfer of power in the north and east. These included a coordinating committee consisting of representatives of all the ethnic and political groups in that part of the country; a security coordinating group with an Indian general, a Sri Lankan official of similar rank, and the chief minister of the North Eastern Province; and a military observer group led by the head of the IPKF and the commander of the Sri Lankan army. Together they would ensure that the transfer of authority would not lead to turmoil.

The IPKF: The Penultimate Phase, September–December 1989

In early September the rate at which the IPKF's units left Sri Lanka was increased. This acceleration took place against the background of dramatic political events in the two countries, beginning with the destruction of the JVP's leadership by the Sri Lankan army and the virtual collapse of the JVP as an insurgent and political force, and then the calling of a general election in India.

The agreement reached between the two governments in August and September 1989 did little to alleviate anxieties in India and in the IPKF about the fate of the EPRLF government and the EPRLF cadres once the IPKF left. President Premadasa, if not the Sri Lankan government as a whole, did not share the Indian suspicions about the LTTE; on the contrary, relations between the Premadasa government and the LTTE were now so cordial that the latter was permitted to move into the areas evacuated by the IPKF. This was contrary to the terms and spirit of the understanding reached with India, which assumed that the Sri Lankan army would take control and that the Sri Lankan police would take over the normal law-and-order functions of a civilian administration.

The anxieties stemming from this drove the Indian government and the IPKF to take a most shortsighted decision, to create an IPKF-sponsored Tamil National Army (TNA) linked to the EPRLF, and to supply it with sophisticated weapons, all in the hope that the TNA could stand up to the LTTE in the inevitable conflict between them. Mistake followed mistake in the pursuit of this disastrous policy. Large quantities of weapons, including light artillery, were supplied to the TNA. The Sri Lankan authorities, civil and military, were aghast at this new development, but their protests against establishing the TNA and arming it were not heeded.

The LTTE was the principal beneficiary of the Indian government's shortsighted and hasty attempt to establish the TNA as a military arm of the EPRLF. First, it enabled the LTTE to coordinate an anti-IPKF policy with the government of Sri Lanka, who, not to be outdone by the Indians in lack of forethought, was persuaded to let the LTTE bring in arms from abroad, through Colombo, allegedly to meet the threat faced from the TNA. Although there were suspicions in political circles in Colombo that the government of Sri Lanka had allowed this, there was no firm evidence about it until December 1991, when the *Hindustan Times* in Delhi published a statement from a Sri Lankan army subaltern to the effect that he had been instructed to deliver a truckload of weapons to the LTTE to be used against the IPKF, and had done so in June or July 1989.[22] (At this time the TNA had already been formed.) Once this Indian newspaper made this sensational disclosure, the Sri Lankan government was forced to admit that it had supplied weapons to the LTTE at this time. What the Premadasa government did not reveal was that the LTTE had been provided with a large sum of money as well.

Second, the TNA eventually succumbed to the LTTE without firing a shot. The LTTE gained access to weapons from two sources: the IPKF and the Sri Lankan government. The supply from the IPKF via the TNA was not only much larger, it included more and powerful weapons such as light artillery. By the beginning of 1991 the disintegration of the TNA was complete.

The irony of arming the TNA was lost on the Indian government. A peacekeeping force brought in to disarm Tamil separatist groups not only failed to do so but, worse, actually ended its stay in the island by arming a ragtag force linked to its puppet regime.

The IPKF: The Last Phase

Rajiv Gandhi's defeat at the general election of November 1989 was greeted by President Premadasa with a sigh of relief. On the morning of 5 December, even before the new Indian cabinet had been sworn in, President Premadasa telephoned the new Indian prime minister, V. P. Singh, to offer his congratulations personally. In the course of the conversation he expressed a wish to send a delegation to see him almost immediately—a delegation consisting of the foreign minister (Ranjan Wijeratne), the foreign secretary (Bernard Tillakaratne), the president's adviser on foreign affairs (Bradman Weerakoon), and the defense secretary (Gen.

D. Sepala Attygalle). The new prime minister agreed to this proposal with some hesitation. The news that a delegation would be in Delhi even before the new prime minister had picked his cabinet took the principal Indian officials of the prime minister's office and the Ministry of External Affairs by surprise. None of them was very receptive to the idea and S. K. Singh, the foreign secretary at the time, actually urged the Sri Lankan high commissioner, Stanley Kalpage, to persuade the delegation to postpone their visit by forty-eight hours—until the weekend or thereafter. Eventually, however, these officials reluctantly agreed to go along with the idea of receiving the Sri Lankan delegation. But there was still a problem—a foreign minister had not been named yet. The official acceptance of the Sri Lankan president's urgent request that the Indian government meet a delegation from Sri Lanka came before the Indian cabinet was announced![23]

The Sri Lankan president's anxiety to establish contact with the new prime minister of India was, naturally enough, the subject of much speculation in New Delhi. Was it done in the hope that the Sri Lankan version of events in the north and east of the island would be given the new prime minister before the Indian officials established their hold on him? If this was indeed so, then it demonstrated the wide difference in the political cultures of the two countries. India had a powerful and highly professional civil service elite who made a major contribution to policy making—in contrast to Sri Lanka—and no prime minister could entirely ignore their views or do without their expertise. Unlike in the situation in Sri Lanka, there was an official "memory" on policy matters that a new government would have to take into consideration even if it eventually decided that a fresh initiative was required. Thus a change of government in India would not necessarily lead to any dramatic changes in India's Sri Lankan policy.

By Tuesday 5 December it was known that a Sri Lankan delegation was due to reach Delhi the next day or the next night. The delegation left Colombo that evening. When they got to New Delhi in the early hours of Wednesday, they found to their chagrin that there was no minister or even minister of state to receive them. The senior officials who greeted them there explained that, for security reasons, Indian ministers did not participate in such welcoming ceremonies at night. The real reason, however, was that the process of cabinet making was not complete; and most politicians preferred to concentrate on that rather than on welcoming importunate visitors. The delegation was lodged at the Taj

Hotel. They had come equipped with an album of photographs of the arms supplied to the Tamil National Army.

The Sri Lankan delegation expected to meet the prime minister and the foreign minister in that order. The Indian officials shrewdly arranged for them to meet the new foreign minister, I. K. Gujral, before they met the prime minister. In this way they would be able to listen to what the Sri Lankans had to say to the foreign minister and prepare their answers for the meeting with the prime minister, since much the same arguments were likely to be used on the second occasion.

Thursday morning saw V. P. Singh and I. K. Gujral (a Punjabi Hindu, elected from a Punjabi constituency) make a visit to the Punjab. From their point of view that was much more urgent than Sri Lanka. Gujral met the Sri Lankan delegation on Thursday afternoon, and later hosted them at dinner.

The interview with Gujral went off very well. He was in a very conciliatory mood, and began by apologizing for not being able to greet them personally when they arrived. The Sri Lankan delegation's sole spokesman was Ranjan Wijeratne, who dwelt on three themes: the need to adhere to the previous agreement on the departure of the IPKF, with 31 December as a possible new deadline; the IPKF's role in arming the TNA; and a friendship treaty as a substitute for the one-sided concessions made by Sri Lanka in the letters which formed part of the Indo–Sri Lanka Accord of July 1987.

Gujral assured his Sri Lankan counterpart that the IPKF would leave as soon as possible. The Indian government would seek to advance the deadline for the departure of the IPKF to 31 December, but if this proved difficult, the two sides—the Indian and Sri Lankan governments—could reach an understanding on a new timetable. The fact is that there were 25,000 troops still in the north and the east. He did appreciate the significance of the points made about the IPKF and the TNA, but gave no indication of his own response to this difficult situation. The Sri Lankan delegates were very impressed by Gujral's sincerity and moderation. He was very accommodating about the friendship treaty.

Earlier in the year, with Rajiv Gandhi and his foreign minister there had been, generally, a rather tense and confrontational atmosphere during discussions. Some of this was blamed on J. N. Dixit, India's envoy in Pakistan, who had participated in the last set of talks (July/August 1989), traveling from Islamabad for that purpose. The Sri Lankans were relieved that Dixit had not been invited to the talks with Gujral.

Apart from the meeting with Gujral, Ranjan Wijeratne had a very successful press conference that evening. Indeed the Sri Lankan delegation was quite elated; it had had a good day; the Indian officials had remained more or less silent.

The meeting with the Indian prime minister took place next day (Friday 8 December) at 11 A.M. V. P. Singh was friendly but not very forthcoming. He listened attentively but did not speak much. Once again Ranjan Wijeratne was the Sri Lankan spokesman. He got a polite hearing, but no more. By now the Indian officials had had time to get their brief ready, and they had briefed the new prime minister. The general feeling was that this second meeting was not as good as the meeting with Gujral from the Sri Lankan point of view.

The communiqué that was issued was a very bland one reflecting the influence of the officials in the South Block. There was no firm commitment about expediting the departure of the IPKF so that they would be away from the island by 31 December. Nor was there any great enthusiasm for the friendship treaty.

The problem was that the IPKF's departure had been at the rate of fifteen hundred a week up to the end of November. With 25,000 soldiers still left in the island by the end of December, it would take at least three more months for all of them to move out, unless the process were expedited by the provision of more transport facilities by sea, or if air transport were resorted to.

The process was not hastened very much. The last IPKF soldiers left the island on 24 March 1991, a week before the deadline of 31 March. They left, ironically enough, to the strains of "Auld Lang Syne." By the time they left they had seen the collapse of the TNA, and were compelled as a matter of humanitarian assistance to help some of the TNA's "soldiers," and supporters of the EPRLF, to escape to safe havens in Tamil Nadu and Orissa.[24] The V. P. Singh government attempted to persuade its political ally, the new chief minister of Tamil Nadu, M. Karunanidhi, to bring the Sri Lankan Tamil factions in Tamil Nadu together, in an attempt to protect them from the vengeance of the LTTE. But all attempts failed. By the time the last IPKF soldiers reached Tamil Nadu, there were already over three thousand Sri Lankan Tamil refugees there belonging to the EPRLF and its allies, the Ealam National Democratic Liberation Front, Tamil Eelam Liberation Organization, and People's Liberation Army of Tamil Eelam.

Retrospect

The departure of the IPKF from Sri Lanka brought to an end India's longest war, and one in which it had over one thousand soldiers killed with three thousand or more wounded. The presence of the IPKF in the north and east of Sri Lanka, and in such large numbers, had proved to be a self-defeating exercise. The IPKF had failed in one of its principal objectives as a peacekeeping force, to disarm the Tamil separatist groups, and especially the LTTE, even if one disregards the timetable set out in the Indo–Sri Lanka Accord as hopelessly optimistic and therefore unrealistic. Nor did the IPKF succeed in eliminating the LTTE as a fighting force after it was decided to turn its guns on them, thus opening themselves to the charge that they had been incapable of doing that, or that it was never intended to do so.[25]

There is considerable evidence that instructions had been issued to the IPKF in 1988 through the Indian high commission that the leadership of the LTTE should be eliminated. A concerted attempt was made in May and June 1988 to eliminate the LTTE leader, Velupillai Prabhakaran, and his second in command, Mahendraraja (known by his nom de guerre of Mahattaya), but the IPKF found it impossible to get to them in their jungle hideouts or elsewhere. The assumption was that, if this had been done, the LTTE would have disintegrated, as indeed the JVP did, when the Sri Lankan army eliminated its leadership in 1990. The LTTE was aware of this threat and took extraordinary precautions to protect its leadership: there were concentric circles of armed men, around them all the time, assigned the task of protecting them at all costs.

Despite all this, the LTTE was driven to the bargaining table because of a perceived weakening of its military strength, sapped in the course of a long and debilitating struggle against the IPKF. Had the LTTE not reached an understanding with the Premadasa government after April 1989, the IPKF would have gone on to weaken them further, and may perhaps have even eliminated the LTTE leadership before leaving Sri Lanka.[26] As it was, the rapprochement with the Sri Lankan government permitted the LTTE to escape a crushing final defeat at the hands of the IPKF. Thus the LTTE was doubly fortunate. In July 1987, the Indian intervention and the Indian army had saved them from further humiliation at the hands of the Sri Lankan army. By the time the IPKF left, the LTTE, which had been cornered and weakened, had been allowed to reestablish itself as a political and military force. Its leadership was intact and safe; its troops battle hardened and ready for combat; its morale high as a result of its "diplomatic" coup in reaching out to the Sri Lankan government. Even before the IPKF left, the LTTE was dominant over the north and east and had begun to eliminate its Tamil rivals.

One final point. The presence of the IPKF in the north and east of the island was not without advantages to the Sri Lankan government. For one thing, the country's defense expenditures dropped noticeably after mid-1987. The Indian government bore the heavy expenditure involved in the pacification—such as it was—of the north and east. This decline in defense spending on the part of Sri Lanka would have been more substantial if the threat posed by the JVP had not been so serious. More important, the fact that the IPKF kept the LTTE at bay in the north and east of the island greatly helped the Sri Lankan security forces, and in particular the army, to crush the JVP militarily and to eliminate it as a political force.

Notes

1. This information was obtained by the author in discussions with senior members of the Indian High Commission staff, in Colombo, at this time.

2. Ibid.

3. See, for example, the *Hindu*, 20 February 1989.

4. *Illustrated Weekly of India*, 11 October 1987.

5. There is surprisingly little information on Dixit's role in Richard Sisson and Leo E. Rose, *War and Secession: Pakistan, India and the Creation of Bangladesh* (Berkeley: University of California Press, 1990). On p. 186, there is a reference to special units set up by the External Affairs Ministry under Peter Sinai and A. M. Dikshit [*sic*] but not to a J. N. Dixit.

6. This is based on discussions I have had with Bangladeshi diplomats, academics, and politicians who knew Dixit in Bangladesh.

7. Ibid.

8. See *Keesing's Contemporary Archives*, 15–25 August 1974 for information on Bhutto's visit to Dacca, which began on 27 June.

9. Information on this incident was supplied by Bangladeshi diplomats and academics who remembered it.

10. Rajesh Kadian's account (see his *India's Sri Lanka Fiasco: Peace Keepers at War* [New Delhi: Vision Books, 1990, 123–24) of a conversation that Dixit is supposed to have had with President Jayewardene with regard to the holding of elections to the North Eastern Provincial Council is clearly a figment of his (Kadian's) imagination or is based on some very unreliable information. That was not Dixit's style of doing things.

11. *Daily News*, 10 April 1989.

12. J. N. Dixit, "IPKF in Sri Lanka," *United Service Institution Journal* (July–September 1989): 248–62.

13. This is based on the testimony of a number of Sri Lankan cabinet ministers of this period. Confirmation of it is available in a summary of proceedings of the cabinet meeting of 12 August 1987 in the J. R. Jayewardene MSS.

14. Ranjan Wijeratne, interviews with the author, April and July 1989.

15. Ibid.

16. Rajiv Gandhi's letter to President Premadasa, 12 June 1989. The correspondence between the two heads of government was published in Sri Lanka in the local newspapers on the initiative of President Premadasa.

17. Ranjan Wijeratne, interview with the author, August 1989; S. K. Singh, interview with the author, 12 April 1991.

18. For discussion of the implications of this, and President Premadasa's reaction to it, see Bradman Weerakoon, *Premadasa of Sri Lanka: A Political Biography* (New Delhi: Vikas, 1992), 77–82.

19. Rajiv Gandhi, interview with the author, 23 April 1990; S. K. Singh, interview with the author, 20 September 1990.

20. At the interview I had with Rajiv Gandhi on 23 April 1990, he stressed the fact that he had intended to destroy the IPKF's military capacity before the IPKF left Sri Lanka. He added that he was prevented from doing so because of the impending Indian elections.

21. I. K. Gujral told me on 18 December 1991 in New Delhi that he and Ranjan Wijeratne had virtually arrived together when he came to his office for the first time as minister of external affairs of the new government.

22. See the *Hindustan Times,* 19 December 1991.

23. The substance of the negotiations in Delhi on this occasion was derived from interviews with S. K. Singh, 12 April 1991 and from a discussion I had with I. K. Gujral in Delhi on 19 December 1992.

24. On the final phase of the IPKF's withdrawal, see Rajesh Kadian, *India's Sri Lanka Fiasco,* 132–38.

25. See the article by P. S. Suriyanarayana in the *Financial Express* (Delhi), 12 June 1988, where he claimed that "Delhi finds it diplomatically and politically advisable to liquidate the Tiger leader, Mr. Velupillai Prabhakaran."

26. A point Rajiv Gandhi made quite emphatically at the interview he gave me on 23 April 1990.

16

Conclusion

India in Sri Lanka: The Costs of Intervention

THE OPENING PARAGRAPH of this concluding chapter begins, as do the opening paragraphs of the introduction, with a reference to the late Indian prime minister, Rajiv Gandhi. We began the introductory chapter by quoting a communiqué issued on Rajiv Gandhi's departure from Sri Lanka after signing what turned out to be an ill-fated accord with the Sri Lankan government. Here we quote an extract from a speech he made at a public meeting in Madras just two weeks later. This is what he said on that occasion:

> This agreement is a major landmark in these four decades of India's freedom. I am told that no such agreement has been signed by any country in the world, at least in this century. It is an agreement without precedent in history. It is an agreement which does not have a parallel in the world. It is an agreement which vindicates the principles of good neighbourliness, peaceful co-existence and non-alignment.[1]

The euphoric tones and the grandiloquent pronouncements were directed at his special audience, the people of Tamil Nadu, who, he hoped and believed, would be grateful to him for the continued intervention in the affairs of Sri Lanka, on behalf of the Tamil minority there, an intervention initiated by his mother. In contrast, his speech in the Lok Sabha on 20 July 1987, introducing what the official record called, the "Sri Lankan Agreement," had been remarkably restrained, indeed very low key. Nevertheless, on that occasion too the emphasis was on the benefits that would accrue to Sri Lanka's Tamil minority from the accord.[2] And he was almost apologetic about the dispatch of the Indian Peace-Keeping Force (IPKF) to Sri Lanka:

In response to [a] formal request from the Government of Sri Lanka, and in terms of our obligations under the just signed Indo-Sri Lanka Agreement, units of the Armed Forces of India have today landed in the Jaffna peninsula. Let me repeat that our troops have landed in Sri Lanka in response to a specific and formal request of the Government of Sri Lanka who have invoked our obligations and commitments under the Indo-Sri Lanka Agreement. Our troops have gone there to end the ethnic strife in Sri Lanka and their despatch underlines our firm commitment to the unity and integrity of Sri Lanka.[3]

Earlier chapters have shown how this exercise in the extension of Indian power ended in failure. The book ends with the last batch of Indian soldiers of the IPKF leaving for India in March 1990. But that was not the end of this story for the regional power or for the small state. We do not intend to deal here with the aftermath within Sri Lanka of the departure of the IPKF. Instead we turn to India where it all began.

On 13 June 1990, an LTTE execution squad operating in Tamil Nadu had raided a block of apartments in which the leadership of the Eelam People's Revolutionary Liberation Front (EPRLF) lived as refugees in Madras and killed thirteen of them, including the secretary general of the party and one of its MPs in the Sri Lankan Parliament. The Liberation Tigers of Tamil Eelam (LTTE) raiders had carried AK-47 assault rifles. While the immediate reaction in Tamil Nadu was one of shocked dismay, little was done to curb the LTTE's activities until the assassination of Rajiv Gandhi by the LTTE on 21 May 1991 in Tamil Nadu compelled a reappraisal of attitudes and policies. When photographs of Rajiv Gandhi's mangled body were carried by news magazines and newspapers throughout the world, they provided grisly evidence of the human costs and the personal tragedies involved in the Indian intervention in Sri Lanka. At last India itself woke up to a realization of the staggering price in money, blood, and decline in prestige it had been called on to pay for the support extended to Tamil separatism in Sri Lanka.

A distinguished Indian journalist evaluating the miscalculations and blunders that characterized India's intervention in Sri Lanka described the LTTE as a Frankenstein's monster that India had helped create.[4] The LTTE had established a government within a government in parts of the Tamil Nadu coast; its smuggling enterprises included a flourishing narcotics trade; it had infiltrated the Tamil Nadu administration; and it had introduced a culture of violence into parts of India which had not known it before.

One part of the reappraisal was a calculation of costs: financial, human, and political. In financial terms the IPKF exercise cost India something like Rs 50 billion (in Sri Lankan rupees) or U.S.$1.25 billion. While it may be argued that some part, if not a great deal, of this money would have been spent on this force even if it had remained in India, the additional costs involved in moving troops to and from Sri Lanka and in maintaining them there must have been very considerable. Furthermore, over one thousand Indian soldiers were killed and over double that number were injured, many of them crippled by land mines and other improvised explosive devices in the laying and making of which the LTTE were experts, an expertise they gained through Indian trainers on Indian soil.

There is also that great intangible—the loss of prestige stemming from the patent failure of a political and military enterprise that had begun with a flourish and such high hopes. At the time the IPKF arrived in the island, only the Sinhalese were hostile and opposed to its presence. After a short time of the IPKF's presence in the north and east, even the Tamils who originally welcomed it as liberators were alienated from it, all except the political groups associated with the marginalized EPRLF. The gains were few, if any.

Sri Lanka: Small State Security

By the early 1990s Sri Lanka's problems had demonstrated the vital importance of considering options for her survival as an independent state. Through the 1980s the Sri Lankan state had confronted two formidable threats. First was a separatist movement that had secured assistance from a regional unit of a powerful subcontinental neighbor, and the neighbor herself. The threat thus created was very complex, involving internal subversion through guerrilla warfare and terrorism, and external danger through linkages established between separatist activists in the Jaffna peninsula and sources of supply and support in southern India. The linkage included an age-old smuggling trade. Second was the threat to the state and civil society from radical forces such as the Janatha Vimukthi Peramuna (JVP) espousing a blend of doctrinaire Marxism and Sinhalese nationalism. This threat was essentially internal, but included (as in 1971 and to a greater extent in 1987–89) systematic subversive activity and the fomenting of widespread civil disorder. There have been up to now no direct or formal systematic links between these two threats. Thus it is all the more difficult to develop a common response to both, apart, of course, from meeting any direct physical assault through the use of the security services and the police.

Sri Lanka's recent history demonstrates the importance of the careful handling of ethnic dissonance, including linguistic and religious tensions, strictly at the level of domestic politics. This is often the first and most vital factor in the regulation of national security. Where such conflicts exist and persist, they provide opportunities for external interference if not intervention—not for nothing is it said that the second law of ethnic conflict is the inevitability of its internationalization.[5] This is especially so when—as in Sri Lanka—a minority has historical and cultural links with ethnic groups in a neighboring state. When that occurs, ethnic or linguistic conflicts will almost certainly stimulate regional tensions and undermine domestic security. If there is any lesson to be learned from the ill-fated Indo–Sri Lanka Accord of 1987, it is the cardinal importance of the principle that states should seek to manage, if not resolve, their own internal problems as far as possible on their own without the involvement of external forces.

The consequences of internationalization of an ethnic conflict such as the one in Sri Lanka reviewed in this book are not necessarily those which the affected parties generally anticipate; nor are they necessarily beneficial to them, as the case of the Tamils of Sri Lanka, and the Indian involvement on their behalf, demonstrates. On the contrary those who initiate internationalization face an abiding inherent dilemma. Internationalization is as likely to prolong a conflict and make parties to the conflict more intractable as it is to make the latter more amenable to a negotiated settlement.

Thus the Indian mediation process in Sri Lanka from 1983 on was prolonged, partly at least, because every principal Indian negotiator except Romesh Bhandari became an advocate not merely of the Sri Lankan Tamil cause but also of the essence and details of the political programs sponsored by the principal Tamil political groups, stopping short only of support of a separate state. And this despite the threat many features of these programs posed to the stability of the Sri Lankan government, and the peace of the country in the Sinhalese areas. Thus the negotiations between 1983 and 1987 were in the nature of a diplomatic war of attrition. Every concession extracted under Indian pressure was followed by persistent demands for yet more concessions that incorporated other parts of the political agenda of Sri Lankan Tamil political groups. We have seen how the signing of the Indo–Sri Lanka Accord provoked widespread rioting in many of the Sinhalese areas of the country, including the capital, in late July and early August 1987. One government party MP was assassinated at that time. President Jayewardene himself narrowly escaped assassination, on 18 August 1987, while several senior politicians were severely injured and one district minister killed. Despite this there was no relaxation of the Indian pressure.

Once the Northern and Eastern Provinces had been amalgamated late in 1988, one of the most controversial and unpopular features of the accord, the Indian government, operating like a reckless gambler riding his luck, began to raise the ante once again. Now diplomatic pressure was initiated to ensure that the amalgamation was made permanent. One of the key features of the Indo–Sri Lanka Accord was the provision for a referendum in the Eastern Province to test the opinion of the people there as to whether they wished the amalgamation of their province to the Northern Province to continue. But the Indians were lending their support to the insistence by Tamil groups that the amalgamation be treated as a fait accompli and no longer negotiable. The most vocal was the LTTE, but other political groups, ranging from the Tamil United Liberation Front (TULF) to the Tamil Congress, not to be outdone, began supporting the LTTE on the perpetuation of the linkage without resort to a referendum. Pressure from India through the Indian high commission in Colombo (especially, but not only, during Dixit's days) was mounted in support of this despite the fact that the beleaguered Sri Lankan government, in the last days of the Jayewardene administration, was in the throes of a complex transition of leadership quite apart from a continuation of the serious insurgency mounted by Sinhalese intransigents opposed to the Indo–Sri Lanka Accord in general and the amalgamation of the Northern and Eastern Provinces in particular.

Indian mediation illustrated the operation of a general principle that, when regional or great powers enter a domestic ethnic dispute playing the role of sponsors and suppliers, the original issues in the conflict are often superseded by the interests of the external contenders. The Indo–Sri Lanka Accord provides another example of this in the exchange of letters between the two governments constituting the second agreement concluded on 29 July 1987.

India was driven as much by its own domestic political concerns, especially those of Tamil Nadu, as it was by anxieties regarding regional security. One of the most remarkable features of the story is the extent to which the state of Tamil Nadu influenced the negotiating process, and the number of persons from southern India (mainly southern Indian Brahmins) involved in the making of India's Sri Lankan policy. The names ranged from G. Parathasarathy in 1983, to P. Chidambaram in 1984–86, to A. P. Venkateswaran in 1986 and K. P. S. Menon, Jr., in 1987. This was quite apart from men like the defense analyst and advocate of the expansion of Indian power, K. Subhramanyan, and General K. Sunderji. There was, finally, the influential journalist G. K. Reddy, one of the chief nonofficial spokesmen for the South Block. India's Sri Lankan policy in the 1980s was a combination of the pursuit of its strategic interests, and its domestic concerns relating to the internal politics of Tamil Nadu, with the support given to the Tamil minority and its principal political parties within Sri Lanka. It was mediation with muscle, with the mediator having a vital stake in the outcome of the mediation. India was at once a principal mediator, as well as a biased mediator.[6]

The regional power equation was also skewed because of a factor that has seldom, if ever, been considered in evaluations of India's role as a regional power, namely Delhi's position as a regional information center. A great many of the world's major newspapers have their South Asia correspondents based in Delhi, and when regional issues affecting India emerge the reporting can often be influenced by information obtained from, if not supplied by, the South Block through official or unofficial channels. This does not always happen, and at least some of the foreign correspondents spot a planted story with great ease. All too often, however, the story travels around the world because the common run of Delhi-based foreign correspondents were either too uncritical of their sources, or were not inclined to check them as carefully as they normally would. Thus, except in the case of a few reporters, Mark Tully of the BBC or Barbara Crossette of the *New York Times* to name two, the reporting on the Indian intervention in Sri Lanka often uncritically reflected Indian sources. The smaller countries of South Asia, Bangladesh, Nepal, and Sri Lanka, have all had to live with the reality that the principal news center in South Asia is Delhi, and that reporting often carries a Delhi flavor, if not a Delhi bias.

On balance, the hard lesson that emerges from India's insistence on bilateral mediation and her interventionist role in Sri Lanka's ethnic conflict is that regional powers have less to offer than they think to those involved in such conflicts, by way of appropriate transferable institutional devices and mechanisms or constructive practical experience in the handling of such problems. This is equally true of great powers. Worse still India did not demonstrate that essential requirement for successful mediation, a thorough grasp of the history behind the issues that led to the breakdown in Sri Lanka. And this in a part of the world where historical metaphor and historical memories have a mesmerizing effect on all sides of the divide.

In a compact but perceptive analysis of strategies of small state survival, Hans Indorf[7] emphasizes the need for new and multidimensional approaches to old practices, to search for a combination of these to make any threats to a small state too costly to be carried out. While a large state has the advantage of an in-depth defense, a small state, lacking physical size and an ability for flexible defense, has to rely on strategic insights, political and diplomatic skills, and shrewd tactics to outwit any potential aggressor. Above all, a small state needs a well-defined strategy for national security, something that should receive the highest priority in the nation's political agenda. In short, a small state must get its own house in order.

For Sri Lanka an essential part of that national political agenda is a realization that, to keep the country together, it is essential to manage its ethnic rivalries and tensions better than has been done since the mid- and late 1950s. Given all that has happened in the 1970s and 1980s and the conflicting perceptions of vulnerability among the parties involved, this will be no easy task. Politicized ethnicity is a potent destabilizing element and multiethnic societies are difficult to govern on the traditional majoritarian principles. Efficient and peaceful governance requires generosity and imagination. It is important to move away from assertion of majority dominance, to policies of accommodation of minority interests, and where conflict has broken out, measures of reconciliation.

An equitable distribution of economic benefits and national wealth among a country's various ethnic groups would be an essential feature of such policies, but economic prosperity, on its own, need not and will not make the management of ethnic conflict any easier in societies with a long history of violent confrontation. The primary importance of political mechanisms needs to be emphasized, especially forms of, and devices for, powersharing. These must range from the national government, through a second tier of government in the form of regional or provincial and district units or autonomous regions, to revitalized local government bodies, and include decentralization of administration at all levels. But even such measures would be inadequate without statesmanship—a very scarce commodity in the political marketplace—and a spirit of tolerance, of live and let live. Together, economic benefits, political and institutional reform, and pragmatic patterns of governance that emphasize practical resolution of controversial issues could bring peace to a nation which confronts the destabilizing passions of politicized ethnicity. Makeshift and expediency are essential, not a rigid adherence to abstract theorizing and the self-righteous intensity of the zealot.

In regard to external security, the choices before a small state faced with a powerful regional power like India, seeking to fill a vacuum left by colonial power arrangements, are limited and intrinsically unpalatable. First, as the Sri Lankan experience of the 1980s shows, when a small state shifts its interests and alignments, or even appears to do so, it can pose a threat to the security (or at least, to the security perceptions) of a regional power. The small state thereby faces long-term vulnerability. Second—and here we deal with an abstract proposition rather than a political reality in the case of Sri Lanka—if it seeks alignment to a great power or to another regional power to obtain security against a neighboring regional power, it will soon realize that such alignment carries a fundamental weakness, namely that it can be summarily (or even not so summarily but just as effectively) abrogated when it no longer serves the interests of the dominant party.

The third option, and one that Sri Lanka has pursued since the mid-1950s, is nonalignment. Yet, as the Sri Lankan situation has demonstrated, nonalignment does not necessarily provide security, especially where the threat emerges from within the nonaligned "bloc" rather than from a predatory great power. Indeed it is all too often the case that an assertive regional power could be as dangerous a predator as any aggressive great power. Thus the margin of maneuverability available for small states will continue to be exceedingly narrow.

Small states like Sri Lanka will need to keep their diplomatic options open to as wide a range of influences as possible without committing themselves to any single course of action. What is required is not a systematic linkage but a partial one. Systematic linkage is an undesirable position for a small state to adopt because any shift in power relationships would impair the prevailing balance and thus increase vulnerability. A partial linkage, on the other hand, keeps a small state outside or at the fringes of great power or even regional power competition. It remains free to pursue other strategies. In most cases small states prefer to retain their flexibility in determining the desired type of linkage. All linkages, however, have the disadvantage that their benefits can be nullified by the inherent liabilities of dependence and of abrupt unilateral curtailment of linkages.

Regional groupings are, by and large, the least disadvantageous, if not the most desirable, by small states. There are several reasons for this. Small states find these regional associations of some security and status benefit and somewhat less economic benefit. Indeed, many small states will find the economic interdependence of regional groupings such as the South Asian Association for Regional Co-operation of dubious value. But there is the inestimable advantage that such groupings and arrangements help preserve sovereign rights, if not fully, certainly to a greater extent than other associations.

There has been a massive disorientation in India's own foreign policy stemming from the winding down of cold war tensions, and a fading away of her links with the former Soviet Union with the latter's dissolution—links which had been the pivot of India's foreign and defense policies since the late 1960s. But all India's neighbors in South Asia will continue to face the common problem of a relationship in which every possible calculation is weighted in favor of India and against her smaller neighbors. Some of India's neighbors—Pakistan, Bangladesh, and the Maldives—have the advantage of belonging to the Islamic world. Sri Lanka does not have this advantage and in that sense is diplomatically and politically more isolated. Her politicians will have to demonstrate much greater tactical skill and show much sharper strategic insights if the country is to survive in the twenty-first century without serious damage to its independent status. As an island located at a convenient point in the trade routes of the Indian Ocean, Sri Lanka is not entirely without advantages. One external link that could be pursued is to the countries of Southeast Asia with whom Sri Lanka has had historic cultural and religious ties. The other important consideration is that the subcontinental giant is not without its own constraints. India is, after the Soviet Union, the second largest (in terms of population—not land area) multiethnic society in the world, and the problems of governing such a country will tax the energies of her politicians, administrators, and security forces to the utmost into the next century.

Ethnic Tensions and Conflict Resolution

In this review of India's intervention in Sri Lanka's ethnic conflict, we encounter one of the critical issues in the theory and practice of conflict resolution, the difficulties inherent in the resolution of conflicts involving ethnicity (as in Sri Lanka) or politicized religion (as in contemporary India). As in other conflict situations in other parts of the world, there are two approaches to the management of social conflict: the structural and the cultural. The first emphasizes the importance of political or institutional change or both as the means of resolving conflict, and its principal underlying assumption is that change and progress are facilitated best by devising new political structures and institutions or revitalizing existing ones to serve this new purpose.[8] At the political level the structural approach emphasizes negotiations and a search for compromise between political representatives of groups in conflict. In contrast, the cultural approach emphasizes the need for reconciliation between communities in conflict, through mutual understanding and shared responsibility. It operates at the level of the community, concentrates on relationships between communities in conflict and emphasizes the importance of nongovernmental community relations organizations in the processes of reconciliation.[9]

This duality in practical approaches in conflict resolution has its parallel in two clear strands of thought in conflict resolution theory. One emphasizes the need for negotiating, bargaining on the sharing of power, and emphasizing the need for compromise. The other concentrates on communication, relationships, and mutual problem solving as the basis of enduring resolution. It would be true to say that the first of these, the structural approach, has been preferred to the cultural approach in the resolution of ethnic conflicts in South Asia in general and Sri Lanka in particular.

The emphasis on the structural approach is in many ways a reflection of the formidable difficulties that confront mediators seeking to resolve ethnic conflicts, especially where these have persisted over long periods of time.[10] Indeed, ethnic conflict is less amenable to mediation than other conflicts, including conflicts between states.[11] In many cases—Punjab and Sri Lanka are good examples—there is a multiplicity of interested and conflicting parties, as well as divided authority on one or more sides, all of which makes it difficult to reach agreement, or to make an agreement stick once it has been reached. Furthermore, leaders of extremist groups, including some of the factions of the Akali Dal in Punjab or the LTTE and many of its rivals in Sri Lanka, see few gains in a peaceful outcome, and have little or no interest in the give and take of mediation. External forces with a stake in the outcome—India in the case of Sri Lanka—are complicating factors. Generally, however, the principal sources of the intractability in South Asia's ethnic conflicts have been indigenous forces rather than external allies and mentors.

There is also the mediation-with-muscle aspect of the structural approach of resolution theory and practice. We have seen in previous chapters how the Indian army was used, in Sri Lanka and in the Punjab, in a calculated demonstration of military power to impose the will of the Indian government in support of what were seen to be India's national strategic interests. The difference was that in Sri Lanka the use of the Indian army followed the signing of an accord and flowed from its clauses, while in the Punjab the accord itself had to deal with the consequences that flowed from the army's intervention. In both instances the use of the army did little to resolve the conflict; on the contrary, the consequences were nearly disastrous for India's own national interests, and not least for the two leaders who ordered the resort to force. Mrs. Gandhi was assassinated by her Sikh bodyguards within a few months of Operation Blue Star, as the army assault on Amritsar's Golden Temple was called; Rajiv Gandhi was assassinated not quite four years after he sent the Indian army to the north and east of the island, an assassination carried out by the LTTE presumably to avenge the deaths caused by the Indian army in Jaffna and elsewhere in the north and east of the island. Mrs. Gandhi was destroyed by the very separatist forces she had helped set in motion in the Punjab, just as her son was eventually destroyed by the separatist forces in Sri Lanka which she had actively encouraged, a policy he himself had been unable to repudiate. The full story of the Indian involvement in Sri Lanka has yet to be written from the Indian end. Kuldip Nayar, a distinguished Indian journalist, made the point in 1992 that "the bureaucrats, the guilty ones still occupy the position of power. Some day the story will come out. When it happens all Indians will have to hang their heads in shame."[12]

This study of the Indian intervention in Sri Lanka's ethnic conflict serves two purposes: to reveal first, the complexities that confront mediators in situations of prolonged and violent disputes and the narrow range of options available to a mediator; and second, the unique nature of the Indian intervention in exhausting the four options for mediation identified here.

Of the many forms that the process of mediation can take, the first is to assist one or another of the participants; such assistance can be terminated whenever it is necessary or possible to do so. This assistance is designed to do one of several things—to encourage the continuation of struggle, to persuade one or another of the parties to the dispute to change its strategy, or even to encourage a settlement. Second, the intervenor may try to resolve the conflict itself by acting as a mediator, applying sanctions to one, some, or all parties, or underwriting a settlement. Third, the intervenor may become the common enemy that unites the warring factions or the principal parties to the dispute (for example, the Sri Lankan government under President Premadasa and the LTTE) against it. Fourth, the intervening regional power could face the same forces of politicized ethnicity in its own territories as a consequence of its intervention. Thus the stability of its own polity could be put at risk by the stimulus provided by cross-border tensions from the state it intervenes in. Its own leadership, no less than others', is vulnerable to cross-border acts of violence engineered by disaffected individuals or groups in the ethnically divided country whose problems the mediator seeks to resolve. The Indian mediation in the Sri Lankan conflict has the unique distinction of taking on the first three forms, and also demonstrating the fearful reality of the fourth feature, mutual vulnerability to aroused and competing politicized ethnicities.

Notes

1. The extract is from M. Rasgotra, ed., *Rajiv Gandhi's World View* (New Delhi: Vikas, 1991), 191, cited in H. L. de Silva, "The Indo-Sri Lanka Agreement (1987) in the Perspective of Inter-State Relations," *Ethnic Studies Report* 10, no. 2 (July 1992): 10.

2. Lok Sabha, official record, 30 July 1987, col. 343.

3. Ibid., col. 345.

4. Kuldip Nayar, discussion with the author in Delhi, December 1992.

5. For discussion of this theme, see K. M. de Silva and Ronald J. May, eds., introduction to *Internationalization of Ethnic Conflict* (London: Pinter Publishers, 1991), 1–10.

6. On this theme see Saadia Touval, "Biased Intermediaries," *Jerusalem Journal of International Relations* 1, no. 1 (1975): 51–69.

7. H. H. Indorf, *Strategies for Small State Survival* (Kuala Lumpur: Institute for Strategic and International Studies, 1985).

8. For a statement of the views of this school, see I. William Zartman, *Ripe for Resolution: Conflict and Intervention in Africa*, 2nd ed. (New York: Oxford University Press, 1989); I. William Zartman and Maureen R. Berman, *The Practical Negotiator* (New Haven, Conn.: Yale University Press, 1982).

9. See particularly Edward E. Azar, *The Management of Protracted Social Conflict: Theory and Cases* (Aldershot: Dartmouth, 1991); E. Azar and John W. Burton, eds., *International Conflict Resolution: Theory and Practice* (Sussex: Wheatsheaf, 1986); John W. Burton, *Resolving Deep-Rooted Conflict: A Handbook* (Lanham, Md.: University Press of America, 1987).

10. See K. M. de Silva and S. W. R. de A. Samarasinghe, eds., introduction to *Peace Accords and Ethnic Conflicts* (London: Pinter, 1993), 1–15.

11. For a somewhat different perspective on this, see Marc Howard Ross, "Ethnic Conflict and Dispute Management," in Austin Sarat and Susan Silbey, eds., *Studies in Law, Politics and Society*, vol. 12 (Greenwich, Conn.: JAI Press, 1992), 155–95.

12. Kuldip Nayar, "LTTE: India's Embarrassment," The *Tribune*, 3 June 1992.

Appendix

Introduction

THIS APPENDIX CONTAINS eight documents relating to the negotiations between Sri Lanka and India from 1983 to 1987. Documents I through III mark the beginning of the process of Indian mediation in Sri Lanka's ethnic conflict, described and analyzed in chapters 4, 6, and 7 of this book. The first three documents are referred to as Annexures A, B, and C. The use of the term "annexure" in this instance is more than a little misleading because there is no principal document—at least none that we know of—to which the annexures belong. There has been no official reference to such a document and one has not been published in Sri Lanka or India. Indeed, the annexures stand on their own. The most important of them is Annexure C, because it contains the essence of the agreement reached in late November 1983 in New Delhi between President J. R. Jayewardene and G. Parathasarathy (referred to in the text of Annexure A as "G. Parathasarathi"), the principal negotiator for the Indian government. Annexures A and B are published here because they provide essential background to understanding the principal features of Annexure C.

The terms used in Annexure C need no clarification except for the reference to "cess" in clause 6. A cess is a tax or a levy, generally an export levy, from which the revenue is used for a specific purpose.

Documents IV through VIII are part of the controversial Indo–Sri Lanka Accord signed on 29 July 1987, the background to which is reviewed in chapter 11 of this book. The Indo–Sri Lanka Accord consists of three parts: the first is the agreement proper (Document IV), the second is the annexure to the agreement (Document V), and the third contains the correspondence incorporated in the accord (Documents VI, VII, and VIII). The correspondence consists of two letters from the Indian prime minister to the Sri Lankan president (Documents VI and VII) and a very brief reply from the Sri Lankan president (Document VIII).

Document I. Annexure A: Press Statement Issued by His Excellency the President, J. R. Jayewardene, on His Return from New Delhi on 1.12.83

On my visit to New Delhi to attend the Meeting of the Commonwealth Heads of Government, I had an opportunity to discuss with Her Excellency Shrimathi Indira Gandhi, the Prime Minister of India, the problem of Sri Lanka Tamils in Sri Lanka.

2. Before leaving for New Delhi, I had had consultations on this matter with various political leaders in Sri Lanka. The Special Envoy of the Prime Minister of India, Mr. G. Parathasarathi, had also discussed this matter with me during his visits to Sri Lanka and in India.

3. It will be recalled that I had made it clear that I could resume any discussions with the TULF to discuss the possible lines of a solution only if they give up their call for a separate state.

4. I am happy to say that according to available information the TULF is prepared to give up its call for a separate state, if a solution of the Tamil problem that is acceptable to them is worked out.

5. I am also happy to say that the Government of India has stated in clear terms that India is against secession and stands for the independence, integrity and sovereignty of Sri Lanka.

6. Mr. G. Parathasarathi, the Special Envoy of the Prime Minister of India, has had discussions with the Members of the TULF who are in New Delhi and has obtained their response to the proposals that have emerged as a result of the discussions in Colombo in November. I will first consult all political parties in Sri Lanka on the modalities of summoning an all party conference to discuss these proposals. Once the modalities for this conference are settled, I will communicate to all parties the various proposals that have emerged, so that they will have an opportunity of studying them, before participating in the conference. Thereafter, I propose to summon a conference of the political parties at which these proposals will be discussed.

Document II. Annexure B: The Following Matters Have been Suggested for the Formulation of an Agenda by the All Party Conference

1. The giving up of the idea of a separate state.

2. The merger of the District Development Councils within a Province after acceptance by the Councils' members and a Referendum in the District. This proposal would be applicable to the whole island.

3. Regions that have Regional Councils to establish a convention that the Leader of the Party which commands a majority in a Regional Council would be formally appointed by the President as the Chief Minister of the Region. He will work with a Committee of Members of the Council constituted by him.

4. The President and the Parliament to continue to have overall responsibility for all subjects not transferred to the Region and generally for all other matters relating to the maintenance of the Sovereignty, Integrity, Unity, Security, Progress and Development of the Republic as a whole.

5. The list of subjects to be allocated to the Regions to be worked out in detail. With regard to these subjects the Regional Councils to be empowered to enact laws and exercise executive powers in relation thereto. The Council to have the power to levy taxes, a cess or fees and to raise loans and also to receive grants and allocations from the Central Government.

6. The recognition of the administration of Trincomalee Port as a Central Government function.

7. High Courts to function in each Region while the Supreme Court of Sri Lanka will exercise separate and constitutional jurisdiction.

8. The constitution of a Regional Service of those serving in the Region and those who will be seconded to the Region.

9. Regional Public Service Commissions to be created for recruitment and disciplinary action.

10. The Public Services of Sri Lanka, the Armed Services to reflect the national ethnic composition.

11. The Police Services for internal security to reflect the ethnic composition of the Regions.

12. A national policy on land settlement to be worked out.

13. The Constitution and other laws dealing with the Official Language Sinhala, and the National Language, Tamil, to be accepted and implemented as well as similar laws dealing with the National Flag and Anthem.

14. United opposition to the use of violence (terrorism) to attain political objectives.

Document III. Annexure C

In terms of paragraph six of the President's statement of December 1st 1983, the following proposals which have emerged as a result of discussions in Colombo and New Delhi are appended for consideration by the All Party Conference. These proposals are in the context of the unity and integrity of Sri Lanka and will form a basis for formulating the Agenda of the All Party Conference.

1. The District Development Councils in a Province be permitted to combine into one or more Regional Councils if they so agree by decisions of the Councils and approved by Referendum in that district.

2. In the case of the District Councils in the Northern and Eastern Provinces respectively, as they are not functioning due to the resignation of the majority of Members, their union within each province to be accepted.

3. Each Region will have a Regional Council if so decided. The convention will be established that the leader of the party which commands a majority in the Regional Council would be formally appointed by the President as the Chief Minister of the Region. The Chief Minister will constitute a Committee of Ministers of the Region.

4. The President and the Parliament will continue to have overall responsibility over all subjects not transferred to the regions and generally for all other matters relating to the maintenance of the sovereignty, integrity, unity and security and progress and development of the Republic as a whole.

5. The legislative power of the Region would be vested in the Regional Councils which would be empowered to enact laws and exercise executive powers in relation thereto on certain specified listed subjects including the maintenance of internal Law and Order in the Region, the Administration of Justice, Social and Economic Development, Cultural matters and Land Policy. The list of subjects which will be allocated to the Regions will be worked out in detail.

6. The Regional Councils will also have the power to levy taxes, cess or fees and to mobilise resources through loans, the proceeds of which will be credited to a Consolidated Fund set up for that particular Region to which also will be credited grants, allocations or subventions made by the Republic. Financial resources will be apportioned to the Regions on the recommendations of a representative Finance Commission appointed from time to time.

7. Provision will be made for constituting High Courts in each Region. The Supreme Court of Sri Lanka will exercise appellate and constitutional jurisdiction.

8. Each Region will have a Regional Service consisting of (a) officers and other public servants of the Region and (b) such other officers and

public servants who may be seconded to the Region. Each Region will have a Regional Public Service Commission for recruitment and for exercising disciplinary powers relating to the members of the Regional Service.

9. The armed forces of Sri Lanka will adequately reflect the national ethnic position. In the Northern and Eastern Regions, the Police forces for internal security will also reflect the ethnic composition of these Regions.

10. A Port Authority under the Central Government will be set up for administering the Trincomalee Port and Harbour. The area which will come under the administration of the Port Authority as well as the powers to be assigned to it will be further discussed.

11. A national policy on land settlement and the basis on which the Government will undertake land colonization will have to be worked out. All settlement schemes should be based on ethnic proportions so as not to alter the demographic balance subject to agreement being reached on major projects.

12. The Constitution and other laws dealing with the official language Sinhala and the national language, Tamil, be accepted and implemented as well as similar laws dealing with the National Flag and Anthem.

13. The Conference should appoint a committee to work out constitutional and legal changes that may be necessary to implement these decisions. The Government would provide its Secretariat and necessary legal offices.

14. The consensus of opinion of the All Party Conference will itself be considered by the United National Party Executive Committee and presumably by the executive bodies of the other Parties as well, before being placed before Parliament for legislative action.

Document IV. Indo–Sri Lanka Agreement to Establish Peace and Normalcy in Sri Lanka (29 July 1987, Colombo)

The Prime Minister of the Republic of India, His Excellency Mr Rajiv Gandhi and the President of the Democratic Socialist Republic of Sri Lanka, His Excellency Mr J. R. Jayewardene having met at Colombo on July 29, 1987.

Attaching utmost importance to nurturing, intensifying and strengthening the traditional friendship of India and Sri Lanka and acknowledging the imperative need of resolving the ethnic problem of Sri Lanka, and the consequent violence, and for the safety, well-being and prosperity of people belonging to all communities of Sri Lanka.

Having this day entered into the following Agreement to fulfil this objective.

1.1 **desiring** to preserve the unity, sovereignty and territorial integrity of Sri Lanka;

1.2 **acknowledging** that Sri Lanka is a multi-ethnic and a multi-lingual plural society consisting, inter alia, of Sinhalese, Tamils, Muslims (Moors), and Burghers;

1.3 **recognising** that each ethnic group has a distinct cultural and linguistic identity which has to be carefully nurtured.

1.4 **also recognising** that the Northern and the Eastern Provinces have been areas of historical habitation of Sri Lankan Tamil speaking peoples, who have at all times hitherto lived together in this territory with other ethnic groups;

1.5 **conscious** of the necessity of strengthening the forces contributing to the unity, sovereignty and territorial integrity of Sri Lanka, and preserving its character as a multi-ethnic, multi-lingual and multi-religious plural society, in which all citizens can live in equality, safety and harmony, and prosper and fulfil their aspirations.

2. **Resolve that:**

2.1 Since the Government of Sri Lanka proposes to permit adjoining Provinces to join to form one administrative unit and also by a Referendum to separate as may be permitted to the Northern and Eastern Provinces as outlined below:

2.2 During the period, which shall be considered an interim period (i.e.) from the date of the elections to the Provincial Council, as specified in para 2.8 to the date of the referendum as specified in para 2.3, the Northern and Eastern Provinces as now constituted, will form one administrative unit, having one elected Provincial Council. Such a unit will have one Governor, one Chief Administrator and one Board of Ministers.

2.3 There will be a referendum on or before 31st December, 1988 to enable the people of the Eastern Province to decide whether.

(a) The Eastern Province should remain linked with the Northern Province as one administrative unit, and continue to be governed together with the Northern Province as specified in para 2.2, or

(b) The Eastern Province should constitute a separate administrative unit having its own distinct Provincial Council with a separate Governor, Chief Minister and Board of Ministers.

The President may, at his discretion decide to postpone such a referendum.

2.4 All persons who have been displaced due to ethnic violence, or other reasons, will have the right to vote in such a referendum. Necessary conditions to enable them to return to areas from where they were displaced will be created.

2.5 The referendum, when held, will be monitored by a committee headed by the Chief Justice, a member appointed by the President, nominated by the Government of Sri Lanka, and a member appointed by the President, nominated by the representatives of the Tamil speaking people of the Eastern Province.

2.6 A simple majority will be sufficient to determine the result, of the referendum.

2.7 Meeting and other forms of propaganda, permissible within the laws of the country, will be allowed before the referendum.

2.8 Elections to Provincial Councils will be held within the next three months, in any event before Dec. 31, 1987. Indian observers will be invited for elections to the Provincial Council of the North and East.

2.9 The emergency will be lifted in the Eastern and Northern Provinces by August 15, 1987. A cessation of hostilities will come into effect all over the island within 48 hours of the signing of this Agreement. All arms presently held by militant groups will be surrendered in accordance with an agreed procedure to authorities to be designated by the Government of Sri Lanka.

Consequent to the cessation of hostilities and the surrender of arms by militant groups, the Army and other security personnel will be confined to barracks in camps as of May 25, 1987. The process of surrendering of arms and the confining of the security personnel moving back to barracks shall be completed within 72 hours of the cessation of hostilities coming into effect.

2.10 The Government of Sri Lanka will utilise for the purpose of law enforcement and maintenance of security in the Northern and Eastern Provinces the same organisations and mechanisms of Government as are used in the rest of the country.

2.11 The President of Sri Lanka will grant a general amnesty to political and other prisoners now held in custody under the Prevention of Terrorism Act and other emergency laws, and to combatants, as well as to those persons accused, charged and or convicted under these laws. The Government of Sri Lanka will make special efforts to rehabilitate militant youth with a view to bringing them back to the mainstream of national life. India will cooperate in the process.

2.12 The Government of Sri Lanka will accept and abide by the above provisions and expect all others to do likewise.

2.13 If the framework for the resolution is accepted, the Government of Sri Lanka will implement the relevant proposals forthwith.

2.14 The Government of India will underwrite and guarantee the resolutions, and co-operate in the implementation of these proposals.

2.15 These proposals are conditional to an acceptance of proposals negotiated from 4.5.1986 to 19.12.1986. Residual matters not finalised during the above negotiations shall be resolved between India and Sri Lanka within a period of six weeks of signing this agreement. These proposals are also conditional to the Government of India co-operating directly with the Government of Sri Lanka in their implementation.

2.16 These proposals are also conditional to the Government of India taking the following actions if any militant groups operating in Sri Lanka do not accept this framework of proposals for a settlement, namely:

(A) India will take all necessary steps to ensure that Indian territory is not used for activities prejudicial to the unity, integrity and security of Sri Lanka.

(B) The Indian Navy/Coast Guard will co-operate with the Sri Lanka Navy in preventing Tamil militant activities from affecting Sri Lanka.

(C) In the event that the Government of Sri Lanka requests the Government of India to afford military assistance to implement these proposals the Government of India will co-operate by giving to the Government of Sri Lanka such military assistance as and when requested.

(D) The Government of India will expedite repatriation from Sri Lanka of Indian citizens to India who are resident there concurrently with the repatriation of Sri Lankan refugees from Tamil Nadu.

(E) The Government of India and Sri Lanka, will co-operate in ensuring the physical security and safety of all communities inhabiting the Northern and Eastern Provinces.

2.17 The Government of Sri Lanka shall ensure free, full and fair participation of voters, from all communities in the Northern and Eastern Provinces in electoral processes envisaged in this agreement. The Government of India will extend full co-operation to the Government of Sri Lanka in this regard.

2.18 The official language of Sri Lanka shall be Sinhala. Tamil and English will also be official languages.

3. This agreement and the annexure there-to shall come into force upon signature.

In witness whereof we have set our hands and seals hereunto. Done in Colombo, Sri Lanka, on this the twenty ninth day of July of the year one thousand nine hundred and eighty seven, in duplicate, both texts being equally authentic:

Rajiv Gandhi
Prime Minister of the
Republic of India

Junius Richard Jayewardene
President of the Democratic
Socialist Republic of Sri Lanka

Document V. Annexure to the Agreement

1. His Excellency the Prime Minister of India and His Excellency the President of Sri Lanka agree that the referendum in paragraph 2 and its subparagraphs of the Agreement will be observed by a representative of the Election Commission of India to be invited by His Excellency the President of Sri Lanka.

2. Similarly, both heads of Government agree that the elections to the Provincial Council mentioned in paragraph 2.8 of the Agreement will be observed by a representative of the Government of India to be invited by the President of Sri Lanka.

3. His Excellency the President of Sri Lanka agrees that the Home Guards would be disbanded and all para-military personnel will be withdrawn from the Eastern and Northern Provinces with a view to creating conditions conducive to fair elections to the Council.

4. The Prime Minister of India and the President of Sri Lanka agree that the Tamil militants shall surrender their arms to authorities agreed upon to be designated by the President of Sri Lanka. The surrender shall take place in the presence of one senior representative each of the Sri Lanka Red Cross and the Indian Red Cross.

5. The Prime Minister of India and the President of Sri Lanka agree that a joint Indo–Sri Lankan observer group consisting of qualified representatives of the Government of India and the Government of Sri Lanka would monitor the cessation of hostilities from 31 July, 1987.

6. The Prime Minister of India and the President of Sri Lanka also agree that in terms of paragraph 2.14 and paragraph 2.16(c) of the Agreement, an Indian Peace Keeping contingent may be invited by the President of Sri Lanka to guarantee and enforce the cessation of hostilities, if so required.

Document VI.

Prime Minister of India New Delhi

July 29, 1987

Excellency,

Conscious of the friendship between our two countries stretching over two millennia and more, and **recognising** the importance of nurturing this traditional friendship, it is imperative that both Sri Lanka and India reaffirm the decision not to allow our respective territories to be used for activities prejudicial to each other's unity, territorial integrity and security.

In this spirit, you had, during the course of our discussions, agreed to meet some of India's concerns as follows:

(i) Your Excellency and myself will reach an early understanding about the relevance and employment of foreign military and intelligence personnel with a view to ensuring that such presences will not prejudice Indo–Sri Lankan relations.

(ii) Trincomalee or any other ports in Sri Lanka will not be made available for military use by any country in a manner prejudicial to India's interests.

(iii) The work of restoring and operating the Trincomalee oil tank farm will be undertaken as a joint venture between India and Sri Lanka.

(iv) Sri Lanka's agreement with foreign broadcasting organizations will be reviewed to ensure that any facilities set up by them in Sri Lanka are used solely as public broadcasting facilities and not for any military or intelligence purposes.

In the same spirit, India will:

(i) Deport all Sri Lankan citizens who are found to be engaging in terrorist activities or advocating separatism or secessionism.

(ii) Provide training facilities and military supplies for Sri Lankan security forces.

India and Sri Lanka have agreed to set up a joint consultative mechanism to continuously review matters of common concern in the light of the objectives stated in para 1 and specifically to monitor the implementation of other matters contained in this letter.

Kindly confirm, Excellency, that the above correctly sets out the agreement reached between us.

Please accept, Excellency, the assurances of my highest consideration.

Yours Sincerely,

(Rajiv Gandhi)

His Excellency
Mr J.R. Jayewardene,
President of the Democratic Socialist Republic of Sri Lanka, Colombo.

Document VII.

President of Sri Lanka

July 29, 1987

Excellency,

Please refer to your letter dated the 29th of July 1987, which reads as follows:

"Excellency,

Conscious of the friendship between our two countries stretching over two millennia and more, and recognizing the importance of nurturing this traditional friendship, it is imperative that both Sri Lanka and India reaffirm the decision not to allow our respective territories to be used for activities prejudicial to each other's unity, territorial integrity and security.

2. In this spirit, you had, during the course of our discussions, agreed to meet some of India's concerns as follows:

(i) Your Excellency and myself will reach an early understanding about the relevance and employment of foreign military and intelligence personnel with a view to ensuring that such presences will not prejudice Indo–Sri Lanka relations.

(ii) Trincomalee or any other ports in Sri Lanka will not be made available for military use by any country in a manner prejudicial to India's interests.

(iii) The work of restoring and operating the Trincomalee Oil tank farm will be undertaken as a joint venture between India and Sri Lanka.

(iv) Sri Lanka's agreements with foreign broadcasting organisations will be reviewed to ensure that any facilities set up by them in Sri Lanka are used solely as public broadcasting facilities and not for any military or intelligence purposes.

3. In the same spirit, India will:

(i) deport all Sri Lankan citizens who are found to be engaging in terrorist activities or advocating separatism or secessionism.

(ii) provide training facilities and military supplies for Sri Lankan security forces.

4. India and Sri Lanka have agreed to set up a joint consultative mechanism to continuously review matters of common concern in the light of the objectives stated in para 1 and specifically to monitor the implementation of other matters contained in this letter.

5. Kindly confirm, Excellency, that the above correctly sets out the agreement reached between us.

Please accept, Excellency, the assurances of my highest consideration.

Yours sincerely
Sd/-
(Rajiv Gandhi)

His Excellency
Mr. J.R. Jayewardene,
President of the Democratic Socialist Republic of Sri Lanka,
Colombo

Document VIII.

This is to confirm that the above correctly sets out the understanding reached between us. Please accept, Excellency, the assurances of my highest consideration.

Sd/-
(J.R. Jayewardene)
President

His Excellency
Mr. Rajiv Gandhi,
Prime Minister of the Republic of India,
New Delhi

Bibliography

I. Manuscript Sources

H. L. de Silva MSS.
Gamini Dissanayake MSS.
J. R. Jayewardene MSS.

II. Interviews

Sri Lanka.
The principal sources were
President J. R. Jayewardene (in particular).
Lalith Athulathmudali.
Gamini Dissanayake.
Ranjan Wijeratne.
There were occasional interviews and discussions with
A. C. S. Hameed.
Ronnie de Mel.
Among the officials interviewed were
Ernest Corea, Sri Lankan ambassador to the United States, 1983–87.
W. T. Jayasinghe, secretary, Ministry of Foreign Affairs, 1977–88.
Bernard Tillakaratne, Sri Lankan high commissioner in Delhi, 1982–88;
Secretary, Ministry of Foreign Affairs, 1989–94.
Bradman Weerakoon, advisor on foreign affairs to the president, 1989–94.
There have been occasional interviews with other officials involved in these negotiations, including
W. M. P. B. Menikdiwela, secretary to President J. R. Jayewardene, 1978–88.
K. H. J. Wijayadasa, secretary to President R. Premadasa, 1989–93.
Several military officers were interviewed but I must protect their identities. One such officer can be mentioned, the late Major General Vijaya Wimalaratne, commanding officer, Jaffna.

India

Romesh Bhandari, foreign secretary, 1985–86.
Rajiv Gandhi, prime minister, 1984–89.
I. K. Gujral, minister of external affairs, 1989–91.
S. K. Singh, foreign secretary, 1989–91.
A. P. Venkateswaran, foreign secretary, 1985–87.
There were short discussions with
K. Shankar Bajpai.
G. Parathasarathy.
Among the Indian journalists interviewed were Pran Chopra; M. Ram, deputy editor of the *Hindu* and editor of *Frontline;* and the late Dilip Mukherjee. I had a brief discussion with Kuldip Nayar.

III. Bibliographies on Sri Lanka

de Silva, Daya, and C. R. de Silva. *Sri Lanka (Ceylon) Since Independence (1948–1976).* Hamburg: Institute of Asian Affairs, 1978.
———. *Sri Lanka Since Independence: A Reference Guide to the Literature.* New Delhi: Navrang, 1992.
Goonetileke, H. A. I. *A Bibliography of Ceylon: A Systematic Guide to the Literature on the Land, People, History and Culture Published in the Western Languages from the Sixteenth Century to the Present Day.* 5 vols. Zug, Switzerland: Inter Documentation Co., 1970–83.

IV. Books and Monographs on Sri Lanka—History and Politics

Alles, A. C. *Insurgency 1971.* Colombo: Colombo Apothecaries Co., 1976.
———. *The JVP 1969–1989.* Colombo: Lake House, 1989.
Bond, George. *The Buddhist Revival in Sri Lanka: The Religious Tradition, Reinterpretation and Response.* Columbia: University of South Carolina Press, 1988.
Chandraprema, C. A. *Sri Lanka, the Years of Terror: The JVP Insurrection, 1987–1989.* Colombo: Lake House, 1991.
Committee for Rational Development. *Sri Lanka: The Ethnic Conflict, Myths, Realities and Perspectives.* New Delhi: Navrang, 1983.
Coomaraswamy, Radhika. *Sri Lanka: The Crisis of the Anglo-American Constitutional Traditions in a Developing Society.* New Delhi: Vikas, 1984.

Cooray, J. A. L. *Constitutional and Administrative Law of Sri Lanka (Ceylon): A Commentary on the Constitution and the Law of Public Administration of Sri Lanka.* Colombo: Hansa, 1973.

de Silva, K. M. *A History of Sri Lanka.* London: C. Hurst, 1981.

———. *Managing Ethnic Tensions in Multi-Ethnic Societies: Sri Lanka, 1880–1985.* Lanham, Md.: University Press of America, 1986.

——— ed. *History of Ceylon,* Vol. 3. Peradeniya: University of Ceylon Press Board, 1973.

———, ed. *Sri Lanka: A Survey.* London: C. Hurst, 1977.

———, ed. *Universal Franchise, 1931–1981: The Sri Lankan Experience.* Colombo: Department of Information, 1981.

———, ed. *Sri Lanka: The Problems of Governance.* New Delhi: Konark, 1993.

Dewaraja, Lorna S. *The Kandyan Kingdom of Ceylon, 1707–1782.* Rev. ed. Colombo: Lake House, 1992.

Dharmadasa, K. N. O. *Language, Religion and Ethnic Assertiveness: The Growth of Sinhalese Nationalism in Sri Lanka.* Ann Arbor: University of Michigan Press, 1992.

Dissayanake, T. D. S. A. *The Agony of Sri Lanka: An In-depth Account of the Racial Riots of July 1983.* Colombo: Swastika, 1983.

———. *The Dilemma of Sri Lanka.* Colombo: Swastika, 1993.

Fernando, Tissa, and Robert N. Kearney, eds. *Modern Sri Lanka: A Society in Transition.* Syracuse, N.Y.: Maxwell School of Citizenship and Public Affairs, Syracuse University, 1979.

Gunaratna, Rohan. *Sri Lanka, A Lost Revolution? The Inside Story of the JVP.* Colombo: Institute of Fundamental Studies, 1990.

———. *Indian Intervention in Sri Lanka: The Role of India's Intelligence Agencies.* Colombo: South Asian Network on Conflict Research, 1993.

Hulugalle, H. A. J. *The Life and Times of Don Stephen Senanayake.* Colombo: Gunasena, 1975.

Jayanntha, Dilesh. *Electoral Allegiance in Sri Lanka.* Cambridge: Cambridge University Press, 1992.

Jayawardena, Visakha Kumari. *The Rise of the Labor Movement in Ceylon.* Durham, N.C.: Duke University Press, 1972.

———. *Ethnic and Class Conflicts in Sri Lanka.* Dehiwala, Colombo: Centre for Social Analysis, 1986.

Jayewardene, J. R. *Men and Memories: Autobiographical Recollections and Reflections.* New Delhi: Vikas, 1992.

Jeffries, Sir Charles. *Ceylon: The Path to Independence.* London: Pall Mall Press, 1962.

Jennings, Sir Ivor. *The Economy of Ceylon.* 2nd ed. London: Oxford University Press, 1951.

Jennings, Sir Ivor, and H. W. Tambiah. *The Dominion of Ceylon.* London: Stevens, 1952.

———. *The Constitution of Ceylon.* 3rd ed. London: Oxford University Press, 1953.

Jiggins, Janice. *Caste and Family in the Politics of the Sinhalese, 1947–1976.* Cambridge: Cambridge University Press, 1979.

Jupp, James. *Sri Lanka, Third World Democracy.* London: Frank Cass, 1978.

Kapferer, Bruce. *Legends of People, Myths of State: Violence, Intolerance and Political Culture in Sri Lanka and Australia.* Washington, D.C.: Smithsonian Institution Press, 1988.

Kearney, Robert N. *Communalism and Language in the Politics of Ceylon.* Durham, N.C.: Duke University Press, 1967.

———. *Trade Unions and Politics in Ceylon.* Berkeley: University of California Press, 1971.

———. *The Politics of Ceylon (Sri Lanka).* Ithaca, N.Y.: Cornell University Press, 1973.

Kemper, Steven. *The Presence of the Past: Chronicles, Politics and Culture in Sinhala Life.* Ithaca, N.Y.: Cornell University Press, 1991.

Kodikara, Shelton U. *Foreign Policy of Sri Lanka: A Third World Perspective.* 2nd ed. New Delhi: Chanakya, 1992.

———. *Indo-Ceylon Relations Since Independence.* Colombo: Ceylon Institute of World Affairs, 1965.

Leitan, G. R. Tressie. *Local Government and Decentralized Administration in Sri Lanka.* Colombo: Lake House, 1979.

Manogaran, Chelvadurai. *Ethnic Conflict and Reconciliation in Sri Lanka.* Honolulu: University of Hawaii Press, 1987.

Manor, James. *The Expedient Utopian: Bandaranaike and Ceylon.* Cambridge: Cambridge University Press, 1989.

———, ed. *Sri Lanka in Change and Crisis.* London: Croom Helm, 1984.

Marga Institute. *Inter-Racial Equity and National Unity in Sri Lanka.* Colombo: Marga Institute, 1984.

Mendis, Garrett C. *Ceylon Under the British.* Colombo: Colombo Apothecaries Co., 1952.

Moore, Mick. *The State and Peasant Politics in Sri Lanka.* Cambridge: Cambridge University Press, 1985.

Namasivayam, S. *The Legislatures of Ceylon, 1928–1948.* London: Faber, 1951.

Nyrop, Richard, et al., eds. *An Area Handbook for Ceylon.* Washington, D.C.: U. S. Government Printing Office, 1974.

Pfaffenberger, Bryan. *Caste in Tamil Culture: The Religious Foundations of Sudra Domination in Tamil Sri Lanka.* Syracuse, N.Y.: Maxwell School of Citizenship and Public Affairs, Syracuse University, 1982.

Phadnis, Urmila. *Religion and Politics in Sri Lanka.* New Delhi: Manohar, 1976.

Ponnambalam, Satchi. *Sri Lanka: National Conflict and the Tamil Liberation Struggle.* London: Zed Books, 1983.

Ratnatunga, Sinha. *The Politics of Terrorism: The Sri Lanka Experience.* Canberra: International Fellowship for Social and Economic Development, 1988.

Roberts, Michael. *Caste Conflict and Elite Formation: The Rise of a Karava Elite in Sri Lanka, 1500–1931.* Cambridge: Cambridge University Press, 1982.

———, ed. *Collective Identities, Nationalisms, and Protest in Modern Sri Lanka.* Colombo: Marga Institute, 1978.

———, ed. *Documents of the Ceylon National Congress and Nationalist Politics in Ceylon, 1929–1950.* 4 vols. Colombo: Department of National Archives, 1978.

Ross, Russell R., and Andrea Matles Savada, eds. *Sri Lanka: A Country Study.* U.S. Library of Congress, Federal Research Division. Washington, D. C.: U.S. Government Printing Office, 1991.

Russell, Jane. *Communal Politics Under the Donoughmore Constitution, 1931–1947.* Colombo: Tisara Press, 1983.

Ryan, Bruce. *Caste in Modern Ceylon.* New Brunswick, N.J.: Rutgers University Press, 1953.

Singer, Marshall R. *The Emerging Elite: A Study of Political Leadership in Ceylon.* Cambridge, Mass.: MIT Press, 1964.

Smith, Donald E., ed. *South Asian Politics and Religion.* Princeton, N.J.: Princeton University Press, 1966.

Snodgrass, D. R. *Ceylon: An Export Economy in Transition.* Homewood, Ill.: R. D. Irwin, 1966.

Spencer, Jonathan, ed. *Sri Lanka: History and the Roots of Conflict.* London: Routledge, 1990.

Tambiah, Stanley J. *Sri Lanka: Ethnic Fratricide and the Dismantling of Democracy.* Chicago: University of Chicago Press, 1986.

———. *Buddhism Betrayed? Religion, Politics and Violence in Sri Lanka.* Chicago: University of Chicago Press, 1992.

Vijayavardhana, D. C. *The Revolt in the Temple.* Colombo: Sinha Publications, 1953.

Wilson, A. Jeyaratnam. *Electoral Politics in an Emergent State: The Ceylon General Elections of May 1970.* Cambridge: Cambridge University Press, 1975.

———. *Politics in Sri Lanka, 1947–1979.* London: Macmillan, 1979.

———. *The Gaullist System in Asia: The Constitution of Sri Lanka (1978).* London: Macmillan, 1980.

———. *The Break-up of Sri Lanka: The Sinhalese-Tamil Conflict.* Honolulu: University of Hawaii Press, 1988.

———. *S J V Chelvanayakam and the Crisis of Sri Lankan Tamil Nationalism, 1947–1977.* London: C. Hurst, 1994.

Wiswa Warnapala, W. A. *Local Politics in Sri Lanka: An Analysis of the Local Government Election of May 1991.* New Delhi: South Asian Publishers, 1993.

———. *The Sri Lankan Political Scene.* New Delhi: Navrang, 1993.

Wiswa Warnapala, W. A., and L. Dias Hewagama. *Recent Politics in Sri Lanka: The Presidential Election and the Referendum of 1982.* New Delhi: Navrang, 1983.

Woodward, Calvin. *The Growth of a Party System in Ceylon.* Providence, R.I.: Brown University Press, 1969.

Wriggins, W. Howard. *Ceylon: Dilemmas of a New Nation.* Princeton, N. J.: Princeton University Press, 1960.

V. Articles and Pamphlets on Sri Lanka

Amunugama, Sarath. "Buddhaputra and Bhumiputra? Dilemma of Modern Sinhala Buddhist Monks in Relation to Ethnic and Political Conflict." *Religion* 21 (1991): 115–39.

de Silva, C. R. "The Constitution of the Second Republic of Sri Lanka (1978) and Its Significance." *Journal of Commonwealth and Comparative Politics* 17, no. 2 (1978): 192–209.

de Silva, K. M. "Buddhist Revivalism, Nationalism and Politics in Modern Sri Lanka." In *Fundamentalism, Revivalists and Violence in South Asia*, ed. James W. Bjorkman, 107–58. New Delhi: Manohar, 1988.

Fernando, Tissa. "Elite Politics in the New States: The Case of Post-Independence Sri Lanka." *Pacific Affairs* 46, no. 3 (1973): 361–83.

Gunatilleke, Godfrey, Neelan Tiruchelvam, and Radhika Coomaraswamy. "Violence and Development in Sri Lanka: Conceptual Issues." In *Ethical Dilemmas of Development in Asia*, ed. Godfrey Gunatilleke, Neelan Tiruchelvam, and Radhika Coomaraswamy, 129–78. Lexington, Mass.: D. C. Heath, 1983.

Halliday, Fred. "The Ceylonese Insurrection." Reprinted in *Explosion in a Subcontinent: India, Pakistan, Bangladesh, Ceylon*, ed. Robin Blackburn, 151–220. First published in *New Left Review* (October 1971). Harmondsworth: Penguin, 1975.

Kearney, Robert N. "Sinhalese Nationalism and Social Conflict in Ceylon." *Pacific Affairs* 37 (1964): 125–36.

———. "Ethnic Conflict and the Tamil Separatist Movement in Sri Lanka." *Asian Survey* 25, no. 9 (1984): 898–917.

Kearney, Robert N., and Janice Jiggins. "The Ceylon Insurrection of 1971." *Journal of Commonwealth and Comparative Politics* 13, no. 1 (1972): 40–64.

Obeyesekere, Gananath. "Religious Symbolism and Political Change in Ceylon." *Modern Ceylon Studies* 1, no. 1 (1970): 43–63.

———. "The Sinhalese-Buddhist Identity." In *Ethnic Identity: Cultural Continuities and Change*, ed. George De Vos and Lola Romanucci-Ross. Palo Alto, Calif.: Mayfield, 1976.

———. "The Origins and Institutionalisation of Political Violence." In *Sri Lanka in Change and Crisis*, ed. James Manor, 153–74. London: Croom Helm, 1984.

Perinbanayagam, R. S., and Maya Chadda. "Strategy of Internal Relations: An Examination of the Conflict in Ceylon." In *Nationalism and the Crises of Ethnic Minorities in Asia*, ed. Tai S. Kong, 132–38. Westport, Conn.: Greenwood Press, 1979.

Pfaffenberger, Bryan. "The Cultural Dimension of Tamil Separatism in Sri Lanka." *Asian Survey* 21, no. 12 (1980): 1145–57.

Roberts, Michael. "Elites, Nationalism, and the Nationalist Movement in Ceylon." Introduction to *Documents of the Ceylon National Congress*. Vol. 1, ed. Michael Roberts, xxix–ccxxii. Colombo: Department of National Archives, 1978.

———. "Ethnic Conflict in Sri Lanka and Sinhalese Perspectives: Barriers to Accommodation." *Modern Asian Studies* 7, no. 3 (1978): 353–76.

Russell, Jane. "Sri Lanka's Election Turning Point." (The General Election of 1977). *Journal of Commonwealth and Comparative Politics* 16, no. 1 (1978): 79–97.

Samarasinghe, S. W. R. de A. "Ethnic Representation in Central Government Employment and Sinhala-Tamil Relations in Sri Lanka, 1948–81." In *From Independence to Statehood: Managing Ethnic Conflict in Six African and Asian States*, ed. Robert B. Goldman and A. Jeyaratnam Wilson, 86–108. London: Pinter, 1984.

Samaraweera, Vijaya. "Sri Lanka's 1977 General Election: The Resurgence of the UNP." *Asian Survey* 18, no. 12 (1977): 1195–1206.

Schwarz, Walter. *The Tamils of Sri Lanka*. Minority Rights Group Report 25. Rev. ed. London: Minority Rights Group, 1979.

Smith, Donald E. "The Political Monks and Monastic Reform." In *South Asian Politics and Religion*, ed. Donald E. Smith, 489–501. Princeton, N.J.: Princeton University Press, 1965.

———. "The Sinhalese-Buddhist Revolution." In *South Asian Politics and Religion*, ed. Donald E. Smith, 453–88. Princeton, N.J.: Princeton University Press, 1965.

Stiratt, R. L. "The Riots and the Roman Catholic Church in Historical Perspective." In *Sri Lanka in Change and Crisis*, ed. James Manor, 196–213. London: Croom Helm, 1984.

Wilson, A. Jeyaratnam. "The Tamil Federal Party in Ceylon Politics," *The Journal of Commonwealth Political Studies* 4, no. 2 (1966): 117–39.

———. "Oppositional Politics in Ceylon 1948–1968." *Government and Opposition* 4, no. 1 (1970): 54–69.

Wriggins, W. Howard. "Impediments to Unity in New Nations: The Case of Ceylon." *American Political Science Review* 55, no. 2 (1961): 313–21.

VI. Indo–Sri Lankan Peace Accord, Select Bibliography

Bhaduri, Shankar, and Afsir Karim. *The Sri Lankan Crisis*. Lancer Paper 1. New Delhi: Lancer International, 1990.

Crossette, Barbara. "Hatreds, Human Rights and the News: What We Ignore." *SAIS Review* (Winter–Spring 1993): 1–11.

de Silva, H. L. "The Indo–Sri Lanka Agreement (1987) in the Perspective of Inter-State Relations." *Ethnic Studies Report* 10, no. 2 (July 1992): 10–17.

de Silva, K. M. "Indo–Sri Lanka Relations 1975–89: A Study in the Internationalization of Ethnic Conflict." In *Internationalisation of Ethnic Conflict*, ed. K. M. de Silva and Ronald J. May, 76–106. London: Pinter, 1991.

———. "The Prelude to the Indo–Sri Lanka Accord of July 1987." *Ethnic Studies Report* 10, no. 1 (January 1992): 1–16.

———. "The Making of the Indo–Sri Lanka Accord: The Final Phase— June–July 1987." In *Peace Accords and Ethnic Conflict*, ed. K. M. de Silva and S. W. R. de A. Samarasinghe, 112–55. London: Pinter, 1993.

Fernando, Tyronne. *100 Days in Sri Lanka '87*. Colombo: The Author, 1988.

Gunaratna, Rohan. *War and Peace in Sri Lanka, with a Post-Accord Report from Jaffna*. Colombo: Institute of Fundamental Studies, 1987.

Gunasekera, S. L. *Indo-Lanka Accord: An Analysis*. Colombo: Mahajana Publications, nd.

Hoole, Rajan, et al. *The Broken Palmyra: The Tamil Crisis in Sri Lanka— An Inside Account*. Rev. ed. Claremont, Calif.: Sri Lanka Studies Institute, 1990.

Jayawardena, Kumari. "Ethnic Conflict in Sri Lanka and Regional Security." In *Asia: Militarization and Regional Conflict*, ed. Yoshikazu Sakamoto. Tokyo: United Nations University; London: Zed Books, 1988.

Jayaweera, Neville. *Sri Lanka: Towards a Multi-Ethnic Democracy?* (Report of a fact-finding mission). Oslo: International Peace Research Institute, 1990.

Kadian, Rajesh. *India's Sri Lanka Fiasco: Peace Keepers at War*. New Delhi: Vision Books, 1990.

Kodikara, Shelton U., ed. *Indo–Sri Lanka Agreement of July 1987*. Colombo: University of Colombo, 1989.

———. *External Compulsions of South Asian Politics*. New Delhi: Sage, 1993.

Merchant, Minhaz. *Rajiv Gandhi, The End of a Dream*. New Delhi: Penguin, 1991.

Mohandas, K. *M G R: The Man and the Myth*. Bangalore: Panther, 1992.

Muni, S. D. *Pangs of Proximity: India and Sri Lanka's Ethnic Crisis*. Oslo: PRIO; Newbury Park, Calif.: Sage, 1993.

———. "Indo–Sri Lankan Relations and Sri Lanka's Ethnic Conflict." In *Internationalisation of Ethnic Conflict*, ed. K. M. de Silva and Ronald J. Mays, 115–24. London: Pinter, 1991.

O'Ballance, Edgar. *The Cyanide War: Tamil Insurrection in Sri Lanka 1973–88.* London: Brassey's, 1989.

Premdas, Ralph R., and S. W. R. de A. Samarasinghe. "Sri Lanka's Ethnic Conflict: The Indo–Lanka Peace Accord." *Asian Survey* 28, no. 6 (June 1987): 676–90.

Ram, Moham. *Sri Lanka: The Fractured Island.* New Delhi: Penguin, 1989.

Ratnatunga, Sinha. *Politics of Terrorism: The Sri Lanka Experience.* Canberra: International Fellowship for Social and Economic Development, 1988.

Roberts, Michael. "Nationalism, the Past and the Present: The Case of Sri Lanka." *Ethnic and Racial Studies* 16, no. 1 (January 1993): 133–66.

Rupesinghe, Kumar. "The Sri Lanka Agreement of 1987 and Conflict Resolution in Sri Lanka." *South Asian Journal* 2, no. 3 (January–March 1989): 271–94.

Samarasinghe, S. W. R. de A. "The Dynamics of Separatism: The Case of Sri Lanka." In *Secessionist Movements in Comparative Perspective*, ed. Ralph R. Premdas, S. W. R. de A Samarasinghe, and Alan B. Anderson. 48–70. London: Pinter, 1990.

Samarasinghe, S. W. R. de A. and Kamala Liyanage. "Friends and Foes of the Indo–Sri Lanka Accord." In *Peace Accords and Ethnic Conflict*, ed. K. M. de Silva and S. W. R. de A. Samarasinghe, 156–72. London: Pinter, 1993.

Sardeshpande, S. C. *Assignment Jaffna.* New Delhi: Lancer, 1992.

Seevaratnam, N., ed. *The Tamil National Question and the Indo–Sri Lanka Accord.* New Delhi: Konark, 1989.

Sen Gupta, Bhabani. *Rajiv Gandhi: A Political Study.* New Delhi: Konark, 1989.

Singh, Depinder. *The IPKF in Sri Lanka.* New Delhi: Trishul, 1992.

Suriyanarayana, P. S. *The Peace Trap: An Indo–Sri Lankan Political Crisis.* New Delhi: Affiliated East-West Press, 1988.

Vanniasingham, Somasundaram. *Sri Lanka: The Conflict Within.* New Delhi: Lancer, 1988.

Venkateswar, Rao P. "Foreign Involvement in Sri Lanka." *Round Table* 309 (1989): 88–100.

Weerakoon, Bradman. *Premadasa of Sri Lanka: A Political Biography.* New Delhi: Vikas, 1992.

Wiswa Warnapala, W. A. *Ethnic Strife and Politics in Sri Lanka: An Investigation into Demands and Responses.* New Delhi: Navrang, 1994.

VII. General Works on Ethnicity and Politics

Alter, Peter. *Nationalism.* London: Edward Arnold, 1989.

Anderson, Benedict. *Imagined Communities: Reflections on the Origin and Spread of Nationalism.* Rev. ed. London: Verso, 1991.

Assefa, Hizkias. *Mediation of Civil Wars: Approaches and Strategies— The Sudan Conflict.* Boulder, Colo.: Westview, 1987.

Ayoob, Mohammed. *India and South East Asia: Indian Perspectives and Policies.* London: Routledge, 1990.

Azar, Edward E. *The Management of Protracted Social Conflict: Theory and Cases.* Aldershot: Dartmouth, 1990.

Azar, Edward E., and John W. Burton. *International Conflict Resolution, Theory and Practice.* Boulder, Colo.: L. Rienner; Sussex: Wheatsheaf, 1986.

Banton, Michael P. *Racial and Ethnic Competition.* Cambridge: Cambridge University Press, 1983.

Barnett, Marguerite R. *Politics of Cultural Nationalism in South India.* Princeton, N.J.: Princeton University Press, 1976.

Barth, Fredrik, ed. *Ethnic Groups and Boundaries: The Social Organization of Culture Difference.* London: Allen and Unwin, 1969.

Beazley, Kim C., and Ian Clark. *The Politics of Intrusion: The Superpowers and the Indian Ocean.* Sydney: Alternative Publishing, 1979.

Bjorkman, James W., ed. *Fundamentalism, Revivalists, and Violence in South Asia.* New Delhi: Manohar, 1988.

Brass, Paul B., ed. *Ethnic Groups and the State.* Totowa, N.J.: Barnes and Noble, 1985.

Brecher, Michael. *Crises in World Politics: Theory and Reality.* Oxford: Pergamon Press, 1993.

Breuilly, John. *Nationalism and the State.* Manchester: Manchester University Press, 1982.

Brown, Sherlyn J., and Kimber M. Schraub, eds. *Resolving Third World Conflict: Challenges for a New Era.* Washington, D. C.: United States Institute of Peace, 1992.

Burton, John W. *Resolving Deep-Rooted Conflict: A Handbook*. Lanham, Md.: University Press of America, 1987.

Chatterjee, Partha. *Nationalist Thought and the Colonial World: A Derivative Discourse*. London: Zed Books, 1991.

————. *The Nation and Its Fragments: Colonial and Postcolonial Histories*. Princeton, N.J.: Princeton University Press, 1993.

Cohen, Stephen Philip, ed. *The Security of South Asia: American and Asian Perspectives*. New Delhi: Vistar; Urbana: University of Illinois Press, 1987.

Connor, Walker. *The National Question in Marxist Leninist Theory and Strategy*. Princeton, N.J.: Princeton University Press, 1984.

————. *Ethnonationalism: The Quest for Understanding*. Princeton, N.J.: Princeton University Press, 1994.

de Silva, K. M., et al., eds. *Ethnic Conflict in Buddhist Societies: Sri Lanka, Thailand, Burma*. London: Pinter, 1988.

de Silva, K. M., and Ronald J. May, eds. *Internationalisation of Ethnic Conflict*. London: Pinter, 1991.

de Silva, K. M., and S. W. R. de A. Samarasinghe, eds. *Ethnic Peace Accords and Ethnic Conflicts*. London: Pinter, 1993.

Deutsch, Karl W. *Nationalism and Social Communication: An Inquiry into the Foundations of Nationality*. Cambridge, Mass.: Harvard University Press, 1966.

————. *Nationalism and Its Alternatives*. New York: Knopf, 1969.

Deutsch, Morton. *The Resolution of Conflict*. New Haven, Conn.: Yale University Press, 1973.

de Vos, George, and Lola Romanucci-Ross, eds. *Ethnic Identity: Cultural Continuities and Change*. Palo Alto, Calif.: Mayfield, 1976.

Dowdy, William L., and Russell B. Trood, eds. *The Indian Ocean: Perspectives on a Strategic Arena*. Durham, N. C.: Duke University Press, 1985.

Edwards, John R. *Language, Society and Identity*. Oxford: Basil Blackwell, 1985.

Emerson, Rupert. *From Empire to Nation: The Rise to Self-Assertion of Asian and African Peoples*. Cambridge, Mass.: Harvard University Press, 1960.

Enloe, Cynthia H. *Ethnic Conflict and Political Development*. Boston: Little Brown, 1973.

————. *Ethnic Soldiers: State Security in Divided Societies*. Harmondsworth: Penguin, 1980.

Fisher, Glen. *International Negotiation: A Cross-Culture Perspective.* Chicago: Intercultural, 1980.

Fisher, Roger, and William Ury. *Getting to Yes: Negotiating Agreement Without Giving In.* New York: Houghton Mifflin, 1981.

Fox, Annette Baker. *The Power of Small States: Diplomacy in World War II.* Chicago: University of Chicago Press, 1959.

Gellner, Ernest. *Nations and Nationalism.* Oxford: Basil Blackwell, 1983.

Ghosh, Partha S. *Cooperation and Conflict in South Asia.* New Delhi: Manohar, 1989.

Glazer, Nathan, and Daniel P. Moynihan, eds. *Ethnicity: Theory and Experience.* Cambridge, Mass.: Harvard University Press, 1975.

Gupte, Pranay. *Mother India: A Political Biography of Indira Gandhi.* New York: Scribner, 1992.

Gurr, Ted Robert. *Why Men Rebel.* Princeton, N. J.: Princeton University Press, 1971.

Hafiz, M. Abdul, and Abdur Rob Khan, eds. *The Security of Small States.* Dhaka: University Press, 1987.

Heraclides, Alexis. *The Self-Determination of Minorities in International Politics.* London: Frank Cass, 1991.

Hobsbawm, Eric J. *Nations and Nationalism Since 1780: Programme, Myth, Reality.* Rev. ed. Cambridge: Cambridge University Press, 1993.

Horowitz, Donald L. *Ethnic Groups in Conflict.* Berkeley: University of California Press, 1985.

Husain, Syed Anwar. *Superpowers and Security in the Indian Ocean: A South Asian Perspective.* Dhaka: Academic Publishers, 1992.

Ikle, Fred Charles. *How Nations Negotiate.* New York: Harper and Row, 1964.

———. *Every War Must End.* New York: Columbia University Press, 1971.

Irschick, Eugene F. *Politics and Social Conflict in South India: The Non-Brahman Movement and Tamil Separatism.* Berkeley: University of California Press, 1969.

———. *Tamil Revivalism in the 1930s.* Madras: Cre-A, 1986.

Isaacs, Harold R. *Idols of the Tribe: Group Identity and Political Change.* New York: Harper and Row, 1976.

Jayakar, Pupul. *Indira Gandhi: A Biography.* New Delhi: Viking, 1992.

Kang, Tai S., ed. *Nationalism and the Crisis of Ethnic Minorities in Asia.* Westport, Conn.: Greenwood Press, 1979.

Kedourie, Elie. *Nationalism.* London: Hutchinson, 1966.

————, ed. *Nationalism in Asia and Africa.* London: Wiedenfeld and Nicholson, 1971.

Kellas, James G. *The Politics of Nationalism and Ethnicity.* London: Macmillan, 1991.

Kuper, Leo. *Race, Class and Power: Ideology and Revolutionary Change in Plural Societies.* London: Duckworth, 1974.

Levite, Ariel E., Bruce W. Jentleson, and Larry Berman, eds. *Foreign Military Intervention: The Dynamics of Protracted Conflict.* New York: Columbia University Press, 1992.

Lijphart, Arend. *Democracy in Plural Societies: A Comparative Exploration.* New Haven, Conn.: Yale University Press, 1977.

Little, Richard. *Intervention: External Involvement in Civil Wars.* Totowa, N.J.: Rowman and Littlefield, 1975.

Malhotra, Inder. *Indira Gandhi: A Personal and Political Biography.* London: Hodder and Stoughton, 1989.

Mansingh, Surjith. *India's Search for Power: Indira Gandhi's Foreign Policy, 1966–1982.* New Delhi: Sage, 1984.

Mitchell, C. R., *Peacemaking and the Consultant's Role.* London: Gower, 1981.

Mitchell, C. R. and K. Webb, eds. *New Approaches to International Mediation.* Westport, Conn.: Greenwood, 1988.

Montville, Joseph V., ed. *Conflict and Peacemaking in Multiethnic Societies.* Lexington, Mass.: Lexington Books, 1991.

Moraes, Dom. *Mrs. Gandhi.* London: Jonathan Cape, 1980.

Moyall, J. *Nationalism and International Society.* Cambridge: Cambridge University Press, 1990.

Moynihan, Daniel P. *Pandaemonium: Ethnicity in International Politics.* New York: Oxford University Press, 1993.

Nash, Manning. *The Cauldron of Ethnicity in the Modern World.* Chicago: University of Chicago Press, 1989.

Nordlinger, Eric A. *Conflict Regulation in Divided Societies.* Cambridge, Mass.: Cambridge Center for International Affairs of Harvard University, 1972.

Nugent, Nicholas. *Rajiv Gandhi: Son of a Dynasty.* London: BBC Books, 1990.

Patterson, Orlando: *Ethnic Chauvinism: The Reactionary Impulse.* New York: Stein and Day, 1977.

Phadnis, Urmila. *Ethnicity and Nation Building in South Asia.* New Delhi: Sage, 1990.

Pillar, Paul R. *Negotiation of Peace: War Termination as a Bargaining Process.* Princeton, N.J.: Princeton University Press, 1983.

Porter, Jack Nissan, and T. Taplin. *Conflict and Conflict Resolution: A Historical Bibliography.* New York: Garland, 1978.

Premdas, Ralph R., S. W. R. de A. Samarasinghe, and Alan B. Anderson, eds. *Secessionist Movements in Comparative Perspective.* London: Pinter, 1990.

Princen, Thomas. *Intermediaries in International Conflict.* Princeton, N.J.: Princeton University Press, 1992.

Rigo Sureda, A. *The Evolution of the Right to Self Determination.* Leiden: Sijthoff, 1973.

Rizvi, Hasan Askari. *Pakistan and the Geostrategic Environment: A Study of Foreign Policy.* New York: St. Martin's Press, 1993.

Ronen, Dov. *The Quest for Self-Determination.* New Haven, Conn.: Yale University Press, 1979.

Rosenau, James N., ed. *International Aspects of Civil Strife.* Princeton, N.J.: Princeton University Press, 1964.

Ross, Marc Howard. *The Culture of Conflict: Interests, Interpretations, and Disputing in Comparative Perspective.* New Haven, Conn.: Yale University Press, 1993.

Rothschild, Joseph. *Ethnopolitics: A Conceptual Framework.* New York: Columbia University Press, 1981.

Rudolph, Lloyd I., and Susan Hoeber Rudolph. *In Pursuit of Lakshmi: The Political Economy of the Indian State.* Chicago: University of Chicago Press, 1987.

Rupesinghe, Kumar, ed. *Ethnic Conflict and Human Rights.* Oslo: United Nations University, 1988.

Ryan, Stephen. *Ethnic Conflict and International Relations.* Aldershot: Dartmouth, 1990.

Samarasinghe, S. W. R. de A., and Reed Coughlan, eds. *Economic Dimensions of Ethnic Conflict.* London: Pinter, 1991.

Schaeffer, Robert. *Warpaths: The Politics of Partition.* New York: Hill and Wang, 1990.

Seton-Watson, Hugh. *Nations and States: An Enquiry into the Origins of Nations and the Politics of Nationalism.* Boulder, Colo.: Westview, 1977.

Shafer, Boyd C. *The Faces of Nationalism: New Realities and Old Myths.* New York: Harcourt Brace Jovanovich, 1972.

Smith, Anthony D. *The Ethnic Revival in the Modern World.* New York: Cambridge University Press, 1981.

———. *State and Nation in the Third World: The Western State and African Nationalism.* Brighton, Sussex: Wheatsheaf, 1983.

———. *Theories of Nationalism.* 2nd ed. New York: Holmes and Meier, 1983.

———. *The Ethnic Origin of Nations.* Oxford: Basil Blackwell, 1987.

———. *National Identity.* Harmondsworth: Penguin, 1991.

Smith, C. *India's Ad hoc Arsenal: Direction or Drift in Defence Policy.* Oxford: Oxford University Press, 1994.

Stavenhagen, Rodolfo. *The Ethnic Question: Conflicts, Development, and Human Rights.* Tokyo: United Nations University, 1990.

Stein, Janice Gross, ed. *Getting to the Table: The Processes of International Prenegotiation.* Baltimore: Johns Hopkins University Press, 1989.

Stone, John. *Racial Conflict in Contemporary Society.* Cambridge, Mass.: Harvard University Press, 1985.

Suhrke, Astri, and Lela Garner Noble, eds. *Ethnic Conflict in International Relations.* New York: Praeger, 1977.

Thomas, Raju G. C. *The Defence of India: A Budgetary Perspective of Strategy and Politics.* New Delhi: Macmillan, 1978.

Tinker, Hugh. *A New System of Slavery: The Export of Indian Labour Overseas, 1830–1920.* London: Oxford University Press for the Institute of Race Relations, 1974.

———. *Separate and Unequal: India and the Indians in the British Commonwealth, 1920–1950.* London: C. Hurst, 1976.

———. *The Banyan Tree: Overseas Emigrants from India, Pakistan and Bangladesh.* Oxford: Oxford University Press, 1977.

Touval, Saadia. *The Peace Brokers.* Princeton, N.J.: Princeton University Press, 1982.

Touval, Saadia, and I. William Zartman, eds. *International Mediation in Theory and Practice.* Boulder, Colo.: Westview, 1989.

van den Berghe, Pierre L. *The Ethnic Phenomenon.* New York: Elsevier, 1991.

van Dyke, Vernon. *Human Rights, Ethnicity, and Discrimination.* Westport, Conn.: Greenwood, 1985.

Vincent, R. J. *Nonintervention and International Order.* Princeton, N.J.: Princeton University Press, 1974.

Vital, David. *The Inequality of States: A Study of Small Powers in International Politics.* New York: Oxford University Press, 1967.

———. *The Survival of Small States: Status in Small Power/Great Power Conflict.* London: Oxford University Press, 1971.

Weiner, Myron. *Sons of the Soil: Migration and Ethnic Conflict in India.* Princeton, N.J.: Princeton University Press, 1978.

Wilson, A. Jeyaratnam, and Dennis Dalton, eds. *The States of South Asia: The Problems of National Integration.* New Delhi: Vikas, 1982.

Wriggins, W. Howard, ed. *Dynamics of Regional Politics: Four Systems on the Indian Ocean Rim.* New York: Columbia University Press, 1992.

Young, Crawford. *The Politics of Cultural Pluralism.* Madison: University of Wisconsin Press, 1976.

Young, Oran R. *The Intermediaries: Third Parties in International Crises.* Princeton, N.J.: Princeton University Press, 1967.

Zartman, I. William. *Ripe for Resolution: Conflict and Intervention in Africa.* 2nd ed. New York: Oxford University Press, 1989.

Zartman, I. William, and Maureen R. Berman. *The Practical Negotiator.* New Haven, Conn.: Yale University Press, 1982.

VIII. Articles and Pamphlets—General

Anderson, Walter K., and Leo Rose. "Superpowers in the Indian Ocean: The Goals and Objectives." In *The Indian Ocean as a Zone of Peace.* International Peace Academy Report 24. Dordrecht: Martinus Nijhoff, 1986.

Arthur, P. "The Anglo-Irish Agreement: Events of 1985–86." *Irish Political Studies* 2 (1987): 99–107.

Ayoob, Mohammed. "The Quest for Autonomy: Ideologies in the Indian Ocean Region." In *The Indian Ocean: Perspectives on a Strategic Arena,* ed. William L. Dowdy and Russell B. Trood. Durham, N.C.: Duke University Press, 1985.

———. "The Primacy of the Political: South Asian Regional Cooperation in Comparative Perspective." *Asian Survey* 25, no. 4 (April 1985): 443–57.

———. "India in South Asia: The Quest for Regional Predominance." *World Policy Journal* 7, no. 1 (1989): 107–33.

Banks, Michael, and C. R. Mitchell. "Conflict Theory, Peace Research, and the Analyses of Communal Conflicts." *Millennium: Journal of International Studies* 3, no. 3 (1974–75): 252–67.

Barry, Brian, and Harry Beran. "A Liberal Theory of Secession." *Political Studies* 33, no. 4 (1984): 596–602.

Birch, A. H. "Minority Nationalist Movements and Theories of Political Integration." *World Politics* 33 (1978): 325–44.

Burton, John W. "The Resolution of Conflict." *International Studies Quarterly* 16, no. 1 (1972): 5–30.

Connor, Walker. "Ethnology and the Peace of South Asia." *World Politics* 22, no. 1 (1969): 51–86.

———. "Nation Building or Nation Destroying?" *World Politics* 24, no. 3 (1972): 318–55.

———. "The Politics of Ethnonationalism." *Journal of International Affairs* 27 (1973): 1–21.

———. "Ethnonationalism in the First World." In *Ethnic Conflict in the Western World*, ed. Milton J. Esman, 19–45. Ithaca, N.Y.: Cornell University Press, 1977.

———. "A Nation is a Nation, is a State, is an Ethnic Group, is a . . . ." *Ethnic and Racial Studies* 1, no. 4 (1978): 377–400.

———. "The Impact of Homelands upon Diasporas." In *Modern Diasporas in International Politics*, ed. Gabriel Sheffer, 16–68. New York: St. Martin's Press, 1986.

Coser, Lewis S. "The Termination of Conflict." *Journal of Conflict Resolution* 5, no. 4 (1967): 347–53.

Crocker, Chester A. "Conflict Resolution in the Third World: The Role of Superpowers." In *Resolving Third World Conflict: Challenges for a New Era*, ed. Sherlyn J. Brown and Kimber M. Schraub, 193–210. Washington, D.C.: United States Institute of Peace, 1992.

Das Gupta, Jyotirindra. "Ethnicity, Language of Communal and National Development in India." In *Ethnicity: Theory and Experience*, ed. Nathan Glazer and Daniel P. Moynihan, 29–52. Cambridge, Mass.: Harvard University Press, 1975.

Duner, Bertil. "Proxy Intervention in Civil Wars." *Journal of Peace Research* 18, no. 4 (1981): 353–61.

Enloe, Cynthia H. "Internal Colonialism, Federalism, and Alternative State Development Strategies." *Publius* 7, no. 4 (1977): 145–60.

Esman, Milton J. "The Management of Ethnic Conflict." *Public Policy* 21, no. 1 (1973): 49–78.

———. "Perspectives on Ethnic Conflict in Industrialized Societies." In *Ethnic Conflict in the Western World*, ed. Milton J. Esman, 371–90. Ithaca, N.Y.: Cornell University Press, 1977.

———. "Ethnic Pluralism and International Relations." *Canadian Review of Studies in Nationalism* 17, nos. 1–2 (1990): 83–93.

Fishman, Joshua A. "Nationality-Nationalism." In *Language Problems of Developing Nations*, ed. Joshua A. Fishman, Charles A. Ferguson, and Jyotirindra Das Gupta, 39–51. New York: Wiley, 1968.

Fox, W. T. R., ed., "How Wars End." *Annals of the American Academy of Political and Social Science* 392 (November 1970).

Geertz, Clifford. "The Integrative Resolution." In, *Old Societies and New States: The Quest for Modernity in Africa and Asia*, ed. Clifford Geertz, 105–57. New York: Free Press, 1963.

Gladstone, Jack A. "Theories of Revolution: The Third Generation." *World Politics* 32, no. 3 (1980): 425–53.

Gurr, Ted Robert. "Theories of Political Violence and Revolution in the Third World." In *Conflict Resolution in Africa*, ed. Francis M. Deng and I. William Zartman, 153–89. Washington, D.C.: Brookings Institution, 1991.

Halsey, A. H. "Ethnicity: a primordial social bond," *Ethnic and Racial Studies* 1, no. 1 (1978): 124–28.

Hare, A. P. "Third Party Roles in Ethnic Conflict." *Social Dynamics* 1, no. 1 (1975): 81–107.

Hechter, Michael. "The Political Economy of Ethnic Change." *American Journal of Sociology* 79, no. 5 (1973): 1151–78.

Horowitz, Donald L. "Ethnic Identity." In *Ethnicity: Theory and Experience*, ed. Nathan Glazer and Daniel P. Moynihan, 111–40. Cambridge, Mass.: Harvard University Press, 1975.

Juergensmeyer, Mark. "What the Bhikku Said: Reflections on the Rise of Militant Religious Nationalism." *Religion* 20 (1990): 53–75.

Keohane, Robert O. "Lilliputians' Dilemmas: Small States in International Politics." *International Organization* 23, no. 2 (1989): 291–310.

Keyes, Charles F. "Towards a New Formulation of the Concept of Ethnic Group." *Ethnicity* 3 (1976): 203–13.

Krippendorff, Ekkehart. "Minorities, Violence and Peace Research." *Journal of Peace Research* 16, no. 1 (1979): 27–40.

Lijphart, Arend. "Consociational Democracy." *World Politics* 21 (1969): 207–25.

Lustick, Ian. "Stability in Deeply Divided Societies: Consociationalism Versus Control." *World Politics* 31, no. 3 (1979): 325–44.

McKay, James, and Frank Lewins. "Ethnicity and the Ethnic Group: A Conceptual Analysis and Reformulation." *Ethnic and Racial Studies* 1, no. 4 (1978): 412–27.

McSweeny, W. "The Politics of Neutrality: Focus on Security for Smaller Nations." *Bulletin of Peace Proposals* 18, no. 1 (1987): 33–45.

Mitchell, Christopher R. "Civil Strife and the Involvement of External Parties." *International Studies Quarterly* 14, no. 2 (1970): 166–94.

———. "Evaluating Conflict." *Journal of Peace Research* 17, no. 1 (1980): 61–75.

———. "Ending Conflicts and Wars: Judgement, Rationality, and Entrapment." *International Social Science Journal* 127 (February 1991): 35–56.

———. "Case Analysis and a Willingness to Talk: Conciliatory Gestures and De-Escalation." *Negotiation Journal* (October 1991): 405–40.

———. "External Peace-Making Initiatives and Intra-National Conflict." In *The Internationalization of Communal Strife*, ed. Manus Midlarsky, 274–97. London: Routledge, 1992.

Mitchell, Christopher R., and M. Nicholson. "Rational Models and the Ending of Wars." *Journal of Conflict Resolution* 27, no. 3 (1989): 495–520.

Modelski, George. "The International Relations of Internal War." In *International Aspects of Civil Strife*, ed. James N. Rosenau, 122–53. Princeton, N.J.: Princeton University Press, 1964.

Petersen, William. "Ethnicity in the World Today." *International Journal of Comparative Sociology* 20, nos. 1–2 (1979): 3–13.

Rajan, M. S. "Small States and the Sovereign-Nation-State System." *International Studies* 25, no. 1 (1988): 1–23.

Rejai, Mostafa, and Cynthia Enloe. "Nation-States and State Nations." *International Studies Quarterly* 13, no. 2 (1969): 140–58.

Rose, Lee, and Constance Stillinger. "Barriers to Conflict Resolution." *Negotiation Journal* (October 1991): 389–404.

Rose, Leo E. "The Superpowers in South Asia: A Geo-Strategic Analysis." *Orbis* 22, no. 2 (1978): 398–413.

Rosenau, James N. "The Concept of Intervention." *Journal of International Affairs* 20, no. 2 (1968): 165–76.

Ross, Marc Howard. "Internal and External Conflict and Violence." *Journal of Conflict Resolution* 29, no. 4 (1985): 547–79.

———. "A Cross-Cultural Theory of Political Conflict and Violence." *Political Psychology* 7, no. 3 (1986): 427–69.

———. "The Role of Evolution in Ethnocentric Conflict and Its Management." *Journal of Social Issues* 47 (1991): 167–85.

———. "Ethnic Conflict and Dispute Management." In *Studies in Law, Politics and Society* 12, ed. Austin Sarat and Susan Silbey, 155–94. Greenwich, Conn.: JAI Press, 1992.

Rothchild, Donald. "Ethnicity and Conflict Resolution." *World Politics* 20, no. 1 (1969): 597–616.

———. "An Interactive Model for State-Ethnic Relations." In *Conflict Resolution in Africa*, ed. Francis M. Deng and I. William Zartman, 190–215. Washington, D.C.: Brookings Institution, 1991.

Smith, Anthony D. "The Diffusion of Nationalism." *British Journal of Sociology* 29 (1978): 234–48.

Stavenhagen, Rodolfo. "Ethnic Conflicts and Their Impact on International Society." *International Social Science Journal* 127 (February 1991): 117–32.

Stockwell, A. J. "The White Man's Burden and Brown Humanity: Colonialism and Ethnicity in British Malaya." *Southeast Asian Journal of Social Science* 10 (1982): 44–68.

———. "British Imperial Policy and Decolonization in Malaya, 1942–52." *Journal of Imperial and Commonwealth History* 13, no. 1 (October 1984): 68–87.

Stone, John. "Introduction: Internal Colonialism in Comparative Perspective." *Ethnic and Racial Studies* 2, no. 3 (1979): 255–59.

Subrahmanyam, K. "India's Security Challenges and Responses: Evolving a Security Doctrine." *Strategic Analysis* 11, no. 1 (April 1987): 1–12.

Tellis, Ashley J. "The Naval Balance in the Indian Subcontinent: Demanding Missions for the Indian Navy." *Asian Survey* 25, no. 2 (1985): 1186–1213.

———. "India's Naval Expansion: Reflections on History and Strategy." *Comparative Strategy* 6, no. 2 (1987): 185–219.

Touval, Saadia. "Biased Intermediaries." *Jerusalem Journal of International Relations* 1, no. 1 (1975): 51–69.

———. "Gaining Entry to Mediation in Communal Strife." In *The Internationalization of Communal Strife*, ed. Manus Midlarsky, 255–73. London: Routledge, 1992.

van Dyke, Vernon. "Self-Determination and Minority Rights." *International Studies Quarterly* 111, no. 3 (1969): 226–33.

White, N. R. "Ethnicity, Culture and Cultural Pluralism." *Ethnic and Racial Studies* 2 (1978): 139–53.

Wibers, Hakan. "Self-Determination as an International Issue." In *Nationalism and Self-Determination in the Horn of Africa*, ed. I. M. Lewis, 43–65. London: Ithaca Press, 1983.

Wittman, Donald. "How a War Ends—A Rational Model Approach." *Journal of Conflict Resolution* 23, no. 4 (1979): 743–63.

Wood, John R. "Secession: A Comparative Framework." *Canadian Journal of Political Science* 1, no. 1 (1981): 107–34.

Yapp, Malcolm. "Language, Religion and Political Identity: A General Framework." In *Political Identity in South Asia*, ed. David Taylor and Malcolm Yapp, 1–34. London: Curzon Press, 1979.

Young, Crawford. "The Temple of Ethnicity." *World Politics* 35, no. 4 (1983): 652–62.

Zartman, I. William. "Negotiation as a Joint Decision-Making Process." *Journal of Conflict Resolution* 21 (1977): 619–38.

———. "Prenegotiation: Phases and Functions." In *Getting to the Table: The Processes of International Prenegotiation*, ed. Janice Gross Stein, 1–17. Baltimore: Johns Hopkins University Press, 1989.

———. "Conflict Resolution: Prevention, Management, and Restriction." In *Conflict Resolution in Africa*, ed. Francis M. Deng and I. Wiliam Zartman, 299–319. Washington, D. C.: Brookings Institution, 1991.

———. "Negotiations and Prenegotiations in Ethnic Conflict." In *Conflict and Peacemaking in Multiethnic Societies*, ed. Joseph S. Montville, 511–34. Lexington, Mass.: Lexington Books, 1991.

———. "Internationalization of Communal Strife: Temptations and Opportunities of Triangulation." In *The Internationalization of Communal Strife*, ed. Manus Midlarsky, 27–43. London: Routledge, 1992.

Zartman, I. William, and Saadia Touval. "Mediation: The Role of Third-Party Diplomacy and Informal Peace Making." In *Resolving Third World Conflict: Challenges for a New Era*, ed. Sherlyn J. Brown and Kimber M. Schraub, 239–61. Washington, D.C.: United States Institute of Peace, 1992.

Index

American sympathies of, 40, 41, 52–53, 60, 66–67; and provincial council elections, 281–83; relations of, with Indira Gandhi, 38, 56, 63, 102, 110–11, 113, 124, 127, 137; relations of, with Rajiv Gandhi, 38, 143, 149–50, 157–58, 187–88, 194, 206–15, 226–29, 248–49, 260, 268–70, 275–77, 286, 288–91, 293, 295; search for political settlement of ethnic conflict by, 68–73, 101–2, 104–5, 107, 118–21, 123–30, 132, 137–38, 143–44, 147–54, 156–60, 178–96, 201–15, 222, 226–34, 271–74, 281–82, 286–91; signing of Indo–Sri Lanka Accord by, 15, 238, 248–49, 268; and Tamils' legal rights, 104–5; visits to India by, 44–45, 127, 148, 154, 157–58, 269–70, 275–77; visits to non-Indian foreign countries by, 134–35. *See also* riots, Sri Lankan

Jayewardene, Ravi (son), 128, 132

JVP (Janatha Vimukthi Peramuna), 310, 311; assassination attempts by, 10, 268–69, 274, 292; boycotting of Indian products by, 312–13; destruction of, by Sri Lankan army, 316, 320–22; election violence of, 299–301; goals of, 327; Jayewardene's 1977 amnesty for members of, 126; 1971 insurrections by, 18, 25, 27; opposition of, to IPKF, 265, 299–302, 314; opposition to provincial council elections by, 281, 283, 291, 295; violent opposition to Indo–Sri Lanka Accord by, 233, 237, 254, 259, 272, 274–75

Kachchaitivu (islet), 29
Kadaraman (Jaffna town), 131
Kadian, Rajesh, 323n10
Kalpage, Stanley, 318
Kampuchea (Cambodia), 4, 54n16, 64–67, 114
Kanagaratnam,   Balasubramaniam ("Rahim"), 219n8
Kandyan kingdom, 5, 6, 76, 90, 92–93, 192
Kandyan marriage laws, 192
Kankesanthurai, 204
Karunanidhi, M., 55–56, 108, 320
Kashmir Accord, 103
Kashmir issue, 18, 22, 103

Keenee-Weenee Services. *See* British mercenaries
Khmer Rouge (Kampuchea), 54n16
Khomeini, Ayatollah, 53
Kilinochchi (Sri Lanka), 202, 278
Kittu (Sathasivam Krishnakumar), 219n8, 286
Kotelawala, Sir John, 67
Kotte kingdom, 88
rKrishnakumar,   Sathasivam   ("Kittu"), 219n8, 286
"Kuttumani" (S. Yogachandra), 35n27

Latin America, 8
Laue, James, 100
Lebanon, 4, 245
Lee Kuan Yew, 64–65, 133, 293
Liberation Tigers of Tamil Eelam. *See* LTTE
linguistic nationalism: in Bangladesh, 24; in India, 18–19, 31, 89; in Sri Lanka, 2, 85, 88–89, 328
Li Xian Nian, 134
Lok Sabha (India), 107, 109–12, 152–54, 284, 286, 325–26
London *Observer*, 284
Longowal, Sant Harchand Singh, 168–70
LTTE (Liberation Tigers of Tamil Eelam): assassination of Rajiv Gandhi by, 239, 326, 335; assassinations of Sri Lankan politicians by, 10, 16, 169–70; attempts to disarm, 235, 239–40, 242, 243n24, 245–46, 251–57, 286, 288–91, 315–16, 321; bombing skills of, 173, 262, 263, 327; and Delhi Accord, 168–69, 175, 179, 181, 186–87, 204–5; guerrilla warfare by, 68, 155, 173–74, 181, 185, 205–6, 213–14, 216, 217–18, 221, 228, 258; and Indian government, 229–31, 239–40, 246–47, 253, 278, 283–91, 294; on Indian mediation, 134, 204, 335; Indian payments to, 240, 253–54, 283–85, 290; Indian support for, 173, 219, 226; and Indo–Sri Lanka Accord, 239–41, 246–47, 255–58, 283–86; internecine fighting of, 178, 185, 202, 256, 258, 290, 317, 321–22, 326; IPKF's war against, 252, 254–56, 260–63, 271, 275–78, 284, 291, 294, 310–11, 314–16, 321–22; as main Tamil separatist group, 185, 196, 202, 205, 256; martyrs for, 258–59;

and Northern and Eastern Provinces, 329; plans of, to set up a Tamil state, 203, 205–7, 209–10, 256; power of, in Tamil Nadu, 326–27; and provincial elections, 256–58; regrouping of, in Jaffna jungles, 261, 263–64, 278; seizure of weapons from, 195, 197n27, 202–3; Sri Lankan army's offensive against, 202, 205–10, 213, 215–17, 219, 221, 223, 225, 229, 234, 241–42, 251, 254, 260, 262, 311, 322; Sri Lankan government's negotiations with, 160–61, 163, 167, 203–5, 277–78, 286–87, 310–11, 313, 316–317, 321–22, 336; Sri Lankan payments to, 317. *See also* Balasingham, S.; Prabhakaran, Velupillai

Madras (India), 265
Madras International Airport, 136, 139
Mahajana Eksath Peramuna (MEP), 17
"Mahattaya" (Mahendraraja), 321
Mahavali River project (Sri Lanka), 46, 53, 178, 184
Mahendran, C., 145n12
Mahendraraja ("Mahattaya"), 321
Maheswaran, Uma, 126, 161, 178, 181
Mainstream, 312
Majeed, Abdul, 192–93
Malaysia, 64, 133, 279
Maldives, the, 333
Mannar (Sri Lanka), 131–32
Maran, Murasoli, 108–9
maritime agreement (China and Sri Lanka), 25
Markar, Bakeer, 282
Marshall Plan, for Southeast Asia. *See* Colombo Plan
Mathew, Cyril, 125–26
Ma Tzu-Ching, 27
mediation: All Party Conference efforts at, 130; by Commonwealth countries, 174, 182; difficulty of, within cultures, 189–94; Dissanayake's views of, 223; of ethnic conflict, 334–36; Indira Gandhi's, of Sri Lanka's ethnic conflict, 7, 43, 73, 81, 89, 99–113, 118–21, 133–34, 139–40, 155–57, 174, 325; lack of consensus on, in Sri Lankan cabinet, 223–24, 230, 232–33, 237–38, 241–42, 254; lessons about, 328–31, 334–36; LTTE on Indian, 134, 204, 335;

principal *vs.* neutral, 100, 108, 176, 328–30, 335; Rajiv Gandhi's, of Sri Lanka's ethnic conflicts, 7, 147–48, 151, 154, 156–57, 175–89, 201–2, 206–15, 221, 224–40, 248, 261, 267–70, 278, 312–15, 318, 320, 325–26; Sinhalese opposition to, 124–26; Sri Lanka's decision to accept, 125–26; Tamil and southern Indian dominance in India's, 102, 108, 176–77, 189, 260, 330. *See also* conflict; IPKF; *names of mediators*
Mehrotra, L. L., 309
Menikdiwela, W. M. P. B., 128, 269
Menon, K. P. S., Jr., 206, 330
Menon, V. K. Krishna, 38
MEP (Mahajana Eksath Peramuna), 17
Michiko (Princess of Japan), 50, 67
Middle East, 8, 48–49. *See also names of Middle Eastern countries*
Ministry of National Security (Sri Lanka), 128–29, 208, 302
Mirdha, Mr., 146n28
Mohammed, M. H. (Sri Lankan minister of transport), 232
Mohammed, Dr. Mahathir (Malaysian prime minister), 133
Mohandas, K., 136
Moraes, Dom, 102–3
Mossad, 152, 307. *See also* Israel
Mudaliyar (Tamil underworld boss), 145n27
Mukherjee, Pranab, 107
Mullaitivu (Sri Lanka), 141, 202, 264, 278
Muslim(s), 194; on devolution of power, 81–82; in Eastern Province, 6, 90–91, 186–93, 212, 279; fundamentalism of, 91; Hameed as, 42, 54n8, 311; and IPKF, 251; opposition of, to Tamil ethno-region, 231; as possible bond among Islamic countries, 24, 333; relations of, with Tamils, 4, 85, 88–89, 91, 152, 193, 202, 228; as Sri Lankan minority, 333; and Sri Lankan ties to Israel, 135–36; as Tamil-speakers, 85, 88–91, 152, 189–90, 192–93, 255, 311; as victims of guerrilla efforts, 193

Nagaland (India), 263
Nakasone Yoshihiro, 133